1988

THE BIRTH OF
THE PROPAGANDA STATE

The Birth of
the Propaganda State

Soviet Methods of Mass Mobilization,
1917–1929

PETER KENEZ

University of California, Santa Cruz

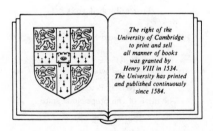

The right of the
University of Cambridge
to print and sell
all manner of books
was granted by
Henry VIII in 1534.
The University has printed
and published continuously
since 1584.

CAMBRIDGE UNIVERSITY PRESS

CAMBRIDGE

LONDON   NEW YORK   NEW ROCHELLE

MELBOURNE   SYDNEY

To P. D. K.
with love

Published by the Press Syndicate of the University of Cambridge
The Pitt Building, Trumpington Street, Cambridge CB2 1RP
32 East 57th Street, New York, NY 10022, USA
10 Stamford Road, Oakleigh, Melbourne 3166, Australia

First published 1985

Printed in the United States of America

Library of Congress Cataloging in Publication Data
Kenez, Peter.
The birth of the propaganda state.

Bibliography: p.
Includes index.
1. Propaganda, Russian. 2. Kommunisticheskaia
partiia Sovetskogo Soiuza – Party work. 3. Soviet Union –
Politics and government – 1917–1936. I. Title.
DK266.3.K43   1985   303.3'75'0947   85-5725
ISBN 0 521 30636 1 hard covers
ISBN 0 521 31398 8 paperback

Contents

Illustrations

Preface

This book took a long time to write, and the final product turned out rather differently from what I had originally planned. The Russian Revolution was one of the great social revolutions in history: People suffered dreadful hardships and saw around themselves a remarkable transformation of their world. My first intention was to study the changing perceptions of ordinary people in extraordinary times. I wanted to know how well people understood what was happening to them, what in fact they thought of their leaders, the political institutions, and of new ideas that must have appeared strange to them.

As I read more and more of the available source material, it became clear to me that I would never be able to reconstruct the world view of the average citizen. Workers and peasants left no memoirs; the thoughts and feelings of the ordinary people appeared in the sources only in a distorted fashion. Under the circumstances, my study gradually turned into an examination of the ways with which the new political elite attempted to bring its message to the common people; I was, in fact, writing a book on propaganda. I did not then, and do not now, believe that the Bolsheviks at the time of their Revolution or in the 1920s were cynical. They had a burning desire to convince their fellow citizens that the new order would bring a better world of social justice. They were certainly manipulative, and that was an attitude born out of their ideology and practical experiences. They came to their task of ruling an almost ungovernable country, however, with no clear ideas about propaganda. They had not given a thought to how exactly the masses should be mobilized; they were creating the instruments and methods of propaganda as they were going along. The Bolsheviks were the great unconscious innovators of twentieth-century politics.

Even though the focus of my study shifted, I have not changed my intention of writing about the experiences of the common people. In this book I have little to say about high-level politics. I spend little time in discussing the work of Party and government bodies that were responsible for the organization of the propaganda network. Instead, I have much to say about the movies people saw, the books and newspapers they read, and the characteristics of the mass meetings in which they participated.

I have used the transliteration system of the Library of Congress. However, in the transliteration of such well-known names as Trotsky, Kerensky, and Gorky, for example, I have sacrificed consistency for the sake of avoiding confusion. Nor did I succeed in maintaining perfect consistency in the vexing matter of sexism in language. By and large I preferred to use the word "humanity" instead of "mankind" and "people" instead of "man." Nevertheless on occasion I did allow "man" to stand for human being. Phrases such as "he or she might have if he or she could have" seemed ludicrously clumsy. Very likely in the not too distant future the English language will evolve so as to reflect changed social consciousness. At this time, however, the language is creaking under the burden of new requirements.

In the revolutionary years, the Soviet leaders created a large number of institutions and introduced many new concepts. Under these circumstances, abbreviations proliferated, and many of these became new Russian words. Therefore this book includes a Glossary, which the reader is encouraged to consult.

Several institutions supported me in the course of writing this book. Through an International Research and Exchange Board–Academy of Sciences of the USSR exchange, I spent three months in the Soviet Union during the fall of 1977. My description of the literacy campaign is based on archival sources that I was able to see while in Moscow. In the academic year 1979–80, I held a fellowship from the Kennan Institute of the Woodrow Wilson International Center for Scholars. The center provided a wonderfully congenial environment for work. I wrote the first draft of the first half of the manuscript while in Washington. The Research Committee of the University of California, Santa Cruz, gave me several grants, which enabled me to hire student assistants and do my writing on a computer. In addition, I received support from the Comparative International Studies Organized Research Activity of UCSC. I am grateful to these institutions.

Of the numerous libraries and archives in which I worked, I enjoyed most the days I spent at the Pacific Film Archives of the University of California, Berkeley. At the Library of the Hoover Institution, I always turned with my problems to Hilja Kukk, who is an exceptionally knowledgeable librarian. I used extensively the inter library loan services of UCSC and was aided by Joan Hodgson and Betty Rentz.

Among the many student assistants I had I would like to acknowledge in particular the help of Richard Johnson and Amy Roitshteyn.

In the course of the many years I was working on this book, I received valuable help from friends and colleagues with whom I discussed my ideas and who read all or parts of the manuscript. At the early stages of my work I benefited from the advice of Victoria Bonnell, Richard Stites, Jeffrey Brooks, David Joravsky, and Tom Gleason. I presented several chapters of the manuscript to the faculty seminar of the Comparative International Studies Organized Research Activity, and I learned from the criticism of my colleagues. Robert Kraft, Charles Neider, Wally Goldfrank, Susan Mann, Buchanan Sharp, Jonathan Beecher, Mark Traugott, Vivian Sobchak, Josephine Woll, and Andrew C. Janos made helpful comments on individual chapters. I am particularly grateful for the extensive criticisms and friendly encouragement of George and Kristina Baer, David and Elizabeth Mayers, Laurence Veysey, Isebill V. Gruhn, Murray Baumgarten, and Paul Hollander. Dorothy Dalby, once again, read the entire manuscript and improved my style. I received by far the most extensive and valuable help from Penelope Kenez.

Introduction: The Soviet concept of propaganda

This book is about the development of Bolshevik propaganda. The subject is an important one, because propaganda played a large role in the 1917 victory of the Communists and an even greater part in their ability to retain power during the extremely difficult years of the 1917–1921 Civil War. In the course of the relatively peaceful 1920s, the revolutionary leadership attempted to transform man and society through mass indoctrination.

The subject also deserves careful study because the institutions of mass mobilization became integral parts of the Soviet system. As we examine how the Leninists saw their task of bringing their message to the workers and peasants and how they built their institutions of indoctrination, we gain essential insights into the Russian form of Marxism.

Furthermore, the Soviet Communists were pathbreakers; they introduced a new approach to politics. In the course of the twentieth century, revolutionaries in various parts of the world often found themselves in a situation similar to that of the Bolsheviks in the early part of their rule. Their solutions to problems frequently mirrored Bolshevik solutions. This was not so much because of any conscious copying, though that also happened, but because circumstances dictated essentially similar approaches. The Bolshevik leadership in the Civil War period and in the 1920s was made up of intelligent and articulate people. It is of enduring interest how they defined their problems and how they arrived at their solutions.

The development of Soviet propaganda is an elusive and difficult subject. The greatest problem is that while we all think we know perfectly well what propaganda is, in fact we have no precise definition that would be value free and valid regardless of time or political culture. Social scientists, no doubt unwittingly, have often defined propaganda in such a way as to make their definition into an ideological weapon. They have searched for a definition that covers only the activities of people whose point of view they do not like. Some have insisted that propaganda is something covert; others have stressed that propaganda appeals to our emotions rather than to our intellect. At a moment's reflection, however, it is evident that such definitions have nothing to do with the real world, where propaganda is covert on some occasions but overt on others; sometimes propaganda is aimed at our emotions, sometimes at our minds.

The problem is further compounded by the fact that, given the common understanding of "propaganda," the word has become a pejorative term in Western societies. It was not always so. Pope Gregory XV in 1622 set up a College of Cardinals and entrusted this college with the task of overseeing foreign missions for the spread of faith. The new institution was called *Congregatio de Propaganda Fide*, Congregation for the Propagation of Faith. The church assumed that it had the one and only correct interpretation of faith, of man's place in nature and in history, and therefore regarded the attempt of bringing its doctrine to others as wholly benign. The concept may have been new in the seventeenth century; the phenomenon obviously was not. Ever since people have lived in politically organized societies, some have attempted to influence the mind, and therefore the behavior, of others. In modern Western history, propaganda became a pejorative term only when man accepted as inevitable that human beings would disagree as to the proper organization of society. Under these circumstances, we suspect that our enemies achieve their successes by underhanded methods of persuasion, that is, by propaganda.

An unqualified hostility to propaganda, nevertheless, is not warranted. When we deplore the very existence of this phenomenon, we in effect reject mass society; it is evident that one could not exist without the other. How propaganda is an integral part of the modern world is a large and complex subject that cannot be discussed here. This book, however, illustrates the part played by the manipulation of opinion in one modern polity, the Soviet Union.

Viewing propaganda as the locus of illness in the modern world, the enemies of mass society (whether on the right, like Jacques Ellul,[1] or on the left, like Herbert Marcuse[2]) make it the focus of their attack. But such views must be rejected, for neither Ellul's aristocratic utopia, posited in the past, nor Marcuse's vague description of an ideal society is a realistic vision of the future. Both thinkers found the political opinions and tastes of the common people appalling and believed that the people lost their way because they had been manipulated by others. The elitism in the writings of both Marcuse and Ellul is barely hidden. Ironically, exactly the same elitism characterizes the attitudes of the successful political propagandist: an unwillingness to believe that people want what they profess to want.

Clearly, propaganda often means telling less than the truth, misleading people, and lying; therefore, a study of Soviet use of this political instrument must reveal some unattractive features of that system. The very decision to undertake a description of Bolshevik methods of indoctrination might seem to some an ideologically motivated enterprise. Yet the goal of this book is most certainly not to "unmask" Russian Communism. Although Bolshevik methods and attitudes were original, the Leninists were by no means alone in attempting to influence the minds and behavior of their own people. We form our opinion of the Bolshevik system on the basis of considerations other than the character of its indoctrination methods. It would be difficult to argue that the Bolsheviks' most reprehensible act was to attempt to bring their ideas to the people.

The greatest problem in attempting a study of propaganda is that the phenomenon does not exist by itself. An abstract discussion of the topic would be no more enlightening than an abstract discussion of altruism, courage, or love. If one defines the subject narrowly and limits the discussion to the use of the media and to explicitly agitational institutions (e.g., the agitational trains during the Civil War), one misses the broader Soviet flavor of propaganda. Also, by discussing methods of manipulation in isolation from policies, one – perhaps inadvertently – creates the impression that Soviet politicians were cynical. In too broad a definition, by contrast, the history of propaganda becomes synonymous with the history of the Soviet state.

To draw a line between a legitimate act of government and a propaganda gesture, between content and form, is often difficult; for example, to win the Civil War, the Soviet leaders introduced policies aimed at attracting support. Lenin's famous decree on land was, among other things, a propaganda instrument, and revolutionary activists spared no effort to acquaint the peasantry with it. Yet a discussion of Bolshevik land policies obviously cannot be a part of a study of Soviet propaganda.

It is even harder to separate the inherent appeal of policies and the accomplishments of successful agitators. Soviet historians get themselves into a curious paradox when they discuss this issue. On the one hand, they stress that Lenin and the Bolsheviks were superb organizers and propagandists; on the other, they imply that such advantages did not matter. The Russian people supported the Bolsheviks in the Civil War because only the Bolsheviks stood for their interests. If we accept the interpretation of these historians, we must also accept that organizational strength and propaganda skills played no role at all in the outcome. A more convincing interpretation of Bolshevik victory is that the Reds won for a combination of reasons: They were in a position to introduce policies preferred by at least a majority of Russians; they had the perspicacity to see when and where to offer concessions to the popular will; and at the same time they possessed the organizational strength and skill to bring their message to a wide audience. No one can say exactly what the relative role of each of these factors was.

But it was not only the inherent appeal of Bolshevik policies combined with the undoubted skill of the propagandists that produced the desired results. The nature of the political system built by the Bolsheviks clearly made a major contribution. It was easy, for instance, for Soviet newspapers to argue a particular point of view, when the coercive arm of the regime had eliminated all the newpapers that might have presented opposing arguments or facts tending to undermine the Bolshevik case. In this study, I will attempt to examine the matter in its political and social context.

Instead of focusing narrowly on propaganda, and trying to establish what it was and what it was not, I will describe the history of those Soviet institutions that have been engaged in the struggle to transform people's opinions and attitudes. By studying the workings of the press, the development of the movie and publishing industries, and so forth, we will be able to form a picture of Bolshevik accomplishments in mass mobilization.

To discuss the matter sensibly, we must abandon the hope of finding a definition of propaganda that would be precise, cover all acts of propaganda and only propaganda, and be usable regardless of time and space. Instead, we must accept the broadest possible definition: Propaganda is nothing more than the attempt to transmit social and political values in the hope of affecting people's thinking, emotions, and thereby behavior. The intent of influencing others is hardly objectionable. When we think we disapprove of propaganda, it usually turns out that we really object to its goals or methods. These methods are frequently repugnant. They include manipulating and distorting information, lying, and preventing others from finding out the truth. We should deplore dishonesty and cheating – though we must be aware that often there are extenuating circumstances – but to rail against propaganda is useless, for it is an integral part of the modern world.

With regard to the Soviet Union, it is not very enlightening to prove that the Bolsheviks carried out propaganda. Of course they did. The task is to analyze the distinctive features of their propaganda and to establish how it fit into the political system.

Soviet publicists are correct when they stress that the October Revolution created a radically new type of political organization: the revolutionary state. In the heady days after their victory, Lenin and his comrades faced problems that were novel; they pursued uniquely ambitious goals; and they built their institutions on untried principles.

One of the unusual elements was the attitude of the leaders of young Soviet Russia toward indoctrination. The Soviet state was more permeated with propaganda than any other. Though such matters, admittedly, cannot easily be measured, it is indisputable that the Bolshevik regime was the first to not merely set itself propaganda goals but also through political education to aim to create a new humanity suitable for living in a new society. No previous state had similar ambitions, and no leaders had paid comparable attention to the issues of persuasion.

Soviet institutions, and to a considerable extent the mentality of leaders who created those institutions, were formed during the difficult days of the Civil War. It is conceded by friend and foe that at least in part the Reds emerged victorious from the life-and-death struggle because they were better than their opponents in getting their message across to the people. The propaganda organization, the system of indoctrination introduced at the time of the Civil War, became the basis of a much larger and more elaborate indoctrination network to be built later.

The skill of the Bolsheviks relative to their Civil War enemies is the subject of the first part of this book. It is, however, necessary at this point to pose the question: Why were they more skillful? A simple, though not very enlightening, response would be that they were better propagandists because they were better politicians; they understood the needs of the moment, the nature of the struggle in which they were engaged, and the crucial significance of getting the support or at least the good will of the uncommitted. But why was the Bolshevik side blessed with more able leaders? The Reds were fortunate in that their past prepared them better for the tasks they had to face. A person who spends years in underground struggle, or even in foreign exile editing a small newspaper, will develop a better understanding of the need to get public support than will a general who spends his working hours giving commands. In this respect, the difference in background between the revolutionary and the counterrevolutionary leaderships was extreme. The Bolsheviks were lucky; their enemies were extremely ill-prepared.

The revolutionaries brought with themselves not merely lessons of underground struggle but also some ideological baggage, which in this case turned out to be extremely useful. First of all, they were Marxists. As Marxists, they assumed the perfectibility of man and the possibility of building a just and rational society. Their ideological commitments impelled them to attempt to appeal to the poor and to the hitherto disenfranchised. A Marxist movement was unthinkable before the era of mass politics, before the development of modern means of communications – that is, before the time of modern propaganda.

The socialists believed that in Marxism they possessed an instrument that allowed them to analyze the process of history. They and they alone had access to "true knowledge." The task of the revolutionaries, therefore, was not to search for knowledge, for that was already achieved. Their duty was instead to bring the fruits of Marxist analysis to the proletariat. This aspect of the Marxist heritage is the most crucial one for understanding the Bolsheviks' attitude toward propaganda.

The Bolsheviks were not only Marxists but also Leninists. As is well known, Lenin's most fundamental revision of Marxist thought was the rejection of the notion that the workers in the process of class struggle would develop the necessary class consciousness to bring about the revolution. As Lenin put it in a famous paragraph in *What Is to Be Done?*,

We have said that there *could not have been* a Social-Democratic consciousness among the workers. It would have to be brought to them from without. The history of all countries shows that the working class, exclusively by its own effort, is able to devlop only trade union consciousness, that is, the conviction that it is necessary to combine in unions to fight the employers, and strive to compel the government to pass the necessary labor legislation, and so forth. The theory of socialism, however, grew out of the philosophical, historical, and economic theories elaborated by educated representatives of the propertied classes, by intellectuals.[3]

From a theoretical, Marxist point of view, Lenin's observation seems questionable. If Lenin was correct, then how can we explain the emergence of class consciousness among intellectuals? What kind of materialist explanation would help to clarify why some intellectuals choose "bourgeois" ideologies whereas others side with the proletariat? If we agree with Lenin that class consciousness comes from "knowledge" rather than from "experience," we have repudiated a fundamental tenet of Marxism and have retreated to Hegel. From a practical point of view, though, Lenin's insight was most valuable; in the given circumstances it was true, and facing reality was a precondition for success.

Lenin's revision of Marxism had far-reaching implications for the development of Bolshevik propaganda. He believed that the workers were to be led, because they were incapable of understanding their own interests unaided. Although he was ambivalent toward the Russian intelligentsia, he assigned important tasks to at least a segment of it. In *What Is to Be Done?*,[4] he approvingly quoted Kautsky, who wrote: "Modern socialist consciousness can arise only on the basis of profound scientific knowledge" – something which only the intelligentsia is likely to possess. In the Leninist conception, the revolutionary intellectuals were above all propagandists, who brought the fruits of their knowledge to the workers.

The instrument used by the revolutionaries to approach and lead the masses was the vanguard Party, Lenin's unquestionably greatest contribution to the theory and practice of revolution making. This was clearly meant to be a manipulative organization, as it aimed to do more than to express the outrage of the oppressed and give form to the already-existing revolutionary spirit. The Party was to lead the proletariat to a successful revolution on the basis of its superior understanding of the process of history.

Lenin at times was wrongly accused of being a follower of the nineteenth-century Russian revolutionary Tkachev. Such an accusation, however, was unfair, for Lenin, unlike his predecessor, did not believe that the elite would actually bring about the revolution. In Lenin's view, the Party alone could not fight a successful battle. The task of the Party was to make the proletariat see its own best interest. Had the Bolsheviks truly followed Tkachev's ideas, they would have had little interest in propaganda.

It is evident that Bolshevik thinking hid a great deal of condescension toward the Russian people in general and toward the proletariat in particular. Lenin and his fellow revolutionaries in this respect were no different from the majority of the Russian intellectuals, who saw little that was valuable in the indigenous culture of the Russian people.

The major elements in the Bolshevik ideological heritage were a clear understanding of the important role of ideas in history and a belief that some people knew better than others; therefore, it was unwise to allow people to look after their own interests. These two notions together created a very good attitude for a successful propagandist. Probably all good propagandists must look down at least to some extent on their audience. But in the Bolshevik case, the condescension was extreme. It was evident in all propaganda activities, in the style of Soviet newspapers, in the organization of various campaigns, and in the meticulous care with which exact instructions leaving nothing to local initiative or spontaneity were sent out from the center to the localities. The condescension of the Bolshevik elite toward the Russian people is a major theme of this book.[5]

The Bolsheviks, like most other revolutionaries working against the tsarist regime, were above all propagandists. Under the circumstances, it was natural that they devoted some attention to the organizational, technical aspect of their major activity. They did not have many original insights. Lenin often pointed out that an underground worker must address the proletarians and peasants in a simple language, but this observation was only common sense. Bolshevik thought and practice on the subject did not differ from those of other socialists at the time. For instance, the distinction between agitation and propaganda, an idea that Lenin and later the Soviet publicists made their own, came first from G. Plekhanov, the great Russian Marxist thinker and activist.

Plekhanov wrote: "A propagandist presents many ideas to one or a few persons; the agitator presents only one or a few ideas, but he presents them to a mass of people." In *What Is to Be Done?*, Lenin illustrated Plekhanov's distinction this way:

The propagandist dealing with, say, the question of unemployment, must explain the capitalist nature of the crisis, the causes of their inevitability in modern society, the necessity for the transformation of this society into a socialist society, etc. In a word he must present "many ideas," so many, ideed, that they will be understood only by a (comparatively) few persons. The agitator, however, speaking on the same subject, will take as an illustration a fact that is most glaring and most widely known to his audience, say the death of an unemployed worker's family from starvation, the growing impoverishment, etc., and utilizing this fact, known to all, will direct his efforts to presenting a *single idea* to the masses, e.g., the senselessness of the contradiction between the increase of wealth and the increase of poverty; he will strive *to rouse* discontent and indignation among the masses against this crying injustice, leaving a more complete explanation of this contradiction to the propagandist. Consequently, the propagandist operates chiefly by means of the *printed* word; the agitator by means of the *spoken* word.[6]

This paragraph expresses a great deal about Bolsehvik attitudes toward propaganda. Lenin assumed that the workers would not understand "complex" explanations of the nature of the capitalist system, and therefore socialist propaganda had to operate on several different planes. Appeals to emotions and demagogy were acceptable weapons in the arsenal of the agitator. At the same time, there was no question of presenting an altogether false picture; the revolutionary agitator was not trained to be a liar.

The distinction between agitation and propaganda is not a helpful one. One suspects that it became part of Soviet parlance only because of Lenin's endorsement of Plekhanov. The Soviet propaganda system has existed on many different planes, from the highly sophisticated Marxist Academy to the sloganeering of wall papers. Such distinctions, however, cannot be meaningfully reduced to a dichotomy. Who was carrying out propaganda and who agitated and on which occasion cannot be established; even if they could be, they would throw little light on the activity. In this study, I will use the terms propaganda and agitation interchangeably.

Aside from Plekhanov's distinction, the Russian socialists have contributed nothing to a theoretical discussion of the techniques of mass persuasion. There was no Bolshevik Goebbels, no Soviet theorist fascinated by the activity itself. As this study will show, Bolshevik successes followed from organizational strength, from dogged attention to problems, and, perhaps most importantly, from an ability of the political system to isolate the Russian people from information and ideas that would have undermined the message. The Bolsheviks never looked for and did not find devilishly clever methods to influence people's minds, to brainwash them.

That the Bolsheviks were not interested in the techniques of mass persuasion followed from their notion of propaganda. They thought of propaganda as part of education. It is noteworthy that in 1920 the supervision of much of this work was entrusted to a body, *Glavpolitprosvet,* that was a department within the Commissariat of Education. Indeed, a synonym for propaganda in early Bolshevik parlance was "political education work" or, according to the contemporary abbreviation, *politprosvetrabota* .

In the view of the Bolshevik leaders, specifically in Lenin's opinion, the Russian people were distressingly backward. This backwardness, rather than the actual political strength of the enemy, was the greatest obstacle to building socialism. The remedy was evident: The people needed to be educated. After 1917, the ever-practical Lenin chose culture and education as major themes of his writings. He wanted the Russians to learn to read and write, he wanted them to enjoy the benefits of Western civilization, and he wanted them to "learn" socialism. Teaching people the fundamentals of knowledge and spreading the Bolshevik message were inseparable in Bolshevik opinion.

The title of this book is *The Birth of the Propaganda State: Soviet Methods of Mass Mobilization, 1917– 1929.* In what sense can we describe the Soviet Union during the first decade of its existence as a "propaganda state"? And, describing it as such, do we imply that the society was totalitarian? The Soviet Union was a propaganda state because of the extraordinarily significant role played by indoctrination in forming the state and in executing policy. At the time, the Bolsheviks employed such phrases as, "Bring

8

enlightenment to the masses," "Create the new socialist man," and "Instill class consciousness among the workers and peasants." To achieve their goals, the new leaders spared neither time nor effort in building an impressive and elaborate indoctrination machinery.

No other political elite before 1917 ever had such an approach. Even in our own times, only communist governments have been fully successful in following the Soviet example. The French revolutionaries at the end of the eighteenth century also thought that they were at the dawn of a new era, and they too hoped to bring enlightenment to their fellow citizens. They appreciated the significance of ideas, and they did not shrink from repression. They did not believe, however, that they possessed a theory that would be able to interpret history and all facets of human behavior. They thought that the mere removal of "unnatural" obstacles would be sufficient to fully develop human potential.

The Japanese modernizers in the late nineteenth century, like many other political elites in our own century, understood that the creation of modernity called not only for the construction of factories and the building of railroads but also for the creation of an extensive education system to instill new values. They therefore encouraged the spread of literacy and attempted to shape the educational system to their own purposes. However, the efforts of these modernizers to change the mentality of the people pale in significance by comparison with those of the Soviet leadership.

As in so much else, the First World War was a turning point in the history of propaganda. The war imposed extraordinary hardships on the belligerents. It was a war in which the solidity of the home front was crucial. All the participating countries, with varying degrees of intensity and success, experimented in the difficult new art of mass mobilization. The democratic countries of the West had an edge. By common consent, they were more successful than the autocracies: They had a larger store of experience in appealing to the common people, and they possessed better instruments for reaching an audience. Adolf Hitler was most impressed. He came to be obsessed by the importance of propaganda, and he always regarded the performance of the Allies, especially the British, as a model to be followed.

The goals and themes of war propaganda were utterly predictable: The propaganda aimed at (1) arousing hatred against the enemy, (2) preserving the friendship of allies, (3) winning the good will and cooperation of neutrals, and (4) demoralizing the enemy.[7] To achieve these concrete and always limited goals, the propagandists, to put it mildly, did not hesitate to wash away the distinction between truth and falsehood. For example, the British press provided pictorial "evidence" of enemy atrocities by reprinting photos of the victims of 1905 tsarist pogroms, and they invented stories about the Germans using their own corpses to make soap.[8] (This grisly invention was an uncanny precognition of the not-too-distant future when the Germans in fact would make soap out of human bodies.) Such petty but

9

nonetheless effective deception dominated the propaganda of all belligerent nations. The future leaders of the Soviet state were, of course, well acquainted with wartime propaganda. To them, the success of such efforts seemed to be yet another example of the ability of the burgeoisie to mislead the working classes.

Bolshevik attitudes toward propaganda differed not only from that of the liberal and democratic governments but also from that of the Fascists. The followers of Hitler and Mussolini, of course, well appreciated the significance of mobilizing the masses. Goebbels, among others, wrote lovingly about mass persuasion. Fascist propagandists were contemptuous of the common people and believed that the views of the public could easily be manipulated. It did not disturb them at all to lie. They thought that covert propaganda was likely to be more effective. Indeed, unlike the Bolsheviks, the Fascists never advertised their activities. It cannot be disputed that Goebbels and his colleagues employed extremely powerful techniques of mass mobilization. Posters, torchlight parades, and mass rallies were essential aspects of German and Italian life in the 1930s. Indeed, one cannot even talk about Fascism without alluding to modern methods of mass persuasion. It is also true that there were numerous superficial and significant similarities between Communist and Fascist propaganda. Some of the similarities were due to Fascist imitation of successful Communist techniques, but most of them followed from the fact that Fascists and Communists faced similar problems and operated in political environments that had much in common. Neither hesitated to repress.

In spite of these similarities, however, Fascist and Bolshevik propaganda remained fundamentally different. The source of that difference was that the Germans and Italians, unlike the Bolsheviks, possessed no all-encompassing ideology. Indeed, fascism was an intellectual void. There was no set of doctrines to be applied to all aspects of human experience — no set of doctrines with a pretense of predictive power that could be presented to intellectuals as a self-contained whole. The Fascists were far less ambitious than their Bolshevik competitors; they lacked the passionate desire to educate. They could not have wanted to foist on others an entire world view, for they scarcely had one themselves beyond the nebulous vision of a "thousand-year Reich."

Among all organizations, it was the Catholic Church with which the Bolsheviks had most in common in matters of propaganda. Like the Catholics, the Bolsheviks saw nothing shameful about attempting to change the people's mind. On the contrary, they considered bringing their message to the people a necessary and noble task of every Party activist. Indeed, how could it be otherwise, since the revolutionaries believed that they knew what the future of mankind would be and also the fastest and best way to that utopia? It is striking that only Communists and Catholics have proclaimed proudly that they were propagandizing.

There are also important differences between Communists and Catholics.

Although the church maintains that its doctrine has relevance to many aspects of human life, it does allow a rather substantial sphere over which it claims no authority. Further, at least in modern times, the church has lacked the secular power with which to enforce its antipluralist views.

The Bolsheviks, who possessed an all-encompassing ideology, assumed that their opponents, the liberal democrats of the West, did so as well. Because they were determined to propagandize their ideology, they took it for granted that believers in other world views were doing the same. When Westerners denied that they carried out propaganda, the Bolsheviks regarded such denials as sheer hypocrisy. Indeed, to some of the Russian leaders it seemed precisely the covert nature of "bourgeois" propaganda that made it so effective.[9]

It is remarkable that the Bolsheviks who paid extraordinary attention to propaganda still regarded the bourgeois politicians and ideologues as examples to follow, at least as far as the technical aspect of propaganda was concerned. In this respect they were not unusual, for it is an amusing fact that members of every political group believe that their opponents are more skillful propagandists then they.

We human beings have difficulty accepting that others see the world differently than we do and that they dismiss as nonsense the notions that seem eternal verities to us. Here the concept of propaganda helps us out. It is consoling to believe that others disagree with us because they have been misled by self-interested, sinister, and wicked agitators. For example, in the early 1920s the Bolsheviks assumed that the very-much-hoped-for world revolution had not occurred primarily because the bourgeoisie had succeeded in blinding the proletarians to their own best interest. From the earliest days of the regime, there has been an ambiguity in the Bolsheviks' self-evaluation of propaganda successes. On the one hand, publicists have been eager to take credit for ingenious methods of bringing the revolutionary message to the people; on the other hand, they have always complained about the subversive enemy, skillfully confusing and misleading the people, who must be mercilessly combated, and not only in the realm of ideas.

Do the references in the title of this book to a "propaganda state" and to mass mobilization imply that I use the totalitarian model to interpret Soviet society and politics? When I talk about totalitarianism, I think of a well-functioning state or Party machinery that successfully controls every aspect of the life of the citizens. Obviously, during the years of the Civil War and of the New Economic Policies (NEP), the Soviet Union had no such machinery. As the following chapters will show, the everyday lives of most people remained largely untouched by the new regime.

Two factors slowed the movement toward the development of a totalitarian regime. First of all, Bolshevik organizations in the countryside were weak; there were too few reliable cadres living in the villages. However much the regime would have liked to teach literacy to the peasants, for example, and use the occasion to indoctrinate, it did not yet have the strength to do so. During the 1920s, Bolshevik penetration into the countryside proceeded at a very slow pace. In the prevailing circumstances, traditional institutions such as the commune and the church continued to be dominant in the peasants' lives. The decisive change occurred with the introduction of collectivization, for the collective farms provided the Party with organizational bases.

Secondly, although Soviet leaders tolerated no competition in politics and would have liked to control or at least influence many aspects of life, they still more or less accepted that much of what we think of as "culture" stood outside the realm of politics. They did not merely tolerate cultural activities; they actively and strongly supported them. Culture was considered both a helpmate of socialism and a good in itself. Consequently, with notable exceptions, they allowed the survival of nonpolitical literature and art. It was only the Stalinist generation of leaders that defined politics so broadly as to kill independent thought.

Although Soviet society in the 1920s was not totalitarian, a study of the methods of mass mobilization will help us understand the development of full-fledged Stalinism, that is, totalitarianism. One of the most interesting debates among Western historians in recent years has been about the relationship between the age of Lenin and that of Stalin. Historians have posed such questions as, To what extent can we hold Lenin responsible for the horrors of collectivization and mass murder in the 1930s? Was the logic of Leninism such as to lead inexorably to Stalin? How great was the difference between the peaceful 1920s and stormy 1930s?[10] The material presented in this book will not provide us with an unambiguous answer. Because in the 1920s a large degree of pluralism in fact existed, the break between the two periods can be seen as most significant. The future is never entirely predetermined, and there were a number of other leaders, most significantly N. I. Bukharin, who might have emerged victorious from the bitter internecine struggles of the twenties to establish an order altogether different from that which in fact emerged.[11]

By contrast, one may equally legitimately stress that much of the mentality that was necessary to force peasants into collectives and put millions into concentration camps was already present in the relatively attractive period of the NEP. Already at this time the Bolsheviks were contemptuous of their people; they were utterly convinced of the righteousness of their cause; they had no respect or tolerance for opposing viewpoints; and they already showed a predilection for coercive measures.

On the basis of the evidence presented here, we cannot say with assurance that given the nature of the Leninist Revolution, Stalinism was bound to follow. On the other hand, it is evident that without the preparatory work of the 1920s a fully totalitarian society could not have emerged. Mass mobilization is possible without totalitarianism, but the reverse cannot be. The education of cadres, the development of a political language, the incessant politicization of an ever-larger segment of life, the substitution of "voluntary" pseudosocieties for independent public organizations – all these were preconditions for the coming of the age of Stalin.

A naive observer of the contemporary Soviet Union will be struck by the strange, stilted language of the newspapers, by the meaningless phrases pasted on billboards, by the numerous propaganda campaigns, and by the existence of seemingly purposeless organizations. Why do the Soviet people decorate their streets with such slogans as, "Glory to work!," "Lenin is more alive than all the living!," "We will fulfill the resolutions of the twenty-sixth Congress of the Communist Party of the Soviet Union!," and so forth? The basic features of Soviet indoctrination policies came into being during the early years of the regime; this book is an attempt to examine the roots of the system.

The type of propaganda that the Bolsheviks carried out is absolutely central to our understanding of the nature of the regime that they had created. The regime could not have existed without its special brand of propaganda, and only a Communist system could have developed those methods of mass mobilization that in fact existed. In this book, therefore, our primary goal will be to describe the interaction of indoctrination and politics. How exactly did the existing political order create its instruments of propaganda, and, conversely, how did the particular methods of mass mobilization contribute to the development of the Soviet style in politics?

From the time of the birth of the regime, Soviet life has been permeated with propaganda to such an extent that it is difficult for an outsider to imagine. It would be, therefore, difficult to trace the history of every instrument of indoctrination. In any case, such an attempt would soon become repetitious. My strategy here will be to concentrate on some methods and ignore others. Admittedly, at times my choices may appear idiosyncratic. For example, I will devote a great deal of space to the establishment and growth of the Soviet film industry. One might have decided to ignore the cinema and pay attention instead to the theater. Indeed, the role of traveling theater groups in spreading the Communist message during the Civil War would be an interesting topic. It seemed wiser, nevertheless, to choose the cinema, for many of the films are still available, and in any case, they reached a much larger group of people than the theater ever did. Similarly, we will have nothing to say about the use of the radio, a method of indoctrination that was increasingly widely used in the 1920s and especially in the 1930s on the collective farms. One could, with profit, study the propaganda use of monuments, music, sports, and even ballet. However, it is worthwhile to sacrifice comprehensiveness for the sake of being able to see the details of the working of the propaganda apparatus in selected areas.

The Bolsheviks had no blueprint for a propaganda system when they came to power. It would also be altogether wrong to imagine that there was an isolated group of leaders who designed propaganda for the masses. Instead, the particular methods of mass mobilization followed from a peculiar combination of circumstances, from the mentality of the Bolsheviks and from the tasks that they had to face. Consequently, we will have little to say about high politics. We will describe the organizations devoted to the supervision of propaganda within the Central Committee of the Party and within the Commissariat of Enlightenment. However, our more important task will be to convey what the people actually experienced: What kind of films could they see? What did the newspapers of the period look like? What kind of political education did the young Party activist receive?

No other book, whether published in the Soviet Union or in the West, has aimed at this level of description. In 1950, Alex Inkeles published a valuable book on the Soviet propaganda machinery.[12] Inkeles's main concern, however, was contemporary propaganda. In any case, he limited himself to the examination of the instruments and paid relatively little attention to the mentality of the propagandists or the development of a political style. Recently, Roger Pethybridge in his *The Social Prelude to Stalinism*[13] raised at least some of the issues with which we are dealing here. His book, which is a series of essays rather than a detailed examination of the empirical material, includes a chapter on the literacy campaign. Pethybridge sets out to examine those aspects of Bolshevik thought that culminated in Stalinism. He is not concerned with propaganda per se.

There are also no adequate studies of the individual topics discussed in this book. There is no history of the Soviet press or of the publishing industry. There is a book on the Komsomol (Communist League of Youth) by Ralph T. Fisher published in 1959. This is an institutional study of the congresses that has almost nothing to say on the role of the youth league in the life of the country.[14] By contrast, there has been a great deal written on the golden age of the Soviet film. These works, however, approach the cinema from an aesthetic point of view and show little interest in the political message. An exception to this generalization is Richard Taylor's book *The Politics of Soviet Cinema, 1917–1929.*[15] Taylor, however, concentrates entirely on the organization of the industry and does not discuss individual films.

Naturally, no Soviet historian would ever pose questions similar to the ones contained in this book. A peculiar bias of Soviet historiography is the rejection of evolution. It is obligatory for Soviet historians to appear to assume that Lenin had the last word to say on all topics and that the system that he created is in existence today. Their arguments must not go counter to the basic myth that the Bolsheviks made every decision with a view to realizing the overarching Marxist-Leninist vision. Under the circumstances, there can be no investigation of the development of Soviet propaganda. For believers in the Soviet system, the peculiar features of the regime do not appear peculiar at all and therefore require no special explanation.

Soviet scholars, however, have published a number of interesting and useful monographs on individual topics. Particularly helpful were the book by V. A. Kumanev on the struggle against illiteracy,[16] the study of publishing by A. I. Nazarov,[17] and A. Z. Okorokov's book on the suppression of the non-Bolshevik press.[18]

The fundamental features of the propaganda system came into being during the time of the Civil War and in the era of the New Economic Policies. Although one might argue that the pattern of Bolshevik thought had developed during the difficult years of underground struggle and that the essence of Leninism was already contained in *What Is to Be Done ?* (published in 1902), it is evident that the distinctive features of Soviet propaganda could surface only when the Bolsheviks possessed the machinery of the state, which enabled them to take charge of the media and to build their own coercive apparatus.

The Civil War was a time of desperate struggle, a time when the survival of the regime was repeatedly in question. In these circumstances, the Bolsheviks were forced to make extraordinary efforts and to try new and unconventional methods. Most of these did not work and had to be abandoned. Some of the newly created institutions, however, later came to be integrated into the Soviet polity. At a time when the resources of the regime were meager and the tasks huge, one had to be something of a utopian to remain a Bolshevik. On the soil of poverty and misery, utopianism flourished. The Bolsheviks came to power against all odds. They defeated or at least held off enemies who had seemed to be far stronger. Now anything appeared possible. The Bolsheviks were acutely conscious that a new era had dawned.

The flavor of the era of the New Economic Policies was different. The Bolsheviks had to learn the meaning of such prosaic virtues as frugality and had to pay attention to such mundane matters as balancing the budget. At first, it was not clear that the Party and the regime would be able to survive the great volte-face. But gradually the revolutionaries readjusted themselves to the new circumstances. The NEP period turned out to be a time of gradual building of institutions, of gathering strength for future assaults, and of creating the propaganda state.

The subject of Part I of this book will be the Civil War period. It is appropriate to begin a study of Soviet propaganda by describing the development of the unusual features of the press. Even in a backward country, which had a relatively low rate of literacy, the printed word had a major role to play in spreading the political message. An analysis of the formative period of the Soviet press will show that the crucial development was the almost instantaneous introduction of censorship. How the Bolsheviks were ideologically and organizationally prepared to take that decisive step is the most important part of the story of the Soviet press, which is told in Chapter 1.

The Civil War was fought over the issue of who could impose control quickest over the Russian people, the great majority of whom were peasants.

To achieve this goal, it was obviously essential to win, if not the allegiance, at least the tolerance of the peasantry. The Bolsheviks thought up innovative ways to deal with the problem. They spared no effort to send their own people into the villages and at the same time combated what seemed to them the ideological arm of the White movement, the Orthodox Church. Chapter 2 will describe Bolshevik attempts to penetrate the countryside.

One of the instruments the Bolsheviks used in the ideological struggle was the movement to eradicate illiteracy. The revolutionaries saw no distinction between propagating enlightenment and spreading their own political ideology. Although at a time of civil war no major advance against illiteracy could be achieved, it is worthwhile nevertheless to study the efforts of the revolutionaries because such a study reveals much about both the Bolshevik attitude toward enlightenment and the utopian frame of mind. Chapter 3 does such a study.

Chapter 4 will describe the establishment of the Soviet youth organization, the Komsomol. The Komsomol will serve as a case study for the political use of "voluntary" organizations. These organizations not only carried out agitational tasks for the regime, but by giving room for activity to enthusiasts, they also cemented their commitment to the revolutionary order.

Part I will conclude with an examination of the relationship of cultural policies and propaganda goals. Chapter 5 will describe the political use of publishing, filmmaking, and poster drawing.

In Part II, which covers the NEP period, we shall return to the examination of some of the same subjects. In the 1920s, however, the relative importance of different propaganda instruments was not the same as at the time of the Civil War. Innovative, ad hoc methods, such as sending agitational trains to distant parts of the country and forcing peasants to read to their illiterate comrades, disappeared, while other ways of reaching the people, suitable for peacetime, developed their full potentials only during the NEP period.

One of the most important ways of conveying the Communist message to the Soviet people was the organization of an enormously elaborate and stratified political-education system. Chapter 6 will describe how the Party built a network of schools to take care of the needs of people from the most sophisticated to the illiterate.

Next, we shall turn in Chapter 7 to the examination of the achievements of the literacy drive in the 1920s. The Party consciously used the literacy drive as an important instrument of mobilization.

The Komsomol, which in chapter 8 is again the subject, grew into an organization of great importance in the period of the NEP. In distant villages, the existence of a Komsomol cell was often the only reminder of Soviet power. The youth organization taught a generation of young people to think and speak in a communist fashion.

In Chapter 9, we shall look at Soviet films in their golden age and examine the extent to which these could be regarded as successful propaganda.

In Chapter 10, we shall describe how Soviet newspapers and the publishing industry developed during the NEP period. The two sections of this chapter will show an interesting contrast: Although in publishing a considerable heterogeneity was tolerated, the Soviet regime insisted that newspapers speak with one voice. This book, which is a study of the Soviet methods of indoctrination, should help us understand how the Bolsheviks brought the Soviet people into the twentieth-century world.

The Civil War

CHAPTER I

The press

In the modern world, the press has had a decisively important role in spreading political ideologies. This was true even in tsarist Russia, a country that had a large percentage of illiterates. Before the Revolution, partisans of the government, liberals, and revolutionaries competed with one another in their newspapers. Under the circumstances, the Bolsheviks also had to be journalists. They spent much of their time writing articles for legal and underground papers, attempting to appeal to workers, peasants, and intellectuals, and at the same time trying to evade the censor and the police. In the process, they developed propaganda skills. Undoubtedly, their journalistic work was one of their formative experiences: They learned the use of Aesopian language and learned that censorship was a part of the political struggle.

The prerevolutionary press

During the last decades of the Empire, Russian journalism developed remarkably quickly. In 1890, 796 periodical publications appeared; in the next ten years, this number grew to 1,002 and by 1910 to 2,391.[1] Newspapers multiplied particularly fast. Their number grew between 1883 and 1913 from 80 to 1,158.[2] Although in the 1880s only the largest papers appeared in printings of 20,000, by the turn of the century there were several papers with a circulation of over 100,000.[3] Institutions of modern journalism, such as telegraph agencies, clubs, and unions of journalists, were formed in Russia for the first time. The rapid growth of journalism, together with the expansion of the educational system and of the publishing industry, was part of the larger process of transformation that was taking place in Russia.

In spite of the impressive growth, however, Russia remained backward according to Western European standards. A contemporary observer pointed out that although in Russia one periodical was published for every 167,000 citizens in 1899, in Germany there was one for every 8,000, and in the U.S. state of Michigan, which he chose for illustration, there was one for every 2,600.[4] Russia obviously had no Northcliffe who aimed to print a mass newpaper for every inhabitant. The distribution system remained elementary. Most of the newspapers limited their circulation to the largest cities, and even here the proper network was missing. In the large industrial city of Kharkov, for example, there were only two newspaper vendors in 1903. In Moscow and Saint Petersburg, though newspapers were easily available in the central district, the suburbs were not well supplied. In 1902, papers could be bought from 227 vendors, kiosks, and stores in Moscow.[5]

It is much more difficult to describe the character of the prerevolutionary press than to demonstrate its quantitative growth. Both in intellectual sophistication and in political content, the press was extremely heterogeneous. The difference between a paper aimed at a mass reader, such as *Kopeika* (Penny paper), published between 1908 and 1917 and sold in printings of hundreds of thousands, and an organ catering to an educated audience, such as *Rech'*, (Speech), published by the Kadets between 1906 and 1917, was great. Especially striking was the contrast between the papers published in the two capitals and the products of the provincial press, most of which constantly struggled to survive and were remarkably primitive in their language and analysis of politics.

Censorship contributed a great deal to determining the character of the press. In particular, it influenced the attitudes of the Bolsheviks, who became accustomed to writing in Aeosopian language. The fact that Russia had experienced a relatively brief period of free press made it easier for the new rulers in 1917 to suppress it.

Russian censorship was as old as educated public opinion. In the 1860s, at the time of the great reforms, the harshness of censorship laws was ameliorated somewhat. Nevertheless, the regulations of 1865, which remained in force until the 1905 Revolution, prescribed precensorship, from which only certain categories of printed materials were exempted. Publishers of books and some newspapers and journals required the censor's approval only after printing. The Ministry of the Interior, however, granted exemptions from precensorship only to the major papers of Moscow and Saint Petersburg.

Censorship was capricious, reactionary, and silly on the one hand and ineffective on the other. The Ministry of the Interior periodically sent out a list of subjects that could not be discussed. Within a short time, the situation became exceedingly complicated. V. M. Doroshevich, a well-known journalist of the period, complained that his paper, *Russkoe slovo* (The Russian word) had to hire a specialist to keep up with the over 13,000 circulars dealing with forbidden matters.[6] Prohibitions dealt with some of the important matters of the day. The government, for example, forbade mentioning the famine in the 1890s. (The Soviet government proved to be incomparably more effective in enforcing a similar ban a few decades later.) At the same time, the government could not stop involving itself in trivia: It directed newspapers not to discuss matters that would cast aspersion on the honor of the wives of the Turkish Sultan.[7]

The government justified censorship by arguing that the simple people had to be protected from subversive ideas. It followed from this paternalistic attitude that the government was most vigilant in censoring material aimed at a mass audience; it was easier to publish long and expensive books than cheap pamphlets. The ironic result was that writers padded their books to make them more respectable looking. Marx's *Capital* could be published but *The Communist Manifesto* could not, for it was too short.

Provincial journalists suffered more than their colleagues in the capitals. The Ministry of the Interior granted only a handful of major reactionary journals the privilege of exemption from precensorship. Zealous provincial censors on occasion even forbade the publication of official proclamations. The journalists had to serve two masters: They had to satisfy both the censor and the governor. Censorship and the lack of means prevented them from dealing satisfactorily with the national and international news. Harassment from the governor's office and local administration made it difficult if not impossible to convey to their readers what was happening in their own localities.

Given these obstacles, the small readership, and the lack of skilled and experienced journalists, the rapid growth of the provincial press is all the more impressive. By the turn of the century, almost all provincial cities had papers, and such cities as Kiev and Odessa had several. Some of these papers received support from the local *zemstvo* (self-government).[8] Many of the papers were hopelessly amateurish. In one incident, for example, an editor simply combined two contradictory editorials into one, arguing that some would like the first half and others the second.[9] Undoubtedly, however, the country benefited from the work of these self-sacrificing half-intellectuals. They wanted to contribute and did contribute to the education of their people, to the formation of an articulate public opinion.

The 1905 Revolution brought essential changes. As autocracy disintegrated, the power of the censor disappeared. From January until the fall of 1905, journalists defied the authorities increasingly openly. At the height of disintegration, in October 1905, the revolutionaries simply disregarded the censor in Moscow and Saint Petersburg and paid little attention to him in the provinces. For a few weeks, "illegal" papers freely appeared. The only form of censorship that might have been said to exist at this time was one excerised by the left. On occasion, organized workers refused to print material they considered reactionary.

At a time when the forces of revolution seemed strong, the new premier, Sergei Witte, gave concessions to bring about the consolidation of his government. The new press law, published on November 24, 1905, and modified on April 26, 1906, was one of these concessions. Although the law was promulgated as "temporary," it remained in effect until the 1917 February Revolution. It was a great step toward the establishment of the principle of a free press: It abolished prepublication censorship and took away the right of the Ministry of the Interior to forbid mentioning specified subjects in print. Although new press organs were required to register, the Ministry of the Interior no longer had the power to discriminate arbitrarily among them. In theory, at least, censorship became a judicial rather than administrative matter. How liberal the system was is shown by the fact that between 1912 and 1914 the Bolsheviks managed to publish a legal daily, *Pravda* (Truth).

This is not to say that censorship disappeared. The publication of "subversive" material led to judicial and even administrative proceedings. Newspapers were closed down; editors were frequently jailed; and worst of all, from the point of view of the publisher, the offenders were frequently heavily fined. However, the papers quickly learned to operate in this environment: If they were closed down, they reopened under another name; they hired dummy editors who had no other task but on occasion to stay in jail for awhile; and they accumulated a fund for paying fines.[10]

Before the 1905 Revolution, the interest of the government in affairs of the press tended to be prophylactic; it wanted to prevent the spread of subversive ideas, but had seldom made sustained efforts to get its point of view across to the people. To the government, any concern with public affairs, unless specifically ordered by the tsar or his agents, was subversive. "Patriotic" Russians, by definition, did not involve themselves with politics.

The traumatic experiences of the 1905 Revolution brought slight changes in this attitude. For the first time since the days of Nicholas I, the government considered it necessary to spread proregime propaganda. It is not surprising in view of history and of the half-heartedness of the bureaucrats that the attempts were clumsy and ineffective. For example, officers, who had been inculcated with contempt for "politics," were now instructed to educate their troops in the spirit of loyalty and to explain to them the "errors" in the program of the revolutionaries. Most of the officers simply ignored this order, and very few carried it out successfully.[11] In February 1906, Witte requested 10,000 rubles from the state budget for the publication of propaganda brochures, but Nicholas refused the request and said that the Ministry of the Interior should find the money from its allocation.[12] The government proceeded simply to subsidize the most reactionary segment of the press.

In spite of the clumsy attempts at bribery and censorship, the overwhelming majority of the press during and after 1905 remained hostile to the existing political order. *Grazhdanin* (Citizen), 1882–1914, *Russkaia znamia* (Russian banner), 1905–17, and *Zemshchina* (The land), 1909–17, expressed the views of the extreme rightists. Interestingly, even these papers did not refrain from attacking the government. By and large, the journalistic efforts of the extreme rightists failed, and none of these papers attracted a mass readership. During the World War, the tsarist ministers became somewhat wiser. The Ministry of the Interior succeeded in bribing a "respectable" paper, *Novoe vremia* (New times), published by A. S. Suvorin, one of the best-known Russian publishers. When the Provisional Government opened the archives of the Ministry of the Interior, it came to light that *Novoe vremia* had received almost a million rubles.[13]

In the semiconstitutional system that was born in 1905, all the newly formed parties acquired their own papers. The limited freedom of the press reflected the limited extent of Russian constitutionalism. The most important paper of the moderate opposition was *Russkoe slovo*, published by I. D. Sytin, which became a major and successful commercial enterprise. In 1916, over 700,000 copies of it were printed, and it had millions of rubles in yearly advertising revenues.[14] The central organ of the Kadet party was *Rech '*, which appeared in much smaller editions, (approximately 40,000 copies during the war) but benefited from the contributions of such important intellectuals and politicians as Miliukov, Struve, Nabokov, and Petrunkevich. *Birzhevye vedomosti* (Stock exchange news), not affiliated with any political group, also expressed a moderately liberal political point of view.

The condition of the socialist press was far worse than that of the liberal. Between the revolutions, the most important Menshevik paper was *Luch* (Ray), which appeared between 1912 and 1914 in printings of approximately 10,000 copies daily. The Socialist Revolutionaries published *Trudovoi golos* (Workers' voice). All the socialist papers were harassed by censors and had to change their titles several times to avoid suppression.

The prerevolutionary Bolshevik press

The revolutionaries were also journalists; much of their activity consisted in writing articles and editing and distributing small newspapers. By reading these old papers, one can reasonably well reconstruct the story of the internal and external struggles of the Russian socialists.

All revolutionary socialist publications were basically similar: Socialist Revolutionaries, Mensheviks, and Bolsheviks alike paid great attention to the press, and they operated more or less in the same environment. The only advantage the Bolsheviks had was that their leader, V. I. Lenin, had an unusually clear understanding of what newspapers could accomplish and therefore used the press more self-consciously.

Lenin in his writings gave an impressive analysis of the role of the newspaper in the revolutionary movement. As always, he was the most clear sighted and insightful when dealing with the problems of organization. In a short but important article, "Where to begin?," published in 1901, he argued that the most important immediate task of the socialists was to establish a national newspaper. In the process of putting the newspaper together, the Party would develop. He also wrote that the work of carrying out propaganda was an instrument of propaganda itself. His insight that propaganda and organization are opposite sides of the same coin because a fundamental principle of Bolshevik policy making.

Soviet publicists made Lenin's sentence famous by quoting it endlessly: "The newspaper is not only a collective propagandist and a collective agitator, it is also a collective organizer."[15] Lenin went on to explain:

The mere technical task of regularly supplying a newspaper with copy and of promoting regular distribution will necessitate a network of local agents of the united party, who will maintain constant contact with one another, know the general state of affairs, get accustomed to performing regularly their detailed functions in the all-Russian work and test their strength in the organization of various revolutionary actions.[16]

In his major and seminal work, *What Is to Be Done?*, published in 1902, Lenin returned to the same theme. It is characteristic of the down-to-earth quality of his thinking that in this study, in which he stated the theoretical premises of Bolshevik ideology, he devoted an extraordinary amount of space to the mundane questions of organizing a single newspaper. He argued that putting out a paper would provide the activists with concrete tasks that would act as a catalyst for organization. Furthermore, he believed that publishing a national newspaper would help the socialists avoid the danger of localism.[17]

Lenin's immediate concern was to strengthen the position of the *Iskra* (Spark) newspaper group within the socialist movement. The paper, founded in 1900, had among its editors the great figures of early Russian Marxism, such as G. V. Plekhanov, Iu. O. Martov, V. I. Zasulich, and of course Lenin. *Iskra* played a decisively important role in directing nascent social democracy before the Party in fact was established. The moment of the greatest influence of the paper was the 1903 founding congress of the Party. The congress, which had the goal of unifying Russian socialists, in fact irrevocably divided them between Mensheviks and Bolsheviks. It also divided the *Iskra* group, which would never again work together. Although Lenin was originally victorious, he soon lost control of the newpaper to the Mensheviks, who continued to print it until October 1905.[18]

As authority disintegrated during the 1905 Revolution, illegal socialist publications transformed themselves into legal newspapers. These played a major role in coordinating the strike movement and other aspects of the revolutionary struggle. When Witte's government succeeded in consolidating its power, it once again closed down the socialist newspapers, including Lenin's *Novaia zhizn'* (New life), which appeared in Saint Petersburg in November and December 1905. The defeat of the Revolution, however, did not mean a return to the pre-1905 situation. The liberalized censorship laws gave the Social Democrats and Socialist Revolutionaries new opportunities.

The revolutionaries put out three types of newspapers. They published their central papers abroad and then smuggled them into the country. They brought out illegal publications, which appeared wherever the movement was strong. Finally, they had legal newspapers. Both the legal and illegal papers were ephemeral; the police would often close them down after a couple of issues. The severity of the repression varied from month to month and from town to town.

Between 1907 and 1912, the Bolsheviks made several attempts at legal journalism. Only two issues of *Zrenie* (View) appeared in 1907.[19] *Zvezda* (Star) was more stable. It came out first in 1910 as a joint venture between Bolsheviks and Mensheviks. Gradually, the Leninists succeeded in taking it over.[20] *Zvezda* started out as a weekly, but later it appeared three times a week. In its year-and-a-half existence, 69 copies appeared, of which 30 were confiscated. On eight occasions, it was subjected to heavy fines.[21]

In 1912, at a time when the revolutionary movement was gaining strength, the Bolsheviks succeeded in establishing a paper, *Pravda,* that had a crucial role in giving direction to the revolutionaries. The paper that first appeared in Saint Petersburg on May 12, 1912 (New Style) came out in printings of 20,000 to 40,000. All the leading Bolsheviks in the capital participated in its work. A worker, M. E. Egorov, became the nominal editor, whose main task was to sit in jail on occasion, while the real editors would continue their activities. N. G. Poletaev, who as a deputy of the Duma enjoyed immunity, was named publisher. In its two-year history, *Pravda* was closed down nine times, and it reopened eight times under a new name.[22]

The authorities observed their own rules in fighting the revolutionary press. They obviously knew who the real editors were, yet they were satisfied with jailing a dummy. They knew the paper that reopened the day after the previous one was closed, with the same editorial offices, the same subscribers, and the same collaborators, would also pursue the same policies. The revolutionaries did nothing to hide the facts; they trusted the government to observe its laws. Seven times out of eight, for example, they chose titles that included the work "pravda" (*Rabochaia pravda* [Workers' truth], *Pravda truda* [Work's truth], *Za pravdu* [For truth], *Proletarskaia pravda* [Proletarian truth], *Put' pravdu* [The road of truth], *Trudovaia pravda* [Workers' truth], *Rabochii* [Worker].[23] The editors went out of their way to emphasize continuity: The word "pravda" was always printed with the same script on the masthead, and yet the government tolerated this charade.

To avoid trouble, the journalists used a transparent Aesopian language. Instead of "Central Committee," for example, they would write "the leading group of Marxists," and instead of demanding nationalization of industry and a democratic republic, they substituted "the full and uncurtailed demands of the year 1905."[24] Out of the 646 issues that appeared in the course of two years, 190 were suppressed.[25]

Considering that Lenin did not set foot in Russia during *Pravda*'s prerevolutionary existence, it is remarkable how closely he was involved in its work. He published 265 articles in it.[26] He settled in Cracow at least in part to be as close as possible to the Russian capital, thus reducing the time for mail to arrive from and to Russia. When the Austrian police questioned him about his profession, he could answer more or less truthfully that he was a "correspondent of the Russian democratic paper, Pravda. " [27]

Lenin was ever watchful for ideological purity. When the Mensheviks started to publish their own daily, Luch, in September 1912, the Bolshevik leader perceived a threat. The socialist Duma deputies, six Bolsheviks and seven Mensheviks, had an understandable desire to unite the two fledgling Social Democratic papers. Indeed, four of the Bolshevik deputies' names appeared on the masthead of Luch, and all seven Menshevik deputies were listed as contributors to Pravda. Lenin was furious. He used all his considerable powers of persuasion to make his comrades in Saint Petersburg change their position.[28] In the following two years, he never stopped sending letters to the editors to encourage them to take an uncompromising attitude toward Menshevism.[29] Because in his view the editorial board was tainted by collaboration, he decided to reorganize it. The Cracow conference that met in January 1913, after criticizing Pravda 's editorial policies, named Ia. M. Sverdlov de facto editor.[30] Lenin was not an easy man to please. Although he had less trouble with the new editorial board than with the previous one, he continued to criticize ideological deviations and write angry letters to the editorial board. On occasion, embarrassed by Lenin's uncompromising policies, the board dared to omit his articles or to print them after a delay.[31] Such insubordination made Lenin furious, and he wrote more angry letters.

The Bolsheviks always maintained that their press from the very beginning was of a "new type." A cursory examination of Pravda and Luch does not bear out such far-reaching claims. In fact, the two papers were remarkably similar in style and content. Lenin instructed his followers to write simply for a worker audience. This was a sensible advice but hardly a major insight. Indeed, one would have had to be obtuse to do otherwise. The Bolshevik journalists were skillful in their appeal to their readers but not more so than other revolutionaries. Lenin was particularly keenly aware of the competition with the Mensheviks. He instructed his followers to make an attempt to outsell Luch in every factory.[32] According to admittedly unreliable Soviet figures, the Menshevik paper sold 9,000 to 12,000 copies daily compared to Pravda 's 20,000 to 40,000.[33] This superiority, however, was achieved by other than journalistic means. The Bolsheviks had more money and were by and large better organized.

The outbreak of the First World War marked the end of an epoch. The socialist movement suffered a brief eclipse. The drafting of workers and the temporary patriotic fervor greatly weakened the strike movement. In addition, under conditions of national emergency, the tsarist police stifled voices of socialist opposition. Pravda was closed down just before the beginning of hostilities, and it could not reopen. The police jailed Bolshevik leaders, and the Party was once again in the situation that had existed before 1905. The focal point of Lenin's journalistic interest became the *Sotsial-demokrat,* a newspaper published in Switzerland, where Lenin moved after the beginning of the war. In Russia, only a few underground presses existed and worked under extreme difficulties, never succeeding in putting out more than an issue or two.[34]

1917

In March 1917, the Bolshevik Party had approximately 25,000 members, its organizations were in disarray, and its influence on the masses of workers was minimal. By November, the Party's membership had grown to 115,000, it dominated the Petrograd and Moscow soviets, and at least temporarily it had gained the support of the workers in two capitals. How important was the press in this remarkable success? On one hand, it is clear that the Leninists were skilled propagandists, and on the other that the soldiers increasingly craved peace and that the peasants insistently demanded land. But was there a casual relationship?

An examination of the press in 1917 reveals that the Bolsheviks were victorious in the political struggle even though their enemies controlled the newspapers. A crucial segment of the Russian people came to hold opinions that the Bolsheviks had already advocated. The liberal order, born out of the March Revolution, was no more able than the tsarist regime to provide the country with a stable government. The Provisional Government disintegrated, and the Bolsheviks were able to pick up the pieces.

One of the first acts of the Provisional Government was to abolish on March 4 (Old Style) the Central Administration for Press Affairs, which in effect abolished censorship.[35] The government clarified the legal position of the press on April 27. It issued a regulation that explicitly declared the press to be free not merely from preliminary censorship but also from administrative penalties. It only required the editors of new publications to register their product.[36]

The legal situation of the press changed considerably as a result of the confusion of the July days. The government, feeling threatened from the left, and attacked by the right for lack of firmness, reimposed military censorship. The General Staff, which had demanded for some time that some form of censorship be reinstituted, now succeeded in closing down Bolshevik publications.[37] From this time on, the inability of the government to prevent the publication of subversive materials resulted not from a lack of legal remedies but from internal weakness.

From the first moment of the democratic Revolution, the Russians lived under dual power: The Provisional Government issued laws and carried the burden of responsibility, and the Petrograd Soviet of Workers' and Soldiers' Deputies enjoyed power because it could call on the workers and soldiers to strike and to demonstrate. The commitment of the socialist Soviet to the principle of the freedom of the press was less unequivocal than that of the "bourgeois" government. Since the Soviet could instruct the printers of any newspaper to go on strike, it was in the position to close down a newspaper if it chose. On March 7, the Executive Committee of the Petrograd Soviet carried out a passionate debate: The right stood for unlimited freedom, but the left and the center were determined to prevent the publication of papers that they considered reactionary. Although on this occasion the left prevailed, three days later the Soviet reversed itself. Evidently the leaders of the Executive Committee realized that for the time being the monarchists posed no danger. The Moscow Soviet, to its credit, never considered censorship.[38]

As a result of the passionate politics of the day, and of the lifting of censorship, the press flourished as never before. Understandably, the non-socialist papers continued to dominate. They had established reputations, and they possessed financial strength that enabled them to hire the best and most experienced journalists. With the exception of the monarchist right, which withered away in the radically changed political climate, almost every political point of view found a journalistic outlet.

Just as before the war, *Kopeika, Malen'kaia gazeta* (Little gazette), and *Russkoe slovo* were the most popular papers, appearing in printings of hundreds of thousands. Papers and such as *Rech ', Den', Novoe vremia, Birzhevye vedomosti,* and *Utro rossii* (Russian morning), which appealed to the educated, also retained their readers. As Lenin pointed out, although socialist parties got 75 to 80 percent of the votes in the municipal elections, the combined circulation of their papers was less than a quarter of the total.[39]

The socialist press could not compete in number of copies printed and in distribution with the bourgeois papers, but it nevertheless experienced a period of remarkable growth. The non-Bolshevik socialists were publishing approximately 150 newspapers by the end of 1917.[40] Considering that before the March Revolution the Socialist Revolutionaries and the Mensheviks were repressed as severely as the Bolsheviks, and that at the time of the revolution they hardly possessed any newspapers at all, this was a phenomenal development. Indeed, a weakness of the socialist press was that it reflected the fragmentation of socialist politics; every group published a paper on its own.[41]

It is remarkable how quickly Russian socialism recovered after the wartime suppression. The Petrograd Soviet started to function simultaneously with the creation of the Provisional Government and immediately, on February 28, started to publish *Izvestiia* (News). The central organ of the Mensheviks, *Rabochaia gazeta* (Workers' newspaper), appeared first on March 7, and the Socialist Revolutionary *Delo naroda* (The people's cause) on March 15. Among the socialist factions, however, the Bolsheviks were the quickest. The first issue of *Pravda* appeared on March 5.[42]

Pravda was created as a joint undertaking between the Russian Bureau of the Central Committee of the Bolsheviks and the Petrograd Committee.

There were considerable ideological differences between the two bodies at this time. The Petrograd Bolsheviks took a more friendly stance toward the newly formed Provisional Government. The first editorial board consisted on Kalinin, representing the Petrograd Committee, and V. M. Molotov and K. S. Eremeev of the Russian Bureau.[43]

It took some time to find a suitable press. The Bolsheviks, with the permission of the Petrograd Soviet, took over the printing establishment of *Sel'skii vestnik* (Agricultural herald), which before the revolution, had been a publication of the Ministry of Agriculture. The finances of the paper were tenuous, to say the least. The editors had at their disposal the ridiculously small sum of 100 rubles by way of working capital. *Pravda* did not pay for the use of the press, however, and the printers gave their services free. The editors acquired paper on credit. The first issue appeared in a printing of 100,000, and it was distributed free.[44]

The shifting political position of *Pravda* during the first weeks following the February Revolution obviously reflected the ideological confusion of the Bolshevik leadership, which was caught off balance by the revolutionary events. In this early period, the accident of personalities determined policy. Since the representatives of the Russian Bureau, Molotov, A. G. Shliapnikov, and P. A. Zalutskii, were the most prominent Bolshevik leaders in the capital, their point of view dominated the party paper. As a result, during the first days of its existence *Pravda* took an uncompromising position against the Provisional Government and denounced the war in terms similar to Lenin's. But the paper's point of view abruptly changed ten days after the appearance of the first issue. M. K. Muranov (an ex-Duma deputy), Stalin, and Kamenev returned from exile, and since they outranked the relatively junior leadership that had been in Petrograd at the outbreak of the Revolution, they took control of *Pravda*. Their policy did not differ much from that tactic advocated by the majority of the Petrograd Soviet: defensism, as far as the war was concerned, and conditional support of the Provisional Government. Naturally, the shift did not please all Bolsheviks. Lenin was furious. It is reported that on his return to Russia on April 3, the first thing he said to Kamenev, who came to meet him at the Finnish border, was: "What is this that is being written in *Pravda*? We saw several issues and really cursed you out."[45] Lenin quickly took command of the newspaper, which became an exponent of his policies and an instrument in the struggle for his April Theses. Between February and October, the Bolshevik leader published 180 articles in *Pravda*.[46]

In March and April, the Bolshevik daily appeared in printings of 80,000.[47] The Communists considered this circulation inadequate but did not have the means to expand it. The Party did not have its own printing press and did not have enough money. Under the circumstances, the paper repeatedly turned to its readers for help. It initiated a campaign in April, aiming to collect 75,000 rubles to buy a press and start another daily. The readers responded generously, and the Bolsheviks reached their goal; however, it turned out that the money was not enough, and therefore it was necessary to start other campaigns.[48]

The history of Bolshevik finances has never been satisfactorily explained. It is clear that the Bolsheviks were poorer than their enemies, in spite of the support they received from the Germans. Although German support helped, it would be mistaken to overstress its significance. Undoubtedly, without foreign money Pravda's circulation would have been somewhat smaller, and some secondary publications would have never appeared, but it would be hard to maintain that the political fortunes of the revolutionaries would have been fundamentally different.[49]

Pravda was the flagship of the Bolshevik fleet of papers. Its special place followed from the role of Petrograd in the political life of the country. The leading figures of the Party worked in the capital, and it was here that the Party was strongest. It was only natural that the other Bolshevik papers all over the country carefully followed the line set by Pravda. Local papers reprinted a great deal of the material from the central organ of the Party. About half the printed copies of Pravda were sent out of the capital.[50] The distribution system in Petrograd worked reasonably well, but the copies sent by mail often did not arrive, partly because of the general confusion and partly because of the hostility of the employees of the postal service and of the military high command. As a result, the direct influence of Pravda remained largely confined to the capital.

The second most important Bolshevik paper was Sotsial-Demokrat, published by the Moscow organization. It first appeared on March 7, which shows that the Moscow Bolsheviks were also quick to take advantage of the changing circumstances. The Bolsheviks occupied a private press, and the Moscow Soviet later sanctioned this revolutionary action. M. S. Ol'minskii, the editor of the paper, spent much of his time traveling between Moscow and Petrograd. The paper had a circulation of 60,000.[51] The Moscow Bolsheviks also had to work under difficult conditions: There was never enough paper, the printing facilities were poor, and the very existence of the paper was threatened by the lack of a suitable printing shop.[52] The Levenson firm, which had been obliged by the Moscow Soviet to do the printing for the Boshevik paper, was unhappy about the arrangement and sold its facilities to the city-zemstvo union. This organization demanded more money from the Bolsheviks than the private firm was able to do. Interestingly, Moskovskie vedomosti (Moscow news), an extreme rightist paper, was printed on the same presses and had priority.[53]

By the end of March, the Bolsheviks published papers in Kharkov, Kiev, Samara, Saratov, Kazan, Tbilisi, Reval, and Riga. In April and May, the network further expanded.[54] In spite of this expansion, the publication of newspapers continued to be a shoestring operation everywhere. Although the other socialist parties, the Mensheviks and the Social Revolutionaries, were not much better off, they enjoyed the advantage of support from the local soviets.

The Bolsheviks clearly saw the importance of taking their message to the soldiers. On March 30, the Kronstadt Bolsheviks succeeded in bringing out a daily, *Volna* (Wave), which became a source of strength of the Party among sailors of the Baltic fleet.[55] From April 15, the Military Revolutionary Organization of the Petrograd Committee published *Soldatskaia pravda* (Soldier's truth).[51] The paper had a circulation of 50,000, of which half was sent to the front. Other Bolshevik-front organizations later succeeded in publishing smaller papers.

In spite of their efforts, the Bolsheviks were heavily out-gunned. For the approximately 7 million soldiers in the army, the Bolsheviks could provide no more than about 100,000 copies daily. Even if we assume that each copy was read by several men, it is evident that the revolutionaries could reach only a small minority. The officers, understandably, did everything within their power to prevent the circulation of subversive, antiwar literature. The military postal service also frequently confiscated papers.[57] Furthermore, the Bolsheviks faced stiff competition. In May, approximately 150 military papers supported the war.[58] In June, the government set up a special committee on the military press under E. K. Breshko-Breshkovskaia, which had the task of improving the morale of the soldiers. The defensist socialists did not lack skillful agitators who knew how to address an audience of soldiers or workers and peasants. No amount of propaganda, however, could overcome the soldiers' ever-increasing distaste for the war. The soldiers came over to the Bolsheviks' side in spite of the relative weakness of their propaganda.

The Bolsheviks were also conspicuously unsuccessful in spreading literature among the peasants. The leadership, above all Lenin, was well aware of the importance of winning peasant support, but given the widespread illiteracy and disrupted communications, the obstacles were formidable. The Sixth Congress of the Party in July recognized the weakness of propaganda efforts in the countryside and called for increased efforts. Only in October, however, did the Moscow and Petrograd organizations start to publish papers designed specifically for peasant audiences. The Moscow paper, *Derevenskaia pravda* (Rural pravda), amusingly, had on its masthead: "Proletarians of the World Unite!" It came out only three times a week and had a circulation of 20,000.[59] *Derevenskaia bednota* (Rural poor) had a slightly larger circulation. It is evident that the few copies of a paper that existed only for a few days before the Bolshevik Revolution could not possibly have had a measurable political impact. The peasants wanted to take landlord property not because the Bolsheviks persuaded them.

The violent demonstrations that occurred in the beginning of July in Petrograd changed the political atmosphere of the country. It was increasingly clear that the Provisional Government was losing control over the situation. Whether or not the Bolsheviks were responsible for the demonstrations, their political opponents took advantage of their failures and initiated a series of attcks. For a short time, it seemed that the Bolsheviks would suffer a political eclipse. This did not happen, largely because the Provisional Government could not provide the country with stability. When a few weeks later the right, in the form of the Kornilov mutiny, attempted to change the status quo, it was the left that benefited from the failure. Counterrevolution once again seemed a more immediate danger than leftism extremism.

After the July days, the political struggle became more violent. From the beginning, the Bolshevik press suffered more than merely verbal attacks. On May 12, for example, unidentified people burned down the editorial offices of *Soldatskaia pravda*.[60] The enemies of the Bolsheviks subjected them to all sorts of petty harassment: In Moscow, for example, newspaper boys who belonged to the union were allowed to travel on streetcars free of charge. But the union, controlled by Socialist Revolutionaries, expelled the newsboys who sold *Sotsial-Demokrat*.[61]

In the increasingly embittered political environment, the Bolsheviks were subjected to passionate press attacks. Almost the entire press was united against them, from the socialist *Edinstvo* (Unity) to the rightist *Zhivoe slovo* (Living word). The most hostile articles accused Lenin of being a German agent. Others maintained that by encouraging demonstrations and disorder the Bolsheviks played into the hands of the enemies of their country.[62] The press campaign was effective. In July 1917, a political party could still be hurt by being described as a German tool. The virulence and success of this campaign had a considerable impact on Lenin. Without doubt, it contributed to his decision, taken after the victory of the Bolshevik Revolution, that all hostile papers should be closed down . The enemy proved that in the struggle of words it could deal effective blows.

The attack was not limited to a press campaign. At 6 o'clock on the morning of July 5, a detachment of Cossacks and military-school students appeared at the editorial offices of *Pravda,* disarmed the guard, arrested the Bolsheviks who were there, and destroyed the offices.[63] On the following day, a hostile crowd destroyed the presses on which both *Pravda* and *Soldatskaia pravda* had been printed. The loss was approximately one hundred and fifty thousand rubles, which was a considerable blow to party finances.[64]

Under the pressure of events, the government decided to close down subversive papers. It was through this order for the reimposition of military censorship that *Pravda* and *Okopnaia pravda* (Trench truth) were closed officially on July 15. These repressive moves put the Bolsheviks in a situation similar to that which prevailed before the war. Once again, they were forced to change the name of their paper. *Rabochii i soldat* (Worker and soldier), the successor of *Pravda*, reappeared only on July 23, with a circulation of 20,000. Although the circulation gradually increased, it never again reached the pre-July level. Anti-Bolshevik measures were taken elsewhere in the country, also. The military command was especially anxious to use the opportunity and close down papers it had long considered subversive.

In this period of repression, the Bolsheviks returned to their old tactic. When on August 10 the government closed down *Rabochii i soldat*, the Bolsheviks immediately brought out *Proletarii*. This paper existed for two weeks, after which it was superseded by *Rabochii*, which lasted for nine days and was in turn succeeded by *Rabochii put'*.[65]

The new revolutionary wave and the general turn to the left that followed the Kornilov mutiny were accompanied by a growth of the revolutionary press. Circulation figures once again started to climb, and Bolshevik organizations in various parts of the country began publishing newspapers. By the time of the October Revolution, the Party had 75 publications, of which 25 were dailies.[66] It is estimated that the combined circulation of these papers was 600,000 daily.

It is possible to correlate Bolshevik strength with the circulation of their newspapers only to a limited extent. It is true that following the July days, which were a period of weakness for the Party, distribution figures declined and that as the Party gained strength the figures started to increase again. It is also evident that the Bolsheviks were strongest in cities where their papers had the best distribution. However, it is difficult to establish a casual relationship. The great change in the mood of the soldiers was not accompanied by a corresponding increase in the circulation of Communist newspapers. The change occurred for reasons independent of the revolutionaries, who were simply there to take advantage of it.

The suppression of the non-Bolshevik press

The Soviet press came into being in a historically unprecedented situation: It was created and protected by a one-party revolutionary state. This fact essentially determined its character. It is understandable that the Bolshevik papers, once relieved of the pressure of competition, developed characteristics that were unique at the time. The decisive development was the immediate suppression of the free press.

Ideologically, Lenin was prepared for such a move. It is not that he had advocated censorship before. The Bolsheviks, as a revolutionary underground party, had to battle censorship, and it was natural that in their writings the revolutionaries should denounce tsarism for limiting the freedom of the press. Nor did Lenin advocate the institution of censorship after the victory of the future revolution. Neither Lenin nor anyone else envisaged the circumstances in which the Bolsheviks would emerge victorious. The revolutionaries assumed that the revolution would be carried out by the great majority of the people, and, consequently, the question of repression would not even arise. However, Lenin was never a liberal. He placed little value on "formal" freedoms, such as freedom of the press, and it was clear from his writings and actions that he would not hesitate to take steps, however brutal, when the success of his movement was at stake.

35

In retrospect, the first warning signal was contained in *What Is to Be Done?* After his famous denunciation of spontaneity, Lenin wrote:

Since there can be no talk of an independent ideology formulated by the working masses themselves in the process of their movement, the *only* choice is – either bourgeois or socialist ideology. There is no middle course (for mankind has not created a "third" ideology, and, moreover, in a society torn by class antagonisms there can never be a non-class or an above-class ideology). Hence, to belittle socialist ideology *in any way, to turn aside from it in the slightest degree* means to strengthen bourgeois ideology. There is much talk of spontaneity. But the spontaneous development of the working-class movement leads to its subordination to bourgeois ideology . . .

A few paragraphs later, Lenin went on:

But why, the reader will ask, does the spontaneous movement, the movement along the line of least resistance, lead to the dominance of bourgeois ideology? For the simple reason that bourgeois ideology, being far older in origin than socialist ideology, is more fully developed and has at its disposal *immeasurably more means of dissemination.*[67]

It is a peculiar notion that bourgeois ideology is more effective because it is older, and it is somewhat surprising to find Lenin, the defender of Marxist orthodoxy, arguing that socialism was insufficiently developed. But he was unquestionably correct in maintaining that the bourgeois possessed far better means for spreading its ideas. Lenin would return to this point again and again, and it ultimately came to be a justification for censorship. However, the main significance of these passages is in showing that even in this early period Lenin did not accept the principle that one fights ideas with ideas and that he did not trust the workers to arrive at "correct" conclusions it two sides of an ideological issue were presented. It would be an exaggeration to say that these statements from *What Is to Be Done?* implied approval of censorship, but they are certainly consistent with Lenin's attacks on the freedom of the press two decades later.

It was during the 1905 Revolution that Lenin first explicitly discussed the question of the freedom of the press. In his article "Party Organization and Party Literature," he argued that literature should be party literature and that the literature of the proletariat should be under the control of the organization of workers, that is, the Russian Social Democratic Worker's Party. Literature should be an instrument in the class struggle.[68] To those who objected that this development would result in control of creativity, he responded with two arguments: First, though individuals have the right to say anything they desire, organizations have the right to exclude those who do not agree with their fundamental principles; second, talk about absolute freedom of the press is hypocrisy, since in bourgeois society writers depend on those who finance them.[69]

In 1905, Lenin did not foresee that his party soon would be in a position to suppress the opposition. He was preparing for a period when the workers would struggle against the bourgeoisie and would only begin to organize for a socialist revolution. Under the circumstances, suppressing nonsocialist papers was not an issue, because it was not a realistic possibility. Once again, however, Lenin made it clear how little regard he had for the "bourgeois" notion of free expression. Most disconcertingly, in his article he failed to draw a distinction between literature and journalism. Present advocates of artistic freedom in the Soviet Union cannot find much encouragement in it.

The February Revolution made freedom of the press a practical issue. The Bolsheviks supported the efforts of the Petrograd Soviet to close down reactionary-monarchist papers. Lenin had only scorn for the March 10 decision of the soviet, which reversed itself and allowed papers to appear without previous permission.

The traumatic events in Petrograd in early July and the new opportunities presented by the failure of the Kornilov mutiny changed Lenin's tactics in the revolutionary struggle in general and his attitude to the press in particular. In his article "How to Assure the Success of the Constituent Assembly?," published on October 15, he wrote:

The capitalists (and many SRs [Socialist Revolutionaries] and Mensheviks following them either through misunderstanding or inertia) call freedom of the press that situation in which censorship is abolished and all parties freely publish any paper they please. In reality, this is not freedom of the press but freedom for the rich, for the bourgeoisie to mislead the oppressed and exploited masses.[70]

Lenin proposed to remedy the situation by suggesting that the soviet would declare a monopoly on printing advertisements. This move would undermine the financial strength of the bourgeois press and help the socialists. Then he went further. He realized that in the short run what mattered most was the availability of paper and printing facilities. Therefore he proposed the expropriation of all paper and printing presses and their distribution according to the political strength of the parties in the two capitals.

Simultaneously, in another article, Lenin advocated closing down the major bourgeois papers such as *Rech'* and *Russkoe slovo*.[71] He did not make it clear how the two sets of suggestions could be reconciled. After all, the Kadets did have substantial voting strength in Petrograd and Moscow.

Throughout the years, Lenin was consistent in his attitude toward the issue of freedom of the press. It is true that in the fall of 1917 he did not renew his call for party-mindedness as developed in his 1905 article. But the reason was not a newly found liberalism. His article "How to Assure the Success of the Constituent Assembly?" was addressed to the socialists in the Petrograd Soviet. It is unlikely that he expected them to adopt his ideas, but he certainly hoped to score debating points. On the other hand, in September 1917 Lenin did not yet envisage a one-party regime in which only a single voice could be heard. Had his recommendation been followed, the Russian people would have been exposed to a multiplicity of opinions. This was, of course, not the policy the Bolsheviks chose after they took power.

On October 25 the Bolsheviks struck, seizing the Winter Palace, the ministries, the post and telegraph buildings, and at the same time the printing presses of *Russkaia volia* (Russian will). The next day the Military Revolutionary Committee (MRC) issued a resolution, temporarily forbidding the publication of bourgeois papers and counterrevolutionary publications.[72]

The MRC at once named a commissar for press matters, N. I. Derbyshev, a Bolshevik printer. In the middle of November, A. F. Minkin took over. He had the right to report directly to the Council of People's Commissars, Sovnarkom. Soon the soviets in major cities formed press departments.[73]

In the first two days of its existence, the new regime attempted to close down hostile newspapers. Since all the major papers opposed what they regarded as a coup d'etat and many of them published Kerensky's manifesto, the Bolsheviks faced a difficult task. The MRC sent soldiers to occupy the offices of the major newspapers of the country; "bourgeois" and socialist papers suffered alike. The MRC attempted to close down twenty newspapers; however, at a time of great confusion the new authorities did not yet have the power to enforce their decisions, and therefore some of the offending papers continued to be printed and distributed.[74]

It is not necessary to search for ideological reasons for trying to prevent the publication of hostile literature. It is perfectly understandable that during the transition period extraordinary measures had to be taken. A far more important question was what attitude the authorities would take toward freedom of expression once their rule was established.

On October 27, Sovnarkom published its decree on the press.[75] This decree, after repeating Lenin's view on the bourgeois notion of the free press, gave Sovnarkom the right to close down newspapers that advocated resistance to the new authorities or attempted to "sow disorder by the publication of clearly slanderous misstatements of facts." The last paragraph asserted that the decree was temporary and that after the return of normal order, complete freedom of the press would be assured.

A few days later, on November 4, an important debate erupted in the Central Executive Committee of the Congress of Soviets (CEC). The issue was even more profound than freedom of the press. What kind of regime would follow the Revolution? At the time it was unclear whether the exclusively Bolshevik Council of Commissars could retain power or the Bolsheviks would accept a compromise and bring the Socialist Revolutionaries (SRs) and Mensheviks into the government. The majority of the supporters of the October Revolution hoped for a socialist coalition. It was demanded in forceful terms by the union of railroad workers, who possessed considerable power through their ability to call a strike. The idea of coalition was obviously also attractive to an important element in the Bolshevik leadership. At this point the issues of coalition and the freedom of the press became intertwined. Obviously it was not possible to suppress the publications of moderate socialists and at the same time to induce them to participate in the government. It seems fitting that the first crucial and bitter debate that took place within the Soviet leadership concerned free expression.

The Central Executive Committee of the Congress of Soviets had sixty-seven Boshevik, twenty-nine Left SR, and twenty other socialist members.[76] When Sovnarkom issued its decree on the press, the CEC did not object. The revolutionaries understood that the exceptional circumstances necessitated exceptional measures. Ten days later, however, when the issue was thoroughly discussed, circumstances had changed. The debate that took place was remarkable not because of the profundity of the views expressed but because the two points of view, both expressed with great passion, represented real and irreconcilable differences in the vision of the coming socialist order.

B. F. Malkin, a Left SR and the editor of *Izvestiia,* said:

We firmly repudiate the notion that socialism can be introduced by armed force. In our view socialism is a struggle not merely for material advantages but for supreme moral values. The revolution's appeal lies in the fact that we are striving not just to fill our hungry bellies, but for a higher truth, the liberation of the individual. We shall win not by closing down bourgeois newspapers but because our programme and tactics express the interests of the broad toiling masses, because we can build up a solid coalition of soldiers, workers and peasants.[77]

Later, in the heat of the debate, he responded to an opponent: "You are dishonoring the socialist movement by depriving it of its moral force."[78]

V. A. Karelin, another Left SR, argued that suppression of views would only make those more attractive. Prominent Bolsheviks, such as Ia. Larin and D. B. Riazanov, also spoke up in the defense of free expression.

The Leninists, by contrast, were willing to subordinate all values to the immediate interests of the Revolution. In their position one can sense a certain ambivalence. They defended suppression by pointing to immediate and presumably temporary needs, but at the same time they made it clear that they had little regard for "formal" notions of freedom.

V. A. Avanesov said:

We defend the freedom of the press, but this concept must be divorced from old petit-bourgeois notions of liberty. If the new government has had the strength to abolish private landed property, thereby infringing the rights of the landlords, it would be ridiculous for Soviet power to stand up for antiquated notions about liberty of the press.

His resolution included these sentences:

The restoration of so-called "freedom of the press," i.e., the return of the printing press to the capitalists, poisoners of the people's consciousness, would be an impermissible capitulation to the will of capital, a surrender of one of the most important strong points of the workers' and peasants' revolution, and thus indubitably counterrevolutionary.[79]

Trotsky in his speech distinguished between the present and the future. "During the civil war it it legitimate to suppress newspapers which support the other side."[80] For the future he promised a new regime in press matters but was not specific, only saying that the press would be in the hands of the soviets.

Lenin based his argument both on expediency and on principles. He put it picturesquely: "If we want progress toward social revolution, we cannot allow the addition of lies to the bombs of Kaledin."[81] He went so far as to say that allowing bourgeois papers to exist was the same as ceasing to be socialists.

The Leninist position prevailed. Avanesov's resolution was adopted by a vote of 34 to 24 with one abstention.[82] It included these sentences:

The CEC repudiates categorically any proposals leading to a restoration of the old regime in press matters, and supports the Sovnarkom unconditionally against pretensions and intrigues dictated either by petty-bourgeois prejudices or by outright servility to the counterrevolutionary bourgeoisie.

The resolution not only affirmed Sovnarkom's press decree, but advocated further action:

The next measure should be to confiscate private printing presses and stocks of newsprint, and to transfer their ownership to organs of Soviet power in the center and in the provinces, so that parties and groups may have technical means to publish in proportion to the number of their adherents.[83]

It was at this point that people's commissars V. Nogin, A. Rykov, V. Miliutin, and I. Teodorovich resigned.[84]

The November 4 meeting of the CEC was a turning point in the history of the revolution. One can well imagine that had Lenin's opponents possessed more political acumen the outcome of the vote would have been different. The concept of the future, inherent in the thinking of the defenders of the freedom of expression, was obviously profoundly different from Lenin's ideas. On the other hand, the likelihood is that if the revolutionaries had repudiated Leninist methods, the regime would not have lasted very long. The events between February and October proved that Russia could not be administered in accordance with liberal principles. Those who refused to learn this lesson were condemned to defeat. Lenin, after all, was correct: The new regime could not tolerate freedom of expression; nor could it repudiate terrorist methods.

The adoption of Avanesov's resolution did not immediately result in a Bolshevik monopoly of the press. First of all, the Leninists did not yet desire such a monopoly. It was one thing to advocate suppression of the forces hostile to the Revolution and quite another to claim that there could be only one correct interpretation of all political events. Time had to pass before the Bolsheviks came to this view. But even if the Bolsheviks did secretly desire such a monopoly, it was good politics to proceed gradually. Prematurely frightening the uncommitted might have had dangerous consequences. But most importantly, the Bolsheviks lacked the means to suppress all enemies, real or potential. The new regime's control of the workers of Petrograd and Moscow was weak, and its control of the rest of the enormous country was minimal. As a consequence, the first eight months of the Bolshevik regime represented a twilight period for the Russian press. It was a period in which liberal and socialist journalists tried to defend themselves by rallying public support and by attempting to circumvent the regulations of the new authorities. Meanwhile the Bolsheviks were making increasingly successful efforts to impose order on the country and to undermine the strength of their enemies; only when they considered themselves strong enough did they carry out frontal attacks.

The Bolsheviks' first obstacle was the Menshevik-dominated printers union. The printers' opposition to the press decree surfaced even before the CEC debate. On November 1, the union notified the MRC that if the press decree was not rescinded, "the Union would use all available means for pressure"; that is, it would call a strike.[85] On November 6, a meeting of union representatives passed a resolution (171 to 69) that made the threat explicit.[86] The MRC was forced to engage in discussion with the printers in which the arguments used at the CEC meeting were repeated. The printers proved themselves to be just as eloquent defenders of freedom as the socialist politicians. However, the position of the printers was seriously weakened by the fact that the Bolsheviks controlled a large enough minority to shatter solidarity in case of a strike. At a time of extremely high unemployment, the Bolsheviks were able to prevent a strike.[87]

As in all other aspects of national life, great confusion prevailed in the regime's policy toward the press during the first weeks following the October take-over. The MRC or Sovnarkom frequently closed down newspapers, which then simply changed their names and continued to appear. Rech,' for example, appeared under five different titles in the course of a few weeks, and the SR paper, Volia naroda (The people's will), had six different names.[88] The Bolsheviks arrested editors and journalists, but almost all of them were freed within a few days. Furthermore, the situation varied a great deal from city to city. In Moscow, for example, repression was far less severe than in Petrograd. The Moscow MRC went on record in support of free expression exactly when in Petrograd the CEC reaffirmed Lenin's position. The decree issued on November 6 forbade only the printing of proclamations calling for armed struggle against the Soviet power, but it allowed all papers to publish.[89] Indeed, moderate socialist publications continued to appear in Moscow until March 1918, when the government moved to that city. In the rest of the country, the views and power of the leading local

Bolsheviks determined the position of the press. In the first few months, hundreds of newspapers were closed down in provincial cities.

During the transition period, the Bolsheviks often did not feel strong enough to carry out frontal attacks and therefore turned to indirect means. In the early days of the regime, they confiscated the presses of such major papers as *Rech'*, *Novoe vremia*, *Birzhevye vedomosti*, *Zhivoe slovo*, and *Kopeika*.[90] These presses were taken over by Soviet publications. The confiscation of printing facilities was, of course, a heavy blow to the bourgeois papers. They were forced to find smaller presses and contract their work. The newspapers that managed to survive did so with greatly reduced circulations.

The worst problem for all the newspapers was a shortage of paper. Publications tried to protect themselves by hiding their paper supplies. Already on October 26 the MRC ordered a complete inventory of paper, and a few days later it forbade the removal of paper from Petrograd.[91] However, in the confusion it was relatively easy to disobey the MRC; indeed, it was necessary to do so to stay in business. But when the Bolsheviks did succeed in confiscating scarce material, it was often tantamount to closing down a hostile newspaper.

As compared to the confiscation of presses, paper, and newsprint, the regulation that outlawed the printing of advertisements was only a petty harassment. Lenin first presented this idea in September 1917 and clung to it with a lack of realism that was uncharacteristic.[92] On his initiative, Sovnarkom passed a regulation on November 15, according to which only government publications would be allowed to print advertisements after November 22, 1917.[93] The newspapers resisted, and the socialist press, which by and large had not carried advertisements, started to do so as a solidarity gesture. A. I. Minkin, the commissar for press affairs, who foresaw the difficulties, asked and was assigned one hundred sailors from MRC to overcome resistance.[94] In many cities the local soviets failed to take any steps to carry out this particular decree.

After the end of the Civil War, Lenin himself admitted that outlawing advertisements had been a mistake.[95] It created a great deal of resistance and focused hostility on the Soviet regime, at the same exhibiting the powerlessness of the government. The damage inflicted by this regulation on the bourgeois press was trivial: With the economy of the nation in ruins, advertisements were no longer an important source of financial strength.

During the first months of the regime, Soviet policy toward hostile journalism was inconsistent. The authorities closed down newspapers for small violations of vague and sweeping laws while allowing others to print truly subversive material. To bring consistency into the confused situation, the Commissariat of Justice on December 18 decided to set up revolutionary tribunals for press matters. I. Z. Shteinberg, the commissar for justice and a Left SR (the Left SRs joined the government as junior partners in mid-November), issued regulations for the operation of these tribunals that appeared much too lenient for the Bolsheviks. They circumvented this leniency by using the Cheka (Extraordinary Commission, the political police), which of course remained safely in their hands. The jurisdictional struggle that erupted between the commissariat and the Cheka was resolved by Sovnarkom in favor of the Cheka.[96] The Bolsheviks had a firm majority in Sovnarkom. On January 24, the government decided that though revolutionary tribunals would deal with newspapers as collective entities, the Cheka could continue to arrest and punish editors as "counterrevolutionaries."

Four days later Sovnarkom issued a decree on the operation of revolutionary tribunals that went much further than Shteinberg's. Although the revolutionary tribunals were previously intended to punish those who printed falsehoods, the new regulations were aimed at those who published "anti-Soviet material," obviously a much broader and vaguer category. The punishments mandated by the new decree were also more severe: Instead of fines, jail or exile.[97] Legal and extra legal repression became ever harsher.

The work of the press tribunals in Petrograd started at the end of January, and they were later introduced in the rest of the country. Although setting up these institutions gave one more weapon to the new regime in the struggle against its enemies, the tribunals themselves could not solve the basic problem, which was the weakness of the government. The decisions of the tribunals remained inconsistent, and anti-Soviet material, for example Gorky's articles, continued to be published.

A study of the material of the revolutionary tribunals gives interesting glimpses of those confused days. One of the first to suffer was the major Menshevik paper, Den '(Day). The charges against the paper were these: It changed its name several times; it described Bolshevik rule as unstable; it reported about conflicts between the workers and the government; and it wrote that the Bolsheviks had intended to hand over Petrograd to the Germans.[98] It is unlikely that any of the leading Bolsheviks appreciated the irony of the situation. After all, Pravda not so long before changed its name just as often as Den ' did, and the Bolsheviks had also accused the Provisional Government with no justification whatever of wanting to hand over the capital to the enemy.

The signing of the Brest-Litovsk treaty caused further dissension, the withdrawal of the Left SRs from the government, and a new series of repressive measures. A tribunal accused Novyi vechernyi chas (New evening hour) with frightening the public about the danger of Japanese intervention. Volodarskii, the new press commissar and chief prosecutor, charged socialist and liberal newspapers with crimes no greater than "creating the impression that Soviet rule was weak."[99] To close down a paper it was clearly not necessary to prove that it had written something untrue.

The final attack on the non-Bolshevik press occurred in June–August 1918. After that time only one point of view could be expressed. Why did Bolshevik tolerance came to an end at this particular moment?

To some extent, the Leninists simply responded to the moves of their opponents. The abortive SR rising in early July finished all possible hopes for cooperating with other socialists. During the late spring and early summer of 1918, the Civil War in the east and in the south assumed ever more serious proportions. Red terror and White terror reinforced one another.

It would be naive, however, to regard the Bolsheviks as merely reactive and to see the repressive regime that emerged from the revolution as entirely the result of the bitterness of the Civil War. The existence of the Red regime was threatened more seriously during the first half of 1918 than during the second. In the first months of that year, the regime was almost destroyed by sheer anarchy; by the inability of the Bolsheviks to feed the cities and make the state machinery function. In the second half of 1918, Bolshevik rule became more repressive at least partly because now the Bolsheviks had more strength to suppress. The final closing down of all liberal and socialist newspapers in the middle of 1918 was a natural step in the process of ever-increasing repression.

The Soviet press during the Civil War

What kind of press did the Bolsheviks create in an environment in which their monopoly was assured? There was general agreement among the revolutionaries who concerned themselves with journalism that the press functioned poorly and could not carry out its assigned tasks. Observers criticized the content and format of the newspapers and also recognized their technical poverty. Worst of all, from the point of view of the Soviet leadership, their circulation remained low.

Immediately after the October Revolution, the Bolsheviks enjoyed the fruits of their victory. They confiscated the paper supply, machinery, and buildings of the bourgeois papers as spoils of war. On October 27, *Pravda* took over the presses of *Novoe vremia*. On the same day, the MRC of Petrograd gave the presses of *Den'* to *Derevenskaia bednota* and those of *Rech'* to *Soldatskaia pravda*.[100] According to a Soviet historian, the Bolsheviks had confiscated 30 presses by the end of 1917, 70 by July 1918, and 90 by the end of that year.[101] With the help of these confiscated goods, the Bolsheviks were able to increase the circulation of their papers and establish new ones. *Bednota* (village poor), *Ekonomicheskaia zhizn'* (Economic life), *Zhizn' natsionalnostei* (Life of the nationalities), *Komunar* (Member of the Commune), *Kommunistka* (Women Communist), *Rabotnitsa* (Worker woman), and *Voennoe delo* (Military affairs), among others, started to appear shortly after the Revolution.[102] At the end of 1918, Soviet Russia had 563 newspapers and 753 journals. The overall circulation of Bolshevik papers had increased approximately tenfold since Lenin's government took power.

The most difficult problem continued to be the lack of paper and newsprint. In 1914 the Russian Empire produced 33 million poods of paper, but in 1920, the worst year, Soviet Russia produced only 2 million. The paper shortage in 1920 was so great that Sovnarkom was willing to use its precious foreign currency to buy 400,000 poods from Estonia.[103] The paper that was available was poor in quality, often hardly better than wrapping paper. The situation in regard to newsprint was almost as bad. The quality was so poor that on occasion entire columns were completely unreadable.

The shortage of paper inevitably resulted in falling circulations. Many papers closed down, the publication schedules of others became erratic, and such major papers as *Pravda* and *Izvestiia* appeared during the second half of the Civil War in editions of only two pages. *Izvestiia* had the largest circulation in 1919, appearing in printings of 300,000 to 400,000 depending on the availability of paper. The average figure for *Pravda* was 130,000.[104] Such popular papers as *Krasnaia gazeta* (Red newspaper), published in Petrograd as an evening daily, had so little paper that they did not accept individual subscriptions, preferring to send their copies to institutions, where they had a larger readership.[105]

The newspapers also suffered from a lack of trained personnel. The Menshevik-dominated printers' union continued to be hostile. There was a dearth of typesetters and of people capable of operating the machinery. As a result the appearance of the newspapers was poor. Trotsky addressed a gathering of printers with the words:

Comrade printers, our printing technique is terrible. Whole series are so blurred that you cannot make out a single line. The number of misprints, jumbled lines are innumerable. To the person who for ten years has become accustomed to reading papers and understands a phrase from two words, it is difficult, often times impossible, to decipher the idea of our newspaper articles. Under the circumstances how much more difficult is it for the young Red Army soldiers, often semiilliterate?[106]

Looking at issues of *Pravda, Izvestiia,* and *Petrogradskaia pravda* (Petrograd truth), just to mention the best papers of the time, one is struck by the dullness of format. The Bolsheviks had learned nothing of the techniques of the yellow press. The central papers did possess means to reproduce drawings and caricatures, but photographs never appeared.

Distribution was a major problem. The postal service did not function adequately, and at least at the beginning of the conflict, it was in the hands of nonsocialist workers. Since postal workers often refused to deliver Bolshevik newspapers, these had to be sent surreptitiously in parcels and practically smuggled here and there by traveling soldiers and activists, just as before the October Revolution. Local Party organizations constantly complained that newspapers and other propaganda material did not arrive from the center. *Pravda,* for example, wrote on October 27, 1918, that the Vitebsk Party Committee had received only two or three copies of *Izvestiia* per month.[107] In 1957 Soviet historians published the correspondence between the secretariat of the Party's central committee and local Party organizations in 1917 and 1918. Complaints about the unavailability of newspapers in the villages is a constant refrain in these letters.[108]

Another difficulty in the development of the press was the lack of qualified journalists. The Soviet regime faced the problem of not having enough trained people in almost every area of reconstruction, but the shortage of journalists was especially acute. The regime could hardly entrust to potential enemies the sensitive matter of conveying its point of view. The task did not attract party activists. Newly converted but uneducated soldiers and workers were capable of carrying out oral agitation among workers and peasants, but they of course could not write effectively. Among the top leaders, journalism did not have as much prestige as work on the front, in industry, or in administration. Lenin had to admonish his colleagues repeatedly to write more often for the newspapers. Naturally, in the provinces skilled journalists were even more scarce, and as a result the state of local journalism was indeed pitiful.

Because every local soviet and army unit wanted to have its own paper, even one incapable of producing effective propaganda, there was a great proliferation of publications. At the end of the Civil War, more periodicals were printed in Russia than had been printed in peacetime. Soviet historians today use these figures to show how quickly the press developed. But at the time the leaders well understood that a few strong papers would have been more beneficial, and they regarded proliferation both as a sign and as a cause of weakness.

The Party, wisely, stressed the need to improve agitation among the peasantry. This policy was used to justify claims for paper on the part of local organizations. It was one thing to publish a newspaper, however, and another to carry out successful agitation. The provincial papers failed to make contact with village life. By and large they reprinted articles from *Pravda* and *Izvestiia* and filled their pages with the texts of laws and regulations. Without village correspondents and journalists willing and able to travel and investigate, information on village life came from hearsay. Papers appeared irregularly, and their "original" articles were even duller than the ones they copied from the central press.[109] At the same time a large share of the central papers was sent out of the major cities. In 1920, for example, of the 350,000 copies of *Izvestiia*, 279,000 were sent out of Moscow; of the 250,000 copies of *Pravda*, only 41,000 remained in the capital. *Bednota*, aimed at the peasants, was distributed almost entirely in the villages. All in all, 65 percent of the papers printed in Moscow were sent to the provinces.[110]

The Red Army was politically a most powerful organization. During the second half of the Civil War, when the number of civilian papers declined for the lack of resources, the military press continued to expand. At the end of 1918 there were 90 newspapers published by various military units, and in the course of 1919 the number grew to 170.[111] For the army, distribution was no problem, and the investment in indoctrination definitely paid off.

The Bolsheviks published newspapers not only for their own soldiers but also for the enemy. They were particularly interested in reaching the soldiers of the interventionist armies. The Commissariat for Foreign Affairs established a propaganda section in December 1918, which published *Call*, an English-language weekly, in printings of 15,000 to 20,000.[112] After the Comintern was formed in 1919, it took over responsibility for agitation among foreign troops. The demoralized soldiers, who did not want to be in Russia to begin with and had only the vaguest understanding of political circumstances, were willing listeners. It is quite likely that the Bolsheviks contributed to the resounding fiasco of French intervention in South Russia by further undermining the morale of the foreign soldiers.

Agitation among the soldiers was a relatively easy task compared to creating a network of newspapers for the entire country. Journalists and party leaders alike were aware of the technical and ideological weaknesses of the press and discussed these problems repeatedly. L. S. Sosnovskii, editor of *Pravda*, reported to the Eighth Party Congress in March 1919 on the situation of the press. He talked about the confusion in the provinces concerning the financing of newspapers. He complained about the ideological unreliability and lack of education of provincial editors and journalists.[113] Then he submitted a set of resolutions, which the congress accepted. This was the first:

The general weakening of party work at the time of the civil war badly damaged our Party and Soviet press. A general weakness of almost all Party and Soviet publications is a remoteness from local and often from general political life. The provincial Party and Soviet press almost completely ignores local life and chooses its material on general issues extremely unsuccessfully. They print long, uninteresting articles instead of responding with short, simply written articles to the main issues of national and local life. On occasion entire pages are printed with decrees, instead of explaining in a simple and understandable language the most important point of the decree. Newspapers print rules and regulations of different offices and departments instead of making from this material a lively chronicle of local life.[114]

The resolution blamed the failures of the press on the fact that most experienced party leaders paid too little attention to newspapers. In view of the importance of propaganda, the congress directed local organizations to send their most experienced and talented people into press work. It assigned the task of supervising the local press and commenting on questions of Party construction to the central press. The task of the local paper was exclusively to appeal to a mass audience, to discuss their problems in simple language. That this resolution had little effect can be seen from the fact that the Eleventh Congress in 1922 found it necessary to repeat all the main points.

Two congresses of journalists at the time of the Civil War, in November 1918 and May 1919, also looked for ways to improve the work. The deliberations show that the Soviet press was still in a formative stage and that journalists still held a variety of opinions about shaping its character.

The first congress was called by the Moscow committee of journalists, which invited all who were willing to cooperate with the Soviet government, Communists and noncommunists alike.[115] The top leadership of the Party paid great attention to the congress, and such important figures as Kamenev, Radek, Lunacharskii, and Kollontai gave addresses. All speakers agreed that the press should pay more attention to life in the villages and factories. There was, however, an interesting disagreement over the question of audience. Sosnovskii argued that all papers should be written for simple people, but the resolution of the congress spoke of "leading" papers and "mass" papers. In spite of this resolution, the intellectual level of such leading papers as *Pravda* and *Izvestiia* was not appreciably higher than that of local papers, even if those in the capital were more professionally produced.

The journalists devoted considerable attention to the organizational aspect of their work. The resolution called for the establishment of a Central Council of Journalists (Tsentrosovet), which would not only protect the professional interests of journalists but would also be responsible for such matters as the distribution of paper and information. Nothing came of these plans. Tsentrosovet was an organization of little influence, which within a few months ceased to exist. The Party was not about to give control of crucial matters to an outside authority; the journalists were simply disregarded. The political-ideological orientation of newspapers and the appointment of leading cadres continued to be the responsibility of the Central Committee of the Party; distribution of paper, newsprint, and machines was handled by the Central Economic Council (VSNKh); and Sovnarkom set up the Russian telegraph agency (Rosta) to distribute information.

The mood and character of the second congress of journalists in May 1919 was altogether different.[116] The organizers understood that in the developing system there could be no such profession as journalism but simply a party function for publishing newspapers. The press would have no other task than to spread and advertise the policies and decisions of the Party. But the Party did not support even such a modest conception. The newly elected central committee of journalists soon fell apart when the Party sent its members to different parts of the country. The Party had no interest in supporting even the slightest degree of professional independence among journalists: It wanted no mediators between its policies and the publicizing of those policies.

The Civil War years were the formative period of the Soviet press. The Bolsheviks repudiated the principles governing the bourgeois press, but they did not have a clear idea of the kind of newspaper that would be appropriate for the new age. There were no models to follow and many questions. What subject matter should the Communist press emphasize? What should be the style? On what level should the journalists address their readers? Lenin made a major contribution to these discussions in an article in *Pravda* in September 1918.

48

The article "About the Character of Our Newspapers" began with the practical statement that it was necessary to write simply and concisely for the masses. Lenin recommended that to be effective, journalists should deal with concrete situations. But he went much further. He argued that Soviet newspapers should devote less space to politics.

Instead of 200–400 lines, why don't we talk in 20–10 [*sic*] about such matters as the treachery of the Mensheviks, who are the lackeys of the bourgeoisie, or such as the Anglo-Japanese attack for the sake of reestablishing the sacred rule of capital, or such as how the American billionaires gnash their teeth about Germany. These matters are simple, well-known, and to a considerable extent already well understood by the masses.[117]

What should the press write about then? In Lenin's opinion more attention should be given to economics. He did not have in mind, however, the discussion of such issues as war communism, the effects of outlawing free trade in grain, or the consequence of the workers' control of the factories. He wanted detailed reports of which factories did their work well, of which ones did not, and of how success was achieved; above all, he wanted to unmask the guilty—those who did not do their work. They were class enemies. The press should be an instrument of the dictatorship of the proletariat, exposing those who through poor work in fact helped the enemy. These were the last lines of the article:

Less political noise. Less intelligent-like discussions. Closer to life. More attention to how the masses of workers and peasants *in fact* build something new in their everyday work. More *documentation* of just how *communist* this new is.

Lenin was implying that there was no point in discussing the political and economic issues of the day, for those had been decided. It is significant that this article was written exactly at the time when the last vestiges of a critical, non-Bolshevik press disappeared. There remained no one to polemicize against. Politics as a conflict of opinion, as a presentation of alternatives, no longer existed. The public realm of discussion was drastically narrowed and remained so for decades.

It would be naive to think that the Soviet press developed as it did because editors followed the advice of the founder of the system. But Lenin's article was prophetic. Today's *Pravda* would please him: The journalists admonish workers to do their job well, they single out specific factories for praise or blame, and they most certainly waste no space on "intelligent-like" discussion of large political issues in terms of alternatives.

49

CHAPTER 2

The struggle for the peasants

The Russian Revolution is best understood as a process in which authority collapsed. The institutions of the tsarist regime could not stand the test of a modern war, and the ideology of the tsar and his ministers was inappropriate at a time when circumstances demanded mass mobilization. The liberal ideology of the Provisional Government was no more capable of holding the country together at a time of war and extraordinary hardships than the ideology of the tsarist government had been. During the revolutionary year of 1917, anarchy threatened the Russian people.

The Civil War, which inevitably followed the Revolution, was a time in which several groups of people experimenting with different ideologies, and drawing support from different social groups, competed in trying to recreate order. Among the many contenders only two groups had a chance, the Whites and the Reds. This was not because they were the most popular. Anarchist rebel leaders best understood the mentality of the peasants, and the elections to the Constituent Assembly clearly showed that among politicians the Russian people preferred the Socialist Revolutionaries. Only the Bolsheviks and the ex-tsarist generals, however, approached the conflict with principles on the basis of which it was possible to organize functioning armies and to administer territories.

It is impossible to understand either the Whites or the Bolsheviks in isolation. They had much in common: They faced similar problems and, perhaps surprisingly, shared some attitudes to those problems. But, of course, the differences between them were more striking. Their ideological background, their training, their goals, and their social support impelled them to deal with significant issues differently. An examination of these issues will help us understand the outcome of the Civil War.

A civil war is usually a contest between the weak and the weaker. Even a most cursory study of the 1917–21 period will show that both Reds and Whites were weak and disorganized and had a great deal of trouble in winning peasant support. Bolshevik policies and accomplishments, specifically propaganda, seem impressive only in a comparative context.

The Bolsheviks had no special propaganda institution for work among the peasants. It was clear to them from the very beginning that administration and propaganda were inseparable, and therefore it was most important to establish their presence in the villages. They needed to show the peasants that they had the strength and determination to enforce their will. Building administrative institutions, that is, authority, and carrying out propaganda always went hand in hand.

The oral-agitation network

The inability of the Provisional Government to, on the one hand, satisfy peasant demands for land and, on the other, prevent unauthorized land seizures obviously greatly contributed to the collapse of the liberal regime. Although the Bolsheviks encouraged peasant activism, their contribution to the spreading anarchy was minimal; they simply benefited from it. After their Revolution their task became much more difficult: Instead of undermining authority, they had to create it. The new rulers could not be satisfied any longer with allowing events to take their course but had to attempt to bring order out of chaos and to establish themselves in the countryside.

Lenin was clearly aware of the importance of gaining peasant support. He and the other leading Bolsheviks spared no effort and were extraordinarily inventive in finding ways to bring their message to the peasants. Their base was the Party. This institution embodied the Leninist principles of organization, and it proved to be extremely useful in the hands of the revolutionaries in every aspect of national life. The difficulty was, of course, that the Party was weak in the countryside. The crucial local Party organization of the time was the city committee, *gorkom,* of which approximately 300 existed at the end of 1917.[1] It was the task of these committees to coordinate the work of factory cells, organize propaganda among the soldiers, and, most importantly, extend control over the local soviets. The decisive political struggle that was taking place in Russia at the time was the ultimately successful attempt of the Bolsheviks to take over the hitherto independent soviets. They succeeded in this effort because their enemies were disorganized and politically naive.

Russia both before and after the October Revolution was deeply politicized. It was a country of mass meetings, oratory, slogans, and posters. A variety of viewpoints competed for attention. The simple people, who had never heard the idea before, were told again and again that they held the future of their land in their hands, and in a limited sense this was true.

It was in this environment that the Bolshevik agitators had to operate. Anarchy seemed uncontrollable. One district after another voted for Socialist Revolutionary resolutions. The anti-Bolsheviks, although disorganized,

51

remained active. They spread silly rumors about how the Bolsheviks planned to set up communes, how they wanted people to share their property and even their wives. The Bolsheviks by no means had a monopoly on demagogy.

The Bolshevik position had both strengths and weaknesses. The city-based Communist ideology had little inherent appeal to the backward peasantry. Talk about revolution was not attractive to those who craved peace. Worst of all, the new regime had to feed the hungry cities and could offer little or nothing in exchange for food. Consequently, to stay in power the Bolsheviks could not avoid requisitioning, and given the circumstances, such an undertaking was bound to be brutal. On the other hand, the Leninists had a trump card. Unlike their enemies, the Whites, they could allow the peasants to take the land.

Lenin, the master politician, produced his decree on land on the first day of his regime. The decree was a compromise between commitment to an eventual socialist agriculture, in which the revolutionaries continued to believe, and political expediency. Lenin consciously drew up his decree so that it was a propaganda instrument.[2]

Distribution of the land decree became the major task of the propagandist during the first weeks of the regime. The Bolsheviks used all available means. When returning home, each delegate from the Second Congress of Soviets was given a propaganda package, including the latest issues of newspapers and the land law.[3] The Bolsheviks also used demobilized soldiers to take their message to the peasants, and each was given a copy of the land decree.

Lenin's secretary, M. Fofanova, described in her reminiscences the days following publication of the land law. No doubt she exaggerated the joy with which the peasant soldiers received these pieces of paper, but she is completely believable when she talks about Lenin's interest in matters of distribution.

Knowing that I conducted agitational work among the soldiers and peasants who came into the Smolnyi, Lenin asked to me explain to each the meaning of the decree on land. "Discuss with each," underlined Lenin, "what we should do with the land that now it became national property." I remember with what eagerness the peasants took from our hands these pieces of paper with the text of the decree. They took them in bunches, they took them carefully as bread, hiding them in their knapsacks. At times some added: "It is better to put them in the bottom, otherwise you might accidentally use such important paper to make cigarettes." I read often these first decrees of Soviet power aloud and every time as I looked at the faces of the listeners I became convinced of the correctness of the Leninist thought: that the Bolsheviks not only took power but that they were going to retain it. The Bolsheviks attempt to give to the toilers the most important things: peace, bread, and land. And every time Ilich met me, he asked keenly, I would even say passionately, about what do the peasants and soldiers say about this decree and what were their wishes.[4]

Bonch-Bruevich described an even more colorful and striking story.[5] He too wrote about Lenin's great interest in explaining to the soldiers the land decree, and he described how involved the great leader was in the mundane issues of distribution. But in his version it was Lenin rather than the soldiers who were worried about the important document going up in smoke.

"Here is a problem. There is no paper, no newspaper, and one must smoke. From the decree he is going to roll a cigarette." Vladimir Ilich became silent and a few minutes later with a sly smile he turned to me: "You know what, Vladimir Dmitrievich, go to the Sytin firm [a major publishing house]and ask them whether they have some old calendars. Let them give us some . . . Then the decrees will get further in the soldiers' bags. They won't touch them until they get to the village. For cigarettes we will give them each a calendar.[6]

Bonch-Bruevich was not an altogether reliable witness. It is suspicious, for example, that the paragraph just quoted appears only in the later versions of the article "How Vladimir Ilich Wrote the Decree on Land." Nevertheless, the picture is so marvelously vivid and fits so well with our image of the immensely practical statesman finding a simple solution to a genuinely important problem that we are inclined to believe it.

In the crucial months immediately after the Bolsheviks took power in Petrograd, the decisively important agitational work was done by people who went from the cities to the country to report on the mood of the peasants, to agitate, and to organize. Some of these people were experienced Party workers, but the great majority of them were novices: demobilized soldiers and sailors, and simple workers who volunteered for the task. Almost all of them came from humble backgrounds. Consciously or unconsciously they were attracted to the new regime because it gave them an opening; they had a chance to become members of a new elite. Many of the future Soviet leaders began their carrers in these months. The leatherjacketed Communist functionary became a familiar figure in the countryside. Some of these people were tactless, and their condescension and imperiousness alienated the peasants. Nevertheless, on balance, the revolutionary authorities benefited from the services of a committed minority. The ability of the Bolsheviks to offer something to talented young men, and on occasion women, distinguished them from their enemies, the Whites.

The activists who were sent to the countryside to acquaint the people with Leninist land policies were also instructed on how to establish soviet power in the villages. Already at the end of October the Central Committee turned to the Petrograd rayon organizations to select agitators for work in the villages. To train these people, the Party set up brief courses in agitation.[7] The military organization of the Party was especially important in selecting candidates from demobilized soldiers. According to the estimate of a Soviet historian, in the postrevolutionary months 10,000 activists went from Petrograd into the countryside; and by July 1918 approximately 50,000 people were participating in this work all over the country.[8]

The Party published a pamphlet by Ia. Burov in January 1918 to help the agitators.[9] This little pamphlet is revealing of the Bolshevik mentality at the time. The work is full of down-to-earth advice: The author explained to his readers how to prepare for their trip in both practical and ideological terms. He included the addresses of organizations that the agitators might need and explained to them how they could get further information. In a few pages, Burov summarized Bolshevik programs and policies in remarkably simple language, clearly aimed at untutored people. After these essentials, he turned to more difficult matters. He told the agitators what to do if a questioner raised the issue of the dispersal of the Constituent Assembly. They were to tell the peasants that the elections had been invalid, for the uneducated electorate had been misled by the name of the party, "People's Freedom," into believing that it really stood for the people's freedom.[10]

On the question of organizing Soviet power in the villages, Burov, addressing himself to ex-soldiers, used a military analogy. The village was the platoon, *volost'* was the equivalent of the battalion, *uezd* should be thought of as a regiment, and the province was the same as the division.[11] Then the author advised the agitator how to behave. As a soldier, he should understand the importance of reconnaissance.[12] He should spend his first days acquiring information: Do the peasants know about the peace decree? Do they know about the land decree? Do Soviet authorities exist? Most important, who are the leading figures in the village and what is their political attitude? The next task of the agitator was to find five—but if there were not five then two or three—intelligent and reliable people among the poor peasants to whom he should explain the political situation and the needs of the moment. Only then should he turn to the third task, which was to convene the village assembly. Here he had to have the aid of the local peasants who had already been initiated. The village assembly should discuss the questions of land and peace and soviet power, preferably in such a way that the agitator remained in the background. The agitator should see to it that the assembly elected as leaders reliable poor peasants.

Once in secure control of the village, the activist could proceed to organize on the volost' level. If in the volost' or in the district power is in the hands of the anti-Bolsheviks, the activists must insist on new elections. Then, finally, the activists must get in touch with those regional authorities that were already in Bolshevik hands.

The reports of Bolshevik activists are our best source on what was happening in the countryside. In the enormous country conditions greatly varied, and in some places the revolutionaries were stronger than elsewhere, but nontheless the same themes were repeated: The country was in the throes of anarchy; Party organizations hardly existed; Bolshevik printed propaganda did not reach the peasants.

For example, D. Arkhipov from Tambov province reported on December 7, 1917:

I arrived in Narovatovo in Temnikovskii district. Complete chaos. In the summer a few cells were organized, but now they all fell apart. To the extent one can understand it from the explanation of the local peasants, the organizational collapse and anarchic events occurred as a result of the efforts of the Kadets, who received armed help from the local kulaks. The people do not know anything about newspapers and decrees, that is, these do not appear here. When you explain to the peasants the complete October turnover and the new government, the peasants relate to this positively and are upset that they had been deceived by their enemies. The local priests, in their majority, I am told, carry out propaganda for the monarch. There is need for many workers, for the task is enormous.[13]

A certain Ankudovich, writing to the Military Revolutionary Committee in Petrograd on November 14, drew a somewhat more sanguine picture:

On November 8th of this year, according to the instructions of the Military Revolutionary Committee of the Soviet, I left for Vilna province, Disnetskii and Vilna districts, as an agitator. On my arrival in the little village of Glubokoe I turned to the committee of the 11th transport battalion for cooperation. The Glubokoe garrison, which has four platoons of Ussuri Cossacks, two shock battalions, and other units, organized a general meeting. On November 12th, those who gathered there heard my report about the current moment and about events in Petrograd and accepted the resolution which I offered with one absention out of five hundred.

Later I went to the village of Mal'kovichi, Vilna district, where the entire population was called together, that is, 19 households. Following my report, I suggested that the village join the resolution passed by the Glubokoe garrison, and this was unanimously accepted. On November 14th, I went to the little village of Dunilovichi, Vilna district, on a day on which a fair was held. I suggested to the peasants that they gather in the volost' building and they eagerly agreed. Here also the peasants unanimously and eagerly joined the resolution passed by the Glubokoe garrison.

In conclusion I must say that the peasants are very interested in the revolutionary events, but unfortunately they are confused by village kulaks who attempt to win them over to the position of the defensists. Also, the social-parasitic newspapers are widespread in almost every village, though I did not see anywhere Bolshevik newspapers with the exception of Petrograd *Izvestiia,* and that rarely. The Bolshevik literature that I took with me turned out be so little that it disappeared immediately, and many, many who wanted our newspapers could not get them. Volost' committees, even where they exist, are made up of such elements that try to confuse the peasants rather than improve the situation.[14]

A. A. Rozhkov, reporting to the Military Revolutionary Committee on November 26 from Tver province, found particularly unfavorable conditions.

Allow me to inform the agitational bureau on the course of my agitational work. It cannot be said that Korcheva, Tver province and district, sympathizes with the new, people's power, in the form of the Bolshevik People's Commissars . . .

Korcheva district, especially the elected officials, is completely bourgeois-SR-Kadet. They do not wish to recognize the real, people's power, in the form of the People's Commissars of Lenin and Trotsky and others. They say that they operate on the basis of the Provisional Government of Kerensky. I told them that I was empowered to dismiss the zemstvo and recommended and demanded dismissal and new elections in view of the fact that they were elected at the time of Kerensky . . . I demanded to speak at the zemstvo meeting, but they did not let me. They postponed my report to next week. They do not want to know about the existing government.[15]

Gradually the Bolsheviks succeeded in emasculating autonomous peasant organizations. Their agents took over most of the soviets, and they dispersed those elected bodies that were uncompromisingly hostile. They did not recoil from the use of force. Slowly they created a network of Party committees. These, located in provincial and district towns, to use a military analogy much favored by the Bolsheviks at the time, became bases in a hostile environment.

From about the beginning of 1918, the character of the work of the emissaries from the cities changed. The new authorities' greatest problem in the spring of 1918 was hunger in the cities. The Party organized detachments of workers to requisition food from the peasants. These workers had the extraordinarily difficult task of combining taking food from the peasants by force, without adequate compensation, and carrying out propaganda. The strategy of the Party was to sharpen the hostility between the poor and not-so-poor peasants. Activists from the cities formed committees of poor peasants, *kombedy*. At this time the Bolsheviks regarded only the poor peasants as reliable allies.

Bolshevik requisitioning, which was necessary for the survival of the regime, alienated the majority of the peasants and made the work of agitators difficult. Decrees of the government and resolutions of Party congresses showed an awareness of the need to improve work. The leaders believed that the greater the hostility, the more important it was to expand the propaganda network, and to do so it was essential to devise an organizational framework and to impose at least some control.

From the point of view of the Party, the problem was that individual agitators enjoyed considerable independence, since effective supervision in the prevailing conditions was impossible. In an attempt to strengthen discipline, from early 1918 the local Party organizations that requested agitators from the cities had to assume responsibility for them. After returning from the countryside, the agitators were required to fill out standard questionnaires on their experiences.[16]

From the beginning and throughout the Civil War, the main difficulty was that the Communists did not have enough reliable and able people to work among the peasants. The Bolsheviks attempted to overcome this problem in an imaginative, albeit utopian, fashion. The Soviet government in December 1918 published a decree that mobilized the literate citizens of the country for reading aloud to their less fortunate fellows. If we can believe N. K. Krupskaia, the initiative came from Lenin himself.[17] The decree obliged Narkompros (People's Commissariat of Enlightenment) to select readings and the local soviet and party organizations to draw up lists of literate citizens suitable for this work. The readers had to read aloud articles from the press and, in particular, acquaint the population with the laws and regulations of the Soviet government. The reading was compulsory and without compensation. The decree obliged the local soviets to send monthly reports to the district and provincial executive committees.[18]

It is impossible to establish to what extent the instructions of the Soviet government were carried out. One suspects very little was actually done. Where reading aloud was most important, in the remote villages, Party strength was not sufficient to force compliance. The decree, however, is a testimony both to the Bolsheviks' determination to take their message to the people and to their optimism about their ability to do so.[19]

The Eighth Party Congress, in March 1919, addressed itself to the question of how to improve propaganda work in the villages. The resolution, drawn up by Lenin himself, recommended the combination of propaganda with the spread of agricultural information and general education.[20] The congress directed local Party organizations to set up village reading rooms, *izba chital'nia*, for literate peasants. These institutions, which were to be supplied with newspapers, pamphlets, and the classics of Marxist literature, were to grow into Communist strongholds in the countryside.

The resolution paid special attention to reaching the illiterate. It repeated the call to set up sessions of reading for the peasants, and it sensibly pointed out that to make these reading sessions attractive, it was advisable to combine political readings with literature texts and showings of films.

The delegates understood that teachers were important in village life, but they doubted the educators' political reliability. Therefore their resolution made the teachers responsible not only to their superiors in the educational hierarchy but also to the local Party organizations. To improve the political training of all agitators, the congress recommended setting up regional committees of propagandists to train and supervise activists.[21]

The Party was constantly concerned with the political reliability of the agitators. The regional Party organization in Smolensk, for example, instructed agitators to discuss all matters at cell meetings before taking the issues to the peasants. The Smolensk organization also betrayed a concern with the private life of the Party workers. It advised its workers not only to study the theoretical questions of Marxism but also to set a personal example by leading irreproachable lives.[22]

Within a short time, the agitational network expanded enormously. It was difficult to coordinate agitation because every major Soviet institution in one way or another participated in it. The overlapping responsibilities created misunderstandings and institutional jealousies.

The trade unions were particularly important. On the one hand, they carried out important work among their own members, and on the other, they provided the unorganized part of the population with worker-activists, traveling theatrical groups, and lecturers. The trade unions indicated again and again that they were not content to remain executors of policies made elsewhere.[23] The Central Council of Trade Unions (VTsSPS) demanded that its representatives join the presidium of the Extramural Education Department of Narkompros. Leaders of the trade-union movement argued that in cultural work full initiative had to be given to the workers themselves, that is, the trade unions. In their view, the Commissariat of Enlightenment had only to finance the work among the workers on the basis of budgets prepared by the cultural sections of the unions.[24] To Lunacharskii, to Krupskaia, and to the other Narkompros leaders, who professed to believe in decentralization and local initiative, the unions' arguments were difficult to refute.

The Extramural Education Department of Krupskaia also had disagreements with the Political Department of the Army (PUR), which was responsible for agitation among soldiers.[25] PUR, which carried out essential work of indoctrination, did not have enough trained agitators and therefore needed help from civilians. In the dispute over jurisdiction, Narkompros prevailed. At the end of 1920, the Party allowed the commissariat to take charge of indoctrination among soldiers, with the exception of front-line units.

Perhaps the most difficult task was to delineate responsibility between the Party and the Commissariat of Enlightenment. Often the national network of education and the local Party organizations did not work together harmoniously. In theory the relationship between the two organizations was simple: The Party was to provide guidance and supervision, and the government bodies were to do the practical work. The problem was that the Party committees, which possessed the resources, frequently did not show much interest in education. In any case, Party leaders in the provinces did not trust the educational hierarchy. The dispute over how the tasks should be divided was resolved only after the Civil War.

Agitational trains and ships

An unusual and yet typical Bolshevik method of oral agitation was to send agitational trains and ships into the ountryside. As long as the Civil War continued and the front lines moved back and forth, and as long as the government apparatus and the Party remained weak, it made good sense to bring the government, however temporarily, to the people.

This idea, like many others at this time, came from the military. In the earliest period of the Civil War, much of the fighting occurred along the railroad lines. This was the so-called echelon warfare: Each side tried to send its meager forces quickly to places where they were most needed. The train had many uses. Trotsky, for example, set up his headquarters in a railroad carriage, and he went from one trouble spot to another, taking charge of, punishing, or inspiring troops. Railroads also carried a great deal of propaganda material to the soldiers at the front. In August 1918, the Military Section of the Executive Committee of the Soviets decided that instead of sending only printed matter, it would be desirable to equip a train with agitators who could do more than merely distribute leaflets. The first agitational train, named *V. I. Lenin,* was sent to Kazan, where the eastern front was developing and crucial battles were taking place.[26] The organizers evidently considered the trip a success, for the same train a short time later undertook another journey. From September 1918 to March 1919, *V. I. Lenin* visited little towns in Belorussia, Lithuania, and the Ukraine. With the defeat of the Germans, the Western borderlands acquired military significance, and the Red Army moved into the vacuum left by the German withdrawal.

The success of *V. I. Lenin* inspired the Executive Committee of the Soviets to create a commission in January 1919, headed by Ia. I. Burov, which had the responsibility to organize and then supervise the work of other agitational trains and ships. This commission also oversaw the establishment of agitational stations, *agitpunkty,* at major railroad stations. These agitpunkty contained libraries stocked with propaganda material, lecture halls, and often theaters. In the chaos of those days, passengers were often stuck for several days waiting for their trains and were eager to listen to anyting that offered diversion.

The most important task of the commission, however, was to supervise the work of agittrains. The task of these, according to a 1919 resolution, was "to establish ties between the localities and the center, to agitate, to carry out propaganda, to bring information, and to supply literature."[27]

The brain and heart of the agittrain was the political section. It drew up the itinerary and assigned responsibility to each co-worker. Its chief, the political commissar, was also the commander of the train. The section was responsible for directing and carrying out agitation and for providing help to the local authorities. It included representatives of the Central Committee of the Party, of various commissariats, of the Komsomol, and even of the Cheka.[28] In provincial towns and villages where the train stopped, members of the political section established contact with the local authorities: The man from the Cheka inspected the secret police, the representative from Narkompros inquired about the problems of schools, and so on.

The Bolshevik leadership attributed great significance to the trains, and the other major figures of the Party and of the government at one time or another participated in their work. For example, the *Oktiabrskaia revoliutsiia* (October Revolution), the most famous and important of the trains, had among its activists D. K. Kurskii, commissar of justice, N. A. Semashko, commissar of health, G. I. Petrovskii, commissar of the interior, and V. A. Lunacharskii, commissar of enlightenment.[29] In this way the leading figures of the regime could gain firsthand acquaintance with problems. Since they were among the most powerful people in the country, they were in a position to make immediate decisions: They could remove local leaders when they considered it necessary, and they could promise help when conditions warranted.

The task of the other important section of the train, the bureau of complaints, could not easily be separated from the responsibilities of the political section. When Kalinin embarked on his first trip in April 1919, he gave an interview to *Izvestiia* in which he stressed the importance of listening to complaints.[30] The trains accepted thousands of petitions and complaints. It was good policy to convince the peasants that Soviet power was interested in their problems and in listening to them.

The information section was responsible for organizing lectures and distributing brochures. It also controlled a most important piece of equipment carried on the train, the film projector. The infant Soviet film industry produced special films for the agittrains. In addition, the film performances included newsreels and films for children, which were usually shown during the day, in order to reserve the evenings for the adults. The peasants, the overwhelming majority of whom had never experienced this particular wonder of technology, were fascinated. Watching newsreels and seeing the leaders of the Soviet state, Lenin and Trotsky, gave the peasants a feeling of intimacy that had considerable political impact. The films attracted the audience, and the agitators took advantage of the opportunity by scheduling their lectures either before the show or during an intermission. Lenin, with his customary practical sense, quickly grasped the films' propaganda potential. After evaluating the work of agittrains in January 1920, he proposed investing precious foreign currency to buy raw film and projectors abroad.

Each agittrain also carried a press, which permitted it to print its own newspapers and leaflets. And each train's radio station enabled it to keep in touch with the capital. When the trains visited Red Army units, the commissars could report to Moscow on the conditions they had found. One coach on each train was a garage for small automobiles and especially motorcycles so that the activists could go even to remote villages far from a railroad line.

In Russia at the time of the Revolution, the trains were still considered symbols of the new age. The Soviet regime, consciously or unconsciously, used this symbol. To enhance the festive atmosphere, the trains were brightly decorated. At first they were covered with modernist paintings, but this was clearly a mistake, for the peasants did not care for abstract art. The Bolsheviks soon learned the lesson and repainted the trains with pictures of heroic soldiers, peasants, and workers and with bright slogans.[31] The trains themselves, as moving posters, were instruments of propaganda.

On the average, a train carried about a hundred people. Only fifteen to twenty of these were engaged in political agitation. The rest were support staff, who operated the presses and projectors and drove cars. The trains were composed of sixteen to eighteen carriages and had internal telephone systems.[32]

The best-known agittrain was *Oktiabrskaia revoliutsiia.* M.I. Kalinin was the political commissar of this train, and he spent most of the Civil War period traveling. In the course of 1919, *Oktiabrskaia revoliutsiia* made twelve trips of approximately three weeks each. The leaders had the military situation in mind as they chose the itinerary. The train visited the front to raise the morale of the soldiers and the districts just behind the front line to make the rear more stable. The train also frequently went to districts that had just been freed from the enemy. For many peasants, the agitators who came to their villages on these trains were the first representatives of Soviet power they had encountered. Since the Southern and Eastern fronts were the most active, most of the journeys of *Oktiabrskaia revoliutsiia* were in those areas.

Kalinin and his fellow agitators chose different themes to appeal to peasants, soldiers, and Cossacks. When talking to soldiers, Kalinin frequently spoke of the purpose of the war. He played up his peasant background. For example, in September 1919, M. Frunze introduced him to his soldiers this way: "Comrade Kalinin is himself a peasant, a most simple person, and none the less he heads the many millions of Russian people. This fact, unthinkable before, this fact shows the great transformation that the working class and the peasants of Russia have accomplished.[33]

Among peasants, Kalinin's strategy was to make his audience talk about problems. It seems Kalinin was especially skillful in this. He would call a village or volost' meeting and ask the participants whether they had received payment for requisitioned food, whether the division of land had taken place to everyone's satisfaction, whether the land put aside for Soviet farms had been well cultivated.[34] He would purposely bring up subjects considered sensitive by others. He, of course, knew that the peasants resented the special taxes, were suspicious of soviet farms, and did not like the restrictions on grain trade. He explained again and again the Bolshevik position: Outlawing free trade in grain was necessary to prevent speculation; soviet farms would benefit Russian agriculture and therefore, in the long run, the peasants themselves; special taxes were necessary to win the war against the enemies of the peasants, the Whites. He, and the other agitators, made special efforts to persuade the peasants to give up their food voluntarily to feed the hungry cities.

The Bolshevik agitators promised the Cossacks that Soviet power did not wish to destroy their way of life and did not want to force them into communes. They attempted to persuade their audiences that the really significant differences were not between Cossacks and non-Cossacks but between the rich and the poor. Here, as elsewhere, the Bolsheviks tried to increase class antagonism and champion the poor against the rich.

In the second half of 1919 and in 1920 a degree of specialization developed among agittrains: *Krasnyi vostok* (Red east) spent the first half of 1920 in Turkestan, and it had on board a special group of agitators capable of dealing with Central Asian and Muslim affairs. *Krasnyi kazak* (Red Cossack) specialized in work among Cossacks, touring the Don region when major battles were taking place between Denikin's armies and the Red Army.

Krasnaia zvezda (Red star) was an agitational ship. Its political commissar was V. M. Molotov. N. K. Krupskaia, who represented Narkompros, was a participant. *Krasnaia zvezda* made two long trips on the Volga and Kama rivers. Since it operated in areas with large minority populations, and since the Party did not possess enough agitators who could address these people in their native languages, film was an especially important medium. The ship pulled a large barge, which was a floating cinema capable of accommodating six to eight hundred people.[35] Krupskaia left behind a diary in which she described her experiences. The diary conveys vividly the confusion that prevailed in these frontier districts and the weakness of Soviet power.[36]

In January 1920, Burov's section on agitational trains and boats reported to Lenin. Lenin in his response suggested that the work of the agitators be enlarged. He recommended the addition of agronomists and other technical experts, who could provide immediate help to the peasants. Further, he encouraged the agitators to leave the beaten track and seek out remote settlements by means of motorcycles or bicycles.[37] It is clear that Lenin appreciated the value of this type of agitational work.

Burov's section required the agitators to submit reports on their trips. In these reports the participants counted up all the metings, film performances, and even the audience. Very likely the figures were inflated, for it was impossible to check. However, there is no reason to doubt that much was accomplished. According to these reports, in the course of 1919 and 1920 the activists held 1,891 meetings, gave 1,008 lectures, visited 4,000 Soviet establishments and offices, accepted 14,000 complaints, printed and distributed 1.5 million leaflets and newspapers, and attracted between 2.5 million and 3 million people to their meetings and more than 2 million to their movie performances.[38]

The experience of agitational ships and trains shows Bolshevik inventiveness in propaganda. It also shows that the Bolsheviks understood that administration and agitation could not and should not be separated. This understanding was one of the important reasons for the superiority of Bolshevik propaganda to that of their enemies.

The Soviet leaders regarded the experience of agitational trains, ships, and stations as a success. Following the Civil War, *Oktiabrskaia revoliutsiia* continued to make journeys until the middle of the 1920s. At the time of the Second World War, the regime revived the trains to contribute to the indoctrination of soldiers. In civilian life agitational stations came to assume an important role in mass mobilization at the time of the numerous elections carried out by the state. Since the 1930s, agitational stations have been features of Soviet life.

The Whites, the church and the Bolsheviks

One of the main reasons for the Bolsheviks' victory in the Civil War was the political incompetence of their enemies. The White leaders lacked the ability to understand and face the political problems of the country. As officers, they searched for solutions on the battlefields, not realizing that their primary task was political rather than military.

In the earliest stages of the conflict, at a time when the anti-Bolshevik officers were operating under very difficult circumstances, they had only limited means to reach the Russian people. At this time the public statements of the leading generals were largely confined to appeals for patriotism. In their mind it was clear that the Bolsheviks were traitors, bent on destroying "Russia," and they simply could not understand that reasonable and honest people could see matters differently. As officers who commanded troops in battle for years, they so strongly believed in the justice of Russia's cause in the World War, and in the wickedness of the German enemy, that they saw their immediate political adversaries, the Bolsheviks, simply as German tools.

Generals Kornilov and Alekseev, the two organizers of the movement, asked the Russian people to overthrow illegitimate Bolshevik rule for the glory of the fatherland and for the opportunity to get on with the really important struggle against the foreign enemy. Such an attitude, increasingly far removed from the real world, was self-defeating. It was this almost ludicrous inability to understand the nature of Bolshevism and the sources of its strength that allowed them to believe that they could postpone the resolution of the crucial issues facing the country until order was restored.

After the passage of a year, after the World War ended, and after the Whites in South Russia came to control a substantial territory with a large population, the Whites were forced to build an administrative structure. By this time the need for propaganda was so evident that even the White leaders could not fail to see it. A part of the new skeleton government of the South Russian anti-Bolshevik movement was a propaganda department, Osvag (from Osvedomitel'noe-agitatsionnoe otdelenie, informational-agitational department). That the Whites had a special propaganda organization was more a sign of weakness than of strength. By contrast, all Bolshevik agencies, most importantly the Party, carried out agitation. As we have seen, the Reds combined administering and propagandizing.[39]

The Communists were much more conscious of the need to take their message to the people. Perhaps because of this awareness, they were better propagandists than their enemies, as is universally agreed. Nevertheless, the White and the Red appeals each had strengths and weaknesses; this is why the Civil War lasted for three years.

There were several reasons for the Whites' relative weakness as propagandists. The most important was that they possessed no coherent ideology. They did not understand the significance of ideas in the political struggle, and therefore they never felt the need for clearly articulated goals. Since they were basically comfortable in Imperial Russia, they did not desire the civil war. Their allegiance to the antiquated social and political system was unquestioned, unexamined, and inarticulate.

The men hired to carry out propaganda could not provide the movement with an ideology and goals that the movement's leaders did not possess. They had a great deal of trouble in stating what the Whites were fighting for, and they fell back on a narrow, patriotic position: The goal of the movement was to restore the glory of Russia. This message aroused little enthusiasm among those who were the most important in determining the outcome of the civil war, the peasants, and it fatally alienated the national minorities, who might have provided crucial aid against the Bolsheviks.

The Whites had no unifying ideology. Since they had no generally agreed upon interpretation of the momentous events that had been taking place in the country, they were not in the position to impose a "Party line" on the press. The generals, of course, were not liberals and had little interest in the protection of civil liberties; nevertheless, they permitted a much broader spectrum of publications in territories under their control than the Bolsheviks allowed. In anti-Bolshevik cities, Menshevik and Socialist Revolutionary newspapers suffered occasional harassment, but they were able to appear. White repression was haphazard.

The military men were deeply suspicious of propagandists and politicians, and they did not understand the importance of the contribution civilians could make. In their understanding, which they had acquired during tsarist days, politics was itself something subversive that decent people avoided. Such a position, of course, was an unconsciously conservative one. Under the circumstances, it was not surprising that Osvag possessed little prestige within the hierarchy and did not succeed in attracting able workers. Nor did the propaganda agency ever receive enough moral and material support.

A major weakness of White propaganda was the lack of a network that could penetrate the countryside. (When one contrasts the two sides in the Civil War, it becomes clear that the Bolshevik Party made a very significant contribution to victory.) In the cities the Whites set up propaganda bureaus that organized lectures and published pamphlets, but they could not reach the peasants. They were painfully aware of Bolshevik superiority and therefore attempted to copy Bolshevik methods. In 1919, for example, the Kharkov bureau set up an agitation school that trained twenty-six propagandists for work in villages.[40] The impact of the work must have been small. The report of the Kharkov propaganda bureau mournfully concluded: "Our propaganda tried to copy the Bolsheviks, but we did learn from them what was the most important: the ability to go to the masses."

Each side attempted to mobilize the population under its direct control and penetrate the territory held by the enemy. In the second task the

Whites were singularly unsuccessful. The Bolsheviks, after their armies evacuated a region, quickly reorganized their cadres and rebuilt their cells and more or less successfully carried out subversion behind enemy lines. The Communists profited from their extensive experience in underground work. The counterrevolutionaries, who possessed no comparable organization, could not compete. In the last phase of the Civil War, when the anti-Bolshevik movement was headed by General Wrangel, the Whites did publish some manifestos that aimed to appeal to Red Army soldiers and attempted "black" propaganda, that is, issued pamphlets that purported to be Bolshevik products. These attempts, however, were clumsy and ineffective.[41]

The Whites, however, were capable of delivering some blows in the battle of words. They played on peasant fears and prejudices and successfully exploited weaknesses in the Bolshevik position. Their newspapers attempted to spread the misinformation among the peasants that the Bolsheviks did not distribute land but forced everyone into communes.

Anti-Semitism was a particularly powerful weapon. The Whites managed to harm both Jews and Communists by maintaining that they had an unholy alliance against "Russia." The majority of the officers genuinely believed that the destruction of their country was the result of the subversion of "aliens," that is, Jews. Their vocabulary was the same as the vocabulary of twentieth century anti-Semites elsewhere. They spoke of Jews as microbes who brought infection to the healthy body politic of Russia. They expressed a desire to cleanse the country of this unclean element. White posters and pamphlets depicted Communist leaders as Jewish, and commanding officers legitimized the peasants' anti-Semitism by not preventing or stopping pogroms. The leaders allowed the most rabid anti-Semitic agitation. For example, a crazed priest, Father Vostokov gave such incendiary sermons that his listeners came to chant with him "Beat the Jews! Save Russia!"[42]

In the struggle of ideas, on balance, the Whites proved themselves to be feeble fighters. The Bolsheviks, however, did have a powerful ideological opponent that controlled an extensive national network of experienced propagandists. This opponent was the Orthodox Church.

The Bolsheviks did not choose this fight. From the time of Peter the Great, the church had been little more than a government department, an ideological mainstay of autocracy. Almost all the village priests were conservative, and the hierarchy in particular was in the hands of reactionaries. These men consistently and enthusiastically supported tsarist policies, inclusing Russia's war effort.

How strong an influence the church, indeed religion, had among the peasants is a debated issue. Undoubtedly, many priests had led unworthy lives and therefore lost the respect of their parishioners. In the twentieth century, anticlericalism was an increasing force in the countryside. On occasion even believers were hostile to their priests. Nevertheless, the experience of the civil war shows that when priests were persecuted, the peasants often came to their defense. The church in persecution acquired a new authority.

It was hardly surprising that the great majority of the priests was hostile to the February Revolution. The events of 1917 the nationalization of schools, education reforms, and increasing anticlericalism of peasants and soldiers—pushed the churchmen even further to the right.[43] During the era of the Provisional Government, the church hierarchy supported efforts to create a "strong authority," that is, to remove soviets from the political arena and to entrust the future of the country to a military leader. A Church Sobor (council) met in August 1917, and it remained in session until the Bolshevik takeover. The Sobor gave an opportunity to the delegates to air their reactionary political views. This gathering elected Tikhon patriarch of Moscow, and he came to be a leader in the struggle against Bolshevism.[44]

Given the character and traditions of the church, no conceivable set of Bolshevik policies could have gained the good will or even the neutrality of the priests. The Bolsheviks were for their part, of course, atheists who regarded religion as an instrument in the hands of the defeated ruling classes. Therefore the issue was not what attitude the Party should take toward religion in general or to the Orthodox Church in particular but rather what would be the best strategy in facing a hostile force. How could the power of the church be undermined without alienating the peasants, many of whom were religious? How could the Bolsheviks, masters of propaganda, counter the propaganda of their enemies?

The church was provocative. Priests who lived under Bolshevik rule took a more consistently and courageously anti-Soviet position than any other segment of the population. During the early months of the Soviet regime the hierarchy assumed that the government could not possibly last and therefore there was no need to search for a modus vivendi. The Sobor denounced the revolutionaries who had just taken power: "May God arise and scatter His enemies and may all who hate Him flee from his countenance!"[45] The proclamation also denounced the Bolsheviks' effort to conclude peace with Germany.

Bonch-Bruevich described in his memoirs the struggle carried out by the church during the first days of Bolshevik rule:

Only a few days after the dismissal of the Provisional Government news came from everywhere that priests in their sermons and through other means came out against the Soviet regime. Our commissars reported to me that everywhere in Petrograd and even in the most remote back streets printed proclamations appeared in which Soviet power was cursed and which called for bringing down God's anger on the heads of "atheists and terrorists" and which turned to all believers in "our Lord, Jesus Christ" to oppose with all means this new, devilish power and in no circumstances should people obey.[46]

According to Bonch-Bruevich, his agents picked up in the streets of Petrograd old women who were posting these hostile proclamations on the walls. After the frightened old women were treated to tea, they confessed everything and implicated the highest level of church leadership.[47]

The church assisted the White movement from its inception. Priests participated in a commission set up by the White Army to investigate Bolshevik terror, and by their presence they lent prestige and credibility to the undertaking; they celebrated White victories with special services; they signed appeals to Western European clergymen, in which they described the atrocities committed by the revolutionaries and requested help. One of them, Georgii Shavelskii, in December 1918 joined the propaganda agency of the South Russian White movement.[48]

It was the village priests who provided the most valuable service to the anti-Bolsheviks. In their sermons they denounced the revolutionaries and described Bolshevik ideas as contrary to the teaching of Christ. Some went so far as to lead partisan detachments against the Red Army. The Orthodox Church, which had a poor record on anti-Semitism, during the Civil War contributed to anti-Jewish agitation. The church lent its prestige to authenticating such "miracles" as the story of the Jewish commissar who was killed by a bullet that he himself fired at an icon.[49]

The Bolsheviks were confronted with the difficult issue of how to deal with the challenge presented by the church. The new government regarded as one of its first tasks the completion of the process that began under the Provisional Government, the separation of church and state. On January 23, 1918, Sovnarkom issued an important law that regulated the church's position in society. The church lost its right to maintain schools, lost its property, lost its authority to register officially births, deaths, and marriages, and ceased to receive a state subsidy. On the other hand, the law promised freedom of conscience, freedom of private religious instruction, and free use of religious objects and buildings on the basis of arrangement with local or central authorities.[50]

The Soviet constitution of July 1918 reaffirmed the principle of separation of church and state. It once again explicitly recognized freedom for religious propaganda. However, the constitution differed from similar bourgeois documents: It excluded priests, together with imbeciles, criminals, capitalists, and former members of the police, from the right to vote and hold elective office.

It was easier to issue decrees and publish a constitution than to introduce changes into the life of the people. State support of the church immediately ended, and the confiscation of church lands, carried out by the peasants themselves, was a heavy blow. Members of the clergy were quickly removed from schools. On the other hand, the state did not yet possess the machinery to register births and deaths, and therefore it was a long time before this part of the reform could be realized.[51]

The Bolshevik leaders well understood the dangers of a frontal attack on religion. Lenin already in 1910 wrote that if antireligious propaganda was pushed too strongly, it would play into the hands of the church.[52] Although the Soviet government introduced a series of measures against the interest of the Church, and took repressive steps against provocative priests, it allowed the great majority of churches to function and avoided making martyrs out of the leading figures of the hierarchy. The government also did not interfere with the functioning of seminaries. The Bolsheviks, however, did not hesitate to arrest priests for participating in demonstrations, for preaching hostile sermons, or for resisting the laws and regulations of the Soviet government. Individual churchmen on occasion became victims of the Red terror. The most notorious case was the murder of Metropolitan Vladimir of Kiev on January 25, 1918. In the provinces, where control from the center was weak, priests were more likely to suffer. During the short but bloody existence of the Don Soviet Republic (Feb.–May 1918), according to a commission later established by the Whites, fifteen priests were killed. But even this commission acknowledged that the killings were not done on orders from above but by unruly sailors and soldiers.[53]

In particular, the government handled Patriarch Tikhon gingerly. When Bonch-Bruevich, after linking the posting of hostile proclamations on the streets of Petrograd to the patriarch, asked Lenin what should be done, Lenin answered that the patriarch must be left alone but that those who were caught posting the proclamations should be arrested. Bonch-Bruevich in his memoirs admitted a grudging admiration for the courage of the patriarch.[54] In the same way, the Bolsheviks simply ignored the hostile pronouncements made in the Sobor. There was no other institution that the Bolsheviks treated as patiently as they treated the church.

Gradually, however, antireligious propaganda gathered force. In May 1918 the Comissariat of Justice set up a special section dealing with the church. This section was headed by P. A. Krasikov, who came to assume the leading role in the ideological struggle against religion. In 1918 and 1919 the Commissariat of Justice published antireligious pamphlets and books.[55] The circulation of this literature was small, and it was unlikely that it reached its target audience, the peasantry.

An associate of Krasikov, M. V. Galkin, suggested the publication of an atheist journal. Under Galkin's editorship, in February 1919 the Commissariat started to publish *Revoliutsiia i Tserkov'* (The Revolution and the Church). According to the editor, the goals of the journal were: (1) to propagandize the separation of church and state on the basis of scientific communism, (2) to struggle against clericalism in all forms, and (3) to establish contact between the center and local authorities in antireligious activities. The journal, which appeared in twelve issues during the next two years, aimed at a peasant audience. However, the articles were abstract and the circulation small, and therefore it is unlikely that the publication served its purpose.[56]

In the first issue of the journal, Krasikov described Bolshevik strategy.

He wrote that the experience of the French Revolution and recent history had shown that closing down churches and the use of force against priests led only to the strengthening of "fanaticism." "A well-organized Soviet farm is more likely to undermine prejudices than the arrest of dozens of priests."[57] It was proper, however, to oppose the reactionary church. The journal established a section called "under the flag of religion" that gave examples of cooperation between the church hierarchy and the White armies. Articles by such prominent Bolshevik leaders as Iaroslavskii and I. I. Skvortsov-Stepanov stressed the reactionary role of the church in the past and in the present.

Bolshevik agitators did not always follow the principle of moderation recommended by such strategists as Krasikov and Lenin. The line between struggle against the church and struggle against religion was often hard to draw. In the provinces, for example, some party organizations set up crude antireligious exhibits that no doubt brought more harm than benefit.[58] As the civil war became increasingly bitter, the tone of antichurch propaganda became ever more shrill. The authorities especially favored exposing "miracles." The church taught that the miraculous preservation of the bodies of some saints was proof of divine intervention. The party propagandists, therefore, compelled priests to be present at the openings of graves and filmed the proceedings. On such occasions the humiliated priests were compelled to sign affidavits disavowing miracles. At times churchmen were charged with criminal fraud on account of some supposed miracle.

It was not, however, easy to defeat religion; the Bolshevik leaders had reason to be wary. During the Civil War, the persecution of priests often led to violent resistance on the part of the peasants, and in the coming decades religion continued to be an alternate mode of interpreting reality.

CHAPTER 3

Liquidating illiteracy in revolutionary Russia

Lenin, the Marxist, was deeply preoccupied with the question: Was Russia ready for the Revolution? He could not lightly dismiss Menshevik criticisms according to which the economy and society had not yet properly developed. Obviously he ultimately rejected these objections and rejected them passionately; but at the same time, he was deeply aware of the backwardness of the country. His solution in principle was simple: While fighting a life-and-death struggle against their opponents, the Bolsheviks at the same time had to raise the cultural level of the people. Consequently, Lenin, the supreme realist, chose "cultural revolution" as one of the major themes of his writings during the last years of his life.

Where Lenin and his comrades spoke and wrote about "culture," they rarely had in mind mankind's highest creative and artistic achievements. For them culture was the opposite of backwardness, a combination of a certain economic well-being, industrial and technical accomplishments, modern attitudes to the problems of existence, and certain very basic intellectual accomplishments. It is in this context that we must place Lenin's famous preoccupation with electrification and understand such striking statements as "Socialism without postal and telegraph service is the emptiest of phrases"; and, of course, it is in this context that we can understand the remarkable literacy drive undertaken by the young Soviet republic.

The early history of the literacy drive deserves study for three reasons. First, it reveals a great deal about the mentality of the Bolshevik leaders and about their perception of the task of the revolutionary transformation of society. Second, it was during the Civil War that the basic organizational framework of the later campaign was created, and that campaign in the 1920s and 1930s brought results. Third, there is an uncanny similarity between the methods and institutions of this early Soviet experiment and the literacy drives introduced in the course of the twentieth century by other regimes. It is not that the Cubans, Nicaraguans, and others learn from Soviet experience; the similarity results from the similarities in national conditions and in the mentalities of revolutionary leaderships. In this respect, as in much else, the Bolsheviks were the first to face problems that turned out to be crucial for twentieth-century politics: problems of mass mobilization.

As with so many other aspects of national life, the Bolsheviks found after coming to power that they were ill-prepared to deal with the problems of adult education. Their prerevolutionary ideas on this subject and about education in general were rather conventional. They believed that education was a necessary step in developing class consciousness and assumed that the tsarist Ministry of Education understood this fact as clearly as they and that therefore it sabotaged popular education. They firmly linked education with politics and argued that talk of a culture that was above classes was hypocritical. They attacked tsarist schools for indoctrinating students with a monarchist-orthodox ideology, but they were also convinced that this could not be otherwise. The 1903 Social Democratic Party's program plank on education was noncontroversial. It called for compulsory and free education up to the age of sixteen and for outlawing child labor, and it advocated teaching the student in his mother tongue and removing the church from the business of education.[1]

N. K. Krupskaia in her memoirs gives us a particularly interesting glimpse of Lenin's views on adult education. In prerevolutionary Russia, the Ministry of Education took almost no interest in fighting illiteracy among adults. Therefore adult education, to the extent it existed, took place outside the competence of the ministry and was largely financed by private philanthropy. Lenin had a contemptuous attitude toward the philanthropists and regarded them as "do-gooders." He was suspicious of the ideological material that was transmitted and did not in any case believe that the work of a few individuals could make a dent in illiteracy. Krupskaia describes one of her very first meetings with Lenin, in 1893, as follows: "Someone was saying—I think it was Shevlyagin—that what was very important was to work in the Committee for Literacy. Vladimir Ilich laughed, and somehow his laughter sounded bitter. I never heard him laugh that way on any subsequent occasion. 'Well,' he said, 'whoever wants to save the fatherland on the Committee for Literacy, it is all right, we will not hinder him.' "[2]

Let us contrast this quotation with a statement from Lunacharskii, written in 1924: "Next day after the revolution when he [Lenin] asked me in and told me that the Ts.K. considered it essential to place me in the post of People's Commissar of Enlightenment, he said: 'You must overcome illiteracy in Russia'—these were his first words."[3]

How are we to account for the change? The difference was not the result of inconsistency or hypocrisy but rather of the fact that the party faced different tasks before and after the Revolution. Lenin saw education, as he saw everything else, from an exclusively political point of view. Before 1917 he assumed that universal literacy, together with other preconditions of socialism, would be created, consciously desired or not, by a capitalist Russia. At that time the party had far more important concerns than mass education. In November 1917, the issue looked very different. The Bolsheviks had acquired power, basing themselves on the support of the largely literate workers and soldiers. But to retain power, the party had to expand its base of support and win over the peasantry or at least gain their benevolent neutrality. One of the important obstacles to gaining support among the peasantry was illiteracy. In a speech to the Second Congress of Political Education, Lenin discussed with remarkable candor why he was interested in overcoming illiteracy: "As long as there is such a thing in the country as illiteracy, it is rather hard to talk about political education. To overcome illiteracy is not a political task, it is a condition without which one cannot even talk about politics." Later he said, "The illiterate person stands outside of politics. First it is necessary to teach him the alphabet. Without it there are only rumors, fairy tales, prejudices, but not politics."[4] The struggle against illiteracy was thus a "precondition of politics" and the campaign itself a method of indoctrination.

However strong and firm was Bolshevik commitment to combating illiteracy, it is evident that in the conditions that prevailed during the civil war little could be accomplished. The Bolsheviks lacked the material resources that were necessary and, even more important, lacked the organizational framework with which to reach the illiterate among the peasantry.

How great was the task? We often think of the Russia of 1917 as a land of illiteracy. Indeed, a majority of Russians were untutored, backward, and cut off from much of the modern world. However, we tend to imagine illiteracy as even more widespread than it was. It is in the interest of Soviet historiography to stress Bolshevik achievements, and one way to underline them is to exaggerate the degree of backwardness at the time of the revolution. An unqualified assertion of illiteracy is misleading not only because a substantial part of the population could read and write but, more important, because illiteracy was unevenly distributed; politically crucial segments of the population could be reached by the printed word.

Although the overall situation is fairly clear, the exact degree of literacy and the magnitude of the change in the preceding decades are difficult to establish. It is hard to define literacy, and different census takers worked with slightly different definitions. Our knowledge is based largely on three censuses: (1) The 1897 census (published only in 1906) collected figures from the entire Empire, included everyone (even children under eight), and defined a literate person as one who, according to his own self-evaluation, could read. (2) The trade unions carried out a census in 1918, which has the advantage that it came immediately after the revolution. Unfortunately, it provided figures only for urban workers. (3) The most important census was carried out in August 1920 by the newly established Central

Statistical Bureau to facilitate discussions of the subject by the Tenth Party Congress. The census takers asked about both the abilities to read and write and excluded children under eight.

In 1897, 21.1 percent of the population was literate.[5] In 1920 in the Russian Socialist Federal Soviet Republic) (RSFSR) and in the Ukraine 31.9 percent said that they could read and write, and if we exclude, as we should, children under eight, the proportion rises to 40.1 percent.[6] To put it simply, two out of five adults in the newly established socialist state could be reached by the printed word. When we break down the figures according to age, sex, and place of residence, however, we notice enormous variations. In 1897, a third of those between ten and twenty were literate, but only 14.8 percent of those over sixty.[7] Thirty-one and eight-tenths percent of the men, but only 13.1 percent of the women could read. Of the city dwellers, 45.3 percent considered themselves literate, as against 17.4 percent of those who lived in villages.[8]

One cannot but be impressed by the high rate of literacy in the cities and by the impressive improvements in the course of the last two decades of tsarist Russia. Petrograd in 1910 was 76.6 percent literate, and Moscow in 1912 70 percent.[9] In 1913, 68.8 percent of the army recruits were literate [10] and according to the trade-union census of 1918, almost two-thirds of the workers living in cities could read and write.[11] The 1920 census shows how different literacy standards were among the nationalities. Although only about 1 percent of the Chechens, Ingush, and Balkars were literate, the corresponding figures among the Jews and among the Latvians were over two-thirds.[12]

Clearly, the educational standards of tsarist Russia in its last years could not fairly be compared to those of the countries of the third world in the middle of the twentieth century. Further, however slowly, the Imperial educational system was overcoming illiteracy. It is necessary to remember these facts when we evaluate Soviet accomplishments in the interwar period.

Few groups of human beings have ever consciously attempted to transform a society as thoroughly as the Bolsheviks hoped to do in November 1917. At the same time the Russian people were experiencing the painful effects of the most profound anarchy. This dichotomy betwen ambitious goals and nonexistent means was one of the most characteristic features of the situation in which the Bolsheviks found themselves after their victory.

Their victory was unexpected even to themselves. It is perhaps understandable that, under the circumstances, at least for a while anything seemed possible. If they succeeded in defeating their fearsome-looking enemies, why should they not also succeed in changing Russian people? Interestingly, and from a psychological point of view not surprisingly, the very meagerness of the available means encouraged utopian thinking. What good would it do to match carefully resources and tasks when resources were almost nonexistent and tasks enormous? Even Lenin, that great realist, was attracted to some of the utopian schemes, and he seemed to have believed that the problem of illiteracy could be fought by passing decrees and by exhorting the literate to teach their less fortunate compatriots.

The primary responsibility for organizing the literacy campaign belonged to the People's Commissariat of Enlightenment (Narkompros). Sovnarkom entrusted the building of the commissariat entirely to its first head, A. V. Lunacharskii, a leading Bolshevik intellectual. He could choose his subordinates as he saw fit, though Lenin suggested that he seek out the cooperation of his wife, N. K. Krupskaia.[13] She was an obvious choice for such work. She had worked as an unpaid schoolteacher in 1891 and remained interested in the problems of education. Before the Revolution she had given considerable thought to questions of progressive and polytechnical education. Lenin was disposed to take a more active interest in educational issues because of Krupskaia.

It was difficult to build Bolshevik institutions, and the organizing of the Commissariat of Enlightenment presented particular problems. The officials of the ex-ministry by and large refused to cooperate, so the work started slowly. At the outset, Lunacharskii set up a special section devoted to adult education under L. R. Menzhinskaia. In December the commissariat created an Extramural Education Department under Krupskaia, which in a short time incorporated Menzhinskaia's section.[14] In 1920, Krupskaia's department was reorganized, renamed the Department of Political Education, and became responsible for all educational and propaganda work among adults. Although Krupskaia enjoyed considerable power, partly because she could call on Lenin's support, she did not succeed in centralizing all propaganda work. Propaganda was too important to be entrusted entirely to Narkompros; major institutions of the regime continued to be involved in this work.

The commissariat attempted to reorganize national education. Lunacharskii and Krupskaia envisaged local, elected councils on the volost' level, which would direct all educational work, including the fight against illiteracy; but in these plans the coordination of responsibilities with local Party and soviet organizations remained hazy. The new leaders wanted to do away with the tsarist system of school districts, but at the time there existed no organizations to take their place.[15] One suspects that at least one of the appeals of putting greater responsibilities on local organs was the fact that the central bureaucracy did not possess the means to carry out the ambitious policies in any case. Both Krupskaia and Lunacharskii deeply and genuinely believed in the principle of decentralization. However, their policies were one more example of a situation in which commitment to rather utopian principles coexisted well with powerlessness and anarchy.

The hostility of the nation's teachers seriously hindered the Bolsheviks in organizing education. The literacy campaign in particular progressed slowly. The teachers' national union was under Menshevik and Socialist Revolutionary influence. Only after considerable struggle were the Bolsheviks able to create a union of "internationalist" teachers that was willing to accept orders and direction from the new rulers.[16] Illiteracy work also suffered a shortage not only of teachers but also of textbooks and even paper and pencils.

In the first two years of Soviet power, the war against illiteracy was largely fought with words: speeches, announcements, meetings, but little instruction. In August 1918, for example, in a congress on education, Krupskaia spoke in the name of the Extramural Department (Vneshkolnyi otdel') of Narkompros. She called for the creation of a network of *likpunkt* (literacy schools; from *likvidatsiia negramotnosti*, elimination of illiteracy).[17] The congress passed a resolution that called for freeing illiterate workers an hour or two each week from labor to participate in these likpunkt. From the point of view of later developments Krupskaia's ideas were significant, and in the 1920s thousands of these little schools were indeed created and became the major tools in the struggle. For the time being, however, the resolution remained on paper only: No national network existed. The national congress was followed by a series of regional meetings. Although one may argue that the practical accomplishments of the regional meetings were even slighter, it is also true that the large number of speeches devoted to this issue drew the attention of party activists to it and prepared the soil for a later, more successful campaign.

In May 1919, a large congress was called devoted entirely to extramural education. The fact that 1,500 delegates were invited at this militarily difficult moment is an indication of the Party's concern about the problem. In fact, because of the confusion and the military situation only 800 delegates arrived in Moscow.[18] Besides Lunacharskii, Krupskaia, and other leaders of Narkompros, Lenin himself addressed the meeting twice. In welcoming the delegates on May 16, Lenin, the realist, pointed out that though the fight against illiteracy was the single most important cultural task, exceedingly little had been accomplished so far. He repeated his idea that the literate segment of the population should be obliged to teach the illiterate.[19] For those who knew that in the course of the nineteenth century, in Russia and in other countries, such teaching occurred rather frequently, the idea might not have appeared altogether unrealistic. However, given the extreme weakness of Bolshevik influence in the countryside, passing a law would have made no greater impression than a good-natured exhortation. It was naive to think that a law alone, without expanding Bolshevik power in the villages and without great investment, could change reality.

The decisions of the congress were important in signaling a turn away from the utopian notion of decentralization. Also, for the first time the delegates faced the problem of compulsion. They agreed that as far as teaching adolescents was concerned, local departments of education could use any method they saw fit, including coercion.[20]

The next interesting and important step in the rhetorical struggle against

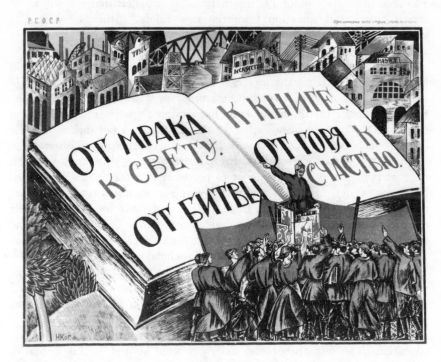

Plate 1. Literacy poster, n.d. Text: From darkness to light. From battle to the book. From sorrow to happiness.

illiteracy took place on December 26, 1919, when Sovnarkom issued its famous decree on illiteracy. Speaking on the tenth anniversary of the publication of this decree in 1929, Krupskaia admitted that at the time of the Civil War not a single paragraph of the decree was realized.[21] Yet the content and the story of the writing of the decree deserve close attention. The law was drawn up to be an instrument of propaganda, and indeed, especially in the course of the 1920s, it was used even more extensively than its framers envisaged. The Party organized national celebrations to mark the anniversaries of the publication of the law. December 26 became one of the phony Bolshevik holidays, one more occasion to organize campaigns, to give speeches, to put together exhibitions—briefly, to mobilize the Russian people.

Such an important law, of course, according to Soviet historians, had to come from Lenin himself, and they customarily refer to it as a "Leninist" law. In fact the decree was drawn up by N. Gudz, a minor official in the Extramural Education Department of Narkompros, who was given three days for the task.[22] After the leaders of his commissariat discussed and accepted this draft, it was published by Sovnarkom, and Lenin signed it in his capacity as chairman of the body. The decree then was printed, and hundreds of thousand of copies of it were distributed.

The first sentence of the law states explicitly why the government was fighting illiteracy: "For the purpose of allowing the entire population of the Republic to participate consciously in the political life of the country, the Council of People's Commissars decrees: . . ."[23] The government, then, gave no other reason than a political one for its struggle to overcome illiteracy.

The nine paragraphs of the decree are impressive in their comprehensiveness and generosity. The government gave responsibility for the work to Narkompros and to its local institutions, except in the case of the Red Army, where the work was to be organized by the political departments of army units. At the same time the decree directed party and mass organizations, such as trade unions, the Komsomol, and the Zhenotdel to provide help in this effort. (The Zhenotdel was an organization of women that existed from the time of the Revolution until the period of collectivization.)

In the crucial paragraph, the government obliged all illiterates between the ages of eight and fifty to study, and at the same time it gave the right to Narkompros organizations to draft literate citizens as teachers. In its most generous provision, the decree freed from work for two hours per day (without reduction in their salary) those who studied as long as the instruction continued. The teachers were to receive wages comparable to those of schoolteachers. Further, the government directed relevant state institutions to provide the likpunkt with necessary teaching materials, giving priority to their needs over the others.

Perhaps the most novel paragraph was the penultimate one, which made it a criminal offense to refuse to teach or to study. It must be added, however, that no citizen of the republic was ever prosecuted under this law.

It is, of course, far easier to summarize resolutions of congresses and laws and regulations than to establish what in fact was accomplished in the struggle against illiteracy. It would be futile to try to guess exactly how many people received instruction. We must be satisfied with a description of the general picture. In the course of 1918 very little was done and the situation began to improve only when, in 1919, Narkompros opened four- to six-week-long courses for instructors. These instructors then traveled to the countryside and organized likpunkts. It is obvious that the training of teachers had to be the starting point of any sustained and serious effort.

The greatest achievement of the regime at the time of the civil war was in teaching the soldiers of the Red Army. It is perfectly understandable that at a time of anarchy the work proceeded best among those who, by definition, were organized. Also, for obvious reasons, the regime was most interested in bringing enlightenment, and therefore political indoctrination, to those who were fighting with weapons in their hands. In the distribution of resources, the teaching of soldiers had absolute priority.

However, even in the army, the work started only slowly: The military command was not always committed to the task; there were not enough instructors or suitable textbooks. Although some military districts organized a few likpunkts as early as 1918, few soldiers were affected. In the winter of 1919 the Military Revolutionary Committee of Petrograd, in collaboration with the Extramural Education Department of Narkompros, set up short training courses (three weeks long) for instructors.[24]

Only in the second half of 1919 did the work accelerate. The Military Revolutionary Committee of the Republic on September 4, following the decision of the extramural education congress in May, ordered compulsory education in the army. Political commissars on down to the company level were instructed to compile list of illiterates within two weeks and to organize the instruction of soldiers. Since the army still did not have enough qualified instructors, civilians, often women, had to be used.[25]

Once again it is difficult to go beyond resolutions to evaluate the degree of success. Conditions varied from military unit to military unit. The Petrograd garrison, perhaps the most politicized one, started three kinds of schools: for illiterates; for those who knew the rudiments of reading; and for those who could both read and write.[26] Elsewhere the work progressed more slowly. The success of literacy work was intimately connected with the major task of building a larger and more disciplined Red Army. In the course of 1919 and in 1920 the size of the fighting force grew impressively, and at the end of the Civil War 5 million men were under arms. At the same time, Trotsky's efforts to impose discipline also began to bear fruit. The great majority of the young men who were drafted by the Bolsheviks were already literate; in the course of the Civil War tens of thousands of young peasants who had not received formal education before now learned the alphabet.

Since by far the best literacy work was done in the army, it is understandable that the first successful Soviet textbook for adults was developed for soldiers. In 1918 the lack of a suitable textbook was a serious problem. At this time the most widely used text was by V. A. Flerov. This book included such offensive phrases as "God's wide world" and "search for God's eternal truth." The message of the simple stories was no better from the Bolshevik point of view. One of them advocated peace between the poor and the rich in the village, whereas another sought to prove that the peasant should be satisfied with what little land he already had. In 1919 the publishers attempted to remedy the situation in the simplest way: They brought out a new edition that eliminated the obnoxious phrases and stories and added a political message. They reprinted "The Internationale"; printed some poems by Dem'ian Bednyi; and included some new readings under headings such as 'The tsar, the priest and the kulak," "What should the poor do in the village?," "Life is struggle," and "Land of capital and the fate of the workers."[27]

However, the revision of an old textbook could only be a stopgap measure. In 1919 a new text was published, the work of B. A. Zelenko and G. G. Tumin. The book never achieved much success, evidently because the reading material, though of course not hostile to the new regime, was not as thoroughly political as the instructors wanted. A much more successful and widely used textbook was composed by D. Iu. El'kina.

El'kina was an ex–Socialist Revolutionary who joined the Bolsheviks only in 1919. In the same year she was sent to the Southern front to do political-agitational work and teach soldiers to read and write. Forty years later El'kina recounted her experience as a literacy teacher among the soldiers and told the story of her decision to compose a suitable textbook for her students.[28] Her description is marvelously vivid. She described how she managed with considerable difficulty to get some old texts and a bit of chalk but could not get paper or pencils for her fourteen students. When the soldiers started to make out the first phrase she wrote on the board, "Masha ate the kasha," they snickered. She was on the verge of tears according to her report, but she turned this unpromising situation into an agitational triumph by discussing with her students why they could not be with their Mashas and why there was so very little kasha. Then she wrote this phrase on the board: "My ne raby" (We are not slaves).

Soon this sentence became famous, for it became the opening line of El'kina's teaching pamphlet. She used her teaching experience to compose her simple text. All her sentences were relentlessly political, and it was this that made her little booklet widely used. She used sentences such as "The defense of the revolution is the duty of the entire working class"; "We are building a new world, without the tyrants and slaves"; and "The Communists defend the interests of the working classes of the entire world."[29]

Whatever one thinks of El'kina's overly simple political message, and indeed of the Bolshevik policy of turning literacy classes into political-indoctrination sessions, there is something genuinely moving about the picture of unwashed peasant lads leaning over their texts and making out for themselves their first written phrase, "We are not slaves."

In late 1919 and in 1920 Narkompros published several new textbooks, including some in national minority languages and even one for the use of the deaf. Among these textbooks one written by V. V. Maiakovsky stands out. The great poet composed satirical two-liners on each letter of the alphabet and illustrated each in his own remarkable style. As Maiakovsky himself wrote about his work, the humor in it was not meant for good society but for soldiers in the trenches. It is hard to say whether the intended audience enjoyed the humor, but over sixty years after they were written, the lines now appear simply strange. The poet, for example, illustrated the letter *M* with the drawing of a Menshevik, holding with one hand a money bag and with the other hand his mother's hand. This is the caption: "Mensheviks and such good people—they can go to their mothers."

79

Plate 2. Literacy poster by Alexander Aspit, 1919. Text: Set up village reading rooms.

The letter *K* is illustrated by a grotesquely sitting Kerensky. The caption reads: "It is hard for the cow to run fast. Kerensky was Prime Minister."[30]

In 1919 and especially in 1920 Narkompros made great efforts to provide the developing literacy drive with the necessary number of textbooks. How committed the government was can be seen from the fact that it was willing to use its small supply of precious foreign currency for this purpose. It hired a foreign firm to print half a million copies. Altogether, by the end of 1920 Soviet Russia had distributed 6.5 million textbooks, out of which 2 million were printed in laguages other than Russian.[31] This major undertaking was a precondition for the success of the campaign of the 1920s. Nonetheless, in spite of large printings, even in the mid-1920s there were never enough textbooks.

In 1920 the literacy drive began to produce impressive results. A precondition of the success was the building of an administrative structure to direct the campaign. In early 1920, in spite of all the talk and resolutions concerning the importance of combating illiteracy, there were only two people in Narkompros who worked full time on organizing and coordinating the literacy drive.[32] However, in the spring, as momentum was gathering for an extensive campaign, Narkompros decided to set up a special section within Krupskaia's Extramural Education Department. On May 27 M. Pokrovskii, Lunacharskii's deputy, addressed the small Sovnarkom with an argument for the formation of a special commission for literacy work. He asked permission to name this commission Special Committee for the Elimination of Illiteracy (Chrezvychainaia Kommissiia po likbez, abbreviated VChk/1b). Some opposed Pokrovskii, arguing that calling the committee Cheka/likbez would contribute to the confusion. In general, those present blamed Narkompros for not having taken advantage of powers already granted and for the lack of local preparation for the campaign.[33]

But Pokrovskii's position prevailed, and on June 19, 1920, Sovnarkom published a decree that established VChk/1b, empowering it to issue regulations with the force of law.[34] This committee was placed within Narkompros, but it was instructed to establish close relations with various mass organizations. Its first director was I. P. Brikhnichev, a teacher. Other prominent figures who participated in the work were D. Iu. El'kina, N. I. Podvoiskii, and L. P. Menzhinskaia, who later took Brikhnichev's position.[35]

VChk/1b gradually built an impressive administrative structure that became involved in all aspects of literacy work. VChk/1b ordered the printing and distribution of textbooks and bought paper and pencils from abroad. In Civil War conditions, the organization had to concern itself with such mundane matters as providing food, clothing, and shoes for the teaching personnel. It established sections for work among peasants, soldiers, national minorities, and trade-union workers; a special section under El'kina was responsible for attracting organizers and teachers to literacy work.[36]

VChk/1b received very significant help from mass organizations, such as the Zhenotdel, the Komsomol, and, by far the most important, the trade unions. Although the Zhenotdel and the Komsomol were still relatively small and in the process of organizing themselves, the trade unions were well-established mass institutions. The workers, aside from the soldiers, were the best-organized part of the population, and therefore it was easiest to establish schools for them and encourage them to attend.

Although the trade unions were the first to respond to the call of VChk/1b to compile lists of illiterates and establish likpunkts, from the very beginning there were jurisdictional and ideological disagreements between the Soviet institutions. The trade unions jealously guarded their autonomy and resented outside interference with the disposition of their cultural funds.[37] Also, not all unions regarded literacy work as their highest priority. For example, the presidium of the textile workers in Vladimir province passed this resolution in March 1920: "Fully agreeing with the usefulness of the elimination of illiteracy among the population, but recognizing the necessity of improving textile industry and considering that the shortening of the working day for illiterates will be one of the reasons for the falling of productivity, the Presidium considers it necessary to ask the Ts.K. of the all-union Trade Union organization to request Sovnarkom permission to study reading and writing after eight hours of work. . . ."[38]

It was ironic that the trade unions concerned themselves with productivity and the government, the ultimate manager of industry, with literacy. However, the trade-union leaders were correct that it was essential to establish priorities and that the young republic could not achieve everything that seemed desirable at the same time. With the introduction of the New Economic Policies, greater realism prevailed both in the organization of the national economy and in the running of the literacy campaign.

With the aid of the trade unions, an impressive network of likpunkts was built in 1920. According to figures collected by VChk/1b, in November 1920 the country had 12,067 likpunkts teaching 278,637 students.[39] At the Seventh Congress of Soviets in December 1920, Lunacharskii reported that 3 million illiterates had already received instruction, a figure undoubtedly grossly exaggerated, as even Lunacharskii admitted a few years later.[40] It is futile to ask for precise numbers of how many illiterates learned to read and write during the Civil War or try to establish the drop in illiteracy in precise percentages. Obviously, many of those who had spent six to ten weeks learning to read and write quickly forgot everything. Reporting agencies, such as trade unions, had an incentive to show success and no doubt overstated the number of pupils. Also, since the school system barely functioned, many of the adolescents who grew up at this time joined the army of illiterates.

Nonetheless, we may assert that the early Soviet literacy drive was a success. During the Civil War many Soviet citizens, especially soldiers and workers, learned to read and write. Soviet power succeeded, if not in mobilizing literate people to teach the illiterate, at least in hiring teachers to do this work as a regular job. Much less was accomplished in the villages than in the cities, even though it was in the countryside that the great bulk of the illiterates lived. To the extent any literacy work was done in the villages, it was focused in the village school and the instruction was provided by the teacher.

From the point of view of the leaders of the regime, the success or failure of the undertaking could not be expressed exclusively in numerical terms. The literacy drive was one of the means through which the regime attempted to spread its ideology and to mobilize the population for its purposes. It was a weapon in the Bolshevik arsenal; not the most important one, but helpful nonetheless.

CHAPTER 4

The Komsomol in the Civil War

Soviet publicists have usually depicted their society in terms of mechanistic images. The Party is the "engine" of society, which provides the force necessary for change and development. Ideas generated by the Party come to the "masses" by "transmission belts." These transmission belts are the mass organizations, such as the trade unions, the Zhenotdel, and the Komsomol.

As with so many other aspects of political life, in exploiting these organizations for the purposes of mass mobilization the Soviet regime was advancing on uncharted territory. Sometimes consciously and sometimes unconsciously the Bolshevik leadership found solutions that then became permanent features not only of the Soviet state but also of many modern states, not all of them communist.

The mass organizations were genuinely important: They popularized ideas developed elsewhere, and they carried out policies introduced by the Soviet leadership. They enabled the regime to tailor its propaganda for certain segments of the population, and they extended the reach of the Party. They were involved in all propaganda campaigns initiated by the Party, whether the goals were long term and far reaching, such as educating the future communist man and woman, or short-term and immediate, such as collecting scrap metal or bringing in the harvest in record time. The Soviet political landscape has been dominated by these campaigns ever since the Bolshevik Revolution.

The mass organizations served another propaganda purpose, perhaps less evident but nonetheless even more important than organizing campaigns. They provided a sphere of activity for tens of thousands of enthusiasts. At the time of the Civil War, the Reds were immensely more successful than their enemies in attracting new talent, in mobilizing elements of the population who had, in the past, been left out of political life. By accepting work in the Komsomol, or the Zhenotdel, a young person committed himself or herself. Such organizations thus became training grounds for

84

Party work, and many important political figures of later decades emerged from them. Associating with the Bolsheviks was often dangerous: The Whites were likely to shoot Komsomol or Zhenotdel organizers if they had a chance. The activists well understood that they could expect no mercy from the enemy if their side lost the struggle and therefore redoubled their work for the victory of communist revolution. Drawing thousands of people into politics was a decisive development. Often the involvement of the new recruit was gradual. A person accepted office in one of the mass organizations without fully agreeing with communist aims. But as the person was carrying out propaganda on behalf of the new regime, he or she was won over. The propagandists usually were the first to become victims of their own propaganda. There is no better method of convincing someone than by asking him or her to convince others.

The mass organizations, however, presented considerable danger to the Party. Their success depended on their ability to understand the mentality and speak to the concerns of particular segments of the population. To do their work well they needed a degree of autonomy; without it, their legitimacy was in doubt. The Party leadership was worried that these organizations might become advocates of their constituencies, and it was determined not to tolerate such a development. The leaders refused to concede that the interests of the young or of women might diverge on some issues from the interests of the public good as determined by the Party. More important, in the communist state there could be no intermediaries between the Party and the individual citizen. The individual could have no other advocate than the Party. Under the circumstances, the leaders of the mass organizations in these formative years had to walk a tightrope. During the civil war much of their energy was taken up by a painful process of self-definition, by establishing the character and limits of competence of their organizations.

Because the Zhenotdel and the Komsomol provided similar opportunities and similar issues arose in connection with their work, I examine only one of them, the Komsomol, in detail.[1]

Soviet historians of the Komsomol usually begin their story with the establishment of the Bolshevik Party. Indeed, it is true that the ideas of revolutionary socialism found particularly fertile ground among the youth, both students and young workers. Further, it is also probable that, as Soviet historians claim, after the split between Bolsheviks and Mensheviks the young were more likely to follow the Leninists. Bolshevik stress on direct action attracted them.

However, neither the Mensheviks nor the Bolsheviks organized a special youth section before 1917. A separate organization would have made little sense. The Bolsheviks, like the Mensheviks, had only a limited number of activists to carry out revolutionary tasks, and a disproportionate number of them were very young. To create two overlapping organizations, each involved in dangerous underground work, would have been self-defeating. Also, such an organization would have violated the principles of centralization and unity of command. It was hard enough for the Leninist leadership to control the local organizations that grew up in the country; it would have been even more difficult to control the work of the impulsive youth.

The February Revolution radically changed the political situation. The collapse of governing institutions was followed by attempts on the part of various groups to organize to make their political weight felt. The politicization of the population stimulated the formation of unions, congresses, organizations, special-interest groups, etc.

The Bolsheviks were not the first to organize the young. In May 1917 a group of Mensheviks, Socialist Revolutionaries, Anarchists, and some Bolsheviks created a proletarian youth group called Trud i Svet (Labor and light). Its leader, P. Shevstov, proposed a program to unify the socialist young people by deemphasizing factional-political differences. The core of the program – similar to the one advocated by Gorky in *Novaia zhizn'* – was to spread enlightenment among the working youth. The organization grew quickly, and within a few weeks it had 50,000 members.[2]

The Leninists saw in Trud i svet a great threat, and its existence compelled them to develop a policy toward youth organizations. They set themselves two tasks: They attempted to capture the leadership of Trud i svet and then destroy it from the inside and at the same time to build their own organization for Bolshevik youth. The first task turned out to be easier than the second. As Bolshevik power and influence grew in the capital, so did the number of their followers within Trud i svet. In August a conference of working youth decided to dissolve Shevstov's organization and endorse instead a much smaller group controlled by the Bolsheviks.[3] This organization, headed by V. Alekseev, was called the Socialist Union of Working Youth; by the time of the October Revolution it had only 10,000 members.[4] In major cities around the country the Bolsheviks attempted to build their own organizations and at the same time to capture organizations created by their Socialist competitors.

N. K. Krupskaia, who had taken an interest in questions of education and youth from the beginning of her revolutionary career, played an important role in defining Bolshevik attitudes toward youth organizations. In her articles in *Pravda* and in her speeches she advocated organizational autonomy for the youth. She pointed out that according to Western European experience only those organizations became successful that were in fact led by young people.

Both the Sixth Party Conference session in July and the Sixth Congress session in August in Petrograd devoted considerable attention to youth organizations. These meetings began the work of defining the character and competence of the Communist Youth League. The issue was the nature of Party control. Some advocated an organization that would be directly and explicitly controlled by the Party. Others were more sophisticated. They foresaw an "independent" youth organization but called for the establishment of Communist cells within the league. Obviously, the purpose of these cells would have been to transmit Party directions. However, the resolution adopted by the Sixth Congress on August 15 (New Style) spoke of establishing a broadly based mass organization, only indirectly controlled by the Bolsheviks.[5] This framework seemed the most effective for bringing revolutionary, Bolshevik ideas to the young people. The text of the resolution deserves attention, for some sentences show how careful a balance the Communists sought between organizational autonomy and Party leadership.

The intervention of the Party in the building of the organization of the working youth should not have the character of guardianship over it. Learning from the experience of Western Europe where independent organizations of the socialist working youth – in contradistinction to those established by the official parties – everywhere supported the leftist, internationalist wing of the labor movement, our Party should, also in Russia, aim for the establishment of independent organization, organizationally not subordinated, but only spiritually connected with the Party. But at the same time the Party should assure that this organization should have a socialist character from the very beginning of its existence . . .

The resolution of the congress had only long-term and theoretical significance, for organization was progressing very slowly. The country had many small, poorly coordinated youth groups. Communist strength and control varied from place to place. The Bolsheviks frequently faced the danger of losing control of the existing groups. As late as January 1918 they had to fight against the anarchists for control of the Petrograd youth group, the most important in the country. Other Bolshevik-dominated groups remained extremely small. At the time of the October Revolution, membership in these groups had further declined. In the entire country there were no more than 15,000 young people in Communist groups, of whom 10,000 were in Petrograd, 2,000 in Moscow, and 3,000 in the rest of the country.[6]

Because the Sixth Congress agreed on the basic principles on which the future Komsomol would be built, one wonders why, in fact, so little was accomplished in the following year. Very likely the main reason was that the Bolsheviks could not spare enough activists for this work. The confusion of the day was so great, and the tasks faced by the Party so many faceted, that the available cadres had to be committed elsewhere. The dissolution of the Trud i svet group in August 1917 lessened the pressure; for the time being there was no competition. Further, responsible Party leaders feared that if they acted prematurely, at a time of extreme Bolshevik weakness all over the country, the newly formed organization might slip out of their hands. The attempts of the anarchist youth to wrest control of the tiny Petrograd organization in January 1918 was a warning.[7]

After the regime had survived the precarious first six to eight months, it became evident that in the developing Civil War the support or at least tolerance of the peasantry would be decisive. Expanding agitational work, spreading the message to groups of people hitherto untouched by Bolshevik propaganda, acquired a new significance. The Bolshevik leadership resumed its organizational role. That the leaders attributed great significance to the future youth league can be seen from the fact that they prepared it most carefully. In July 1918 the Central Committee set up a bureau that had the task of organizing the first Congress.[8] The Party obviously made little effort to hide its role in the creation of the organization. At first, provincial meetings were convened by bringing together the existing Communist youth organizations and unaffiliated activists. These provincial groups called together the first national, founding congress of the Komsomol in Moscow on October 29, 1918.

The first three Komosomol congresses are interesting because on these occasions the details of the future mass organization were hammered out. Although the Party clearly created the basic framework, the details were subject to discussion, and therefore the deliberations of these early congresses were not altogether meaningless.

One hundred seventy-six delegates came to the First Congress. Of these, 88 were members of the Bolshevik Party, 38 called themselves Bolshevik sympathizers, and 45 were without party affiliation. Interestingly, one delegate described himself as an anarchist, one as a Left Socialist Revolutionary, and three as Social-Democrat-internationalists.[9] The six individuals who were elected to chair the sessions were all Party members. The Bolshevik organizers of the congress prepared a list of their names and submitted them to the delegates as a group. This was the way the Party wanted this mass organization to be. Had all the delegates been Party members, it would have significantly narrowed the potential membership of the Komsomol. At the same time, the leadership was firmly in the hands of reliable people.

The congress elected a Central Committee of fifteen (and seven candidate members) who were all Party members. This Central Committee had extensive powers, and it ran the Komsomol in between Congresses.

The name of the organization occasioned considerable debate. Some delegates argues that including the word "communist" might alienate potential recruits, especially from the peasantry. Nonetheless, the great majority of the delegates accepted the name "Russian Communist League of Youth."[10] The first two points of the program – that the league was to be "in solidarity with the Communist Party" on the one hand and "independent" on the other – were accepted without any disagreements. Another point of the program described the youth as "the forward section of the international proletariat in its struggle for socialism." Later, Bolshevik theorists repudiated some points of the program. They could not accept assigning privileged position to the young. They also disliked the bald assertion that the youth league was to be independent. These points were dropped from future programs. Evidently Party leaders feared that this theoretical independence might at some future time become genuine.

The delegates who came to the First Congress claimed to represent 22,000 members, but it is likely that even this small number was exaggerated. The Komsomol was not yet a mass organization, but the Party was ready to help. Immediately after the founding congress Ia. M. Sverdlov, in the name of the Party Central Committee, sent a letter to local party organizations, in which he instructed them to support Komsomol cells where they existed and to help establish them where they did not. He also instructed Party members younger than twenty-three to join the youth movement.[11] In spite of the solicitude of the highest level of Party leadership, the growth of the youth organization was rather slow. In September 1919, at the time of its Second Congress, the movement claimed a membership of only 96,000.[12]

The interest of the Party was not limited to fostering growth. It was determined to suppress all possible competition to the Komsomol and to prevent the emergence of deviations within the organization. Whether anticipated at the time of its establishment or not, one of the main functions of the Komsomol was to prevent the existence of genuinely independent youth organizations. The Soviet regime would tolerate neither hostile organizations nor organizations over which it had no control.

The first and most prominent victim was the boy-scout organization. This movement had been established in Russia before the First World War. As an international movement, claiming to stand above class divisions, it was intolerable to the Soviet regime. At first the Party did not make a frontal attack. It set up a movement called Young Communists (Iuk as its abbreviation and the name under which it became known) that had exactly the same functions as the scout movement, that is, organizing excursions, participating in sports and games, and so forth, but in addition it carried out indoctrination and was under Party leadership through the intermediary of the Komsomol. The Iuk movement was established at the end of 1918. Party cells agitated among scouts to leave that movement for the Iuk. The regime's apparent hostility to the scouts and obvious favor for the Iuks presumably persuaded many parents to avoid trouble by transferring their children to the new organization. The strategy, however, did not work. The Party did not have enough activists to control and operate yet another movement. The Second Komsomol Congress, probably on instructions from above, decided to disband the Iuk.[13] This move, of course, did not mean that the Party was ready to tolerate the scouts. That organization was declared to be an instrument of the enemy, and its troops were gradually closed down. It continued to live a precarious, almost underground existence for the next several years, after which it finally disappeared.

It was much easier to prevent the creation of an organization of Jewish students. According to the boast of the Komsomol leadership, the Bolsheviks successfully undermined the organizational attempt from within. Enough Communists participated in the founding meeting to dissuade the delegates from setting up an organization.[14]

Since the regime would not tolerate a heterogeneity of views outside of the Komsomol, it would have made little sense to accept divergent views within it. The most serious opposition in this formative period came from a group led by V. Dunaevskii. At the First Congress, some delegates advocated setting up "Houses of Proletarian Youth." The idea was that through these houses Komsomol, and therefore Communist influence, could be quickly extended among the working youth. The Komsomol would remain a basically elitist institution, closely affiliated with the Party, and it would supervise the Houses of Proletarian Youth, which would be something like clubs. The Party leaders opposed the idea. Presumably they saw no need for another elite institution sharing a leadership and supervisory role. As a result, the congress voted down the suggestion. However, Dunaevskii and his comrades revived the plan in a somewhat modified form in April 1919. They advocated establishing youth sections within the trade unions. According to this plan the already existing trade-union framework would have enabled the young to organize more effectively. The Party leaders once again opposed the idea. They were suspicious of Dunaevskii and feared that the youth sections might assert the interests of the young workers against the rest.[15] Dunaevskii's followers raised this plan at the Trade Union Congress which met in April 1920. Here, again, it was defeated. Since Dunaevskii did not learn his lesson quickly enough and continued to persist, the Party applied discipline; it suspended Dunaevskii's membership for six months and ordered him to cease participation in work among the young.

The Second Congress of the Komsomol met on October 5, 1919. This time, out of the 429 delegates were 286 Party members and 103 "sympathizers." Oskar Ryvkin, speaking in the name of the Central Committee, told the delegates that his committee was subordinated to the Central Committee of the Party. This subordination was in conflict with the Komsomol program, which called the organization "independent"; however, there was no one to point out the contradiction.[16] This congress went further than the Komsomol previously had in its struggle against competition. It came out in opposition not only to the scouts but also to the existence of sport clubs. The Komsomol proposed to integrate all these activities within its own organization. The congress met at an unpropitious time. In early October Denikin, having taken Orel, was threatening Moscow. In view of the grave military situation, the meeting was dissolved prematurely on October 8.

The Third Congress was convened under much more favorable circumstances. It met in October 1920, at a time when the victorious end of the civil war was in sight. Lenin himself addressed the congress with a major speech in which he summarized his unsurprising ideas about the tasks of the youth.[17] This congress formally changed the Komsomol program by officially dropping the offending passages about an "indepencent" youth organization and about the youth being the vanguard of the proletariat.

The crucial political struggle was fought over the control of the villages. The Bolsheviks well understood the significance of agitation among the peasants. In March 1919, the Eighth Party Congress placed special emphasis on this work, and the delegates to the Second Komsomol Congress, which took place a few months later, followed the example of their elders. The Komsomol Central Committee set up a special section for work among village youth.[18] But the task was difficult and progress slow. Naturally, it was far easier to establish cells in factories and schools in the cities where the Party was strong than in the countryside. At the end of 1918 out of 22,000 Komsomolites, only 2,000 were villagers. A year later the corresponding figures were 10,000 out of 100,000. Only in 1920 did the work improve. At the time of the Third Congress approximately one fifth of the members, about 100,000, were peasant youth.[19]

The report of the Smolensk Party Committee from April 1920 provides interesting examples of how the work among the peasant youth was carried out and, incidentally, throws light on the attitude of the Bolsheviks toward propaganda.[20] After complaints about the looseness of Komsomol organization in the province, the report suggested concrete steps to prevent further disintegration: (1) Organize Communist Saturdays (*subbotniki*), (2) organize the celebration of Communist holidays, (3) organize military instruction among the members of the Komsomol, and (4) organize clubs.

The subbotnik movement, at the initiative of the Party, started in the spring of 1919. At that time some railroad workers undertook unpaid work on their day of rest in order to overcome a crisis in transportation. Communist activists immediately recognized the value of this movement not only for the economy but also as an instrument of propaganda. The movement started in Moscow, spreading from there to Petrograd and within a short time to the rest of the country. It is striking that already in 1920 the Smolensk Committee clearly saw that it was not so much the practical goals of the subbotnik campaign that mattered but rather the fact that the movement could be turned into an organizational tool. The ostensible task was to aid the families of Red Army soldiers, but the more important goal was to strengthen the Komsomol.

The second point in this program is equally remarkable.

Splendor, grandeur, and pomp have an extraordinary effect on the psychology of people, especially on children and on the young. It is not in vain that priests of different religions take care that their ceremonies be surrounded with splendor and pomp. Monarchist and bourgeois governments have always known the significance of influencing the youth and have taken all sorts of measures to turn this influence to their own benefit. The Russian Communist Party, leading the working class and the poorest peasants, is in the avant-garde of the workers on the road to a communist society. It cannot ignore methods of influencing workers and peasant youth in order to turn them into revolutionaries, into fighters for the interests of the working classes. One way of influencing the youth is to organize magnificent revolutionary holidays, which should become a widespread phenomenon in Smolensk Province in the coming summer.[21]

It is noteworthy that already in 1920, middle-level Party leaders were assuming a cynically manipulative attitude; they drew a sharp line between themselves and the "masses," who by implication were seen as childlike. The program then gave precise and detailed instructions on organizing holiday celebrations. For example, it pointed out the advantages of organizing celebrations on the dates of traditional festivals.

The third and fourth points of the program require little explanation. Without making it compulsory, the Party wanted to give military instruction to all Komsomol members. Concerning the work of clubs, the report sensibly recommended that during the summer it was especially important to avoid school-type work and instead to organize excursions, sport activities, and so forth.

During the Civil War, naturally, the Komsomol had a special importance as a recruiting agency and as an instrument for maintaining and raising the morale of the young soldiers in the Red Army. At particularly difficult moments, such as during Kolchak's advance in April 1919, Denikin's approach to Moscow in October of the same year, and the Polish war in the summer and fall of 1920, the youth organization carried out special mobilization campaigns. According to the perhaps exaggerated figures compiled by the Komsomol itself, the organization provided 30,000 volunteers during the civil war.[22]

In October 1919, the Second Congress debated the idea of setting up separate cells in the army. The Party leadership opposed the proposition. It wanted to retain control of indoctrination work in this crucially important section, and it feared a division of responsibility.[23] Since the great majority of soldiers were in the Komsomol age group, the establishment of yet another network within the army would have led to a duplication of effort. It is, however, interesting that in October 1919 a Komsomol congress could still carry on a spirited debate on a crucial issue on which the Party had already made its position known. The Party position, in fact, prevailed by only a narrow majority (120 against 94).[24] Clearly the leaders of the Komsomol were greatly attracted by the power that they would have enjoyed through the establishment of such a network. Although the Komsomol did not establish cells, it had a significant role within the Red Army. Some units were made up exclusively of Komsomol members, and the youth organization was able to send agitators to other units. After the war Komsomol activists claimed that underground cells had been particularly important in territories occupied by the enemy, where they had organized sabotage and espionage. They proudly pointed out that the enemy had punished Komsomol activity as severely as participation in the Party.

The army that the Party sent to the villages to take food away from the peasants was as important as the one that faced the enemy on the battlefields.

The starving cities had to be fed, and the peasants had no incentive to give up their grain. In this unattractive but nevertheless necessary work, the Komsomol played a considerable role. One of the tasks of village cells was to identify *kulaks*, that is, those peasants whom they suspected of hiding grain.[25] Factory cells sent their members to help in the task of "collecting."

The Komsomol was above all an instrument of mass indoctrination. Its task was to carry the message of the Party—whether concerning long-term goals or some immediate and temporary problem—to the young. The work of indoctrination was many faceted. Komsomol cells in middle-level schools and in universities supervised the ideological education of the students and reported on the political reliability of the faculty. Agitation outside the schools, however, was both more difficult and more important.

A chief problem here was the lack of qualified personnel. To overcome this difficulty, the Central Committee of the Komsomol, with the aid of the Party, established a school for agitators in Moscow in March 1919. In a two-and-a-half-month course the students studied Party history, political economy, and the history of the youth movement in Western countries. The first graduating class consisted of 170 young people, who were immediately sent to work in various parts of the country.[26] In the summer of 1919 the Party greatly transformed and expanded this school. It became the Ia. M. Sverdlov Communist University, the most elite institution for Party workers and agitators. The Komsomol Central Committee obtained the right to choose 10 percent of the students.

In September 1919, the Moscow Komsomol Committee assumed the obligation to train young people for setting up cells in villages. This "school" had hundreds of graduates. When the activists arrived in a village, they undertook to set up clubs, reading rooms, and libraries. The members of the newly formed cell were all obliged to participate in a "political circle" where they discussed current events on the basis of their reading of the Party and Komsomol press.

The existence of the Komsomol press preceded the organization itself. In August 1917 the Sixth Party Congress had decided to establish press organs for agitation among the young. The Moscow Party organization began publication of *Internatsional molodiozhi* (Youth international) on October 14 and on November 28; the Petrograd Committee brought out the first issue of *Iunyi proletarii* (Young proletarian).[27] Perhaps more important, *Pravda* began to include a column of Komsomol news. At the time of the Civil War, not only the Komsomol Central Committee but also regional organizations started to issue their own newspapers and journals. As was the case in general with the Soviet press of the period, the Komsomol newspapers and journals were numerous but incompletely written, edited, and printed.

Only the most naive would suggest that the Komsomol was from the moment of its inception anything other than an instrument in the hands of the Party. But how important an instrument was the youth organization?

How much did it contribute to Bolshevik victory in the life-and-death struggle that was the Civil War? It is difficult to answer these questions, for the benefits that the Komsomol provided were intangible (though doubtless real), whereas the weaknesses of the youth organization were self-evident. At the time of its Third Congress, the Komsomol had 482,000 members. In other words, by the end of the Civil War this "mass organization" had managed to mobilize less than 2 percent of the relevant age group.[28] Furthermore, much of the organization existed only on paper; for the great majority of Komsomolites membership in the organization involved very little disciplined group activity. For example, evaluating work among the youth in April 1920, the Smolensk Provincial Party Committee wrote proudly that 12,000 young people had joined the youth organization. The report also noted, however, that "the peasant youth, even those who are united in the youth organization, represent a completely undisciplined mass." The authors went on to warn: "The organization is threatened with complete disintegration in the course of the summer unless all agencies, both Party and Soviet, take extraordinary measures in time."[29] There is every reason to believe that the situation in Smolensk province was typical.

However, it would be a mistake to see only the weaknesses of the Komsomol. The Civil War was a contest between the new regime and its numerous enemies; to understand that contest, every aspect of it must be looked at in a comparative perspective. The Bolsheviks may have managed to reach only a small number of the young, but their enemies never made a comparable, sustained effort. In every major task the regime attempted, such as winning the war, requisitioning food, or improving work discipline, the Komsomol provided at least some assistance.

CHAPTER 5

The political use of books, films, and posters

The Bolsheviks, constantly aware of the importance for winning the Civil War of bringing their message to the people, experimented with such novel methods as sending out agitational trains and ships, building a network of oral agitators, and using the youth organization for indoctrination. Of course, they also did not neglect more conventional means, for example, printing pamphlets and pasting slogans on the wall.

The attitude of the new leaders to the publishing trade, the film industry, and graphic artists was at least partially determined by propaganda needs. However, policies of the Soviet regime in this area were also affected by considerations that went beyond the problems of agitation. These policies followed from Bolshevik ideas about culture and from their ambivalent relationship with the intelligentsia. On the one hand, the revolutionaries had a high appreciation for the role of ideas in the historical process and an admiration for "culture"; on the other, they distrusted intellectuals and despised traits that were traditionally associated with them, such as moral scruples, interminable and seemingly aimless discussions, and sentimentality.

In the eyes of the Bolshevik leaders, publishing had a far greater importance than making movies or drawing posters. The book, after all, was the chief vehicle of culture, and the printed word an essential method of propaganda. By contrast, in the prevailing conditions the cinema could not play a truly important role. After all, how could a vital political message be reliably conveyed to a large group of people through the medium of film when there was often no electricty even in the city? Filmmaking was a complex, slow, and expensive business, and the regime needed cheaper and more flexible ways of winning over the people. Yet a discussion of Soviet methods of mobilization must not slight this subject. The way in which the regime's film policies developed reveals much about Bolshevik attitudes toward propaganda.

Books

Paradoxically, Imperial Russia was a country of mass illiteracy with a flourishing publishing industry. During the decade preceding the First World War, publishing experienced a most impressive growth: In 1907, 9,600 titles appeared; in 1913, more then 34,000.[1] To place this achievement in perspective, we should note that it put Russia in second place in the world, immediately after Germany and far ahead of Britain, France, and the United States.[2]

Although the Russians did not produce their own printing machines, and the technical quality of books was somewhat behind European standards, it is clear that the large output presupposed a relatively sophisticated publishing and distribution system. The country also had a large pool of skilled printers. When the Bolsheviks after their victory wanted to realize their goal of bringing education and enlightenment to the people, in publishing at least they had a firm foundation to build on.

Economic problems caused by the World War were particularly severe in the printing trade. As the region that had most of the paper-making factories came under enemy occupation, there was an increasingly acute shortage of paper. When the foreign-made printing machines broke down, they could not be replaced, and since spare parts were not available, they could not easily be repaired, either. The total output of books fell sharply: In 1917, Russia produced 13,000 titles; in 1918, only 5,326.[3] The number of copies printed was also greatly reduced. Before the war the total was 133 million, but by 1918 it had shrunk to 77 million, and a very large share of these were not books but short pamphlets.[4]

The reduction of the total output led to severe unemployment among the printers. Their union had traditionally been a Menshevik stronghold, and they greeted the November Revolution with passive hostility. The Bolshevik leaders showed no interest in nationalizing the entire trade. But even if they desired to introduce such radical policies, they must have realized that complete nationalization of all firms would have meant a further deterioration of conditions and an increase in unemployment. They compromised: They nationalized those shops that they needed for printing government and Party papers and agitational materials but allowed others to continue privately owned for the time being.[5]

The first year of Soviet power was a period of uneasy coexistence for private and government publishing. In 1917 government-managed firms printed only 11.2 percent of all titles, and this figure grew to 21.5 percent in 1918. During the same time, the share of private publishers fell from 79.8 to 58.4 percent. (The remaining titles were published by political parties, scholarly societies, and cooperatives.)[6] For all practical purposes, during the first months of its existence the Soviet government exercised no censorship over the publication of books. The contrast between the policies toward nespapers and those toward books could not have been greater. In

January 1918, for example, at a time when their newspapers were being closed down, the Kadets were still able to print their party program.[7] The chief problem private publishers faced was not censorship but the collapse of the economy. Although the old, well-established firms, such as Sytin, M. D. Wolf, A. F. Marks, Konovalov, Sabashnikov, and Granat, continued to dominate publishing, each month they printed fewer and fewer books. As capitalists, naturally, they produced for the market. The majority of the titles that they brought out were potboilers, but they also issued some religious books and others equally undesirable from the Soviet point of view.[8] The lack of paper and the disintegraton of the normal book-distribution system led to the closing of more and more publishing firms in the course of the first half of 1918. Private publishing was dying before it was killed by government decree.

The growth in government publishing was uncoordinated. Every commissariat, every powerful Soviet institution wanted to have its own publishing office. Such a situation led to a waste of resources at a time of great scarcity.

As in other branches of the economy, the Soviet leadership attempted to impose order by constant reorganizations. The first government agency that had the task of coordinating state publishing was the literary-publishing department of Narkompros. The new department, which was set up in December 1917, was headed by P. I. Lebedev-Polianskii, a close friend and associate of commissar of enlightenment A. Lunacharskii and a leading figure in the Proletkul't (Organization of the Representatives of Proletarian Art) movement. The difficulty was that in the Soviet hierarchy Narkompros was a weak institution, and it therefore could not well fulfill its coordinating role. The new department's authority was further reduced when in April 1918 VSNKh set up a poligraphy section that assumed responsibility for all government-managed printing shops.[9] The lack of coordination between two agencies, one subordinated to the Commissariat of Enlightenment and the other to the Supreme Economic Council, greatly complicated matters. The leaders of Narkompros felt that the only way to impose order was to extend their own authority, and in the course of the Civil War they made several attempts to do so. These, however, remained unsuccessful.

The Soviet state very early embarked on a relatively large-scale publishing venture. The story of this undertaking is interesting neither because of the large number of books produced nor because of the contribution that these books made to the enlightenment of the Russian people but rather because it reveals much about the mentality of the new leaders in their utopian period. In spite of anarchy and lack of means, at a time of great danger both from foreign and domestic enemies, Bolshevik leaders devoted their time and energy to the problems of bringing Russian classics to the people. According to the reminiscences of Lebedev-Polianskii, it was Lenin's friend Bonch-Bruevich who thought up the idea of nationalizing the works of Russia's greatest authors.[10] On the basis of Bonch-Bruevich's idea, and at Lunacharskii's request, Lebedev-Polianskii drew up a draft, which was then presented to the Executive Committee of the Soviets on December 29. The project envisaged two types of publications: cheap editions for a mass audience and scholarly, fully annotated editions. The decree, approved by the Soviets' Executive Committee, gave a monopoly to Narkompros for the publication of fifty-eight authors. The most interesting part of the decree was the first paragraph, which stated frankly that the major reason for this envisaged large-scale publishing venture was to give jobs to unemployed printers.[11] Lebedev-Polianskii recalled later that Lenin, who was constantly concerned with immediate and practical matters, was particularly interested in this aspect of the issue.[12] The decree, however, did not pass the Executive Committee without controversy. Sukhanov, perhaps mischievously, for a time objected that the decree implicitly recognized the right of the descendants of great authors to receive royalties.[13]

One may argue that the government's domination over the cultural life of the country began with monopolizing the classics.[14] But if it was a step, it was a small one, for the Bolshevik leaders at this time did not want to suppress; they wanted to spread enlightenment.

To embark on this publishing task, Narkompros formed a commission in which representatives of trade unions, the Executive Committee of the Soviets, Proletkul't, and other organizations participated. The Soviet state also wanted to attract the services of well-known artists, writers, and intellectuals. The farsighted probably understood that it would be politically beneficial to associate the respected names of authors with the new regime. The publication of classics was obviously such a worthwhile task that intellectuals could hardly object to it. Yet the history of the commission shows the difficulties the Bolsheviks had in this early period in gaining the cooperation of intellectuals. The new regime genuinely needed the help of the intellectuals. There were not enough Bolshevik experts, and those Party figures capable of doing the job had other tasks that they understandably considered more important.[15] Several well-known figures in the world of art and literature refused to participate in the work of the commission. Others, however, such as A. N. Benois, A. Blok, D. B. Sterenberg, and N. N. Punin, agreed to serve. The sterile debates must have reinforced the visceral dislike of some Bolshevik activists for the impractical intellectuals. The commission spent a great deal of time on secondary matters. For example, Blok objected furiously to the majority view that the classics should be published according to the new orthography. To him that reform seemed aesthetically unacceptable.[16]

When the government moved to Moscow, the work had to be interrupted and a new committee formed. Here the Bolsheviks had even more trouble in attracting intellecutals: Many did not even respond to the invitations. Some objected to the idea of nationalizing classics; others disapproved of the plan to provide commentaries, presumably fearing politically inspired misinterpretation. Among the leading intellectuals in Moscow, Briusov, Grabar, V. V. Veresaev, and E. G. Lundberg participated on the commission, which resumed work only in July. The first volumes started to appear at the end of 1918. In this series Gogol, Zhukovskii, Nekrasov, Upsenskii, Chekhov, and Saltykov-Shchedrin were published, among others. The size of the editions varied between 50,000 and 100,000.[17]

In spite of the publication of literary classics, 1918 was a year of disastrous decline in the printing trade, as it was in other branches of the Soviet economy. The introduction of war communism during the second half of 1918 also brought far-reaching changes in publishing. From the point of view of the Soviet leaders the situation was becoming increasingly intolerable: Private firms wasted paper publishing "useless" books, and state enterprises worked without coordination. From the middle of 1918 to May 1919, when Gosizdat, the state publishing house, was established, the regime experimented with various solutions. The first energetic step was taken by the Moscow Soviet, which on October 23 municipalized the book trade and all publishing.[18] This unilateral action of the city soviet dismayed the leaders of Narkompros, who felt that the authority of the commissariat was being undermined. For example, Narkompros had contracted private firms for the publication of textbooks, and now it was unclear whether the firms could deliver.[19] The printers' union also opposed the move of the Moscow Soviet, because the printers feared that it would lead to a further contraction of publishing and therefore to a loss of jobs. Pokrovskii, deputy commissar of enlightenment, raised the matter at a meeting of Sovnarkom. He extracted a promise from the representative of the Moscow Soviet that the municipalized publishing firms would live up to their contracts and then withdrew his objections.[20] The Moscow Soviet's decree was followed by similar ones in the other major cities. City soviets took over not only publishing firms but also libraries.

In late 1918 and early 1919 the Party and the government considered various ways of imposing order. The leaders of Narkompros suggested the creation of a Central Book Committee, Tsentrokniga, in which representatives of the Party, the Executive Committee of the Soviets, and VSNKh would participate. The chief task of Tsentrokniga was to coordinate municipalization of the book trade.[21] The plan was based on the explicit assumption that under the prevailing conditions of near anarchy it was impossible to nationalize and centralize publishing. Since Tsentrokniga was to be part of Narkompros, the leaders of the commissariat hoped to regain lost ground by introducing the project.[22]

At the same time the central committee of the union of journalists proposed more ambitious changes. In January 1919 the leaders of that union recommended the establishment of independent commissariat responsible for all matters of agitation and propaganda; in this capacity it was to oversee the publication of all newspapers and books in the Soviet Union. The leaders of the Party rejected this plan. According to their view, all agencies of the Party and of the state, and indeed all Party members, were to be propagandists. To separate this crucial activity and to entrust it to technicians, even to reliable Party members, seemed inappropriate.[23] On this occasion Lenin said:

It is impossible to give control of literature to a bureau organized by the Union of Journalists. Literature is a powerful weapon of propaganda, and its control in the present period should be in the hands of government. Leadership in literature is necessary, but it should be in the hands of the State Publisher – this is one of its tasks.[24]

In the course of the debate, the Moscow Union of Writers expressed its concern that centralization in publishing would mean increased regulation and ideological control.[25] By contrast, the leaders of VSNKh wanted more control and coordination. N. P. Gorbunov, an official in VSNKh, attacked the Tsentrokniga project as too timid. He recommended the establishment of a centralized publishing organ, outside of Narkompros, subordinated directly to the Executive Committee of the Soviets. Gorbunov's contribution to the debate was clearly part of the feud between Narkompros and VSNKh.[26]

Ultimately, the Central Committee of the Party decided the matter. It set up a committee to study the problems of unifying government publishing. This committee quickly agreed on all major issues, save one. Some members wanted the future publishing house, Gosizdat, to be directly subordinated to the Executive Committee of the Soviets, that is, to be independent of Narkompros. Lunacharskii, who was a member of the committee, passionately objected.[27] The Central Committee of the Party, when the project was submitted to it on February 5, 1919, supported the commissar of enlightenment.

The decree of the Sovnarkom, which officially established Gosizdat in May, made it an autonomous section within Narkompros. The new publishing house was headed by an illustrious committee: The chairman was V. V. Vorovskii, a Party leader of long standing (at the end of 1920 N. L. Meshcheriakov took this post), and its members included N. I. Bukharin, V. I. Nevskii, I. I. Skvortsov-Stepanov, and M. N. Pokrovskii (deputy commissar of enlightenment).[28] It is evident from this list that the Party attributed great significance to publishing.

Gosizdat was created from five publishers: (1) the literary-publishing department of Narkompros, (2) the publishing section of the Moscow City Soviet, (3) the publishing section of the Petrograd City Soviet, (4) Kommunist, which had been the Party's publisher, and (5) the publishing department of the Central Executive Committee of the Soviets.[29] The establishment of Gosizdat did not by itself concentrate publishing in one agency. The army's political-education department (PUR), and the commissariats continued to bring out pamphlets and even books, and VSNKh retained control not only of paper producing and printing but also of publishing technical literature. Nevertheless, the authority of the new publishing house gradually expanded. In the course of 1919 and 1920 it took over provincial firms, which then became its local agencies. By September 1920 it had sixty such agencies.[30]

Initially Gosizdat had six departments: (1) scientific, (2) agitation-propaganda, (3) scientific-popular, (4) scientific-popular for the social sciences, (5) pedagogy and children, and (6) literary-artistic.[31] The largest and most important section, not surprisingly, was the agitation-propaganda one: In 1920, out of a total output of 37.5 million copies, it produced 25.2 million.[32]

Relations between the leaders of Gosizdat and Narkompros were not the best. Vorovskii and his comrades did not always approve of Narkompros's policy; they disliked the fact that Narkompros for a time continued to contract private publishers to print textbooks, even though Gosizdat was capable of doing the job; nor did they like the fact that Krupskaia's Extramural Education Department continued to maintain a national book-and-propaganda distribution network, duplicating Gosizdat's. Sovnarkom, to avoid any misunderstandings, reaffirmed Gosizdat's subordination to Narkompros in October 1919.[33]

The problems of the Soviet publishing industry could not be solved by a reorganization. The difficulties followed from the conditions of the economy, most particularly the shortage of paper. To use the available paper most rationally, the government had established a paper monopoly in May 1919, simultaneously with the creation of Gosizdat. A new agency, Glavbum, had complete authority to distribute paper, and all supplies not issued by it became subject to confiscation.[34] One suspects, however, that this decree was no more effective than a series of other emergency measures taken by Sovnarkom. Private publishers hid their supplies.

Statistics best show the magnitude of the decline in the paper industry. In 1914 Russia produced 23 million poods and imported 10 million from Finland; in 1920 the country produced 2.1 million and imported 400,000 from Estonia. Of these 2.5 million, less than 1.5 million could be used for printing. From the 1.5 million, the central newspapers of Moscow and Petrograd claimed 880,000, and Gosizdat for all its needs got just over a half a million for the entire year. In 1921 the situation further deteriorated. In April, for example, the state publisher received only 23,000.[35]

The economic hardships led to a gradual concentration of the industry. In 1919 and in 1920 the printing sections of various commissariats came to be amalgamated into Gosizdat. The nationalization of private firms progressed slowly because the government did not need more printing shops. In October 1920, 185 private firms still continued a precarious existence.[36] The final move against the private firms took place at the very end of the period of war communism and coincided with the regime's ability to free the printers' union from Menshevik influence. By the end of 1920, even the smallest private printing shops had disappeared.

As long as the private firms existed, however, Gosizdat's function went beyond publishing books. It controlled and supervised all publishing activities in the country. In the summer of 1920, Knizhnaia palata, the national book-registering service, became part of Gosizdat. As a consequence, the state publisher was supposed to receive a sample copy of very book printed.

Gosizdat had an ambivalent relationship with the private firms: It both supervised them and competed with them. It was easier to deal with the largest firms, which had skilled workers, machinery, and distribution systems. These firms received almost all the state contracts. Gosizdat's power was based on the fact that it could allocate scarce paper. Its announced policy was to support the publication of "useful" books by giving paper; it promised neutrality in reference to books, which were irrelevant from a social-political point of view; and it tried to prevent the publication of what it considered harmful. As time went on, censorship became slightly more stringent. Nevertheless, in the confusion of the Civil War, even in 1920, especially in the provinces, it was possible to publish books that were written from an anti-Marxist point of view.

Although Gosizdat was the giant of publishing, it was not the only state-supported firm. Vsemirnaia literatura, a publishing house established by Maxim Gorky, also had an ambitious program. After Gorky's paper, Novaia zhizn', was closed down in the middle of 1918, he made his peace with the Soviet regime. Perhaps because of his international reputation and because of his friendship with Lenin and Lunacharskii, Gorky was allowed a considerable degree of independence. He used his position to protect and support intellectuals who found themselves in increasing trouble with the new authorities. He gathered around himself an ideologically heterogenous group, which included on the one hand Briusov and Blok and on the other Merezhkovskii, Gipius, Gumilov, Aikhenvald, and Sologub.[37] He gave work to hundreds of unemployed intellectuals as translators and as editorial consultants by drawing up extensive publishing plans. He hoped to publish more than 800 volumes of first-rate literature in the course of three years. In fact, up to 1922 Gorky's firm produced only 59 volumes. Even this accomplishment was an astounding achievement and obviously the result of the support that Gorky enjoyed in the highest levels of leadership. Vorovskii and others at Gosizdat were resentful that Narkompros allowed Gorky to compete with them for talent and raw material. In December 1920 they succeeded, over Gorky's protest, in amalgamating Vsemirnaia literatura into Gosizdat.

Other firms that retained their independence had much less ambitious publishing plans. Most of them came to depend for their survival on contracts with Gosizdat. By 1920 paper was so scarce and the printing shops in such disarray that most of the still-existing firms could not undertake new contracts. In April 1920, a Party commission decided that because the domestic printing industry could not fulfill even the minimum needs, it was necessary to contract foreign firms. That the regime was willing to invest precious foreign currency shows on the one hand the extent of the deterioration of the Russian printing industry and on the other what a great significance the regime attributed to the production of books.

In this venture also, Gorky played an important role. For some time he had been interested in the idea of producing and selling Russian books abroad. From the profits of this enterprise he intended to print books for the Russian reader. Gorky knew A. I. Grzhebin, the head of a publishing firm, and acted as an intermediary between him and the Soviet government. Grzhebin's firm had been established in Petrograd in 1919, but because of the prevailing conditions, in 1920 the firm moved to Berlin.

The Soviet government provided the publisher with an investment capital of 2.5 million German marks, and large editions of such classics as Lermontov, Chekhov, and Leskov indeed appeared. This cooperative effort, however, was troubled from the beginning. The venture was not as commercially successful as hoped, and the leaders of the Soviet government wanted more control over the publisher. Many of the books produced by Grzhebin were judged by the Soviet authorities, including Lenin himself, as unsuitable for a Soviet audience. When Gorky showed some of Grzhebin's publications to Lenin, the Soviet leader was disturbed that these included a collection of Indian tales. Gorky argued in vain that the stories were excellent and the publication cheap; Lenin considered it wrong to spend gold on such matters at a time of misery and hunger.[38]

The split, however, came not over questions of economics but over politics. The Bolsheviks initiated a series called *Letopis' revoliutsii* (Annals of the Revolution). To their horror, Grzhebin included the writing of such "counterrevolutionaries" as Dan, Martov, Chernov, and Sukhanov.[39] From 1921 on, the contacts between Grzhebin and the Soviet government became increasingly limited and were broken off completely in 1923.

Publishing suffered not only from material deficiencies and organizational chaos but also from the collapse of the distribution network. Until the fall of 1918 the Soviet government imposed no limitations on selling books. Then in October the Moscow Soviet and later other soviets in the major cities of the country municipalized the book trade. This move completed the disintegration of the publishing and bookselling business.

An even more radical step was taken by Sovnarkom in April 1920. The government at that time outlawed the selling of books and nationalized book supplies. Of all the strange laws passed during the period of war communism, this was among the strangest.[40] In Moscow and Petrograd, Narkompros supervised the process of nationalization. In the provinces, this task fell on local commissions made up of Narkompros and Rabkrin representatives. As with so many other acts of war communism, it is hard to establish how much of the regulaton was actually put into effect. From negative evidence it seems that the decree was largely ignored. For example, the September-October issue of *Kniga i revoliutsiia* (Book and Revolution) mentioned a book sale organized by the press section of the Petrograd Soviet. The sale was in Dom Iskusstv, where tables were set up for selling books. Such a sale was contrary to the announced intention of the law.[41]

In November 1918, the Executive Committee of the Soviets set up a distribution agency, Tsentropechat', for books, pamphlets, newspapers, and all sorts of propaganda material. The network of Tsentropechat' was based on the previously nationalized network of A. S. Suvorin, a major publisher in prerevolutionary Russia. The new agency could not deal with the difficulties. Meshcheriakov, reporting on the work of Gosizdat, mentioned the poor performance of Tsentropechat' as one of the main problems of the state publishing house. He wrote:

An enormous obstacle in the work of Gosizdat was the bad, fabulously bad work of Tsentropechat'. Books did not get to the provinces, they did not get where they were most needed. Books did not get to the reader. This killed the energy of the authors, who did not see the fruit of their literary work.[42]

It was perhaps self-serving for Meshcheriakov to blame another government agency. It is hard to see how the problems could have been solved. The postal service and the railroads hardly functioned. Under the system of war communism, newly printed books and propaganda pamphlets were distributed free and were given to libraries: There was no profit motive to support the links of the distribution network. The Civil War, obviously, was not a propitious time for the spread of enlightenment.

Films

A year before the outbreak of the First World War, the police submitted a report to the tsar dealing with the correspondence of a Duma deputy and an American moviemaking firm. The tsar wrote on the margin of the report: "I consider that cinematography is an empty matter, which no one needs. It is something even harmful. Only an abnormal person could place this farcical business on the level of art. This is silliness, and we should not attribute any significance to such trifles."[43]

The tsar was obtuse. During the first two decades of the twentieth century, movies amazingly quickly came to play an important role in every country of Europe, including Russia, and of course in the United States. Up to 1907 only foreign films appeared on Russian screens.[44] The interest of the public, however, was so great that Russian companies also tried their luck. At first the Russians attempted to make only newsreels; in this field they could give something to their audiences that foreigners could not easily do: a photographic portrayal of some interesting domestic event. In 1908 a Russian company ventured further and made a feature film. Between 1909 and 1913 the number of domestically made films grew from an annual 10 to 129. Even so, before the war, the Russians controlled only 20 percent of the domestic market.[45]

In these early days, both the technical and artistic quality of the films was low. Raw film, cameras, and all other equipment had to be imported. Directors had not yet found the special language of the cinema. Instead of working with original material, they preferred to dramatize literary works. It did not occur to them to rework the classics in such a way as to fit the needs of the film. They were content to provide photographic illustrations.[46]

The war brought major changes. On the one hand, it made the task of the filmmakers more difficult. From this point on and for a long time to come, there was a shortage of raw film and every kind of equipment. On the other, being cut off from abroad, Russian filmmakers were more or less liberated from foreign competition. In 1916, domestically made film conquered 60 percent of the market. The market itself was swelling as popular enthusiasm for this form of entertaiment grew. In 1916, 150,000 movie tickets were sold, which meant that for every theatergoer there were twelve moviegoers.[47]

The world conflict had a special significance for the development of newsreels. The English, the French, and the Germans used the new medium with skill to mobilize domestic opinion for the war. The Russians were once again behind. They lacked the technical means, but more importantly the leaders in government lacked the necessary mentality. Few among those who were responsible for the war effort were as obtuse as the tsar himself, but ministers, bureaucrats, and generals also did not fully understand the significance of the home front. These were essentially nineteenth-century people, who believed that it was the duty of "good Russians" to obey. They did not see that to win a modern war, the people had to be brought into politics; their opinions had to be manipulated; they had to be won over.

The Russians made some attempts at propaganda, but it is striking how feeble those attempts were. A committee was formed that was charged, oddly enough, with carrying out both philanthropy and propaganda. The committee, nominally a private organization but in fact closely connected with the government, was named after a famous nineteenth-century general, Skobelev. The government gave monopoly of war documentary making to this group. On the enormously long front line, however, only five cameramen operated, and two of them were foreigners.[48] However dedicated and talented these people might have been, they could not possibly have produced an adequate pictorial history of the war. The movie section of the Skobelev committee lacked everything: It had few able propagandists and an inadequate distribution network. As a consequence, ironically, Russian audiences saw a far more detailed account of the fighting on the Western than on the Eastern front.

The Skobelev committee became an official part of the government apparatus and continued its work after the February Revolution. Administrative confusion was so great at that time that in the course of eight months the committee passed under the authority of four different ministries.[49] The Socialist Revolutionary and Menshevik leaders had a far clearer appreciation of the significance of propaganda than their tsarist predecessors. The newsreels reflected the spirit of the Revolution, though it would be difficult to argue that in 1917 they played an important role in the formation of public opinion.

No one at the time had a clearer appreciation of the propaganda potential of the cinema than Lenin and his colleagues. The Leninists, with their impatience and their voluntaristic view of history, were constantly searching for ways to bring their beliefs to the people. Cinema was one among the many usable instruments.

If we are to believe Lunacharskii, Lenin in February 1922 told him: "In our country you have the reputation of being the protector of the arts. So, you must firmly remember, that for us the most important of all arts is the cinema."[50] This purported statement of Lenin has been quoted so often that it has become a cliché. Lenin spoke of cinema as the "most important art" not because he understood the artistic potentials of the medium. He obviously did not foresee the emergence within a few years of a group of first-rate artists, such as Kuleshov, Eisenstein, and Pudovkin. Given his conservatism in matters of art, it is unlikely that he ever believed that films could compete with the theater on an aesthetic plane. He attributed great significance to this medium because he believed in its potential as an educator. He was a politician, and naturally he was primarily interested in movies as an instrument of political education. But that was not the only kind of education he envisaged. He had great faith in the use of movies in spreading all sorts of information among the people, for example, about science and agriculture. To Lenin cinema was yet another achievement of Western technology, something that could help the Russians to overcome their appalling backwardness. Lenin's great interest in films as a vehicle of knowledge soon had practical consequences. The young Soviet state invested scarce resources in filmmaking, and the Soviet Union started to make shorts for the popularization of science at a remarkably early date.[51] For the moment, however, little could be done. In January 1918, a movie subsection was organized within Krupskaia's Extramural Education Department of Narkompros. At this point it had not yet occurred to anyone that this organizaton might take charge of the film industry. The task of the subsection was simply to encourage the use of film in political education. At the time of its establishment, the subsection had in its possession a single projector, a few reels of educational films, and newsreels from the days of the Provisional Government. On occasion, agitators used these materials to accompany their lectures.[52]

The attitude of the Bolshevik leadership to the question of freedom within the movie industry was the same as it was in publishing. The leaders drew a sharp line between newsreels, which dealt with political material, and other films, which had the purpose of entertainment. The Bolsheviks were determined not to allow the making and showing of newsreels that were hostile to them. The Skobelev committee, for self-protection, once again detached itself from the government and formed a "cooperative." As a private organization, it continued to make newsreels. These newsreels expressed Socialist Revolutionary and Menshevik points of view, and so the first newsreels made in Soviet Russia were anti-Bolshevik in their spirit. When the government suppressed hostile newspapers following the filming of the dispersal of the Constituent Assembly, it also closed down the Skobelev committee and confiscated its property.[53]

In May 1918, the Soviet government established a national film organization and named D. I. Leshchenko its director. This All-Russian film committee incorporated the film sections of both the Moscow Soviet and the Extramural Education Department of Narkompros, but in fact it operated autonomously.[54]

Soviet historians at times describe 1918–19 as a transitional period, in which the old gradually died and the new came into being. In terms of film history, the transition meant the collapse of private filmmaking and the first, tentative efforts to take charge of the film industry by the Soviet state.

The regime did not hesitate to interfere in the industry. Already in December 1917 and January 1918, some local soviets confiscated cinemas for their own use. When the owners appealed to the government for protection, the Commissariat for Internal Affairs sustained the soviets.[55] In April 1918, the government introduced monopoly over foreign trade, which of course greatly affected the film industry. Since the government did not easily give permission to buy the necessary material and equipment abroad, individual entrepreneurs acquired them by circumventing the law. The foreign-trade monopoly also affected the distribution of foreign films in Soviet Russia. Gradually, in the course of the Civil War the importation of films ceased.

A regulation issued by the Moscow Soviet on March 4, 1918, promised that film factories would not be nationalized; they would, however, like other factories, be subjected to workers' control. No one knew at the time what exactly workers' control meant. The same decree demanded from the owners of studios an inventory of their property and raw materials and forbade the selling of studios.[56]

It is evident from the decree of the Moscow Soviet that the new authorities were above all concerned with the functioning of the economy. At a time of great unemployment they feared the closing down of studios. The government did not want to nationalize the industry because it did not want to assume responsibility for running it under very difficult circumstances. Lunacharskii in an April 1918 article in *Vecherniaia zhizn'* attempted to alllay the fear of studio owners concerning nationalization. He even promised that Russian factories would start producing raw film, thereby alleviating the crippling shortage.[57]

Censorship was by no means heavy-handed. The authorities only wanted to prevent the showings of explicitly anti-Soviet films and those that the puritanical regime considered pornographic. Both the film committee and the soviets had the right to suppress films.[58] Naturally, the decisions of the Moscow Soviet were particularly important, not only because it controlled the capital, the largest market, but also because these decisions served as examples for the rest of the country. Both the Moscow Soviet and the film committee periodically issued bulletins of proscribed films. For example, in August 1918, the film committee forbade the showing of the films *The Lady of the Summer Resort Fears Not Even the Devil* and *The Knights of the Dark Nights* for "pornography" and *The Liberation of the Serfs* and *Flags Wave Triumphantly* for "distorting history."[59]

It is amazing that under the extraordinarily difficult conditions prevailing in 1918, the industry continued to function. In that year, in territories under Bolshevik control almost 150 films were made.[60] Although one assumes that many of these must have been shorts, a number of ambitious projects were also carried out.

Remarkably, films made in 1918, at a time when the country was experiencing a serious crisis, did not at all reflect the environment. The directors did not know how to deal with the revolution, and in any case had little interest in it. Studios, of course, worked on capitalist principles and made the films the audiences wanted. At a time of privation, moviegoers above all wanted entertainment. Consequently the studios produced detective films, romances, and many dramatizations of classics. For example, in 1918 three dramatizations of the works of L. Tolstoi appeared: *Father Sergei, The Living Corpse,* and *The Power of Darkness.*[61]

By far the most important of the three was Protazanov's *Father Sergei,* which was first shown in Moscow in May 1918.[62] This was one of the finest silent films. It retained Tolstoi's anticlericalism, but it was by no means a political tract. Protazanov made a psychological study of remarkable sophisticaton. Although he would direct close to a hundred films in his long career, he never surpassed the artistic level of this one.

Important figures of the future golden age of the Soviet silent era, such as Protazanov, Turkin, Razumnyi, Zheliabuzhskii, and Perestiani, worked in private studios in 1918. The seventeen-year-old Lev Kuleshov, the most underappreciated genius of Soviet film, made his first work, *The Project of Engineer Prite,* at this time.[63] The ubiquitous Maiakovskii was extremely active in movies: He wrote scenarios and acted in several films. His best-known work was in *The Lady and the Hooligan,* a scenario he wrote on the basis of a French story. Both the scenario and Maiakovskii's acting were undistinguished. The undoubted talent of the poet lay elsewhere.[64]

Private film production gradually came to a halt. The shortage of all necessary materials for filmmaking, the closing down of theaters for lack of fuel and electricity, and the general uncertainty that prevailed finally made moviemaking impossible. Actors, directors, and technical personnel first moved south to the Crimea, Odessa, and the Caucasus and lived for awhile under White rule. Later, the great majority of these people followed the defeated White armies and went to Europe. Most of the best-known figures of prerevolutionary Russian films ended up in various European capitals, especially in Paris and Berlin.[65] The proportion of filmmakers who went into emigration was higher than in the other arts. As the directors went south, they often took with them irreplaceable raw material. It would take a long time for the young Soviet film industry to make up for the loss.

The nationalization of the film industry came as an anticlimax. On August 27, 1919, Sovnarkom decided to eliminate private studios and film-distribution networks. In view of the fact that filmmaking and film distribution had come to a halt in any case, the decree had little practical significance.[66] The state took over empty buildings, stripped of machinery, raw materials, and instruments. To take charge of the film industry, the government upgraded the All-Russian Film Committee to the All-Russian Photo-Movie Department (VFKO) of Narkompros. Naturally, a simple administrative reorganization could accomplish little.

The beginnings of Soviet filmmaking were slow indeed. The first products were, naturally, newsreels. Using the confiscated equipment of the dispersed Skobelev committee, the All-Russian Film Committee started to make some newsreels. The technical quality of the work was poor. Even worse, so little raw film was available that newsreels had to be made in very small numbers, often no more than five to ten copies for the entire country.[67] Since the Russians had little tradition in newsreel or documentary making, young people with very little background could quickly receive responsible assignments. Tisse and D. Vertov started their work at this time, together with other talented young people. They did not achieve anything spectacular during the Civil War, but they gained valuable experience.

Although newsreels were technically poor and in short supply besides, they did have some propaganda significance. The agittrains and ships carried them into the countryside, and the Russian peasants for the first time were able to see their leaders; they also saw film reports on demonstrations in the cities and the accomplishments of the Red Army. The Party activists who traveled on agittrains reported very favorably on the effect of the newsreels.[68]

Soviet newsreels were not particularly innovative. At this time, however, the infant Soviet film industry did make a type of film that had never existed before. These were affectionately called *agitki.*

These were short films, from five to thirty minutes long, with extremely didactic content aimed at an uneducated audience. The simplest of the agitki had no plot at all but were called living posters. One, for example, was called, *Proletarians of the World Unite!*[69] The opening titles told the audience about the French Revolution. These were followed by two or three animated scenes from that great event. A long intertitle then explained: "The French Revolution was defeated because it had no leader and it had no concrete program around which the workers could have united. Only fifty years after the French Revolution did Karl Marx advance the slogan: 'Proletarians of the world, unite!' " Next the audience saw an actor playing the role of Marx, sitting in front of a desk, writing "Proletarians of the world, unite!" There were two or three more pictures showing the suffering of revolutionaries in Siberian exile. The film ended with this text on the screen: "Eternal glory to those who with their blood painted our flags red."

Another agitka simply exhorted the audience to give warm clothes to the suffering soldiers of the Red Army. It consisted of nothing more than a couple of pictures of ill-dressed fighting men.

Most of these short films, however, did have simple stories. Some were humorous sketches, such as *Frightened Burzhui.*[70] As a result of the revolution, a capitalist lost his appetite and became an insomniac. He is ordered to appear in a work battalion. Honest labor cures him immediately. Others were melodramas. In *For the Red Flag,* a father joins the Red Army to take the place of his not satisfactorily class-conscious son. The son, recognizing the error of his ways, goes to search for the father. He finds him at the most critical moment and saves the wounded old man. Then the son himself is wounded, but he exhibits great courage and saves the flag from the enemy.[71] In the film *The Father and Son,* it is the son who is the convinced Communist.[72] As a Red Army soldier, he is captured by the enemy. The guard turns out to be none other than his father, who had been drafted by the Whites. The son explains to his father the superiority of the Soviet system, and the newly enlightened father then frees all the prisoners and escapes with them to join the Red Army. *Peace to the Shack and War to the Palace* is also about joining the Red Army.[73] A peasant lad comes home from the war to poverty and misery. He sees that the landlord still lives well. This contrast between poor and rich makes him understand the correctness of the Bolshevik position.

The Bolshevik notion of propaganda was broader than "political education." Even in these very hard times some of the agitki aimed to educate the people. A particularly naive agitka was *Children – the Flower of Life,* written, directed, and photographed by Zheliabuzhskii.[74] We meet two families. One is the family of the worker, Kuleshov, who does not observe the rules of hygiene; therefore their young child gets sick. Instead of taking him to a doctor, they take him to a sorcerer. The child dies, and the unhappy couple breaks up. By contrast, the other family, which observes the advice of the doctor and appreciates the importance of cleanliness, has a healthy child and lives happily ever after. Other agitki were devoted to the description of the struggle against diseases such as cholera and tuberculosis.[75]

Between the summer of 1918 and the end of the Civil War, Soviet studios made approximately sixty agitki.[76] This is an impressive number if we remember that work had to be carried out under the most difficult circumstances. The studios not only lacked raw material but also trained people of all kinds. There were never enough good scenarios. The film committee and later VFKO experimented with competitions for scripts, but these were not very successful. Such important luminaries of Soviet intellectual life as Lunacharskii, Serafimovich, and Maiakovskii tried their hands at working for movies, but they had little experience and understanding of the special needs of the cinema. Most often the director worked without a script and improvised. The well-known directors and actors stayed with the private studios as long as possible, and few wanted to identify themselves with the Soviet regime. Communists, on the other hand, knew little about filmmaking. The directors who did work in the nationalized sector did what they were told, but their work showed that their heart was not in it. Actors had so little experience in playing workers and knew so little about working-class life that they struck unnatural poses, which often caused hilarity in a working-class audience.[77]

Yet in spite of their primitive execution and simple message, the agitki played an important propaganda role. From the reports of agitators, it is evident that audiences enjoyed the films; the agitators constantly asked for more. From the regime's point of view, the agitki possessed several attractive features. Films were an aspect of modern life, and Communists liked to identify themselves with modernity. Unlike theater groups, films could be sent with relative ease to remote parts of the country. In any case, how could the political commissars be certain that theater groups would perform the right plays in the right spirit? Movies were safer.

The agitki could not by themselves do much for Communist education. What they could do was to attract an audience. Then, if he or she was able enough, the agitator took over and explained to the audience the message of the film, connecting that message with the policies of the Soviet regime. After the Civil War, the agitki gradually disappeared. But at the time of the Second World War, when the regime once again felt itself to be endangered, they were revived with success.

Posters

The poster, like propaganda itself, is a product of the modern age. It is in fact the quintessential form of propaganda: Its message can be quickly grasped by the most unsophisticated viewers; its appeal does not depend on rational argument; and it is as capable of advertising a commercial product as of selling a political idea.

The Bolsheviks appreciated the power of this minor art form. When we think of Lenin's Russia during the Civil War, our mental image, formed on the basis of pictures, newsreels, and cinematic reconstructions, always includes slogans pasted everywhere and posters on the wall.

When we consider that Russians had few traditions in this field, it is striking how quickly the posters became ubiquitous.[78] Although it was possible to find examples of commercial graphic art in Russia going back into the 1840s, Russian industrial development and the nature of the domestic market did not create many opportunities for graphic artists. This situation changed somewhat in the immediate prerevolutionary years, when posters became increasingly widely used to advertise firms. But the artists who would later work for the Bolsheviks had received their inspiration from foreign sources. This inspiration came not only from commercial art but also from the great and sudden effusion of patriotic posters at the time of the Great War. In this respect, too, the Russians were far behind Western Europe. It was not so much that the Russians lacked the technical means to create and distribute these martial commercials but rather that tsarist leaders never felt the need. In this aspect of modernity, the Russians were just as far behind as they were in per capita industrial production.

During the first months following the Bolshevik Revolution, various Soviet agencies published proclamations. On occasion, these were accompanied by pictures, but posters worthy of the name did not appear. In the second half of 1918, the situation suddenly changed. First the publishing section of the Central Executive Committee of the Soviets, and then one publisher after another, started to print posters. Within a few months, posters became so popular that a leading official of PUR, V. Polonskii, spoke of "poster mania."[79] Every Soviet agency responsible for indoctrination, such as local soviets, commissariats, and mass organizations, commissioned artists, and hundreds of new posters appeared each month. The Red Army was particularly important: It became a munificent patron of graphic artists, and some of the best work of the time was created on military orders and dealt with military themes.

The first posters were weak, from both technical and artistic points of view. One of their unfortunate characteristics was excessive goriness. As Polonskii put it: "The blood flowed in rivers to such an extent that several times we were concerned that red paint would disappear altogether."[80] However, aspiring artists soon found their medium in the poster, and within a short time a new art form flourished in Russia. These posters were among the most impressive contributions Soviet Russians ever made to the fine arts.

It is understandable that Soviet agitators were attracted to the poster. It was cheap: Thousands could be reached with a relatively small investment of that scarce resource, paper. Furthermore, posters could respond quickly to the ever-changing military-political situation. Although many of them became obsolete in a short time, they were efficient in channeling revolutionary energy where it was most needed. Since the graphic message of the posters often required no ability to read, they were an excellent means of reaching the uneducated. As the Bolsheviks understood very well, these people would have a determining influence on the outcome of the war. Finally, drawing posters is inherently a "committed" art. It ideally suited the expression of the Bolshevik mentality, which stressed conflict and simple juxtapositions: proletarian versus capitalist, progressive versus reactionary, good versus evil. The powerful and handsome worker with his hammer smiting the fat and disgusting "burzhui" was the ultimate in simplification – and a staple of early Soviet posters.

Although the Bolsheviks understood the significance of propaganda far better than their enemies, the poster was such an obvious instrument of propaganda in Civil War conditions that the Whites also turned to it. The White regimes, especially the most stable one among them in the South, attracted a number of talented artists who produced good work. In comparison, however, the Reds outproduced their opponents both in quantity and quality.

Most of the well-known artists were hostile to the Bolshevik revolution and preferred to work for the Whites. Under the circumstances, young, inexperienced, and little-known figures could receive commissions from the revolutionary authorities and had an opportunity to develop their talents. Just as in cinema, Soviet poster art in its earliest period was developed by relatively young people who were untrammeled by tradition and had a bent for experimentation. The new rulers enjoyed their ability to reward those artists who would throw in their lot with them. Such government support was extremely valuable at a time when circumstances were unfavorable for art and artists. As journals closed down, there was no need for illustrators; as businesses could not function, no one wanted to hire a graphic artist.

The finest of the Soviet poster painters was D. S. Moor. He was born in 1883, and his real name was D. S. Orlov. He had no artistic training, though he had worked for satirical journals before the war. His politics were generally leftist and revolutionary. However, like so many others he had been caught up in enthusiasm for the war, and during those years he mostly produced cartoons aimed at the foreign foe.[81] In 1918, at the time of the preparations for the celebration of May Day, he received a commission to decorate the facade of the Historical Museum on Red Square. Later he painted agittrains. He started to paint revolutionary posters in 1918 and quickly achieved great success, turning out dozens of posters in a very short time. Given his prolific output, it is understandable that the quality of his work was uneven. Some of his posters were uninspired and frankly derivative, but others were the best examples of the art. His most memorable poster was occasioned by the 1921–2 famine. It depicted in a slightly stylized form an old man with a suffering, pathetic face, his arms held to the sky. The black and white poster had a single word on it: Help. The classic simplicity of this work was reminiscent of icons.

Another person who achieved considerable fame was V. Deni (V. N. Denisov), who, like Moor, had no formal training but had worked for satiric journals before the Revolution. This experience was evident in his poster art.[82] Deni's drawings were often funny, and the text was important for him. He often cooperated with Demian Bednyi, the Soviet poet. In addition to Moor and Deni, P. Aspit, V. Spaskii, N. Kochergin, I. Maliutin, and A. Radakov acquired the best reputation for their works.

Plate 3. The most famous poster by D. S. Moor, n.d. Text: Help.

The themes chosen by the artists were predictable. They addressed themselves to the needs of the front and of the rear; they ridiculed foreign and domestic enemies of the Soviet regime; and they exhorted people to fight and work harder and better. Naturally, there was considerable variation in style among the artists, even though they freely borrowed from one another and also from foreign models. Since the primary goal of the artist was to make a political point rather than to achieve originality, plagiarism did not seem to bother anyone. Moor, for example, produced a recruitment poster for the Red Army, which became one of his most famous works. This poster was only a modified copy of a famous British original.[83]

A particular version of the poster that turned into a valuable propaganda tool was developed by the Bolsheviks during the Civil War. This tool was the Rosta "windows." Rosta was the Bolshevik telegraph agency, established in September 1918. In the spring of 1919, under the leadership of P. N. Kerzhentsev, Rosta expanded its activities by publishing its own newspapers. The great shortage of paper inspired someone to come up with the idea both of pasting short articles and other agitational materials on the walls of the city and also of placing them in the many empty shop windows. Such wall newspapers had to appeal to people who had little time to read; the political points had to be made quickly and powerfully. The remarkable Rosta window of satire grew out of this newly born medium.[84]

The originator of the idea was N. Cheremykh. He was a graphic artist who had worked for the editorial committee of the publishing section of the Executive Committee of the Soviets, until Kerzhentsev invited him to work for Rosta in helping to design wall newspapers.[85] In September 1919, he took over an abandoned shop window on Tverskaia boulevard and posted his drawings, accompanied by texts, written by another Rosta staff member, Gramen (N. K. Ivanov). The experiment was an immediate success; crowds gathered in front of the shop window. Soon Rosta took over the shop windows in the city for the same purpose.

The idea spread from Moscow to the provinces. By the end of the Civil War, Rosta had forty-seven agencies in different parts of the country, each using the idea of putting satirical drawings in shop windows. At first the drawings were hand copied, but later the artists used stencils to make the work more manageable. On occasion Rosta bureaus created their own material or at least reworked what they had received from the center. Most of the time, however, the local agencies were satisfied to display the work of Moscow artists.

Cheremykh gathered around himself a group of talented and congenial men to help in his work. Among the collaborators were I. A. Maliutin, a satirist with considerable experience, and V. V. Maiakovsky, the poet. Maiakovsky was a crucial figure in this small circle because he both drew and wrote texts. He was a font of ideas and had inexhaustible energy. On the basis of his reading of the daily press, he made up two-liners, which either he or some other member of the collective illustrated. It is estimated

Plate 4. Detail from "Rosta window" by V. Koslinskii, 1921. Text: The
dead of the Paris Commune rose again under the Red flag of the Soviets.

Plate 5. V. V. Maiakovsky in front of Rosta "windows." Picture taken in 1930.

that he wrote 90 percent of all texts; clearly, he put his mark on the entire enterprise.

The pace of work was fantastic. The artists aimed to respond to daily news stories to keep the material fresh. Cheremykh on occasion would make 50 drawings a night. He and Maiakovsky engaged in competitions to see who could produce more drawings.[86] In the course of less than three years, this small group of men produced 1,600 "windows" in about 2 million copies.[87]

The usual Rosta window of satire consisted of several small drawings with one- or two-line captions. Often, like a comic strip, the pictures told a story. Also, again like a comic strip, the same, stylized figures such as "the capitalist," "the worker," and "the soldier" appeared again and again. Some of the particularly successful ones were later printed as individual posters. Looking at these drawings today, one is struck by their simple charm; the stylized drawings have not lost their ability to make us smile.

After the establishment of Glavpolitprosvet within Narkompros, that new institution, which was responsible for all political educaton, took over the collective from Rosta. The windows continued to appear for another year, but in the changed circumstances their raison d'être disappeared. Rosta windows and posters flourished in war conditions, as long as it was clear who the enemy was, as long as it was possible to draw simple juxtapositions, as long as the revolutionary enthusiasm of the artists was uncontaminated. The world of the NEP was too complex and too prosaic.

No one can say whether the Rosta windows or the millions of posters, which appeared everywhere in the country, made an impact on the political thinking of the Russian people. Evidently, this question bothered contemporary Bolshevik leaders also, for they reassured themselves with the example of capitalists investing large fortunes in advertising: Surely those businessmen knew what they were doing.[88]

The new economic policies

PART II

The new economic powers

CHAPTER 6

Political education

Glavpolitprosvet

The Leninist version of Marxism, "scientific" Marxism, implies a paradox. On the one hand, it claims that thought and ideology emerge from experience: Specifically, the workers come into possession of this priceless weapon, revolutionary socialist theory, in the course of their daily toil in the factories and their participation in class struggle. On the other hand, since it is a science, scientific Marxism evidently can be fully accessible only to those who have the proper intellectual equipment and background and who have taken the time to study it. Lenin's famous rejection of the spontaneity of the workers' movement, as represented by the trade unions, was based on this understanding. In other words, Marxism cannot be either the ideology of the workers, who do not understand it, or of the revolutionary intellectuals, from whose experience it did not emerge. To square the circle, to transcend this paradox, has always been a central concern for the Bolsheviks. Soviet preoccupation with propaganda must be understood in this context. The help the workers – and peasants – to understand their true interest, to give them the one and only correct interpretation of their immediate and long-range goals, was the Soviet definition of their own propaganda.

The end of the Civil War was the turning point in almost every aspect of Soviet life and politics, including matters of propaganda. As long as the fighting continued and the central government itself was in jeopardy, propaganda had to concentrate on the all-important task of defeating the Whites. It was a utopian period. The Bolsheviks believed that their problems would be relieved by the defeat of their enemies and by the coming of world revolution. In the constantly changing situation, with the Bolsheviks facing a motley but powerful collection of enemies, their propaganda was ever present but inevitably haphazard. In the short run, it was more important to concentrate on the wickedness of the opponents of the Revolution than to attempt to convey a world view.

Soviet leaders and publicists have never tired of emphasizing that their revolution and their regime were radically new. Indeed, they were. For the first time in history, a secular government considered itself to possess a theory with which to interpret and change the world. For the first time, a government considered its task to be not merely to mold the views of the people in this or that matter but to persuade them of the correctness of an entire world view. From such an attitude it followed that an organization must be built to help bring about the appointed goals.

As long as the Party was an organization of revolutionaries with the goal to bring down the tsarist government, creating a propaganda section made no sense whatever. Every Bolshevik as a matter of course was a propagandist: His main task was to explain the goals of the movement and win converts to support those goals. The situation drastically changed on October 25, 1917. From that time on, the Party was responsible for running the country; propaganda and agitation remained important, but they were no longer the only tasks. During the Civil War most Soviet institutions from the Red Army to the universities and commissariats were in some ways engaged in propaganda work. Especially in the last months of the Civil War, Soviet leaders perceived an unnecessary duplication of effort and an unclear division of responsibilities for carrying out propaganda. There was general agreement among activists that it was important to build a centralized organization for this work. During the second half of 1920 and in the beginning of 1921, the Party and the state created a basic institutional framework for propaganda that lasted with very few modifications through the NEP period. The restructuring of the apparatus occasioned a series of debates and discussions in the leadership that revealed some of the underlying attitudes concerning propaganda, or "political education" as it was also called at the time.

The political-education system had two distinct tasks. First, it had to educate a Party elite. During the Civil War, there was a large influx into the Party of ambitious and often able young men and women who contributed to winning the struggle by mobilizing their fellow workers and peasants. That the Reds, unlike their enemies, managed to tap a reservoir of talent among the lower classes was one of the reasons for their victory. Their very strength, however, their closeness in mentality to the average Russian, was from the point of view of the Party a source of serious weakness, for these people knew practically nothing of Marxism. "Old" revolutionaries in their speeches at this time constantly deplored the declining intellectual standards within the Party.[1] The obvious solution was to weed out the unpromising and to educate those who could be made into true Communists. Second, the propaganda network had to win over the people for the new goals: socialist construction, and the creation of the socialist human being.

Although the two tasks of political education were distinct in principle, in reality no definite line could be drawn between them. The Party built a political-education network on every intellectual level – from wall newspapers in factories and villages, in which the socialist message was reduced to the simplest slogans, to the Socialist Academy, where the problems of Marxist theory could be discussed on a sophisticated plane. In theory an individual could proceed from one level to the next to the very top of the hierarchy.

In August 1920, the Central Committee of the Communist Party, at the initiative of the Organizational Bureau, established an agitation and propaganda section, which was headed by R. Katanian. The primary task of this new body was to coordinate the work of all those Soviet institutions that had been engaged in propaganda.[2] The section was divided into five subunits. The first and most important of these was the agitation subsection, which had the task of directing propaganda campaigns. Lenin had often said that propaganda should be a matter of action rather than words. The Bolsheviks interpreted this rather ambiguous phrase to mean that agitation should be tied to some concrete goal. The agitation subsection, therefore, initiated campaigns for occasions such as the Congress of the Third International, the anniversary of the October Revolution, the anniversary of the French Revolution, to encourage the peasants to do good work during spring sowing, to show the nation's gratitude to the soldiers of the Red Army, and to help to organize the fight against famine. This subsection also supervised the local press and gave instructions to Bolshevik journalists on how to present their arguments.

The second subsection was devoted to political education. It helped to develop a curriculum for the Party schools. The third subsection was responsible for the publishing work of the Central Committee. It published two journals, Vestnik agitatsii i propagandy (Journal of agitation and propaganda) and Izvestiia Tsentral'nogo Komiteta, (Proceedings of the Central Committee). The fourth unit dealt with the problems of distributing propaganda literature in the provinces, and the fifth aimed to coordinate the work among the national minority sections of the Party.

As was often the case this time, the Bolsheviks gave impossibly ambitious goals to an institution that did not have the necessary means. During the first months of its existence, the Section had thirteen employees, of whom six were clerical workers.[3] The Bolsheviks wanted coordination and even centralization. The agitation and propaganda section of the Central Committee clearly was not in the position to bring about the desired goal. The bulk of the propaganda work in the young Soviet state was directed not by a Party but by a government agency.

Narkompros almost from its establishment included a section for extramural education, which was responsible for the political indoctrination of adults. In the summer of 1920, in connection with a general reorganization of the commissariat, it was proposed that this section be upgraded into a

Chief Committee on Political Enlightenment (Glavpolitprosvet), which would assume authority for all types of political education by agencies of Narkompros.[4] In October and November 1920, the Executive Committee of the Soviets (Vtsik), Sovnarkom, and the politbureau of the Party all discussed the problem of coordinating propaganda work. Bukharin and Preobrazhenskii drew up a project on the subject. On the basis of their work, Sovnarkom published a decree in November 1920 that greatly expanded the role of Glavpolitprosvet. The first meeting of this organization, still a part of Narkompros, took place on November 11 under the chairmanship of Preobrazhenskii, but N. K. Krupskaia became its permanent head.

Glavpolitprosvet had two tasks. One was to build a national apparatus going down to the volost' level. The fact that Glavpolitprosvet was a part of Narkompros was helpful, for it could build on already-existing machinery. The speed of the establishment of the national politprosvet network varied greatly from province to province. All in all, it took years before the leaders of the Party were satisfied.

The other task was to coordinate already-existing institutions.[5] The two major networks outside of Narkompros that needed to be coordinated were Glavpolitput' and PUR. Glavpolitput' was the political-administration department of the Commissariat of Transport. The reason this comissariat had such an extensive propaganda organization was that it had been responsible at the time of the Civil War for running the agitpunkts, which were located at thousands of railroad stations. Glavpolitput' therefore, possessed a valuable supply of movie projectors. Sovnarkom's decree absorbed Glavpolitput' into Glavpolitprosvet. It was more difficult to incorporate PUR, the Political Administration of the Red Army. The army had been perhaps the most successful propaganda agency during the years of fighting. It possessed an extensive network of agitators, printing facilities, instructors, and libraries. Many among the military leaders disapproved of the idea of losing their independence in agitational matters. They distrusted Narkompros, they were proud of their own accomplishments, and they believed that military life offered special agitational opportunities and problems that civilians could not well appreciate. Nevertheless, the agitational organization of the army, with the exception of front-line units, now became part of Glavpolitprosvet.

It was far more difficult to coordinate the work of the Agitprop Section of the Party's Central Committee and of Glavpolitprosvet. The Party could neither leave agitation and propaganda work entirely to others nor successfully carry it out by itself. *Izvestiia Tsentral'nogo Komiteta* reported that in many provinces Party activists grumbled that such a large share of responsibility for Communist education was given to Narkompros.[6] This complex issue was thoroughly discussed at the Tenth Party congress.[7]

Gradually the relative size and importance of the Agitprop Section of the Central Committee increased as compared to the role of Glavpolitprosvet.

From the mid-1920s on, the Agitprop Section assumed more and more responsibility for overseeing the newspapers and literary life of the country. It also came to have a major role in directing the antireligious struggle. This development was part of a larger change, which was the acquisition of dominance of the Party over the government in Soviet political life.

At the time of the Tenth Party Congress, this development was not yet in evidence. This congress, the first held in peacetime, was decisive in determining the character of the Soviet regime. Among the many major issues it discussed was the proper organization of propaganda. It was the only Party congress to do so.

The historian is struck by the general agreement concerning the underlying assumptions. Every speaker took for granted that propaganda was vitally important; that it was the duty of the Soviet state to carry out "political enlightenment" among the workers and peasants; and, rather amusingly, that not only had Bolshevik propaganda efforts been weak up to this point but also that these efforts compared unfavorably with bourgeois propaganda. On reflection, perhaps it is not surprising that every politician believes that his success is based on the correctness of his views but that his failures can be explained by his opponents' skillful manipulation of opinion. Nonetheless it is remarkable that the Bolsheviks, who had devoted greater efforts than anyone to indoctrination and who had raised it to the level of government policy, giving all necessary means and all available power of the government for the task, still continued to feel that the bourgeois states with their pretended unconcern had been more successful. Riazanov, the most maverick Bolshevik, held up the bourgeois states as examples. Their "superiority," he noted, perhaps with a grain of truth, lay in the fact that they did not advertise the class ideology with which they indoctrinated their citizens.[8]

Preobrazhenskii, one of the creators of Glavpolitprosvet, gave the report on agitation and propaganda.[9] He argued that the psychological attitudes of the people never change as fast as the underlying social and economic realities. The Bolshevik Party had already taken power; it had expropriated the expropriators, but at the same time the people were not yet ready to build socialism. Because the Party controlled the state machinery it had the means to overcome this gap. Political education was essential to explain to the people the importance and extent of victories already won and to win them over to the cause of building socialism.

Preobrazhenskii proceeded to give a short history of propaganda work since the Revolution. At first, he noted, every returning soldier and sailor who organized Soviet power in his village had been a propagandist; in that early period no distinction could be drawn between organizing and propagandizing. During the following stage, most Soviet institutions had set up a propaganda section. Much had been accomplished, but at the cost of a great deal of parallelism. Now the time had come for Glavpolitprosvet to coordinate work. Glavpolitprosvet, in Preobrazhenskii's view, would not take over the propaganda work of other agencies; it would simply coordinate their activities.

Preobrazhenskii devoted much attention to the most difficult question of all, the delineation of functions between the Agitprop Section of the Central Committee and Glavpolitprosvet. He conceded that no satisfactory division was possible. There were functions that clearly belonged to Glavpolitprosvet, such as mass agitation among the people, which required a large government apparatus. Glavpolitprosvet was to organize campaigns for increased productivity and for the reconstructon of the economy, and the Party must hand over the clubs, film projectors, and other resources necessary for this work. By contrast, agitational work, which was connected with the organizational activity of the Party, obviously would remain a Party responsibility. Propaganda carried out within the Party could not be handed over to a government agency. There were also areas in which both the Party and Glavpolitprosvet were bound to play a role. Preobrazhenskii mentioned as an example Soviet Party schools, in which he assigned ideological leadership to the Party and organizational matters to Glavpolitprosvet.

The other speakers, in one form or another, all addressed themselves to defining the authority of Glavpolitprosvet. Riazanov expressed concern that if the Party, and other organizations such as the trade unions and the Komsomol, handed over agitation and propaganda to the government, they would be cut off from the masses and the gap between the common people and the leadership would increase.[10] S. I. Gusev, a representative of PUR, wanted to postpone the integraton of his organization into Glavpolitprosvet.[11] Lunacharskii, not surprisingly, argued for a broader definition of the role of Glavpolitprosvet.[12] He would have liked to have seen it take charge of all agitation and propaganda (with the exception of inner Party indoctrination). By contrast, the opponents of Narkompros demanded the removal of political education from the Commissariat of Enlightenment altogether and wanted it placed under immediate Party authority.

Lenin did not participate in the discussion. He expressed his thoughts on propaganda under the conditions of NEP a few months later in a speech to the second congress of political-education workers. He defined the tasks extremely broadly. In his view, the fight against illiteracy, the work to raise the cultural standards of the people, the struggle against bureaucracy, the attempts to instill a correct, Communist attitude toward work – all were parts of political education. He said:

Gone is the time when it was necessary to draw political pictures of great tasks; today these must be carried out in practice. Today we are confronted with cultural tasks, those of assimilating that political experience that can be and must be put in practice. Either we lay an economic foundation for the political gains of the Soviet state, or we shall lose them all. This foundation has not yet been laid . . . that is what we must get down to. The task of raising the cultural level is one of the most urgent confronting us. And that is the job the Political Education Department

Plate 6. A. V. Lunacharskii, commissar of education. Drawing by Iu. Annenskii, 1926.

must do, if they are capable of serving the cause of "political education," which is the task they have adopted for themselves.[13]

His listeners could be forgiven if they did not understand what exactly he wanted them to do.

The birth of the Glavpolitprosvet network was a paradox. On the one hand, there was a great deal of talk about the far-reaching importance of propaganda. Several Soviet leaders pointed out that under the conditions of the NEP, political education was even more important than it had been during the Civil War. Economic freedom, provided by the NEP, enabled the enemies of socialism to fight back. The Party had to make clear to the Soviet people that economic concessions would not be accompanied by political and ideological concessions. On the other hand, the NEP inevitably brought a sense of financial responsibility and frugality, which had been missing at an earlier time. Consequently, the ringing endorsements of the importance of propaganda were not matched by increased investments in this activity. On the contrary. In spite of the brave talk, the first years of the NEP saw a drastic curtailment of the political-education network. As so

Plate 7. Poster n.d. Text: Electrification and counterrevolution.

often in early Soviet history, the gap between talk and reality was not only extremely broad but also widening.

The political school system

The NEP placed reconstruction at the top of the nation's agenda, and for that task the country desperately needed trained people of all kinds: engineers, scientists, managers of factories, and, very importantly, people to run the political apparatus. The need for specialists was both a source of strength and a source of weakness. Clearly, the lack of skilled and reliable people slowed reconstruction. On the other hand, the regime could promise quick advancement to talented workers and peasants. The possibility of promotion very likely contributed to the identification of the working classes with the new regime. The government wanted to train a new group of specialists, a new intelligentsia, partly because it believed that people who received their advancement from the Communist system would be more loyal to it than those who had been educated before the Revolution, and partly because of a genuine commitment to social mobility. In this respect ideology and political necessity happily reinforced one another.

Those who were to run the government and the Party needed training in Marxism. Obviously, the ambitious young peasants and workers who were selected for leadership had only the vaguest understanding of scientific socialism. This was no minor matter, since the leaders of the Party deeply believed that Marxism alone provided a sure guide to solving the problems facing any society.

Given the belief of the Communist leadership in the power of ideas, and given the need for Party activists, it is understandable that the regime devoted much attention to training cadres from the first moment of its establishment. The unusual feature of this training was that it merged with the general political education of the Soviet people. The political-education hierarchy, administered by Glavpolitprosvet, exactly mirrored the traditional educational system.

At the apex of the hierarchy stood the Socialist (later Communist) Academy, established in 1918. Riazanov proudly asserted at the Tenth Party Congress that the academy as an intellectual center could be favorably compared with European bourgeois educational institutions.[14] It was an empty boast. In fact, during its first years the academy was hardly more than a debating society equipped with a reasonably good Marxist library.[15] The Tenth Congress directed the academy to organize training courses for Party activists. The teaching activity of the Academy continued throughout the decade. The annual intake of students was small, gradually increasing from approximately 50 to 200.[16] Within the framework of the academy, Riazanov organized in 1921 a Marx-Engels Institute, which in time came to be the world's leading publisher of the writings of Marx and Engels.

Those who were chosen for top Party positions attended Communist universities. These institutions grew out of weakness. The Party, understandably, considered professors at best unreliable and at worst openly hostile. Communist universities were organized to circumvent the potentially harmful influence of unreliable professors of social sciences. The chief problem was the limited number of qualified Marxist scholars. Those who enjoyed authority as theoreticians usually held responsible Party posts and were extremely busy people. Now these men were also asked to lecture at several different institutions.

The history of the first Communist university is interesting, for it highlights the connection between the need for agitators and the training for leadership. As the Civil War was getting under way in 1918, the Party felt an acute need for agitators. It set up short training courses, which, at first, lasted for only ten days. In time the courses expanded, and ultimately this makeshift institution was turned into a university named after Sverdlov with a four-year course.[17] Even while the fighting continued, the Bolsheviks established others in the same pattern, and by the 1922–3 school year ten universities existed.

In the early days, any literate person with the support of his Party or komsomol committee could apply for admission. Later, places were assigned to Party and komsomol organizations, which distributed them among their most promising and deserving members. In the early 1920s, admission was restricted to Party members of five years' standing with at least three years' manual-work experience.[18] As one might expect, few were academically prepared; for most of them, even to read a book was a struggle. Institutions that stressed independent reading and seminars as against lectures were not designed for people who had little preparation. At the same time, students in the Civil War period and in the early 1920s had to endure extreme physical hardships. Students starved, and the buildings were hardly heated at all. At Sverdlov University in 1922, 50 to 85 percent of the students suffered from anemia and 16 to 17 percent had tuberculosis.[19] Only in the mid-1920s did conditions improve. When Samuel Harper, an American scholar, visited Soviet educational institutions in 1926, he found Sverdlov University the best equipped of all Russian universities.[20]

The students must have realized that admission to a Communist university meant joining the Soviet elite, and in fact a considerable portion of the later Soviet leadership started their careers in these institutions. The young Communists regarded these universities as their own, and they were encouraged to participate in the governance of the institutions. Even at the depth of privations, morale must have been high.

In 1928 there were 8,400 students enrolled in nineteen universities.[21] Only in the 1930s, when the regime felt strong enough and had enough scholars, did it eliminate the duplication in the educational system.

One step down in the political-edcuation hierarchy stood the two-tiered Soviet Party schools, the *sovpartshkoly*. The early history of these schools was like that of the universities: They were created at the time of the Civil War in response to a deeply felt need for trained agitators. The Party first established short-term and irregular sessions, which were later expanded and standardized. A conference of Soviet Party schools in December 1921 established the length of the first-grade schools as three months and the second-grade schools as nine months.[22] Later they were further expanded, and at the end of the decade first grade was a year long and second grade a two-year course.[23]

In October 1921 there were 255 schools in the country educating 50,000 students. A year later as a result of economies a sharp drop occurred, reducing the number of students to 20,000 in 205 schools.[24] Institutions that trained leaders for Soviet and Party work had at the end of the decade 593 schools with 45,000 students.[25] The candidate for the first grade had to be literate and for the second grade had to have some political knowledge and "be able to write political reports." In practice, Party, Komsomol, trade-union, and Zhenotdel organizations chose activists whom they regarded as capable of middle-level leadership. During the early years of these schools, the criteria for selection varied widely among the recommending agencies. As a result, the students were heterogeneous in both educational background and social composition.[26] What the students had in common was youth: In 1922 78 percent of grade one and 68 percent of grade two were under 21.[27] In 1922 25 to 35 percent of the students were not Party members, but a short time later membership in either the Party or the Komsomol became a requirement for admission.[28]

In the years following the Civil War, attrition was very high. In some schools 60 percent did not complete the course.[29] The high attrition rate was partially caused by indadequte preparation of students. But a much more important reason was the appalling physical hardship the students had to endure. According to budgetary arrangements, local authorities were responsible for heating and maintaining the school buildings, while Narkompros was expected to support both the students and faculty and also to provide for families of students who were not able to take care of themselves.[30] Narkompros could not carry out its responsibility: Deliveries of food were irregular, and the students and faculty were fortunate to get one hot meal a day. On occasion they starved. Fats and meat disappeared from the diet. At Briansk, for example, 46 percent of the students in 1922 had to be sent elsewhere, because their physical exhaustion was so great that they could not study. At the same time in Kazan 75 percent of the students suffered from anemia and 10 percent had tuberculosis. Other schools from all over the country reported conditions not much better.[31] Obviously tremendous dedication, or ambition, was necessary to complete the course. In 1923 material conditions gradually began to improve, and the future elite of the country started to receive more suitable supplies and accommodations.

The curriculum was relentlessly and almost exclusively political. The schools did not aim to provide a general education, even though in the case of the majority of students such a training would have been very desirable. A model curriculum, published in 1926 for Komsomol schools, included the following subjects: (1) the Soviet economy, (2) the dictatorship of the proletariat, (3), the history of the Party, (4) the Comintern, and (5) the Komsomol. Out of the twenty-three lessons, eleven were devoted to Party history. The introduction to the curriculum explained: "It is not necessary to cram in a lot of facts. It is not necessary to demand from a Komsomol member a hard knowledge of these facts. What is necessary, above all, is to achieve that a Komsomol member can, from each fact deduce the correct conclusion: why the party in a particular issue took that particular position and not a different one."[32]

The lowest rung on the ladder of Party education were the schools of political grammar (politgramotshkoly). These schools stood between mass indoctrination and the training of cadres. They aimed to give some knowledge of ideology to every Party member. There was greater variety in the organization and functioning of these schools than in the sovpartshkoly. Almost all of them were evening schools. Students, who of course, held full time jobs met twice a week in the evening for a few months to participate in "conversations."[33] Some courses lasted for five months, but in others the abbreviated curriculum took only two and a half months to complete. In the middle of the decade, to reach the peasantry, the Party set up "mobile schools."[34] These traveled from district to district and provided rather elementary political instruction.

It is striking how committed the Party was to political education and how willing it was to make the necessary sacrifices. The building of the network of schools began at the time of the Civil War and continued even in the years of famine and privation. In 1922 there were 440 such schools. Since most of them had three-month sessions, they were able to graduate four classes per year.[35] By 1927 over 300,000 party members (29 percent of the membership) had studied in these schools.[36] But the schools were never restricted to Party members; approximately 15 percent of non–Party members continued to be admitted. In March 1926 the Central Committee of the Party examined the system of elementary Party schools and decided that the center of work must be in the countryside.[37] Of course it was easier to organize and supervise schools in the cities than to provide instruction to the peasants. Even when a politgramotshkola visited a neighboring village, it was difficult for the activist to arrange transportation to attend classes regularly. Furthermore, the schools were unevenly distributed; Moscow and Leningrad provinces were well supplied, but there were relatively few in outlying provinces, in particular, in national minority areas. To utilize these schools most effectively, the Central Committee ordered that illiterates and semiilliterates should not be admitted but sent to more appropriate institutions. However, the demand for peasant women and national-minority activists was so great that politgramotshkoly were directed to make exceptions in their cases. The Central Committee also reviewed and approved a uniform curriculum for the entire enormous country.[38] Exceptions were made only for minority areas.

One can well imagine that few students came to school because of their love of learning or their serious interest in Marxism. The teachers, most of them graduates of grade two of a sovpartshkola, had a difficult job. The Soviet leadership was impressed by "progressive" pedagogy and demanded seminar-type discussions instead of lectures, but the subject matter was not really suitable for discussion. Obviously, nothing was more alien to the thinking Party leaders than the encouragement of independent thought. Furthermore, the students lacked the necessary background for meaningful discussions. Consequently, the pretense of discussions took the place of lectures. The teacher was not allowed to lecture, but at the same time he had to convey a certain amount of material. The description of a class from Nizhegorod province in 1925 gives us a vivid picture:

The leader begins the session. Afraid that what he says might be considered a lecture and that therefore he would be criticized, he mutters a few words and begins a "conversation": "Tell me, what was the attitude of the Mensheviks to the war?"
A brief answer from one of the students.
"And what was Lenin's position?"
Another brief response from another student.
"And what was the effect of the war on the economy of Russia?"

One responds briefly: "Of course it led to collapse."

"How did the war advance the cause of the Revolution?"

Two answers in the same spirit as before. "Why did power go to the bourgeoisie after the defeat of autocracy?"

Somewhat longer, but incorrect, answers. The leader pays no attention to the errors but goes on.

"What was the attitude of the Provisional Government to the war?"

A few answer immediately. The answers are brief and repetitious.

"And what was the attitude to the war of the workers and peasants?"

Here independence reaches its outer limits. There are many who are eager to say something. An ex-soldier talks about the Caucasian front in lengthy detail. The students have heard enough, and the leader wants to take the questions further.

"And who entered the government of L'vov?"

Silence. They think long. One answers: "Kerensky." Other Kishkins, and Burishkins, and Prince L'vov. An impatient voice is heard: "You tell us."

The leader changes the form of the question, and finally the answer is easily given: The SR and Menshevik parties entered the government.

The discussion starts; they debate about mistakes. The leader tries to talk little, in order not to stifle the independence of the students with his authority. Ten more questions are raised, and they move on to the discussion of October.

"And what kind of disagreements were there within the Party at the moment of the Revolution?"

The two-hour session is about over; some of the students are preparing to leave. The leader asks them to stay for this last but important question.

One worker shyly answers: "Zinovev and Kamenev deserted from Sovnarkom, Lenin scolded them, and they soon understood their mistake and returned."[39]

We can only speculate on the effect of political education on Party members and leaders. In September 1926, Ulianovsk province, probably typical of the rest of Russia, carried out a survey of Party activists. Out of the 300 respondents, almost one half had received some kind of party schooling, and 4 percent had attended Communist universities. Almost one-half of the village activists confessed that they had never read any Marx at all. Only 20 percent of the respondents reported, not that they had read Capital but that they had attempted to read it, which is of course very different. Eleven percent had read Lenin's *What Is to Be Done,* but the majority of the activists knew Leninism from newspaper quotations, from excerpts, and from speeches. On the other hand, almost all of them read the daily press. Four out of five read both the local paper and *Pravda.* Clearly, the activists were not scholars but practical people who needed to keep up with current events.[40]

The effect of the political school system cannot be measured by the Party activists' acquaintance with theoretical Marxism-Leninism. The schools with their catechism-like method transmitted a way of thinking, which assumed that there was one and only one correct answer to any question. The schools taught a language in which Party activists were expected to express themselves. They made a great contribution to the development of the particular Soviet-type political discourse.

Plate 8. Poster by D. S. Moor, n.d. Text: Before: One behind the plough and seven with their spoons. Now: He who does not work, does not eat.

The village reading room

The training of cadres and the indoctrination of the Soviet peoples were part of the same system, based on the same principles. However, bringing the political message to millions of workers and peasants was immensely more difficult than shaping the thinking of the relatively few Party members and activists. For example, Party members could be expected to attend indoctrination sessions voluntarily, out of genuine interest or out of ambition, whereas the great bulk of the people had to be enticed somehow into listening to the propaganda.

The regime used the club in the cities and the reading room or hut (izba chital'nia) in the villages as major instruments of political education. Of the two, the reading rooms were far more important: In the 1920s the Party had not yet fully penetrated the countryside, and it used the reading huts as outposts in a more or less alien, of not hostile, territory. It channeled its indoctrination efforts through them. By contrast, the Party had many ways of reaching city dwellers in general and the workers in particular. A survey of workers, for example, showed that in 1923 90 percent of the male workers regularly reading a newspaper spent forty-five minutes daily.[41] Even more interesting, the average worker spent one evening out of six on some type of political work. Among Party members, the figures were one out of three.[42] Propaganda was ubiquitous. Even the least politically minded had to attend meetings, listen to speeches, and be exposed to propaganda when he picked up his favorite newspaper or went to the movies or theater. Clearly, under the circumstances the clubs played a relatively minor role. There was no reason that the regime should pay the same attention to them as it did to the village reading huts.

Clubs were formed by Red Army units, komsomol organizations, city soviets, and, from January 1922, Party organizations. The best-functioning club system, however, belonged to the trade-union movement. When Glavpolitprosvet in 1922 had to curtail its efforts because of a budgetary emergency, the workers' clubs, which were usually attached to factories, survived the best. During the years of the Civil War, membership in the clubs was bloc membership. That is, every trade-union member, komsomol or Red Army soldier was automatically a member of the club of his organization. During the 1920s, a gradual turn to individual membership meant that the size of the clubs was greatly reduced. On the other hand, interest in their work, presumably, increased.[43] At this time club members had to pay a nominal fee.

The workers' clubs were administered by the cultural departments of the trade unions in conjunction with Glavpolitprosvet. The clubs had small libraries, received the daily papers, organized lectures on a variety of topics – mostly political – and gave theatrical and movie performances. Naturally, they also participated in the innumerable campaigns and celebrations introduced by the Party. The greatest emphasis was placed on so-called productivity propaganda. But they also had their share of antireligious enlightenment work and "internationalist" education. A particular form of Soviet indoctrination effort, the mock court, was also used. Club members played at organizing "trials" of such historical figures as Gapon, the priest leader of the ill-fated demonstration of January 9, 1905.[44]

The clubs suffered from a lack of proper accommodations. They usually took over houses that had belonged to the bourgeoisie. However, most of these buildings were inadequate. Even the largest factories had to squeeze their clubs into cramped quarters in private houses. However committed the regime was to the cause of workers' political education, it obviously was not in a position to build clubhouses.

A constant problem was finding the proper balance between amusement and indoctrination. The workers, after all, had choices. If the fare offered by the clubs became insufferably dull, they could always stay home and read a book, or go to the movies, or, most likely, drink with their friends. Yet it clearly was unthinkable to give the workers what they wanted. It was never a secret that the primary goal of the clubs was political education, that is, indoctrination.

The Glavpolitprosvet report of 1923 expresses the danger this way: "The NEP dealt a serious blow to the cause of artistic enlightenment. The content and character of all forms of art, but especially the theater and the film, are determined today by what the public wants."[45] Clubs began to show films for entertainment. They charged admission and used these performances to increase the cultural funds of the union. The trade-union leadership was concerned.

On January 1, 1926, Seniushkin, the head of the cultural department of VTsSPS, wrote to all cultural sections about the proper role of films in clubs.[46] He recommended setting up film circles, which would be responsible for selecting ideologically correct films and also for integrating them into the general cultural work. Furthermore, these circles would have the task of propagandizing Soviet films against ideologically dubious foreign ones and organizing discussion sessions after the performances, when the audience was to be encouraged to judge the political content and the behavior of the heroes of the films.

The secretary of the union of the workers of community enterprises (Soiuz rabotnikov kommunalnogo khozaistva; SRKKh), Ratmanov, in a letter of August of the same year, spelled out in greater detail the role of films:

Showing films is often not connected with general cultural work, and it is only for commercial purposes. Some clubs charge as much as 50 kopecks. In order to improve the situation, the Union recommends to the cultural department the following: (1) Check on the work of clubs and make clear to them the role of movies. (2) Do not allow films to take up a larger role in the work of the club then other forms of mass work. No more than two evenings per week should be devoted to the showing of films. (3) The cultural sections should contact the film section of the central trade-union organization in order to receive proper films for the clubs. In the selection of the films the needs of the audience should be taken into account. (4) It is essential to organize film circles, and these, with the cooperation of the provincial organizations, should choose ideologically correct films. (5) The price of the ticket should only pay for the film and for incidental expenses. It should not be more than 20 kopecks. (6) In order to use the time properly, the clubs should organize orchestras, drama circles, etc. Organize work in the clubs in such a way that showing films will not disturb the development of other forms of mass work.[47]

However annoying it may have been for the Soviet leaders to see the workers spending their time on "frivolous entertainments," on balance the clubs were useful in contributing to the political education of the working classes.

When the regime embarked on collectivization, approximately four-fifths of the Soviet people lived in the countryside, but among Party members the proportions were reversed.[48] At least half the villages did not have a single Party member. (In 1927 there were over a half million "rural inhabited points" but only a quarter million Communists in the villages.[49]) Although these numbers are suggestive, they cannot in themselves give a picture of the weakness of the Party in the countryside. In the course of the 1920s, Party congresses and conferences again and again emphasized the need to increase Communist influence among the peasantry; however, until the regime completed collectivization, it lacked the organizational strength to bring about a major improvement.

In view of this weakness, it was essential for the Party to concentrate its forces. The district (volost') politprosvet organization was responsible for political education in the villages. This organization belonged to the Narkompros network, but it was expected to operate in conjunction with the agitprop section of the volost' Party organization and with the local soviet. When there was industry in the district, the cultural section of the trade union was also represented. The first task of the politprosvet organization was to attract help from the village intelligentsia, from the teacher, the doctor, and, in the rare instances where he was present, the agronomist.[50]

The main instrument of politprosvet to reach the peasantry was the village reading room (izba chital'nia). The greatest problem was that there were not enough of them; the countryside was by no means covered. In 1920–1 there were 24,413 reading huts. Then, as a result of the cut in Glavpolitprosvet's budget, for the next two years there was a precipitous fall in their numbers. In 1921–2 there were only 16,799 and in the following and worst year only 5,018. From that point there was gradual but not consistent improvement. In 1923–4 there were 11,357, and in 1925–6 the country reached the highest figure for the NEP period: 24,924. This was followed by a slight drop. In the following year, there were only 22,125.[51] In villages where the Party did not have the means to set up reading rooms, it attempted to establish so-called Red Corners. These could be established in the building of the village Soviet, in the school house, or even in a private residence. In these instances the village elected a council and a chairman who assumed responsibility for the work of the Red Corner. The chairman saw to it that books were sent from the nearest village reading room. He, together with his council, organized

137

discussions and reading circles. He either gave his services, or received a salary from the village, but under no circumstances could he be paid from a government budget. In villages where even a Red Corner could not be established, the Party tried to persuade a teacher, a demobilized soldier, or a literate peasant to act as a "Red Reader." This person gathered around himself his interested fellow villagers and read aloud from the daily press or from books that his audience found interesting.

The disjunction between the Party's real strength in the countryside and its far-reaching plans to remake society imposed an extremely ambitious program on the village reading rooms and Red Corners. First of all, the reading rooms dispersed information about government policies and regulations. No firm line could be drawn between information about government policies and agitation for those policies. To help the director of the reading room, the *izbach,* Glavpolitprosvet published a monthly journal, *Izba chital'nia* in which the controversial issues of the day that might come up in conversations with a peasant audience were described. The izbach could arm himself with knowledge on subjects such as the currency reform of 1924, the need for the draft, and the main outlines of Soviet foreign policy.

The reading rooms played a central role in the many campaigns initiated by the Party. Some of these had long-term and agitational goals, for example, to convince the peasantry of the superiority of large-scale, collectivized agriculture, of the need to industrialize the country, and of the need to build a strong defense by maintaining a draft. Others had immediate goals, such as making sure that the peasants paid their taxes on time, paid attention to sanitation, and so forth. The reading rooms also organized special campaigns on the occasion of the election of the village soviet and festivals for celebrating the harvest.

The reading rooms greatly contributed to the development of a particular Soviet style of political life by constantly celebrating anniversaries. The article in the Soviet Pedagogical Encyclopedia on izba chital'nia, published in 1930, gives this impressive list of anniversaries to be marked: January 9, the anniversary of bloody Sunday in 1905; January 22, Lenin's death; February 23, Red Army Day; March 8, Woman's Day; March 12, the anniversary of the collapse of autocracy; March 18, the anniversary of the Paris Commune; April 17, the anniversary of the Lena massacre in 1912; May 1, of course, May Day. In May also, a day was to be chosen as a day of the forest, and in June a day was to be put aside to mark "international cooperation." July 6 was the day of the USSR. In September, the peasants celebrated youth day and the day of the harvest. November 7, of course, was the greatest holiday of all. And December 19 was the anniversary of the 1905 revolution. The Encyclopedia expressed the point of these celebrations honestly: "The political educator cannot be satisfied by explaining what happened in the past. For him the anniversary is a pretext in order to place in context and explain in detail the significance of the event for the present."[52]

The constant campaigns and "celebrations" became part of the daily routine. The izbach put up slogans and pictures on the wall. He gave a speech, he made sure that the wall newspaper contained an article on the subject. It is hard to imagine the boredom these "celebrations" must have imposed on hundreds of thousands of people. One suspects that those who thought up the celebrations were consciously trying to create alternatives to church holidays. The Bolsheviks were creating a civic religion.

An important part of the new religion was the ever-increasing Lenin cult.[53] To the development of the cult the reading rooms definitely made a contribution. In May 1924 the journal *Izba chital'nia* instructed the izbachi everywhere to set up "Lenin corners." An article gave detailed and precise instruction on how to do it. There were to be pictures of him as a child, in exile, on a Party congress, among children, at a Comintern congress, during his last illness, and finally at his funeral. The article concludes: "This way every visitor to the reading room will be acquainted with the life and work of Vladimir Ilich."[54]

No reading room could operate without a wall newspaper. His journal instructed the izbach precisely how his wall newspaper should be edited. Every issue had to have an "editorial" about an important current event in 40–60 lines; short news articles from abroad, each no more than 3–5 lines, for a total of 30 lines; 15–20 lines devoted to Party news; 30–40 lines on the work of the local soviet; 20–30 lines on Komsomol work; and 30–40 lines on the economy and also on the work of the cooperative. The wall newspaper had to contain caricatures, poems, and, very importantly, letters from readers.[55]

Within the reading room, several circles operated, some of them with appointed leaders and others without. Most of these were study circles, which undertook reading and discussion of subjects of common interest. The reading room was the center of "art" in the village, which meant that it organized exhibitions, theatrical performances, and film shows. The izbach also organized question-and-answer evenings, for which, on occasion, he invited the local doctor or agronomist. The journal *Izba chital'nia* advised him to plant a question or two, so that the discussion would get going.[56] The reading rooms also sponsored sewing circles for women, singing clubs, and so forth. These ostensibly nonpolitical activities helped to attract the peasantry.

The success or failure of the reading room largely depended on the character, tact, talent, and charisma of the izbach. It was obviously a hard job, poorly paid and often unappreciated. In the middle of the decade the izbach received the same low salary as the village school teacher, that is 20–30 rubles.[57] It is not surprising there were not enough trained people anxious for the work. Most of those who served in this job were in their early twenties. According to a 1925 report in the RSFSR, out of 1,676 people, 987 were between sixteen and twenty-three and only 47 were between forty and fifty.[58] There was a tremendous turnover. It seems many young men—there were few women—quickly became discouraged. The rapid turnover unfavorably affected the work of the reading room. It was not unusual for four different people to serve in one village in a single year as izbachi. By the time he got to know the villagers, and gained their confidence and accustomed himself to the environment, he was ready to move on.[59]

One of the most frequent complaints of the izbachi was the workload. Whenever the Soviet government needed something from the peasantry, it turned to the izbach for help. Several izbachi pointed out that their influence was undermined when they participated in such unpopular tasks as collecting taxes and making inventories, which obviously had nothing to do with their primary responsibilities. The Party repeatedly passed resolutions promising that the izbach would be freed from all extraneous obligations, but the good intentions were never realized.[60]

We have fragments from a diary of an izbach, published in 1927, that graphically show how the Party piled one responsibility after another on the few people it had in the countryside. This izbach was a member of the village Party cell and the librarian of the cell's small book collection. Not counting his duties as a Party member and his official duties for which he was paid, he had these responsibilities: (1) secretary of the volost' politpros-vet center, (2) organizer of literacy work in the volost', (3) member of the volost' soviet executive committee, (4) member of the Ostrovsk uezd (district) komsomol organization, (5) member of the volost' mutual-aid committee, (6) member of the auditing committee of the uezd teachers' association, (7) member of the uezd teachers' productivity (!) committee, (8) member of the directing board of the Ostrovsk uezd voluntary fire brigade, (9) secretary of the volost' cell of the Society of Friends of the Red Fleet, and (10) member of the village soviet.[61]

This izbach wrote in his diary on March 31, 1925:

Went to Podolsk on library, izba-chital'nia, and likbez business. Went into the uezd division on the ODVF [Society of Friends of the Red Fleet] where they severely scolded me for the bad work I was doing in the Ostrovsk cell of ODVF of which I am secretary. It is true that I really let this work go. But what can I do when on me depends other work of such great importance![62]

Another major complaint of the izbach was that the regime did not invest enough money. The izbach received his salary from the uezd budget, but the operating expenses for the reading room came from the volost', which was not always a reliable source. Although the reading rooms received books and journals at cost, there was often no money to build up a decent library. Frequently the entire collection consisted of the confiscated books of a former landlord. Obviously, such a collection was not useful for the purposes of political education. Placing the burden of support on local authorities meant that some regions were much better supplied than others. Some Siberian izbachi complained, for example, that they received so little support that they could not heat their rooms. One concludes: "It is warmer and cleaner in the house of the peasant. He is more comfortable at home then in the reading room. Why should he come?"[63]

How successful were village reading rooms in accomplishing their stated goals of winning over the peasantry and establishing a Party ideological presence in the countryside? It is easier to see the weaknesses of the system than its successes. Indoctrination, by is very nature, is hard to document, but it would be naive to conclude that all the work was in vain.

There is a great deal of evidence that many of the reading rooms were extremely weak. Perusing *Pravda* for November and December 1924, we find the following interesting references. A correspondent from Armavir uezd wrote on December 5: "The village reading room is well equipped, but no one comes to read the fresh papers. Even Party and Komsomol members do not come. The reading room has a library, which was taken over from the local landlord, but it just sits there, untouched. The reading room has no ties with the teacher and no work is being done among the peasantry."[64] On December 30, a correspondent from Tambov province wrote: "Very little attention is paid to the reading room. There is no information desk because no one comes. People prefer to spend their time in the company of women."[65] On November 23 from the village of Kochenego in Novonikoleavsk province came the report that since no one came to the reading room, the head of the local credit union set up his household on the premises.[66] A striking example of party weakness was reported from Saratov province. The reading room wanted to set up literacy courses for the peasants. However the German colonists of the area remained so obstinately religious that the local pastor continued to be by far the most powerful person. When the local Party organization wanted to establish a cell of the "Down with Illiteracy" Society, no one came. Then the secretary of the Party cell went to the pastor for help. This gesture made all the difference. The next time one hundred and fifty people turned up for the meeting. The *Pravda* correspondent, understandably, expressed his dismay contemplating how the ODN cell was going to carry out its antireligious mission.[67]

In some instances the peasants were so hostile to the izbach and to everything he stood for that he and his family were exposed to physical danger. The izbach from whose diary we have quoted had his barn burned down by his enemies, and he considered himself lucky that his house survived. He commented: "Mother and father cry and scold me and my brother for our too-energetic work. (I in the izba chital'nia and library and my brother in the cooperative.) They suggest that we stop our work, a suggestion that they have made several times in the past. Because of our work, we have many enemies."[68]

These examples of failure and hostility are striking. The historian is more likely to be skeptical about tales of success. In those instances self-serving reports from izbachi and propagandistic exaggerations of

Soviet sources are hard to separate from reality. It would appear, not surprisingly, that accomplishments were greater in certain areas and in certain segments of the population than in others. For example, in Russian and Ukrainian areas the reading rooms operated much better and there were many more of them than elsewhere. In the Central Asian republics the institutions barely existed. Among the 15,000 reading rooms that supplied data in 1926, more than 12,500 served the peasantry only in Russian or Ukrainian.[69]

Ironically, the relatively better educated peasant was more likely to benefit from the services of the reading room than the illiterate. This phenomenon of course had class implications, since the poorer the peasant, the more likely that he was illiterate. A meeting of political education workers in 1925 put the problem this way:

Party organization and Party workers engaged in political-education work must not forget for a moment that for us enlightenment is an instrument of class struggle. It is also an instrument for organizing those class forces in the village on which the Party and the Soviet power must base itself. We should approach all of our cultural work from this class point of view. At the same time in practice this is very often forgotten. This fact is shown even in details in the everyday work of the village reading room. In some places the izbachi do not organize the reading aloud of newspapers, saying that the majority of the people are already sufficiently literate as to be able to read the newspapers themselves. After looking deeper into this question, it turns out that the remnants of illiteracy are strongest among the poorest in the village. This way the izbachi involuntarily and unconsciously bring the center of their work to serving the richest elements in the village and forgetting the weakest and the least cultured.[70]

It is easy to see why the izbach would find it easier to appeal to those who at least were able to read a book.

The village youth was more likely to be attracted to the reading room than the older peasants. The fact that most izbachi were themselves very young contributed to this situation. The reading room often resembled a youth club, an extension of the Komsomol. A Party functionary who visited numerous reading rooms reported to the Central Committee: "The peasants complained to me that it was impossible for them to go to the reading room because the youth there behaved in a rowdy fashion. They gathered there and they smoked and the serious muzhik [peasant] simply found himself out of place."[71] The disproportionate presence of the village youth, who found no other amusement and were more likely to be open to new influences, lowered the prestige of this institution in the eyes of the older, more conservative peasants.

Perhaps the Soviet regime would have accomplished more if it had channeled its scarce resources into fewer reading rooms, equipping them better and providing them with better leadership. It might have improved matters if fewer meaningless holidays, such as the anniversary of the Paris commune, had been celebrated and if the Party had not fragmented the energies of its activists by establishing many phony organizations such as the Friends of the Red Fleet.

Excessive ambition, and a lack of correspondence between means and goals, were characteristic of the Soviet regime in the 1920s. After all, if the Bolsheviks had had no far-reaching plans for remaking society, they would not have undertaken their Revolution in 1917 or collectivization twelve years later.

The village reading room was also the focal point of another peculiar Soviet agitational method of the 1920s, the *shefstvo*. The word shefstvo comes from the French "chef." In Soviet political parlance it meant patronage. A Soviet author, writing in 1927, explained the concept this way: "Societies of shefstvo are one of the instruments of the working class through which, in a voluntary fashion, outside of the official budget and government organizations, the working class helps to overcome the contradiction between the city and the village."[72] To put it more simply, shefstvo meant the sponsorship of a village or village organization of a factory, an army unit, a university or a party school. Usually the izba chital'nia, the reading room, was the mediating agency.

Given Bolshevik ideology, which attributed a crucial role to the proletariat in building socialism, and given the political conditions following the Revolution, when Party strength was concentrated in the cities, the emergence of the idea of shefstvo is understandable. It made good sense to use the considerable Communist strength in the cities in trying to remake the countryside. The Bolsheviks could not but be aware of the deep hostility of the peasantry toward the cities, and they believed, perhaps naively, that sending delegations of workers to aid the peasants in various ways would help to overcome this negative attitude.

The movement started after the October Revolution, and in the course of the 1920s it grew in size and importance. In Moscow province alone, according to contemporary figures, 80,000 to 100,000 people took part.[73] In 1927 in the entire country, an estimated million and a half people were involved in this work. It is impossible to give precise figures. Soviet sources refer not to individuals but to members of societies that participated. Only 59 percent were industrial workers, the rest being soldiers and students.[74] Such a large-scale movement required a large organization. The Party sponsored conferences for exchanges of experiences and for the purpose of coordination; and it published guidebooks that summarized in very simple language the principles of proper behavior and gave practical advice to the visitors from the city. One gets the impression that, as with many other Soviet propaganda efforts, indoctrination worked two ways: The workers, soldiers, and students, while indoctrinating the peasants, were themselves indoctrinated.

Whenever possible, the city organization provided help within its own specialty. A city library would sponsor a village reading room and would provide it with some necessary books. The "shefs" from the cities were expected to appear at least twice a month and organize general meetings at least once every two months. The visitors provided aid to the villages by giving lectures, organizing theatrical performances and excursions, and helping them to interpret Soviet laws. Periodically they invited their village friends to the city and showed them their factories, schools, libraries, and so forth.[75] It was hoped that the shefstvo would establish contact with the village intelligentsia, win them over for Soviet power, and engage them in "building socialism." Also, it was expected that the visits would strengthen the local Party organization and raise its authority in the village.

This was the way shefstvo was supposed to operate. However, there is a great deal of evidence that in most instances little was achieved. The visitors came, brought some gifts, provided diversions, and then returned home without changing very much in country life. At times the haughty behavior of the visitors, who knew little about village life and customs, alienated people.

As with other Soviet propaganda efforts, it is impossible to establish the results, but the inventiveness, the energy, the willingness to try every method to mold peoples' minds are striking.

CHAPTER 7

The literacy campaign

It is impossible to establish how important a precondition literacy is for industrial growth, for the creation of a modern society and polity. Until recently, the commonly accepted wisdom has been that it was extremely important. A short time ago, however, a historian argued persuasively that the correlation was more apparent than real, and that intellectuals, historians, and even politicians have overstated the importance of literacy.[1] Similarly, it has been generally assumed that for mass mobilization, which is a characteristic feature of a totalitarian society, the printed word was crucial. Modern experience, on the contrary, shows that though literacy is helpful, the masses can be reached by other means.

Lenin and his comrades, however, firmly believed that a literate peasantry was essential in order for the Russian people to understand the message of socialism. Nothing expresses this conviction more clearly than Lenin's famous sentences: "The illiterate person stands outside of politics. First it is necessary to teach him the alphabet. Without it there are only rumors, fairy tales, and prejudices, but not politics."[2] After the Bolsheviks had won the Civil War and embarked on the great task of economic reconstruction, a new motive appeared in their public statements about literacy. Now they stressed that literacy was essential for building a modern economy. In this respect the work of the prominent Soviet statistician S. G. Strumilin acquired great significance. In a book published in 1924 he purported to show that a literate worker was so much more productive than an illiterate one that in the course of a year and a half the government regained all the expenses invested in a five-year education. According to his calculations, the prodcutivity of the literate worker was twenty-seven times higher than that of the illiterate.[3]

The Bolsheviks had an instrumental view of culture and therefore an instrumental view of literacy. They did not believe in the existence of values independent from one another but saw all positive goals as closely interrelated. Lenin, in particular, had no interest in education for its own sake and spoke contemptuously of "cultural hairsplitting" (*kulturnichestvo*).[4] Every time he mentioned literacy, he coupled it with a concrete goal, such as the struggle against bureaucracy, the improvement of agriculture, or electrification of the country.[5] The Bolsheviks most definitely did not intend to instill in the peasantry a skeptical attitude; they did not intend to aid the peasants in developing a world view of their own by teaching them to read and write. The VChK/lb letter to instructors, in the early 1920s, using the characteristic Bolshevik military terminology, put the matter boldly: "If you only teach your students to read and write, without giving them the necessary direction to their thoughts, without giving them interests, and an active involvement in the surrounding life, you give your students a weapon without teaching them how to use it. Such knowledge might turn out to be unnecessary and easily forgotten."[6]

As far as the Bolsheviks were concerned, the purpose of culture was to aid socialist reconstruction, and to the extent that culture did not contribute to that goal, it was worse then useless. However, they sincerely believed that the spread of knowledge and enlightenment, for which literacy was a precondition, was an important helpmate. In the course of the 1920s they made impressive attempts to overcome the heritage of cultural backwardness and illiteracy among the peoples of the Soviet Union.

1921–4

One might think that the end of the fighting against their domestic and foreign enemies would have enabled the Bolsheviks to expand greatly their cherished literacy drive. In fact the opposite happened: The introduction of the New Economic Policies was accompanied by a drastic curtailment of effort. On October 1, 1921, there were 37,163 likpunkts (literacy schools) in the country, giving instructions to 854,746 people. A half a year later, on April 1, 1922, there were only 8,802 schools teaching 202,446 people. The decline continued. On April 1, 1923, the nadir, there remained only 3,649 schools with 104,361 pupils.[7] The work was reduced everywhere: It almost disappeared in the villages, and it was significantly cut in the Red Army. Only the trade unions attempted to remain faithful to their commitment, but even they had to diminish the scale of their effort.

The reasons for the drastic reductions were clear. The logic of the NEP demanded a return to financial orthodoxy. The policies of the Imperial and Provisional governments, combined with the effects of the Civil War and war communism, had reduced the value of the ruble to almost nothing. Economic reconstruction now demanded a stable currency, and that in turn entailed the government's balancing its budget. The government lightened its financial burden by, among other things, withdrawing support from literacy work. In name, the burden was transferred from the central to the local budgets (city or provincial). In reality, monies for teaching illiterates simply disappeared. Local leaders were far less committed to literacy work, and in any case, they did not have the means. Also, 1921–2 were years of a devasting famine, causing the deaths of millions. The government invested its small supply of precious foreign currency in buying food abroad. This was hardly a propitious time to induce peasants to go to school.

For the time being on a much smaller scale, the work continued; the valuable legacy of the Civil War period did not altogether disappear. At that time the Party drew attention to the importance of the task, and it created the preconditions for later accomplishments by publishing text-books and, most importantly, by creating the rudiments of an organiza-tion. VChK/lb (or, as it was called at the time, Gramcheka), which was created in 1920, remained the backbone of literacy work. In the course of 1920–2, within the framework of Narkompros, a national network was organized. The provincial gramcheka organizations became responsible for running the local campaigns.

Work in the countryside suffered the most: In provinces hard hit by famine it stopped altogether, and it was greatly reduced elsewhere. The leading cadres of literacy work, who met at the second congress of literacy workers in May 1923, well understood that in view of the difficulties, it made good sense to try to reach the "organized" part of the population first.[8] By this they had in mind soldiers in the army, members of trade unions, and members of such mass organizations as the Komsomol and Zhenotdel. They also agreed that those who needed literacy in their work should be taught first. This consideration made sense not only from an economic point of view but also because it offered the best protection against recidivism. However, this way of setting priorities meant that the least amount of work was done where most of the illiterates were.

Reporters to the congress painted a dark picture of the status of the work in the countryside. Revel'skii, a representative of VChK/lb, said that the Party had failed to mobilize the literate part of the population for the work of helping the illiterates. Further, the existing village reading rooms (izba chital'nia), which were supposed to be the centers of political and cultural work, had not become centers of teaching. Whatever little teaching was done was accomplished by the village schoolteachers, who were greatly overburdened, not only with teaching children but also with various ad-ministrative and political tasks that the Party had imposed on them.[9]

From the proceedings of the third congress, which took place a year later, it is clear that not much had been accomplished. Kurskaia, the head of VChK/lb, confessed that Soviet power had not served the peasants well in the cultural sphere. She said: "There are villages of 15,000 people without a single newspaper or book. Fifty percent of peasant children do not even go to first grade." Epshtein, another leader of VChK/lb, gave an equally pessimistic evaluation. "Our idea was to have at least one izba chital'nia per volost'. This was a modest goal, since most of the volosts are very large and have several villages in them. But even this goal is far away. The lack of culture in the villages is shown by the recruits. Even those who had spent 2–3 years in school often come to the army as illiterates. The peasants do not regard literacy as important. They look down on women and refuse to sit down with them in the same classroom. In the villages the decisive factor is the teacher. It is a hopeful sign that now they seem to come to terms with Soviet power. If this happened, that would have great significance."[10] As a result of the improved conditions elsewhere and the bleak picture presented, the congress decided to reverse the previous policies and give primary attention to teaching the peasants. However, throughout the 1920s literacy work in the countryside remained the weakest part of the campaign. Without resolving this essential and most difficult aspect of the problem, there could be no victory over illiteracy.

Among the national minorities the teaching of literacy presented special difficulties. First of all, the question had to be resolved of whether or not the literacy campaign should be used to encourage russification by attempting to teach Russian. Some of the Party spokesmen took this point of view, but the majority of the third literacy congress disagreed and ordered that everyone should be taught in his or her native language. Some of the minorities were extremely backward, and it was among them that the literacy drive was the weakest. Although there was an adequate supply of textbooks for adults in Russian by the early to middle 1920s, these did not exist in national-minority languages.[11] Whatever teaching was done had to be carried out with the aid of textbooks for children. How little had been accomplished before 1924 can be seen from the fact that the third congress still called not so much for the teaching of minorities as the training of instructors for this task. After the congress, some hundreds of people were brought to Moscow for a special course.[12]

The Party had always had a great interest in bringing literacy to the soldiers of the Red Army. Resolutions of congresses and government and Party proclamations agreed that the highest priority must be given to the creation of a fully literate Red Army. Of course, the army possessed important advantages; it could make studying compulsory and enforce the rule. Already at the time of the Civil War the leaders of the army had made the company commander responsible for the appearance of the soldier at his lessons. If the soldier failed to appear, the company commander had to pay a fine. Under the circumstances, one can easily imagine, attendance at the literacy lessons was very good. The end of the Civil War brought with it an immediate and major reduction in the size of the army: Within a few weeks the army was reduced to one fourth its previous size. On February 28, 1921, the Military Revolutionary Council of the country published an order, signed both by Trotsky and Lunacharskii, which called for the complete liquidation of illiteracy in the army by May 1.[13] This order was not fully carried out in the course of the 1920s. In January 1923 there still remained 7 percent illiterates among the soldiers. The percentage was reduced to 4 two years later, but then, in 1926, illiteracy among the soldiers actually increased to 5.3 percent.[14]

In the early 1920s, the trade unions played the most important and most sustained role of all mass organizations in the struggle against illiteracy. Party control of the unions (and of all other organizations) was complete, as the defeat of the "workers' opposition" at the Tenth Party Congress clearly showed. At the same time, in the changed political and economic environment created by the introduction of the NEP, the union movement was bound to play a genuine and important role. The NEP allowed private enterprise and with it a free labor market, and compensation in wages rather than in kind. The demands of economic rationality quickly led to the firing of many workers, and large-scale unemployment plagued Soviet Russia throughout the 1920s. Under the circumstances the workers needed the protection of their unions. The trade unions, which possessed a more or less well-organized national network, were in a good position to carry out the Party's commitment to bring political enlightenment to the working class.

The nerve center of the movement was the cultural department (Kul'totdel') of the national organization, which communicated with the cultural departments of individual unions. On the factory level, unions maintained cultural commissions that were immediately responsible for the actual work. The first task was to compile a national census in order to appreciate the magnitude of the problem. In the course of 1920–2 each union reported on the number and percentage of illiterates, the number of literacy schools already in existence, and the methods used to attract students. From these reports it is clear that the working class culturally was extremely heterogenous. Some unions, such as the printers or health and education personnel, had hardly any illiterates. Other unions, for example sugar-industry workers, had a manageable task. On the other hand, industries that were based on a work force relatively recently recruited from among the village poor, such as lumbering, had an extremely high percentage of illiterates. The textile industry, with its large portion of women workers, was also in a poor position.[15] Unfortunately but not surprisingly, the poorest unions were the ones that needed to make the largest financial investment in education. Illiteracy rates and the success of the campaign also varied from region to region. The two capitals and the central industrial districts, such as Ivanovo-Voznesensk and Tula, were quite well off, but in remote provinces, in the national minority areas, and in provinces hit by the famine, almost nothing was done. In the Volga region, union "cultural funds" were used to alleviate the famine.[16]

It is difficult to find reliable and meaningful figures for the first half of the decade in order to measure the accomplishment of the unions. According to a union census, at the beginning of 1922 there were a million illiterate union members and a year later there were only 400,000. However, as the writer of the report, Isaev, himself pointed out, in the course of the year hundreds of thousands of workers had left the unions (as a result of unemployment) and among the unemployed the percentage of illiterates was especially high. In the course of the year the unions brought approximately 300,000 workers to literacy schools.[17] As the economy of the country improved and there was a new influx of workers, the percentage of illiterates was bound to go up. There was no way to create a fully literate union movement in isolation.

From an organizational point of view, reaching the unemployed presented special difficulties. At the third congress of literacy workers, in April 1924, union representatives suggested that Gramcheka should give special help to counter illiteracy among the unemployed and that literacy schools should be attached to unemployment offices. The unemployed had time to study.[18]

Since the trade unions were the first to teach literacy to hundreds of thousands, they were also the first to have to deal with the problem of motivating students. As one would expect, although there was a genuine interest among many in learning, there were also hundreds of thousands who had no desire whatever to master the difficult arts of reading and writing. The Soviet leadership was ambivalent on the question of the use of compulsion. The "Leninist" decree on illiteracy of December 26, 1919, obliged every illiterate to learn, even though it was not spelled out what would happen to those who did not. The various government and Party resolutions that promised complete literacy by one part of the citizenry or another also implied compulsion. On the other hand, some leaders commendably shrank from the idea of imposing enlightenment by force. The trade-union leaders in particular, who recalled that a very short time ago, during war communism, labor itself had not been voluntary, but workers had been drafted and unable to change jobs, wanted to avoid the use of force. The picture that emerges from a study of union reports is that different methods of coercion were widely used and that, in general, it was difficult to draw a line between legitimate incentives and harsh punishments.

The Kremenchug miners, for example, reported in May 1921: "The schools are filled in the first place by people who want to study. Those who decline without sufficient reason are subjected to the following methods of compulsion: In the first place, they are deprived of their various privileges and compensations that are passed out through the union. In the second place, they are temporarily removed from the union. Finally, they are completely excluded."[19] These were serious punishments. In 1921 a large share of the wages passed through the unions in kind rather than in worthless money. Exclusion from the union at the time of growing unemployment implied a serious threat to a person's livelihood.

The union of transport workers wrote in January 1923 that they encouraged firing the illiterates first.[20] The construction workers expressed themselves this way: "Considering the low level of consciousness among the workers in our trade, as a consequence of the specific conditions of work and life, it is essential to use methods of compulsion in the struggle against illiteracy."[21] By contrast, the union of metal workers in January 1923 disapproved the use of force to make adults study at a time when children were not in school. They also repudiated the use of economic coercion.[22]

The matter of "moral coercion" was less controversial. The union of textile workers, for example, used these methods: (1) public "scolding"; (2) being called in for an "interview" by the factory committee; (3) putting the name of the recalcitrant on a blackboard of shame.[23] Although some trade-union leaders considered the use of public shaming inadmissibly harsh, the cultural department of the national union, meeting in June 1924, authorized the use of such methods.[24]

Positive measures of encouragement were the other side of the coin. The choice of incentive varied from place to place and from union to union. In Ivanovo-Voznesensk in some textile factories the unions gave textiles to those who had successfully completed the literacy course. When the higher authorities found this method unacceptable, and the next graduating class did not receive the same presents, the students decided to complain about it in the local newspaper.[25] Monetary rewards for students were rare, but they existed. Public praise was the most widely used reward.

The generous policy of the Soviet government, which allowed illiterates to study at government expense by freeing them from their jobs several times a week for a couple of hours, was gradually eroded during the early years of the NEP. Trade unions, which were concerned with productivity, by and large supported this concession less enthusiastically than Gramcheka organizations, whose only task was the elimination of illiteracy.[26] Private enterprises often balked at the idea of paying workers who did not produce. State enterprises whose contracts included this clause by and large honored them, but when it was necessary to renew the contracts, this point was usually dropped. The new labor code, drawn up for the conditions of NEP, did not say anything on the subject.[27] As time went on, the government attempted to place the burden increasingly on society itself; although the regime continued to exhort and to organize, it was less and less willing to pay the cost.

The trade unions, of course, were not responsible alone for teaching literacy; they shared that responsibility with VChK/lb. As one might expect, the cooperation of the two organizations, each having different priorities and representing different points of view, was not without friction. In the course of 1923 and 1924, the local union and Gramcheka organizations were instructed by their national headquarters to draw up contracts. These followed a common pattern: Gramcheka promised to provide "methodological leadership"; and send instructors to an appointed teaching place on the basis of plans drawn up ahead of time; and provide teaching material. The union, for its part, promised to send every illiterate to school, providing teaching facilities, equip the students with paper and pencil, and help pay the instructor.[28]

When the local unions reported to the Cultural Department of VTsSPS on the nature of cooperation with Gramcheka, their response varied. Many described cooperation as satisfactory. Others complained that Gramcheka did not send them enough teachers, or sent unsatisfactory teachers. (Isaev, the head of the cultural department, informed these unions although Gramcheka had the responsibility of selecting teachers, the unions did not have to accept them passively.)[29] There were unions that reported no contacts at all with their Gramcheka organizaton. The Gramcheka organizations, on their part, complained that the poorer unions, which required the most work, did not have the means to support the necessary effort.

The heart of the matter was financing. In January 1923, Narkompros, the parent organization of VChK/lb, invited the representatives of VTsSPS to discuss short-term and long-range planning of the literacy campaign and to prepare budgets.[30] The participants assumed that in order to eliminate illiteracy in the eighteen-to-thirty age group by the tenth anniversary of the Revolution, they would have to teach 17 million people in the coming five years. (This was, of course, a less ambitious goal than envisaged by the decree on illiteracy of December 1919, which spoke of the eight-to-fifty age group.) Calculating that the teaching of a single individual cost 3.75 rubles, they arrived at the approximate figure of 64 million rubles for the cost of the entire effort.

The representatives also worked out a budget for the first year, during which they hoped to give instruction to 2 million people, out of which a half million were to be trade-union members. According to these plans, local governments were to pay 5.4 million, trade unions 1.8 million, and the central government 700,000 rubles. The central government planned to bear only the costs of printing textbooks and of organizing conferences for instructors. This way it was assumed that the ideological leadership would remain firmly in reliable hands. Placing the bulk of the burden on provincial and city budgets almost assured that the plans would not be realized. The local governments had neither the means nor the commitment.

Indeed, the plans turned out to be wildly unrealistic, and instead of 2 million people, only 621,000 received instruction, that is, somewhat less than one third.[31] As far as the more distant future was concerned, the gap between the plans and reality became ever wider. The minutes of the planning session are interesting to us only because they show the thinking of the responsible leadership of the literacy campaign on the question of proper distribution of the financial burden.

By the middle of the 1920s, though the regime's utopian plans had not been realized, the achievements in the struggle against illiteracy were still considerable. The program had recovered from the great slump of 1922, and every year more and more people acquainted themselves with the alphabet. The drive that was organized during the first half of the NEP, in contradistinction to the time of the Civil War, was based on a firm foundation. Especially in the cities, more or less reliable lists of illiterates were drawn up, and classes met regularly, reasonably well equipped with text-books, paper, and pencils. However, both as a result of financial difficulties and of organizational weakness, the Bolsheviks could reach only a part of the population. To overcome these problems, the Bolsheviks decided to create a "voluntary" organization, the "Down with Illiteracy" Society (Obshchestvo "Doloi Negramotnosti" or, as it was invariably called at the time, ODN).

ODN

The "Down with Illiteracy" Society was one of several single-issue "voluntary" organizations. In the course of the 1920s there also existed societies to fight alcoholism and the "remnants" of religion. It is proper to place "voluntary" in quotation marks, for none of these institutions from the very moment of its establishment was independent of government control and leadership. Although the regime, the Party, did not succeed in establishing its presence everywhere in the countryside, it was certainly strong enough to prevent the formation of any truly independent movement. The government-sponsored mass societies came to play a genuinely important role within the Soviet political system. They contributed to the development of the particular flavor of Soviet totalitarianism: They represented counterfeit spontaneity, they filled a void, and they became instruments of mass mobilization. Participation in the work of these societies became part of the experience of an entire generation of Soviet citizens. The societies enabled the regime to channel genuine enthusiasm; they allowed the government to identify itself, in the case of the fight against illiteracy and alcoholism, with popular causes; they gave room for the activities of young workers and potential cadres. Since the eradication of alcoholism and illiteracy were "good causes," some people who would otherwise have avoided helping the regime were willing to participate.

The myth of spontaneity was, of course, crucial. According to Soviet publicists and historians, the idea of forming ODN came from local activists in the Ukraine.[32] They maintain that individuals and organizations, such as the Komsomol, turned to Narkompros for help, which was then gladly provided by the commissariat. However, the contemporary Narkompros report on the subject is both more prosaic and more believable:

It became clear that government and local budgets were not in a position to finance such work [literacy]. The scale of the undertaking, such as establishing thousands of likpunkts, giving them books, paper, and other material, and attracting teachers, made it impossible for the government to finance everything. For this reason workers in Glavpolitprosvet decided to organize social forces in the struggle against illiteracy.[33]

It is clear from this document that the question of financing was a major incentive. The regime wanted to place the burden of educating society on society itself. The government's primary contribution was to be organizational know-how. It seems that the Soviet leadership only gradually realized that ODN could bring beneifts far beyond alleviation of this financial burden.

On September 2, 1923, leading Narkompros functionaries met, decided to form ODN, and laid out the basic features of the organization. Krupskaia, Kurskaia, El'kina, Epshtein, Erde, Brikhnichev, Menzhinskaia, and Demian Bednyi participated in this meeting and made up the provisional leadership of ODN. Epshtein, who later became deputy commissar of enlightenment in the RSFSR, was elected president.[34] The growth of the central organization was remarkably fast. The government decided to give the initiative full support, and the entire Soviet leadership joined the organization to become its first members. The organizers of the society appreciated the significance of naming a prominent Soviet figure as titular head of ODN and they so recommended to the Party leadership. A few months later, the Central Committee of the Party made M. I. Kalinin president of the organization. It is unclear how active a role Kalinin in fact played. He gave speeches at ODN congresses, his signature appeared on recruiting letters, and his prestige was clearly an important asset, but the day-to-day affairs of ODN continued to be directed by Epshtein.

The Soviet leadership instructed local Party, Soviet, and Narkompros organizations to form chapters and to help in the work of recruiting. The growth in numbers was rapid. In January 1924 ODN already had 100,000 members and 2,066 cells. A year later it had almost a half-million members and 8,274 cells. From this point on, the increase was spectacular. In April the society had over a million members and almost 16,000 cells. By July it had reached 1.4 million people and 24,000 cells, and in October the corresponding figures were 1.6 million and 28,000.[35]

This organizational achievement was the result of a giant campaign. National newspapers promised to provide space for propagating the ODN and its principles. Goskino agreed to include ODN slogans in its newsreels. Glavpolitprosvet borrowed money from Sovnarkom to establish an ODN publishing house, which was, in part, used to print agitational pamphlets. ODN planned to raise two to three hundred thousand rubles a year by introducing a book lottery.[36]

In the course of 1924 and 1925, ODN cells mushroomed all over the country. Schools, universities, factories, village soviets, and military units all established organizations of their own. However, from reading the reports of provincial ODN chapters, it is clear the organization was largely a paper achievement rather than a functioning body of workers. The local Party, Soviet, Komsomol, or trade-union leaders, urged by their headquarters to participate in this campaign, wanted to report success, and consequently they and their fellow activists joined.

The fact that ODN had far more members than the total number of students in literacy schools clearly shows the illusory aspect of this massive organizational effort. Indeed, on the provincial level, the organization barely functioned. Every provincial report indicates that they were in no position to supervise what was happening in areas under their nominal control and that they had no contact with, or even knowledge of, local cells. The Archangel organization of ODN, for example, wrote in January 1925 that it had no knowledge of the existence of district (uezd) chapters and that whatever evidence it had on local cells came not from the cells themselves but from newspaper reports.[37] In Briansk province, the local politprosvet department described the situation in its letter to ODN headquarters. In the first half of 1924 nothing happened. In June the provincial ODN organization consisted only of a president and a secretary. They sent out a questionnaire to the districts and villages but received no responses. They attempted then to communicate with the villages through the politprosvet network but in vain. Finally cells were instructed through the newspapers to register with politprosvet offices. The report concludes that it was impossible to comment on the extent of illiteracy in the province or on the nature of ODN work, because there was no reliable information. The writer of the report correctly noted that in Briansk ODN did not exist on the provincial level.[38]

The provincial reports are our best sources for understanding the operation of individual cells. Certain common themes emerge. First, as we would expect, cells were a great deal more active in the cities than in the countryside. In the village, the local Party secretary or his wife often became the head of the ODN cell, the directing board was made up of the Komsomol secretary or chairman of the soviet, and so forth. Apart from constituting themselves a cell (and possibly paying the necessary membership fees), they might do nothing at all. Some of the reports show that board members either forgot or never even knew that they were supposed to be members. In a well-functioning cell, every member had a function and a title; one person was responsible for organization, another for agitation, a third for accounting, a fourth for supervision of schools, and so forth. But such cells were rare.

Second, there was a constant complaint about the lack of money. Members had to pay according to a sliding scale: Those who earned over 60 rubles a month had to pay 20 kopecks on entry and 6 kopecks per month. Those who earned under 60 paid 5 on entry and 3 per month. Those who did not pay for three months were automatically excluded. The unemployed, the soldiers, and the students paid nothing.[39] Aside from these dues, the cells made money by soliciting voluntary contributions from organizations, by staging theater and film performances, and by selling books. The local cells were obliged to pass 5 percent of the dues and 15 percent of other income to the higher bodies.[40] How little these monies amounted to can be seen from the fact that the provincial organizations were all extremely poor. The richest in the country in October 1924 was the Don organization, which had at its disposal 9,766 rubles. The next one, Tula province, had only 4,276. Others, such as Iaroslav, Archangel, Briansk, and Kaluga, had no money at all.[41]

Third, it is clear that, since provincial organizations could provide no supervision, the functioning cells were very much left to their own resources. Local activists could introduce methods and ideas that were reprehensible from the point of view of higher authorities. A village cell, for example, decided to attract the peasants by teaching them to play billiards and to charge them for the use of the tables. Another came up with the idea of levying extremely high dues on each member. Everyone had a choice: either to teach an illiterate himself or to pay the cost of teaching one, that is, four rubles, which was a considerable sum in those days.[42] Other cells offered bribes to illiterates to encourage them to attend schools. In some localities activists combined the struggle against juvenile delinquency with the struggle against illiteracy, an idea that, understandably, was unacceptable to central ODN.[43]

It is hard to be balanced in our evaluation of the contribution of ODN to the illiteracy drive. On the one hand, it is clear that the organization greatly exaggerated its successes and padded its rolls. The weaknesses of structure paralleled Soviet weaknesses in the countryside. The Party did not have enough adherents in the villages to build yet another network, and this situation changed only with the collectivization of agriculture. On the other hand, ODN did extend the reach of the government and of the Party. Some well-functioning cells helped in drawing up lists of illiterates and aided likpunkts by providing them with rooms for teaching, and so forth. ODN members taught individuals and groups of illiterates, especially those who were hard to reach, such as peasant women. Also, ODN cells reported on village meetings and thereby brought important publicity to the issue. They rewarded those who did particularly good jobs and set up "comradely courts" for those who did not and who refused to study. The idea of using a mass organization in the struggle against illiteracy turned out to be a valuable one.

1925–9

It is impossible to arrive at a correct understanding of Soviet accomplishments in the fight against illiteracy in the NEP period by reading the works of modern Soviet historians. The most prominent scholar of the subject, V. A. Kumanev, compared the results of the 1897 census with those of the 1926 census, dishonestly pretending that all the accomplishments were made not during the last two decades of the Empire but during the 1920s. He deliberately presented data from the important 1920 census in such a way as to make direct comparisons with the results of the 1926 census impossible.[44] However, fortunately, ODN in 1929 published a mass of data that enables us to form a reasonably accurate picture, both of the previous accomplishments and also of the magnitude of the remaining problem. The figures are sobering.

Between 1920 and 1928, 8,161,000 people attended literacy schools.[45] Since on the average only 70 percent completed the course and since there was obviously considerable recidivism, the number of newly literate was much smaller. Further, we must recall that in the Soviet Union approximately 1 million people reached adulthood (age 16) yearly and that in the RSFSR, which was typical of the entire country, only about three quarters of the children received any education at all during the school year of 1928–9.[46] Thus, the number of newly literate only slightly surpassed the number of newly illiterate; progress was slow. According to the 1926 census, out of every 1,000 citizens of the country, 445 were literate, as compared to 223 in 1897 and 319 in 1920.[47] (These figures somewhat exaggerate the rate of illiteracy for all three censuses because they include the entire population, including children under eight.)

Another interesting aspect of the 1929 data, also deliberately obscured by Kumanev, is that they show that progress was far from constant. After the tremendous decline of the early NEP period (indeed, for some years), there was improvement. The country equaled the achievements of the 1920–1 school year only during 1924–5. Then in the following year it achieved its greatest success, by teaching 1,639,000. However, in the next year there was a sizable drop: Only 1.1 million were educated, and during the last year of NEP, 1.3 million.[48] It would appear that in spite of the great propaganda effort of the regime, in spite of the good work of ODN, the campaign was running out of steam; the problem of illiteracy could not quickly be solved by methods developed during the relative freedom of the NEP period.

It was among the poorest of the peasants that illiteracy was the highest. According to contemporary Soviet estimates, 70 to 80 percent of the peasants described by Soviet statistics as "poor" were also illiterate in the late 1920s.[49] The poorer the peasant, the more likely that he or she was illiterate. Bolsheviks found it galling that it was the better-off elements who were most likely to take advantage of the literacy schools provided by the regime. Some observers complained that on occasion likpunkts were made up of kulaks alone. By contrast, illiteracy among the collective and Soviet farm workers was particularly high.[50] Activists paid lip service to proper "class policy," which called for teaching of the poor, but it was a difficult policy to carry out.

The majority of illiterates were women. In 1920–2 more than half the students were female, but later the proportion was reversed, and in the 1923–4 school year less than a third of the students were women. Later the situation improved and in the rest of the decade the gender composition of the student body was balanced.[51] As one would expect, the more backward and poor a province, the greater the gap between male and female illiteracy.

The situation was especially bad in the national-minority regions. In rural regions of Turkmenistan, for example, in 1927 there were 97 percent illiterates[52] and in rural Armenia, over 80 percent. Ninety percent of all

Plate 9. Poster by Elizaveta Kruglova, 1923. Text: Woman! Become Literate! Eh! Mama, if you were literate you could help me!

Kalmyks were still illiterate in December 1926.[53] The relative position of the minorities within the Soviet Union hardly changed at all in the 1920s. The Jews and Germans were the most literate and the Central Asians and Siberian nomads the least.[54]

In view of the continuing high rural illiteracy, the regime was not even able to reach the goal to which it had consistently given the highest priority: literate recruits. In 1912, 67 percent of the recruits were literate, and this percentage increased to 80.7 in 1924. In the following year the Soviets reached their best figure for the decade, 87.7 percent, but after that date there was a slight decline, and the country never again in the course of the 1920s achieved the same high percentage.[55]

In the second half of the decade the contribution of the unions to literacy work gradually diminished in importance. The unions found that their investment brought gradually diminishing returns: Some unions for all practical purposes became fully literate, whereas others could not make permanent improvements because of the constant influx from the village and because of the large percentage of seasonal workers. The tone of correspondence between the unions and VChK/lb offices became increasingly acrimonious: Each felt that the other was not doing enough. Many union leaders came to resent having to use a substantial part of the cultural funds on the seemingly endless task of literacy work. Between 1926 and 1928 the number of union members increased from 9.2 million to over 11 million, and a large percent of new members were illiterate.[56] At the same time the unions reduced their expenditure on literacy work by almost 50 percent; while in 1925 the unions spent 947,000 rubles, in 1928 they spent approximately half a million.[57]

On the basis of a wealth of data, we can form a fairly accurate picture both of the extent of illiteracy in Soviet Russia at the end of the 1920s and of the accomplishments of the literacy drive during the NEP period. It is much more difficult, and inevitably subjective, to put the statistics in context and evaluate those accomplishments. It is clear, on the one hand, that the tempo of the elimination of illiteracy increased in the Soviet period as compared to the last two decades of the Empire, although Imperial Russia, too, had been on the way to overcoming the problem. Had compulsory education in fact been introduced in the course of the 1920s, as had been planned, illiteracy would have disappeared in two or three decades. On the other hand, it is also evident that in the international context the results of the Soviet literacy drive were not extraordinary. The Balkan countries offer the only meaningful comparison, for the rest of Europe, including East-central Europe, was essentially literate by the time of the First World War. When we look at these countries, we find that major steps in bringing education to the entire people were taken during the interwar period. Rumania's illiteracy rate was reduced from 60.7 to 23.1 percent between 1910 and 1948 and Yugoslavia's from 51 to 25.5 percent between 1921 and 1948. Most interesting are the Bulgarian figures where the Soviet accomplishments were duplicated: between 1926 and 1934 illiteracy declined from 52.1 to 31.6 percent (and, looking at a longer period, from 1880 to 1939 from 96.9 to 22–5 percent).[58]

Obviously, the uptopian provisions of the "Leninist" literacy decree of December 1919 were not carried out, and Soviet Russia remained an extremely backward country at the time of the introduction of the industrialization drive. There were three reasons. First, although the government paid lip service to the cause and organized an impressive campaign, it was unwilling to make serious financial investments. As a share of the budget, expenditures on the literacy drive declined from 2.8 percent in 1924–5 to 1.6 percent in 1927–8.[59] Although the Bolsheviks obviously believed in public education, enlightenment, and literacy, they believed, partly for ideological reasons, that the people should achieve these goals on their own.

Second, Soviet Russia chose the wrong strategy. Had the regime's primary goal been to overcome illiteracy, the best use of scarce resources would have been to educate all children and organize only an auxiliary drive for interested adults. However, those who recommended this solution were branded as class enemies.[60] The regime refused to give up the attempt to influence the politically crucial adult population; after all, the literacy drive from the very beginning was also a political-indoctrination campaign.

Third, and most important, the success of the literacy drive was limited because most of the illiterates lived in precisely those areas where the Party was weakest. Bringing literacy and expanding the rule of the Party over the countryside were parts of the same process. Both problems, illiteracy and the weakness of the Party among the peasantry, were to be resolved by the same revolution: collectivization of agriculture.

It would be a mistake to regard the literacy drive solely as an educational venture; after all, this was not the way its organizers regarded it. For them, bringing "political enlightenment" to the people was equally important. Accomplishments in that sphere are almost impossible to evaluate. The likelihood is, however, that Soviet power had made considerable gains by this method of indoctrination. The use of the literacy drive as a propaganda instrument was twofold: The campaign itself was used for mass mobilizaton, and, more immediately, the lessons were deeply politicized.

To see how literacy was used as a Soviet propaganda theme, let us look at the instructions sent out by Glavpolitprosvet to various organizations all over the country concerning a three-day campaign, May 1–3, 1925. This campaign was, of course, only one of many. It is, however, best to examine in detail one set of instructions in order to appreciate how all-inclusive and how manipulative Soviet propaganda was in the mid-1920s.[61]

First of all, it was necessary to prepare from a much earlier date to the very last moment – local organizations were told. This preparation included the following. (1) Articles on the subject were to be placed in the local, provincial, and national press, "not less often than three times a week." (2) Politprosvet organizatons were to draw up an account of the achievements of the past academic year and plans for the next. (3) Gramcheka organizations were to plan a three-day holiday, including festive graduations from likbez courses. (4) Clubs and village libraries together with teachers of literacy schools were to plan an "artistic" program including plays, "agitational-comradely courts" (agit-sudy), and a new edition of the local wall-newspaper. For the "artistic" work, material was to be found in the publication of VChK/lb, *Za gramotu*. (5) Village libraries were to prepare "exhibitions." (6) ODN cells were to carry out inspection of likpunkts and draw up reports on the work of teachers, in order to be able to give out rewards to the most able teachers during the festivities. (7) All organizations involved in literacy work were to consult with one another to coordinate plans.

Then the instructions turned to the subject of how the festivities should be carried out. On the first day, May 1, the sale of buttons, brochures, and newspapers was to begin. The local and provincial presses were each to include an entire page devoted to the occasion. One of the May 1 slogans of the Central Committee of the Party was to be on illiteracy.

The festivities would begin in earnest on the second day. At that time both on the provincial and local levels festive meetings were to be held. On these occasions chairmen of Soviet executive committees were to give reports on the status of literacy work. This was to be followed by representatives of all organizations engaged in literacy work (Komsomol, trade-union, Zhenotdel, etc.) "giving their greetings." The next point in the program was to be speeches by the newly literate and by teachers of literacy. Finally came the "artistic" presentation, "wherever possible a film."

On the third day the heart of the program was to be mass graduations, organized by workers' clubs in factories and village libraries in the countryside. On these occasions ODN was to present gifts to the deserving. The book *Revolutionary Holidays* was deemed to be especially appropriate for the purpose. Once again, "artistic" presentations were to follow.

In addition, the planners also recommended the outfitting of "agitational streetcars" in cities. These streetcars, bedecked with slogans, were to travel to every part of the city, where their staffs were to hand out brochures. Politprosvet even provided the slogans: "We have three tasks: first, to study, second, to study, and third, to study" (Lenin). "We will create a thick network of schools everywhere in the Russian land. There should be no illiterates. There should be no ignorant workers" (Trotsky). "Arm yourself with knowledge, comrade, as you arm yourself with a rifle" (Rykov). "Those who know how to hold a book well, will also hold a rifle correctly in the defense of the Revolution." And, finally, "Only a literate mother is a true support for her child."

It is evident from these instructions that the central planners were willing to leave nothing to local initiative. Every aspect of the campaign was carefully thought out and choreographed.

One is entitled to doubt that such an elaborate campaign, presumably

Plate 10. The cover of a literacy textbook for adults, drawn on the basis of a poster by Aspit, 1918.

imposing excruciating boredom on millions of people, had no other purpose then the ostensible struggle against illiteracy. We can only speculate about the true motives. The hundreds of thousands of speeches and the millions of slogans extolling Soviet power for bringing enlightenment to the people were a pretense of public support. Those who gave the speeches and who pasted the slogans on the walls became committed and, in the process perhaps, to a slight extent, convinced themselves of the truthfulness of what they were saying. Gradually, the regime washed away the difference between genuine and pretended support. What mattered was that Soviet power was strong enough to prevent the enunciation of hostile views and could command compliance. Often the speakers themselves did not know to what extent they were pretending.

The suppression of independent organizations, newspapers, and social movements made the open discussion of societal choices an impossibility. The public sphere became a void. Orchestrated demonstrations covered up this reality. The Soviet people participated in phony elections: That was Soviet democracy. They joined phony organizations and attended meaningless celebrations: That was Soviet spontaneity.

Of course it would be naive to imagine that the leaders had a master plan and that they acted consciously. The typical Soviet political style emerged gradually in response to the existing conditions. The leaders were as much victims as everyone else, and the system acquired a life of its own. In that system the literacy drive, together with other similar causes, had a considerable importance.

However, the political uses of the literacy campaign were also a great deal more concrete and immediate: The lessons from the beginning to the very end were relentlessly political. Instead of attempting a general description of the political content of teaching, it is, perhaps best to give fully one lesson plan as it appeared in a pamphlet for instructors:

Before the lesson the teacher explains to the students the goal of their coming to the likpunkt, the significance of literacy and education for the workers. He briefly explains to the students the influence of literacy on agriculture and on industry. For illustration he introduces data from the writings of Comrade Iaroslavskii. He tells the students about the attitude of the tsarist government to popular education and contrasts this attitude with the actions of Soviet power. Then he turns to the discussion of the first picture in the textbook. The teacher shows the picture.

Question: What do you see in this picture?

The students answer in unison: "We see the building of the village soviet, we see a worker, a peasant, and a Red Army soldier; we see a field and a harvesting machine."

Q: To whom did the land belong before?

A: To the landlords.

Q: And to whom does the land belong now?

A: To us, the peasants.

Q: You said that the land formerly belonged to the landlords. But to whom did the power belong?

163

A: The power also belonged to the landlords and to the capitalists.
Q: And to whom does the power belong now?
A: It belongs to us, the workers and peasants.
Q: And then to whom do the land and power belong?
A: *Nasha sila — nasha niva.* [Our power — our cornfield. This was also the title of the textbook.] Then the last sentence is repeated once again by the students.[62]

This set of instructions, an example of the numerous pamphlets that village teachers received, is a remarkable document. Both the low level of sophistication of the political content and the primitiveness of the teaching methods are striking. To put it mildly, Soviet propagandists did not expect that the truth would emerge from a conflict of points of view; they preferred to indoctrinate through the use of catechism. On the other hand, to say that the political content was primitive is not to imply that the basic thought, namely, that the possession of land confirmed power, is untrue. Indeed, the Russian peasants would shortly learn this lesson anew, to their sorrow.

Further, by giving such minute instructions to teachers, the Party betrayed its lack of confidence in them. In view of recent history this lack of confidence was understandable. The majority of literacy instructors in rural areas were village teachers. In the earliest period, the Soviet authorities found it difficult to gain the services of these people at all; the teachers, as a group, opposed the Bolsheviks and supported the Socialist Revolutionary Party. Only with the end of the Civil War did the organized opposition of the teachers also came to a halt. This was, however, only a partial reconciliation: Many Bolshevik leaders continued to regard teachers with suspicion, and the teachers, for their part, had legitimate complaints about the Soviet order.

Few other profesions suffered as much in the Revolution as the teachers. Their standard of living declined far more than that of the peasantry. In the worst period teachers were often reduced to begging.[63] A. M. Bolshakov, a Soviet sociologist of the 1920s, reported a particularly striking incident from Tver province. To escape starvation, a teacher became a shepherd. However, he was forced to go back to his work by the compulsory labor service, and once again he was incapable of providing for his family.[64] The Sovnarkom decree of September 1921 ordered the peasants to support the teachers by making "contributions." As might be expected in the prevailing circumstances, such a regulation could not be enforced. As the lives of the Soviet people began to improve gradually, the teachers were left far behind. As late as 1926, when the industrial workers and peasants had almost caught up with their prerevolutionary incomes, the teachers were earning less than one half of what they had earned in 1913.[65] The teachers received extra food or money for special services rendered such as helping to carry out censuses and teaching literacy. These material incentives were crucial.

One can imagine that the teachers remained skeptical about the educational innovations that the Soviet authorities wanted to introduce both in the regular schools and also in combating illiteracy. In this respect from the beginning they came into conflict with the preferences of the Soviet authorities. A methodological conference was called in 1920 to give Communist educators an opportunity to present their views on the correct methods of teaching adults.[66] The "progressive" method was to teach illiterates not to voice single letters of the alphabet and construct words but to voice entire syllables. Although its advocates admitted that at the beginning this method was more difficult, they believed that it provided a firmer foundation of literacy. They argued that the literate person reads not by letters but by syllables and that therefore this way of teaching was more "natural." This method was dubbed "American." (The enthusiasts perhaps overlooked the fact that written Russian is quite phonetic by comparison with written English and consequently that different methods of teaching might be more suitable for each.)

Although there was no logical connection, the advocates of the old methods of teaching were content to use textbooks for children that were relatively free of politics, whereas the "progressives" believed in the use of material that consisted entirely of ideologically loaded examples. The "American" method of teaching, saturated with politics, was forced on the majority of teachers and contributed to their alienation. In the course of the 1920s many teachers must have quietly attempted to go their own way, for they were again and again admonished by Narkompros and the Party to be "progressive."

A similar methodological issue was how the curriculum of the likpunkts should be arranged. The "progressives" rejected the conventional notion of division according to subject matter. Instead of teaching reading, writing, arithmetic, geography, and so forth, they believed in a thematic division. The model likpunkt curriculum, as it was drawn up in 1926, recommended the teaching of these five "subjects": (1) life of peasants; (2) agriculture; (3) worker–peasant alliance (*smychka*); (4) organization of Soviet power; (5) the army and the international situation. The widely used textbook *Nasha sila – nasha niva* (Our strength – our cornfield) was arranged accordingly. The teacher who used this "complex method," as it was called at the time, combined the introduction of new material from a variety of conventional subjects in the course of a single lesson. The students used arithmetic, for example, to calculate the income of a model kolkhoz, and so on.[67]

This innovation of breaking down the boundaries among conventional subjects (as well as the experiments of making students voice syllables rather than single letters) was in line with the general Soviet commitment to progressive education. Given the hostility of the majority of the teachers to these experiments, it is unlikely that on the whole they were effective.

The heavy political load that the teaching of illiterates had to carry was an obstacle to success, if success was to be measured purely by the reduction of illiteracy in the Soviet Union. Both students and teachers must have found the material imposed on them unappealing or even irritating. Undoubtedly, the extreme politicization of the literacy drive turned away some students and focused the hostility of the enemies of the regime on this educational effort. Soviet historians give numerous examples of literacy teachers being attacked in the villages. As long as the Civil War continued, hostility took violent forms. At the time of the Tambov rising, the followers of the insurgent leader Antonov killed teachers and burned down schools.[68] There were similar incidents in 1920–1 in the Ukraine and in Central Asia.[69] In the course of the 1920s "kulaks" were said to have spread rumors to the effect that the newly literate would be drafted, would have to pay a special tax, would be sent to work in a distant place,[70] and so forth. At the time of the social upheaval created by forced collectivization, violent opposition once again appeared and teachers of literacy lost their lives at the hands of enemies of the regime.[71]

If the Soviet leaders had been asked in the 1920s whether it was worthwhile to pay the price for the politicization of the literacy drive, they would not have hesitated in their answer. As far as they were concerned, the struggle against illiteracy and the attempt to indoctrinate the Russian people, especially the peasantry, were two aspects of the same effort; the two were inseparable. When in the following decade the Soviet Union did manage to overcome the problem of illiteracy, it did so not by lessening the political content, but, if possible, by increasing it. The new element was the unrestrained use of force.

CHAPTER 8

The Komsomol in the 1920s

The Soviet political order was born out of the anarchy of the Civil War. Russia, which had always been undergoverned, now fell apart: The weak ties between citizen and government snapped. The decisive task was to rebuild institutions, to restructure authority, and thereby to make the political and economic order function. The Bolsheviks, of course, had no plans for the circumstances in which they found themselves; no one could have foreseen the sequence of events that left Lenin at the head of Russia's government. Nevertheless, the Bolsheviks brought with them from their revolutionary past institutions that could be adapted for the new tasks. Even more important, they had developed a mentality that turned out to be timely and conducive to success.

The most visible of these institutions, the one that best embodied Leninist principles, was the Party. Its role in the Civil War and in the period of economic reconstruction has been justly stressed by Soviet historians and publicists. Western scholars correctly described the concept of the Party as Lenin's greatest contribution to twentieth-century government theory and practice. The accomplishments of the Party – as a formulator of policy, as a recruitment agency for a new governing elite, as a supervisory body, and as a purveyor of doctrine in a new and exotic ideology – are self-evident.

Nevertheless, our appreciation of the importance of the Party must not blind us to the fact that it was only a part, albeit the most visible part, of a new political system. A strength of the Party was its elitism. It motivated important cadres by giving them the conviction that they were more important, better, and therefore more powerful than the average citizen. It is one of the ironies of the Soviet form of communism that it proposed to bring about economic equality by explicitly repudiating political equality and devising a system of extremely refined political distinctions between organizations and citizens. The elitist Party needed mass organizations to function successfully. These were simply the other side of the coin, in some ways as important as the Party itself. The mass organizations carried the message of the Party leadership to the average citizen; they attempted to involve him in political action and to mold his opinions; or, as the Bolsheviks put it at the time, they attempted to bring him political enlightenment. These organizations were the trade unions, the cooperatives, the women's organization, the Zhenotdel, and perhaps most important, the youth organization, the All-Union, Leninist, Communist League of Youth, that is, the Komsomol.

The Komsomol had two major tasks within the Soviet political system: The first was to extend the reach of the Party, acting as a semigovernment agency. At a time when the government structure was weak, and indeed in rural areas hardly existed, it was necessary to find as many ways as possible to link the individual and the policymaking bodies in Moscow. The Komsomol was one of these links. As an agency of mass mobilization, the Komsomol was much like the other mass organizations. The second task of the Komsomol, however, was distinctive: It served as a recruitment agency for the Party. It trained its members in "political literacy," and in the behavior patterns that were expected of a Party member.

Let us first examine the structure and composition of the Komsomol and then consider its effectiveness.

The composition of the Komsomol

To be a mass organization, the Komsomol had to attract the young. The following figures show the increase of membership.[1]

	Members	Candidate members
Oct. 1918	22,000	
Sept. 1919	96,000	
Oct. 1920	482,000	
Oct. 1921	400,000	
Oct. 1922	260,000	13,000
Jan. 1923	284,544	19,400
Jan. 1924	406,660	94,000
Jan. 1925	1,020,456	120,250
Jan. 1926	1,640,107	129,412
Jan. 1927	1,964,312	125,000
Oct. 1927	1,912,435	99,708

(Candidate membership was introduced in 1921 for non-working-class youth.) These figures show a remarkably fast growth in the last year of the Civil War; from September 1919 to October 1920 the organization increased its membership fivefold. The introduction of the NEP caused a precipitous decline. This decline demonstrates that Lenin's switch to a set of moderate economic policies caused confusion and a drop in morale among the activists. In the second half of the decade, however, the growth of the league was impressive; it was at this time that the Komsomol became a mass organization.

Fluctuation in membership of the Komsomol closely paralleled that of the Party. The introduction of the New Economic Policies also almost halved Party membership. The difference was that the youth organization, which was not elitist in its recruitment policies, grew much faster. Whereas in 1921 the size of the Komsomol was about half of that of the Party, at the end of the decade the proportions were reversed.[2]

In spite of its impressive accomplishments, the Komsomol in the 1920s did not involve a large percentage of the youth in its work. It is estimated that in 1922 the number of Komsomol-age young in the Soviet population (between the ages of fourteen and twenty-three) was 25 million. Only 1 percent of these belonged to the youth league. In January 1927 the situation was much better. But even at this time only 2 million out of 29 million, that is, 7.4 percent, belonged.[3]

The 7.4 percent of the youth who belonged to the Komsomol were unevenly distributed in the country; both the gender and class composition was seriously skewed. The percentage of women fluctuated between a low of 15.7 percent in 1924 and a high of 21.3 percent in 1927.[4] The percentages seem particularly low when we remember that as a result of the World War and Civil War more than half the relevant age group was made up of women in the middle of the decade. On the other hand, the Komsomol was more successful than the Party in reflecting the gender composition of the population. Female membership in the Party between 1924 and 1928 grew only from 10 to 13 percent.[5]

There was general agreement among the Party and Komsomol leaders that women should be attracted to political life and that therefore it was essential to increase their membership in mass organizations and in the Komsomol in particular. As far as the optimum social composition of the Komsomol was concerned, the matter was far more complicated. The Komsomol was based on two principles, which, if taken to their ultimate conclusion, were mutually exclusive. One principle was that the Komsomol, as a mass organization, should admit everyone, and therefore its composition should mirror the composition of the population of the Soviet Union. The other principle was that the Komsomol, as a training organization for the Party, must have a proletarian spirit, a proletarian leadership, and therefore a proletarian core membership. Most of the debates that took place in the 1920s concerned the nature of the compromise between the two positions. The recruitment policies of the league vacillated between special efforts made in factories and talk about "facing the village," that is, attracting peasant youth. Komsomol congresses and conferences and the Komsomol literature of the period constantly evaluated the social composition of membership. We have every reason to suspect the figures presented: Individual cells exaggerated working-class membership by every means possible, and in the villages the distinctions drawn between *batrak, bedniak, seredniak,* and kulak (very poor, poor, middle, and rich) were impressionistic and served largely political purposes. The contemporary observer was bombarded by figures showing the constant "improvement" of the social composition of the union.

This built-in ambiguity about the nature of the Komsomol created a fertile ground for the appearance of various "deviations." The earliest of these was the *klassoviki,* which was especially strong in the Ukraine and was therefore often referred to as the Ukrainian deviation. This appeared in 1920–1 and had some ideological ties with the workers' opposition that was making a stand within the Party at the time. The klassoviki wanted a basically proletarian youth league. They had a three-point political program: (1) Create a proletarian majority within the league. (2) Create collectives in factories out of working-class youth in order to involve them in the political struggle. (3) Encourage a deeper involvement of the Komsomol in politics. The Ukrainians wanted to use the purges that were taking place in the Party and in the Komsomol to change the class composition of the league. Their representatives at congresses and conferences constantly called for ever more far-reaching purges.[6] Whether the purges in fact changed the social composition of the organization remained a debated issue between the Ukrainians and the representatives of the Central Committee. An even more extreme version of the "Ukrainian deviation" was presented by Garber, a Komsomol leader from Kazan. He wanted to transform the organization into a league of young Communists.[7]

It is clear that these deviations, like the workers' opposition, presented a threat to the political monopoly of the Party, and as such they could not be tolerated. The Party and Komsomol leaders made sure that the original conception of the Komsomol as a mass organization prevailed and that the youth league did not become an autonomous political center. However, in the matter of class policy, the leadership gave concessions. The First Komsomol Conference in 1921 decided to create candidate membership for non-working-class youth. Workers could enter the Komsomol directly, but non-workers had to remain "candidates" for six months and in addition needed the recommendation of two Komsomol or Party members.[8] (Later this was modified: One Party member could substitute for two Komsomol members.)

In 1924, the Komsomol had to struggle against the opposite deviation. Peasant Komsomol leaders wanted to know why there should be a higher percentage of working-class leaders than members. Some even wanted to transform both the youth league and the Party into worker-peasant organizations and thereby deny "the leading role of the proletariat."[9] Naturally such voices were firmly repudiated. The loyal and therefore successful Communist or Komsomol member had to walk a narrow line.

The consequences of the carefully planned class policies and of the objective circumstances in which the Party and the Komsomol had to operate were that the composition of the Komsomol did not reflect the population as a whole, though it came closer to doing so than the Party. According to admittedly unreliable figures, the proletarian membership of the league fluctuated between a low of 40.6 percent and a high of 43.7 percent (the definition of "worker" also included those who worked on state farms). The peasant membership grew from 40.5 percent in 1924 to 47.5 percent in 1927. The increase was at the expense of the amorphous category of "others."[10] More than half of Komsomol members lived in villages in the 1920s, whereas the percentage of peasants in the Party hovered only between 10 and 13.[11] Given the class composition of the Soviet population, it is obvious from these figures that the Komsomol, not surprisingly, attracted a far larger percentage of city than country youth. More than 40 percent of the factory youth belonged to the league, whereas only approximately 6 to 7 percent of their peasant compatriots did.[12]

Like all institutions of Soviet power, the Komsomol was strongest in the cities. The league was most successful in organizing young workers in the largest enterprises of the country. By and large it did better in industrial centers like Petrograd than in, for example, the Volga cities.

The Komsomol was the strongest where it was least needed by the Party, in industrial regions and especially in the largest factories. The league became a competitor of the trade unions. The Party leadership in the Dunaevskii controversy in 1920 explicitly forbade the Komsomol to organize youth sections within the trade unions, so that the Komsomol would not become a defender of the special interests of the young workers. Nevertheless, given conditions in the early 1920s, it was inevitable that it came to perform union functions. Perhaps no other segment of the population suffered as much as the working-class young from the economic changes produced by the NEP. The directors of factories for the first time had to produce for profit. A natural consequence was the firing of superfluous workers. The regulations protecting young workers that had been introduced by the new socialist state were extremely generous. Now the factory management had a great incentive to fire first the young who were less productive and and cost more. Unemployment in general, and among the youth in particular, became a major issue. How unevenly the young were hurt is shown by the decrease from 9.4 to 3.6 percent in the proportion of Komsomol-age trade-union members.[13] The regime could not ameliorate the problem. In 1923 there were 60,000 Komsomol-age unemployed, and this figure rose to 127,000 by 1925.[14] Interestingly, it was the largest factories that fired the inexperienced workers most often, and the situation from the point of view of the young remained best in private industry.[15]

Had the Komsomol remained indifferent to the plight of its members, it would have lost all credibility. The Central Committee devoted most of its attention to the issue of unemployment and soon was being blamed for neglecting political-education work in congress after congress.[16]

The Central Committee of the Komsomol recommended that a certain percentage of the labor force be made up of young workers. This recom-

Plate 11. N. K. Krupskaia and A. V. Lunacharskii at a meeting of the Central Committee Plenum of the Komsomol in 1925.

mendation was not accepted by the trade unions and not supported by the Party and government leadership. Under the circumstances, the youth league could offer only palliatives: It sponsored the establishment of a few trade schools where adolescents could become skilled workers.[17] The hard times led to friction between the Komsomol and the trade unions. Komsomol leader P. Smorodin complained to the fifth congress of his organization that the trade unions were fighting the Komsomol on every issue.[18]

The great drop in Komsomol membership reflected disillusionment, and those working-class activists who stayed in the organization suffered a decline in morale. Many consoled themselves that the New Economic Policies would last for only a few months. A Tula activist put it this way in the spring of 1921: "No matter. In the fall we collect the agricultural tax in kind, then we throw out the new economic policies, hit the specs [specialists] over the head, and then will start a second, a third, and a fourth revolution."[19] The Komsomol leadership, however, had to dispel such illusions.

In the villages the situation was different. Here many youths left the league when the New Economic Policies were introduced because the new economic environment opened up opportunities they thought inconsistent with Communist goals.

However, the drop was only temporary. In the course of the 1920s the Soviet regime scored a major success in building a network of Komsomol cells around the country. These cells truly extended the reach of the Party. There were three-and-a-half times as many Komsomol members in the villages as Communists.[20] In thousands of villages the Komsomol alone represented the new Soviet order. The Party could not easily expand its peasant membership, for there simply were not enough people in the countryside who were well enough educated and loyal to the government. It was different for the youth organization. The regime could take chances; the misbehavior of a young Komsomolite did not cause as much damage as a scandal involving a peasant Communist. Further, although most of the village Party members were aliens who had been sent from the city, the members of the youth organizations were local boys and girls. Although the overwhelming majority of the Communists in the villages carried out some kind of administrative function, which set them apart from their fellow villagers, the Komsomolites were engaged in the same work as everyone else.[21] The Russian village in the 1920s was remarkably untouched by the new social and political order. The Komsomol by its very presence, activities, and campaigns did make a difference.

The Komsomol had to tolerate a lower level of discipline in the villages than in the cities. Much of the organization in the villages existed only on paper. Thousands of members never turned up for a meeting and did not pay their dues. The Russians called them "dead souls." In the early 1920s the Komsomol suffered from very high turnover, which was particularly widespread in the villages. Peasant members were most often excluded for disorderly behavior, habitual drunkenness, and gross violation of discipline.[22] It would be of course naive to imagine that the young people who joined the organization immediately changed their way of life. Furthermore, during the NEP many ambitious people realized that they would do better by engaging in commerce by hiring workers, and so forth, that is, by doing activities that were unsuitable for a Communist; they therefore voluntarily withdrew from the Komsomol.

Many young peasants became acquainted with the Komsomol while serving in the army. The Komsomol had a role to play in strengthening the armed forces. The league carried out campaigns to make sure that the draftees in fact turned up at recruitment points and helped these men by giving them information about army life. At the end of the decade one quarter of the soldiers belonged to the youth organization.[23]

The league had a special relationship with the Red Fleet. The traumatic experience of the Kronstadt rising impelled the Party leadership to take measures to assure the loyalty and ideological orthodoxy of the sailors. The Komsomol was ready to help. At its fifth congress it assumed "protection" over the fleet. This agitational method, "protection," meant that the league assumed a particular responsibility for the indoctrination of young sailors. The Komsomol held hundreds of meetings popularizing the navy, gave presents to individual naval units, provided them with political libraries, and sent an unusually large contingent into the navy. By the middle of the decade, 40 percent of the sailors belonged to the youth organization.[24] The difference between the percentages of Komsomol members in the army and navy, however, was largely because the navy drew a larger percentage of its recruits from cities than the army did.[25]

Remarkably, in spite of all the work the Komsomol did for the armed forces (such as collecting money for the construction of airplanes, participating in establishing a Society of Friends of the Navy, doing political-education work among the draftees, etc.), it was not allowed to have cells in military units. One suspects that the experience of the Revolution and the Civil War taught the Bolsheviks that the existence of even nominally autonomous organizations among soldiers and sailors was harmful for discipline. The Komsomol leadership in vain petitioned for such a privilege. In 1925, however, the Party gave a concession.[26] It still did not allow the formation of cells such as existed in factories, villages, and schools, but it created "Komsomol groups for assistance to the Party." These groups coordinated the agitational work of individual members but had no right to elect their own leaders or to accept new members. The ban on Komsomol cells shows how concerned the Party was to protect discipline within the Army and how jealously it guarded its political monopoly. The armed forces were simply too important to allow Komsomol interference even in matters of detail.

If the first raison d'être of the Komsomol was to enable the Party to penetrate segments of the population that otherwise might have been closed to it, its second was to train a new generation of Communists. An agitational pamphlet entitled "Duties of a Komsomolite" (published in 1924), which was organized in catechism form, posed this question first: "Why do people enter the Komsomol?" After showing the "fallacy" of other answers, it gave the correct one: "The working youth join the Komsomol in order to learn how to become worthwhile members of the Russian Communist Party."[27] This preparatory function of the Komsomol was always regarded as the crucial one by the leaders of the Party.

The Komsomol acted as a halfway house between ordinary citizens and Party members. Those who had political ambitions could show their dedication, loyalty, and talent by joining the youth league and performing well. Working-class and peasant youth evidently understood that the Komsomol was an excellent avenue for social mobility. Ironically, this "working-class organization" was a great help in contributing to the escape of working-class boys and girls from working-class status.[28] More than half the proletarian youth who joined the Party through the Komsomol and two-thirds of the peasants of this category left work in the factories and fields and accepted Soviet, trade-union, Party or Komsomol responsibilities.[29]

A large percentage of Party members went through the Komsomol experience. In 1928 there were 400,000 Communists; that is, one-fourth of all Party members had belonged to the Komsomol.[30] A third of the new Party members in the late twenties joined through the youth league. In the armed forces, made up of young men, more than three-quarters were Komsomol members.[31] In the villages, too, the Komsomol was by far the most important source of new members.[32] Anyone under twenty could enter the Party only through the Komsomol, aside from distant and rare areas where there was a Party cell but no Komsomol cell. The Fourth Congress of the Komsomol decided that a worker youth who belonged to the organization for half a year could apply for Party membership, whereas others had to wait for a full year.[33]

The consequence of entering the Party through the Komsomol was dual membership. In the course of the decade, approximately one-tenth of Komsomol members also belonged to the Party; in the armed forces the proportion was one-third.[34] This dual membership enabled the Party to supervise the youth league. Although only a tenth of the members of the organization were card-carrying Communists, the leadership was in the hands of these people. Delegates to congresses were almost exclusively Party members.[35] It is evident that this 10 percent made up an elite and formed the nerve center of the league. Playing politics within the Komsomol prepared them for careers within the more important political body, the Party.

The relationship between the Party and the Komsomol was at the center of the debates in the 1920s concerning the appropriate age group for league membership. Those who wanted the organization to play an active political role would have liked to exclude those under sixteen. Those who wanted to prevent the Komsomol from functioning as a rival political organization proposed to lower the upper age limit to eighteen. Riazanov, for example, made this suggestion at the Tenth Party Congress.[36] But for the Komsomol to be exactly what the Party wanted, it had to have the age group fourteen to twenty-three.

An organization created for the politically active youth was bound to face the problem of what to do with members when they reached the upper age limit. There was no problem for those who joined the Party for that organization provided suitable arenas for activity. In the cities the solution was relatively simple. The ex-Komsomol member who wanted to engage in social and political work could do so through the trade unions or through a variety of other bodies. In the villages, however, where often there was no Soviet institution but the Komsomol, the problem was serious. The average

age of the membership constantly rose. In 1922 there were only 1.8 percent within the organization older than twenty-three. By 1927 the figure was 16.4 percent.[37] The Komsomol in the 1920s could find no solution to this problem and therefore faced the ridiculous spectacle of middle-aged men and women who continued to belong to the Communist youth organization. Carelessness in the Party leadership often made the situation worse: The local Communist cell on occasion sent out for Komsomol work middle-aged people, sometimes as old as fifty-five.

The close relationship between the Party and the Komsomol inevitably meant that the League became involved – though never in a decisive way – in the ideological disputes and power struggle that took place in the 1920s. Debates within it merely reflected Party disputes. The support of the organization for one or another leader was not such as to make a major difference. Nevertheless, the struggle against the opposition did take up a considerable part of the energies of the league's leadership, and the nature of the factional fight contributed to the shaping of the youth organization.

In the 1920s in the Komsomol the Trotskyist opposition was the most significant. The charismatic ex–commissar of war had a large following among the Communist youth. His utopian-heroic vision of the future society was particularly attractive to those young people who indentified themselves with the new regime. Students and working-class youth found Trotsky's denunciation of the bureaucratization of the Party and the state congenial.

Given the nature of the Soviet political system in general and Party–Komsomol relations in particular, it is not surprising that the battle for leadership was quickly over. After a brief but sharp struggle in late 1923 and early 1924, the dominant majority of the Party's Central Committee imposed its views on the Komsomol leadership. Those who were sympathetic to Trotsky's position at this point hoped to retreat into neutrality, using the argument that the youth organization should not participate in factional struggles. The victors, however, did not accept such a halfhearted concession. The Central Committee of the Komsomol in January 1924 was compelled to denounce neutrality. Only two members of the committee refused to join in.[38]

After the rout of the Trotskyists in the leadership, the followers of Bukharin were dominant. Their power depended almost entirely on the position of their mentor and Bukharin's political demise was accompanied by his supporters' removal from the Komsomol leadership.

It was far harder to eliminate Trotskyist influence among the rank and file. In some local units, notably in Moscow, in the Urals, and in Armenia, semisecret Trotskyist centers continued to operate for some time.[39] But whether it was necessary or not, the Party conducted a mass indoctrination effort in the late 1920s against Trotskyism. The anti-Trotsky ideological campaign became a training ground for Party activists. Proper Communist methods of argumentation and a particular approach to the social world were conveyed in the course of this factional struggle.

The Komsomol in the Villages

More than once in Soviet history, ambition grew out of weakness. The weaker the regime was, the more its leaders were attracted to far-reaching, utopian solutions. In the 1920s when the people suffered from famine, when the majority of the peasants remained untutored, when the Party had hardly established a presence in the countryside, the regime wanted the Komsomol to help in economic reconstruction, to win over the uncommitted, and to participate in the giant project of creating "the new socialist man."

It is hardly surprising that there was a large gap between ambitions and reality. It is easy to demonstrate that the plans failed. It would be an error, however, to dismiss the agitational projects as without substance. First of all, the presence of the Komsomol, above all in the villages but also (even if perhaps to a lesser extent) in the cities, did make a difference. Second, the plans and projects betrayed the mentality of their creators, which must be understood for an analysis of the twists and turns of Soviet history.

The Komsomol had two tasks: to extend the reach of the Party and to train a new generation of Party members. As far as indoctrination work was concerned, the two tasks implied a duality of effort: The Party used the Komsomol to reach as many people as possible with its message, and the Komsomol trained its members in "political literacy" and instilled in them a desirable political behavior pattern. This separation, admittedly, is somewhat artificial. In reality the two types of work were often indistinguishable. While the Komsomol member agitated for the Party's newest policies, he also acquired a political education himself.

This section concentrates on the work of Komsomol cells in the villages. Here, as often the only instrument of Party indoctrination, the Komsomol provided the most valuable service.

The Komsomol started its work in the NEP period under the most inauspicious circumstances. The Party's volte-face meant not only a great reduction in the size of the organization but also a crisis of faith among the activists. It is easy to understand why the young enthusiasts, carried away by the Revolution's utopian promise, found the sober world of the early 1920s disillusioning. In village after village, the cells continued to exist only on paper or disappeared altogether.[40]

The spirit of capitalism was alive in cities and in villages, and that spirit was about to infest the young and impressionable peasants. In a major speech to the Fifth Komsomol Congress in 1922, Bukharin admitted this danger. He spoke of the NEP as something necessary because it would raise the standard of living of the people, but he described the new policies as a source of ideological weakness and confusion. The young saw millions starving and stores full of everything, including luxuries. Such a situation was fertile ground for the spread of antisocialist ideas. Bukharin could suggest only an intensification of the ideological struggle in order to prevent the spread of inner decay.[41]

Was the Komsomol equal to such a task? Many thought not. Riazanov, for example, speaking in March 1921 to the Tenth Party Congress, spoke in the most pessimistic terms. He said that during his numerous visits to factories he saw no evidence of Komsomol work. The leaders were cut off from the membership, and decisions were made in a vacuum and had little relation to reality. Everyone knew that the situation in the country-side was a great deal worse. Riazanov went so far as to suggest the abolition of the Komsomol in its present form. He recommended that the eighteen-to-twenty-three year group be freed from "childish" Komsomol work. The infusion of young blood then would benefit the Party, and the unnecessary duplication would cease.[42] This was an extreme suggestion, born out of desperation at a difficult moment, and Riazanov found no support for his idea among the Party's leaders. Nevertheless, that such a suggestion was made showed the depth of the crisis and the weakness of the Komsomol.

Only slowly did the Komsomol learn to function under the new circumstances. By 1924 the Komsomol once again had a presence in the villages and was ready to assume the tasks the Party had assigned. These tasks were: (1) political education; (2) agricultural propaganda; and (3) struggle for the new way of life and against the survival of the old, which primarily meant struggle against religion.

The notion of political education was remarkably broad. It included studying the classics of Marxism-Leninism (of which presumably there was very little), agitating for every shift in government and Party policies, and participating in campaigns and celebrations. That type of "politcal educa-tion" was ever present. In the villages it was also carried out by other Party organizations and reading huts. Naturally, each used more or less the same principles, worked on the same level of sophistication, and employed the same methods. The large-scale affairs, the celebrations of anniversaries, and the election campaigns were cooperative ventures.

The heart of the Komsomol's political-education system was the "politi-cal reading," the *politchitka*. The cell gathered, usually under the direction of the secretary, and read some political material. The reading was followed by discussions.[43] The intellectual level of the discussions varied, and natur-ally it was much higher in the cities than in the countryside. Some of the cells separated the politically more advanced, but activists complained that this method deprived the politically illiterate from the company of their more advanced comrades and therefore caused more harm than good. By the middle of the decade, thousands of reading circles existed in the coun-try, at least on paper. In 1925 the Komsomol reported that 60 percent of its cells conducted such political readings.[44]

The selection of the reading material was haphazard. Some cells read books, others newspapers. Especially in the early 1920s, the villages were poorly supplied with political literature, and even the distribution of news-papers was far from satisfactory. The cells were also hampered by a lack of money. From the beginning of the NEP, each had to get by on its own financial resources. They collected dues from the membership, and in some instances they cultivated a bit of land and sold the produce to create a "cultural fund." Petr Smorodin, the secretary of the Central Committee, complained to the Fifth Congress: "About the Marxist library – the issue is resolved simply: We request the provincial committees to send us money and say, in an NEP-like fashion [po NEPovski], Put the money on the table. Aside from the Kharkov committee, not a single one sent us money."[45]

A greater problem than the unavailability of proper reading material was the continuing shortage of qualified leaders. The Party did not possess enough reasonably educated young people to take on this work. The Komsomol sent thousands to sovpartshkoly, and as time went on the situation improved somewhat. Nevertheless it was not easy to provide the entire enormous country with competent political educators. Contemporary reports show that some of the leaders exhibited a rather charming naivete. One, for example, started his talk about Lenin's life this way: "Lenin was a peasant, just like we are; he ploughed the land, he fished, and all this time he was thinking: How to help the workers?"[46] Clearly, in most of the circles the political reading was a painful exercise: The reader read his material haltingly, and a forced and boring discussion session followed.

The Party and Komsomol leaderships were interested above all in numbers. The cell reported to the volost' committee, the volost' to the uezd and the uezd to the province about how many people came, what they read, and how often they met. Each agency wanted to show good work by reporting as high numbers as possible. Consequently, cells went through the motions, however low the intellectual level. The Party and the Central Committee of the Komsomol were well aware of the problems. Contemporary sources were full of admissions of failure.[47] The Komsomol leadership attempted to improve matters by various means. The newspapers for the peasants, *Derevenskaia Pravda* (Village truth) and *Komsomolskaia Pravda* (Komsomol truth), included selections in their columns aimed at politchitka audiences. The Central Committee believed that the work could be improved by closer supervision. It instructed the provincial and uezd organizations to check on the protocols of cells and to send out representatives to the villages to see for themselves how the work was progressing. It also recommended closer cooperation with the Party organizations in the field of political education, in view of the lack of trained personnel. It is unlikely that such steps helped much. The political reading was inherently boring. Only unusually charismatic and intelligent leaders could overcome this basic problem, and they were in short supply.

However, it would be naive to conclude that, just because the intellectual level of the political reading sessions was low and because the sessions were often painfully boring, political education was without effect. The peasant boys and girls did not become trained Marxists, but they did learn a certain mode of thinking, a verbiage, and a certain attitude toward political issues. Those who understood almost nothing regarded the endlessly repeated phrases as magic incantations, powerful, unchallengeable. They acquired, too, perhaps not as their intellectual betters intended, a training in how to be citizens of the Soviet Union.

The politchitka was perhaps the heart of political education, but the system was by no means limited to readings. Indeed, the primary characteristic of the political-indoctrination work was that it was ever present. The Komsomol was quite imaginative in introducing political topics in every daily activity. In the normal course of life, young people would meet one another to drink, play, sing, and enjoy themselves. The Komsomol was determined to bring such occasions under its control to the extent possible. The Smolensk Provincial Committee, for example, sent instructions to the activists about how to behave at parties. The instructions show how determined the Komsomol was to influence every aspect of youth activities and how manipulative the Communist regime already was in the 1920s; no detail was too small to escape the attention of Party and Komsomol organs.[48]

First, the Smolensk Committee's instructions described in dark colors the traditional amusements of youth: At parties they drink, carry out practical jokes on each other, dance, and play cards. "Above all, the Komsomol cell must declare war on such activities in the localities. The first task of the Komsomol cell is to assure the influence of the cell over the youth at these parties." To maintain contact with the youth, the Komsomolites were instructed to attend parties. They must not appear to form a sect on such occasions. At the party it is advisable to gain the support of those elements who visibly have the greatest influence. For example, at parties the musician is a most important figure and therefore it is essential to win him over. The document betrayed ambivalence on the subject of dancing, which took up most of the time at parties. Since at least for the time being there can be no comparable amusement, the Komsomol member must not reject dancing in principle, for that would lead to undermining Komsomol influence. He may dance, but must not overdo it. The Komsomol member must also fight against practical jokes, against drunkenness, and against card games. "One of the best means which has been used anywhere is the use of women in this struggle, for women do not like such things. It is only necessary to suggest to her that she should reject a drunkard, and already much has been accomplished."

The next step for the Komsomol was to organize its own parties, "Red parties." The head of the political-education section of the Smolensk Committee instructed the uezd and volost' committes on how to organize these parties.[49] "If it is at all possible, it is necessary to organize Red evenings, which should be just as lively as the old-fashioned ones. There should be dances, new songs, games, and so forth. The Komsomol should invite to the party all non-Party youth." The head of the political-education department also recommended reading aloud humorous journals at the parties. At a meeting, uezd leaders decided that the best way to attract young women to the organization was to set up knitting and sewing circles that could be combined with the discussion of political topics.[50]

The Bolshevik leaders observed a simple principle: All available methods of indoctrination should be used. None was too trivial. Although Communist doctrine was rational, hence the emphasis on reading and the study of texts, the activists did not disdain the appeal to emotions. Bukharin recommended organizing marches and torchlight parades. He confessed to a Komsomol congress that while in prison he had often dreamt of military music and he was overcome with emotion every time he participated in a march, feeling "one with the masses." He also saw the benefit of putting slogans on the wall. As did many others later, he drew a parallel between political slogans and the use of advertisements. Communist leaders had high regard for capitalist efficiency and rightly believed that the capitalists knew what they were doing and were not wasting their money.[51]

In the 1920s parades on the anniversary of the Revolution and on May Day became regular occasions. Feeling one with the masses, as Bukharin had explained, was a powerful agitational tool. In those pre-Nazi days no Bolshevik leader found anything distasteful about the emotional appeal of torchlight parades. Such occasions became the stock and trade of all mass movements, and Bolshevism was no exception.

The Soviet leaders well understood, however, that political education and enthusiasm for the cause of socialism were not enough. The Soviet people wanted to see the benefit of the Revolution in material terms; they wanted to live better. As a result, the Party drew no sharp distinction between political and economic tasks. Unlike many tsarist ministers, the Bolsheviks had a clear conception of Russian backwardness and were determined to overcome it. Because the Party's strength in the villages was still meager, it turned to the Komsomol for help in transforming village life. The Party assigned three tasks: (1) to teach the peasants modern methods of agriculture; (2) to help the poor peasants against the rich in order to acquire a class basis; and (3) to agitate for the socialist form of agriculture, for the collective farms.

In view of the extremely limited success of the collective-farm movement in the 1920s, we may assume that Komsomol propaganda made no perceptible difference. To help the poor against the rich in practice meant that Komsomol cells attempted to influence village Soviet elections to assure a better representation for the landless and for those who had only small holdings. Komsomol activists also organized mutual-help societies for the poor. By far the most important work of the Komsomol, however, was spreading agricultural information among the peasantry.

This is what the Thirteenth Congress said about the tasks of the Komsomol in the villages in May 1924:

The work of the Komsomol organizations in the village should develop from administrative work and from pure "cultural" work [*kulturnichestvo*] into active participation in all aspects of village life, above all in cultural life (participation in the fight against illiteracy; setting up information bureaus, reading huts, and peasant schools) and social and economic work, which can give help to the peasants in the most readily understood forms, and which are beneficial to them (repairing bridges and firefighting equipment, doing the most elementary forms of social work, and carrying out propaganda by example in improving the level of agriculture, etc.).[52]

The Fourteenth Congress, in December 1925, returned to the same themes:

In the area of village work it is decisively important for the Komsomol to participate in the building of new, progressive forms of agriculture, in the struggle against ignorance and poverty on the one hand and in the struggle against capitalist tendencies on the other. The Komsomol should develop and strengthen agricultural study circles, schools of peasant youth, and courses for adults, and participate in the work of these schools and circles in alliance with the agronomist, the teacher, and the culturally and technically enlightened peasant. The League of Youth will show initiative in participating in the cultural and economic transformation and at the same time in propagandizing the organizing cooperative unification.[53]

In conrete terms, agricultural propaganda meant, once again, setting up reading circles. Given the Russian peasants' low level of scientific knowledge and the general backwardness of agriculture, any increase in knowledge brought about by the Komsomol-sponsored reading circles had to bring improvements. However, there were obstacles to achieving meaningful results. The Komsomol often had little prestige in the eyes of the peasants, and consequently few chose to participate in this free education course. The booklets prepared by the authorities for these courses had little to do with the peculiarities of the district where they were read, and there was rarely any close connection between what the peasants read and their practical problems. Most of the peasants, and especially the poorest ones, were not in a position to take advantage of what they had learned.[54]

The Komsomol leadership recognized that theoretical learning would not make a great impression on the peasants. It considered a better way to agitate by example. Therefore in the mid-1920s the Komsomol undertook a rather utopian campaign. According to Komsomol statistics, 10,000 members were heads of households and independent farmers. The Komsomol encouraged these people to embark on scientific agriculture with the aid of agronomists, hoping they would achieve such impressive results as to gain the admiration of the other villagers. It is unlikely that this well-intentioned campaign had much influence. The odds were against the 10,000 poor and young people, scattered and undirected, making such a spectacular success of their small farms as to encourage the rest of the Russian peasantry to experiment with scientific agriculture.[55]

The third task that the Party assigned to the Komsomol was the "struggle against the survivals of the past." Under this heading, the Communists insultingly combined the laudable work against illiteracy and drunkenness with the fight against religion.

The Russian Orthodox Church and the Bolshevik Party were hostile from the outset. Although from the moment of the November Revolution the Bolshevik leadership looked on the church as an irreconcilable enemy, Lenin and his comrades understood that a frontal attack would backfire and counseled patience and tact to their followers. As one would expect under the conditions of civil war, such advice was not often heeded. Even after the armed struggle ended, outrages against churchmen did not cease. In the campaign against religion the Komsomol had a major part, and this organization was guilty of the worst offenses.

In 1922 the Komsomol carried out a large-scale anti-Christmas campaign. Local organizations put on mass carnivals that coincided with the festive season, in which they used the most vulgar satire to ridicule religion.[56] On this and other occasions, Komsomol members disrupted services by singing the International or by marching to the church and singing with the accompaniment of harmonica such ditties: "Down with the priests, down with the monks. We will climb to heaven and chase away the Gods." It was increasingly evident that such tactics were harmful both to the Komsomol and to the Soviet regime.

The increasing recognition of the danger of crude attacks on religion, and in particular the fiasco of the Christmas campaign, coincided with a major debate on the proper methods of fighting religion. Activists expressed three points of view.[57] The left argued that religion was a class phenomenon and that agitation should be directed toward exposing the reactionary nature of the church. The leftists were willing to use satire and did not reject coercive means. By contrast, the right, the least numerous and politically significant faction, argued that religion would wither away by itself and that no special effort was needed. The Party ultimately endorsed the middle position of E. M. Iaroslavskii, the chief organizer and theoretician of the atheist propaganda. According to Iaroslavskii, circumstances demanded a long-term policy of scientific education. He argued that it was not enough to oppose the religious world view; the agitator must provide another, a truly materialist and scientific one.

In the first half of the 1920s both Iaroslavskii's and the left's views influenced the work of the Komsomol. The situation changed only in 1926 when the Party officially repudiated the position of the leftists.[58] However, after the unfortunate experiences of the 1922 Christmas campaign, the Komsomol Central Committee was determined to exercise greater control and issued detailed instructions. No detail was considered too insignificant to be left to local initiative.

The Central Committee called for the organization of a long-term campaign, in which a variety of agitational methods had to be used.[59] The heart of the education was to be a lecture series devoted to scientific topics, such as the creation of the universe and the development of human beings. The lecturers were to point out at every turn that the findings of modern science contradicted the teachings of the Bible. Very importantly, the lectures had to be accompanied by slides that were thought to influence an uneducated audience and be followed by a question-and-answer period. It was this open discussion that in the opinion of the organizers won over the uncommitted.

In addition to the lecture series, the cells were instructed to organize atheist reading circles, exhibitions of material that unmasked the church, and "anti-religious evenings." These evenings combined entertainment with atheist indoctrination. According to the instructions, careful planning of the evenings was essential. This task fell on the antireligious and natural-science circles of the Komsomol cell.[60] The instructions described a model evening in the Easter season.

The evening opened with a short lecture on the subject of religious and proletarian holidays. The lecturer pointed out that religious holidays were times of doing nothing and drinking. The main lecture was on the subject of faith and knowledge. The lecturer spoke about the mythology of Easter. The activists had the task of drawing out the audience through the collective singing and shouting of slogans. Then came the obligatory question-and-answer period. The "serious" part of the evening was followed by entertainment in which passages from the Bible were satirized in the form of dramatic sketches. The evening concluded with games. These instructions from the central organs went so far as to suggest words for charades.[61] The word, rabbi (ra-vin) was to be played out this way: "first syllable: Ra – Egyptian God standing on a dais. A procession walks by headed by a priest. The procession brings a young girl as sacrifice. 'Oh, Great God, Ra,' exclaims the priest, 'we brought you a sacrifice. May the blood of the young maid expiate our sins.' They all dance around their God. Second syllable: vin (wine). The table is covered with bottles. Behind the table sit a priest and a rabbi. They clink their glasses. They drink until they fall under the table snoring. During the scene they shout several times: How much vodka? How much wine? A Jewish woman goes up to the rabbi asking him to give her something that will take away her son from the Komsomol. The rabbi gives her an enormous amulet that includes a hair from Moses' beard. 'I, a rabbi, the representative of God, will now make a miracle.' " According to the instructions, the evening was not to last longer than three and a half or four hours.

Atheist propaganda created great hostility. Without doubt it alienated many peasants, especially among the older generation. Peasants were often tempted to take forceful measures against what they considered sacrilegious Komsomol activities, but they were restrained by fear of retribution from the representatives of Soviet power. Clearly, the Komsomol's failure to attract a large female membership had at least something to do with the commitment to religion of the young women. In many households the young Komsomol member's attempt to remove icons, which he was encouraged to do by his cell, led to family troubles. Peasant parents often forbade their children to join the Komsomol because they objected to the Komsomol's attack on the church.

One cannot but wonder why, under the circumstances, the regime persisted. Naturally, the church and the Party could not be allies. Whatever the Party did, the church was bound to be hostile, and a materialist, Marxist ideology predisposed the Communists to look on churchmen as their enemies. Nevertheless, it was not essential to conduct an active campaign. The Communists might have accepted the advice of the rightists and waited for the withering away of religion. The argument that contemporary activists gave, namely that it was necessary to fight the church because the church supported the kulaks, can be dismissed. Whatever threat the kulaks may have represented to Soviet power was unrelated to active church involvement. The Bolsheviks fought against religion with great determination, because their God was a jealous God; it tolerated no other. Religion presented an alternate world view. The Bolsheviks could not allow the existence of an area of life over which they had no control.

The school for communism

It is always hard to evaluate the effect of propaganda, and it is even more difficult to see how a propagandist changes in the process of carrying out his work. Nevertheless it is evident that a change occurs on a large scale. Soviet publicists have been correct when they described the Komsomol as a school for communism. In it the young people learned to be proper Soviet citizens and learned how to function effectively within their peculiar political system.

Joining the organization was the first formative step. In the large factories, where the great majority of the young workers signed up, receiving a membership card perhaps did not have much significance. In the villages, however, where only a small minority of the young joined the league, choosing to belong implied a commitment. In their own eyes and in the eyes of their fellow villagers, the young people now decided to side openly with the new political and social order.

Why did people join? Obviously different people did so for different reasons, and most had a combination of motives, conscious and unconscious. There is no question that the young were genuinely attracted to what the Komsomol stood for: a promise of a new way of life. The desire among the literate to escape their parents' way of life was widespread even in prerevolutionary Russia. The Soviet regime, unlike the one that preceded it, promised concrete ways to escape. In the mid-1920s in one of the purely agricultural districts of Voronezh province the Komsomol carried out a survey among its members. Of the sample, 85 percent came from peasant families, but only 3 percent indicated that they wanted to work in agriculture in the future.[62] When the Komsomol attacked the traditional village, it obviously found eager listeners.

A second appeal of the Komsomol was closely connected to the first. The league took the side of the young against the old in the generational conflict. The very fact that many parents opposed what the Komsomol stood for must have encouraged some people to join. The Komsomol leadership, of course, was well aware of the generational conflict, and it explicitly encouraged adolescents to oppose their parents. The youth league gave a sense of belonging. The occasional voluntary work on Saturdays, the subbotniki, instead of being a burden for many young people, gave a joyous sense of working together in a common cause.[63] The political lessons, which had to be tedious for most, nevertheless appealed to the young enthusiasts because they were "serious" lessons. It seemed an adult occupation to talk about large social and political issues, even though these discussions were routinized and even though on occasion the young only half understood what was being said.

Opportunism and idealism were not mutually exclusive. Those who realized that joining the Komsomol would advance their careers were just as likely to believe in the promise of a better future as those who were disinterested. It must have been evident that in the villages the road to the Party led through the Komsomol and that there was no better way of escaping the drudgery of village life and heavy agricultural labor than through Party membership. Many in the 1920s joined the Komsomol in the same way that in America a young businessman would join the junior chamber of commerce.

When discussing why people joined the Youth League, we must keep in mind that the regime planned carefully to eliminate all possible alternatives. By the mid-1920s it had achieved a monopoly of organized social life, and it guarded this monopoly carefully. The regime destroyed the scout organization and the organization for Jewish youth. Then it moved against sports clubs. The Central Committee of the Communist Party in July 1925 passed a resolution that shows clearly that the leaders of the Party acted consciously to prevent the appearance of any competition. The resolution said: "Physical education should be an inseparable part of the social-political upbringing and education plan of the relevant social and state organizations and establishments (Trade Unions, Komsomol, Red Army, schools, organs of health-care system, etc.). Therefore physical education should not be separate in an organizational way in some sort of independent sport-health unit, which would inevitably lead to a separation from the basic political-education work and a rift between those who engage in physical culture and basic social organizations."[64] Those who craved some kind of social activity in the village could find only one outlet, the Komsomol. When a young person saw that his friends were joining the league he also felt impelled to do so.

For most people who joined the Komsomol, the act itself did not mean a major change in life style. Those who liked to drink continued to do so. Contemporary reports were full of complaints about disorderly behavior and drunkenness.[65] Many attended meetings only irregularly. It would often happen, for example, that young women when they got married simply allowed their membership to lapse.[66]

There were, however, a few activists for whom Komsomol work meant everything, and attendant political activities filled their lives. The Soviet regime had ambitious goals for remaking society, but it could count on only a small number of cadres. The regime created meaningless organizations, it celebrated empty, political holidays, and it initiated numberless campaigns, all in the hope of involving people in politics. Although the majority of peasants remained aloof, those who were ambitious, or who were simply responsible activists, always had a great deal to do. There were too many meetings, too many schools of political education to attend. N. Bocharov, who wrote his brief reminiscences after emigrating, vividly describes his life in the Komsomol in the early 1920s.[67] He joined the youth league with great enthusiasm and soon achieved prominence in it. At age seventeen, in recognition of his good work, he was made chairman of the local soviet. His authority spread over eight villages. He also became a member of the district soviet and at the same time remained responsible for Komsomol work. Not surprisingly, the young man in two years felt so overburdened that he petitioned to be relieved. When his request was not granted, he saw no solution but escape. He joined his relatives in Leningrad and thus ended his political career.

Bocharov's case was not an isolated one. The Party's Central Committee was aware of the problem of overburdening activists. In April 1925 it passed a resolution that Komsomol meetings should not exceed a prearranged maximum and that the Komsomol-sponsored political schools should limit their requirements.[68] It further advised the activists to engage in sports to protect and improve their health, which was endangered by overwork. However, the substance of the problem remained untouched: The regime wanted to do too much with the help of too few. The pressure on the ambitious or conscientious person remained.

It was perhaps the activists alone who took seriously the Komsomol's message concerning the ethics of everyday life. In the 1920s there was much talk about Communist morality. Party leaders and publicists in newspapers and speeches discussed how human beings should relate to each other. It was generally agreed that a new set of rules would be necessary. For the outside observer it is hard to see the element of novelty. The Komsomol attempted to inculcate in its members conservative good manners and conformity. Aside from the major exceptions of the

THE BIRTH OF THE PROPAGANDA STATE

attack on the authority of the family and of the church, peasant parents could have found nothing objectionable in the overt ethical teachings of the Komsomol.

It is perhaps ironic that revolutionaries who aimed to destroy the old world and construct a new one worried so much about good manners, punctuality, avoiding bad language, and so forth. But it could hardly have been otherwise. The regime needed hard, steady, and obedient workers who were able to get along with one another and who were, above all, willing to participate in a movement. Movements and mass organizations are bound to be conformist. The prominent figures of the regime well understood that the time for revolutionary acts had passed. Bukharin in his talk to the Fifth Komsomol Congress made it clear that since the Revolution was over, behavior desirable in those heroic days was inappropriate during the period of the NEP. He called for the establishment of new norms. He preferred to talk about norms, rather than about "Communist morality" because such a phrase sounded fetishistic to him, and because morality implied to him behavior whose rules could not be rationally established. However, he was only quibbling; In practice there was little difference. He used an interesting parallel. He described the present protest against norms as similar to asking for committeees in the army. What was proper for 1917 was clearly undesirable in a "workers' state."[69]

The genius of the regime was to ask for conservative, conformist social behavior and to justify it with revolutionary phraseology. Those who demanded a thorough "liberation" of the individual, whatever such a utopian demand may have meant under the harsh conditions of the 1920s, could not appeal to a revolutionary heritage. That heritage was the property of the existing system, which jealously guarded it. The individualists and the social malcontents were thus deprived of their traditions and natural ideology of rebellion.

Creating "a new, socialist man," establishing "communist morality," that is, teaching human beings how to deal with one another, was a difficult task, and we may assume that the Komsomol had only limited success. The youth league undoubtedly did better in conveying political instructions and in teaching its members how to function within the existing political system. The primary message was the importance of the collective and the necessity of obedience. A pamphlet entitled *The Duties of the Komsomol Member*, published in 1924, maintained: "Komsomol discipline and Komsomol obligations are the most important of all."[70] The writer made explicit what he meant. The Komsomol member was obliged to attend meetings, even if his family forbade him. If his father gave him commands that were against Komsomol or Soviet rules, he was forbidden to carry out those commands. The authority of the Komsomol superseded the authority of parents.

One section of the pamphlet explains how a Komsomol member should behave in case he disagrees with a Komsomol resolution in a meeting that includes outsiders. "Now arises the question. There are young people who are confused: 'How is it possible to vote always for the resolution of the Komsomol in meetings of non-Party members?' 'If the Komsomol proposes an incorrect resolution, they ask, am I still obliged to vote for it?' Many who entered the Komsomol only recently vote one way in a Komsomol meeting and in the Non-Party meeting they change their minds and vote against the resolution of their own cell. Such behavior is unacceptable." The writer then explains the proper procedure. In case one disagrees with the resolution and considers the matter important, the correct thing is to vote for it nonetheless and then call the attention of the highest authorities to the fact that an error has been committed.[71]

The Komsomol member must not voice his misgivings in front of outsiders but must appeal to the Party, which is responsible for the youth organization. "It is quite unacceptable to fold your hands when you see the Komsomol cell commits an error. No, one must not be silent; the Komsomolite must raise the issue. But not among non-Party members, but in an organized fashion, in front of the Communist Party, which directs the Komsomol and corrects its occasional mistakes, or in front of the higher authorities of the Komsomol. That is the correct Komsomol discipline."[72]

The best way to teach political behavior was by involving the young; the aspiring activist learned by doing. He becomes acquainted with the proper phraseology, with the mentality of the Party leadership, and with the Communist method of argument. One particularly interesting and instructive example was the anti-Trotsky campaign initiated by the Komsomol Central Committee in January 1925. It was a new phenomenon for one of the two major architects of the Revolution and a man who was still a member of the Politburo to be openly and mercilessly attacked. Soviet organizations did not leave such a ticklish matter to local initiative, and therefore it is not surprising that the Komsomol Central Committee sent minute instructions as to how the campaign should be conducted.[73] It was to be divided into three parts: work among the activists, among Komsomol members, and among the population. The center instructed the provincial organizations to give a series of lectures to teach the activists how to approach the subject. The instructions described how the material should be presented. It is striking that many features of later vilification were already present in this 1925 document. Communist thinkers tolerated no ambiguities. They did not present Trotsky as a man who had great achievements to his credit in the service of the Revolution but now propounded an incorrect point of view. Instead, their Trotsky was a person whose every past position was wrong. They gave no concessions even while discussing the matter in the most sophisticated circles, among the city activists.

The Central Committee was most concerned that the discussions in the political circles held by the ordinary cells should be led by reliable and trained leaders. Only Party members were allowed to lead the sessions. The provincial committees had to check on the reliability of each session leader and had to consult with the local Party committee about the reliability of individuals involved and local issues to be discussed. The directive emphasized that there was to be no difference in the subject matter of the sessions held for the activists and for ordinary members; only the "depth" of the lectures was to be different.

How should anti-Trotskyism be discussed in the village? The directive put it this way: "It is necessary to take into consideration the low level of political knowledge among the village activists and among the masses of village Komsomol members. This makes it necessary that the discussion of issues should be freed from details and the matter should be discussed in relation to the issue of the present moment." The Central Committee stressed again and again that it was necessary to explain to a peasant audience that all Trotsky's errors stemmed from his underestimation of the importance of the peasantry.

We can only guess how the majority of peasant Komsomolites responded to the campaign. Apparently the propaganda that depicted Trotsky as antipeasant was successful, and very few villagers had to struggle with their consciences when they voted for anti-Trotsky resolutions.[74] The alert and ambitious Komsomol member learned the ritual of denunciation, which in the following decade came to be an extremely useful skill.

As Trotsky's political fortunes declined, the tone of denunciation became increasingly vicious. After he was expelled from the country, resolutions condemning him became commonplace. Here is a typical open letter addressed to him:

Mister Trotsky, we, Komsomol members of the city of Kamenets-Podolsk gathered here, read with the greatest indignation in the bourgeois newspapers your slander against the first workers' republic in the world. Remembering that the existence of the dictatorship of the proletariat in the country was achieved by the sacrifice of the blood of the workers and progressive peasants, we consider the poison of your treasonous articles as treachery of the cause of the working classes unheard of in history. For pound sterling you sold the conscience of a revolutionary. But the world revolution will soon sweep you into the garbage heap of history together with the lackeys of the bougeoisie and with the executioners of the international working classes. We, 600 Komsomol members, send you our curse."[75]

Here we can see the political language of the mature Soviet society.

The Pioneers

The Party assigned responsibility for the children's organization, the Pioneers, to the Komsomol. The movement developed slowly. The leaders of the regime appreciated the need for such a movement, but the new order lacked the necessary resources, cadres, and organizational know-how. Also, at the time of the Civil War the Bolsheviks had more important things to worry about than the political indoctrination of children. A few local leaders made attempts to include children in Communist activities; however, these attempts were haphazard. The regime was groping for a suitable organizational form and for the principles on the basis of which the movement should be built. A model and at the same time a dangerous competitor was the scout movement, which had appeared in Russia at the turn of the century, Clearly, an organization that claimed ignorance of class struggle, which brought together middle-class and lower-class children in excursions and nature study, which promised "character development" without taking into consideration the interests of class, had no place in the new Soviet society. The first competing Soviet organization was the Young Communists (Iuks). These groups had no national leadership and included a great many local variations. In some places, the old scout units reformed themselves into Iuks without many changes in their agendas and thereby avoided political trouble. In other places, Iuk groups were formed to draw children away from the established scout units. Once the regime decided to get rid of the scouts the Iuk movement also disappeared.[76]

At the time of the Civil War, in a period of utopianism, some activists experimented with strange and exotic ideas. In Tula, for example, a few Communists established a "Children's Communist Party," which published its own newspaper.[77] This and similar attempts were clearly ephemeral and betrayed a lack of central leadership.

In October 1922 the Fifth Congress of the Komsomol discussed the children's Communist movement and decided on the form of the Young Pioneer organization.[78] Although almost all the future ideas and principles of organization were contained in this resolution, the work began slowly. At this time there were four thousand Pioneers, and the number grew only to 161,000 at the beginning of 1924. The years 1924 and 1925 should be regarded as the period of the real birth of the movement. By January 1, 1925, there were 1 million Pioneers,[79] and by the middle of 1926 over 2 million (this number included the newly formed Young Octoberists for the eight-to-eleven age group). This meant that the Pioneers grew to approximately the size of the Komsomol. Although it still embraced only a small percentage of the relevant age group (about 6 percent), the quick growth of the movement was impressive.[80] Like the Komsomol, the Pioneer organizations also first established themselves in the cities and only relatively slowly penetrated the countryside. While the majority of the Pioneers in the late twenties lived in villages, the percentage of working-class youth who joined remained much higher than that of peasant children. The sex distribution of the Pioneers was better than that of the Komsomol; girls were almost as likely to join as boys. In the mid-twenties girls made up almost 42 percent of the membership.[81]

The Pioneer movement was designed for children between the ages of ten and sixteen. The success of the organization encouraged the leadership of the Party to form the Young Octoberists for children between eight and eleven. Soon this organization had almost 300,000 members. Children between ten and eleven could belong to both the Young Octoberists and the Pioneers; and those between fourteen and sixteen could be members of both the Pioneers and the Komsomol. Of course people between eighteen and twenty-three could be members of both the youth organization and the Party. The purpose of this arrangement was to have a cadre of leaders on each level who accepted the discipline of the higher, politically more demanding, more "adult" organization. Each organization prepared its members to join the higher one; and each higher organization was responsible for the one just below. Naturally, the criteria for membership became increasingly stringent as one ascended the hierarchy. The Party was frankly elitist, with an elaborate class policy. The Pioneers, on the other hand, accepted all children; but this organization also liked to have a core of leaders from working-class families. The Bolsheviks did not haphazardly create organizations, each relevant for only one age group; they built an all-encompassing and integrated system.

In their organizational form the Pioneers learned from the boy scouts. Forty to fifty children formed a detachment, which was divided into four or five links, a link being the smallest unit. According to the rules of the organization, the Komsomol cell in each instance chose the leader of the Pioneer detachment from among its own members. In the cities the detachments were attached to factories, workers' clubs, or children's homes. By not basing the Pioneer movement on territorial divisions or attaching them to schools, the regime hoped to stress working-class influence. In the villages, by contrast, the schools were the primary basis of the organization.[82]

There was never the slightest doubt that the primary purpose of the organization was political indoctrination. For someone of a different political culture it is hard to appreciate how single minded the Bolsheviks were in pursuing this goal. In the Bolsheviks' system of values, the indoctrination of children was a major and positive good. They understood that it was essential to start the work as early as possible, and they believed that they were enabling the Pioneers to become useful citizens of a new and better society. The Bolsheviks have always proudly affirmed their intention to indoctrinate. A resolution of the sixth Komsomol Congress in July 1924 put it succinctly:

The children's movement in the Soviet Republic is a new form of Communist education and a first step in the working-class movement. Its task is to prepare socially, culturally, and politically a new generation of workers for class struggle, for their participation in building a Communist society. The educational method of the children's movement is the planned inclusion of children in class struggle and in socially necessary work.[83]

Still, difficult questions remained about the proper methods of reaching the announced goal. After all, children were children; that is why it was necessary to form a separate movement for them. Their attention spans were short, their political knowledge nonexistent. One did not have to be a child psychologist to know that to provide nothing else for the young but a steady diet of lectures on political subjects was bound to be self-defeating. In the first years the Komsomol experimented to find the proper balance of politics and amusements for their younger colleagues. At times the Party criticized the Pioneers for not paying sufficient attention to political education, but another time it was found that too much political work tired and bored children.[84] In April 1925 the Central Committee of the Party expressed its concern that Pioneers were overburdened by tasks imposed on them by their organization.[85]

Indeed, the children participated in all the same types of work that the Komsomol members did. They marched on political holidays, they listened to lectures on agriculture and world politics, they participated in the antireligious campaign. Pioneers appeared at factory meetings and addressed the workers. In one recorded instance a twelve year old was haranguing the adults: "We workers are tired of being exploited."[86] One can only guess what impact such tasks had on the children. They must have learned that there were magic sentences to be uttered and that their words and reality had little relationship. These were important lessons for future Communists.

The Pioneers attracted the children with games, excursions, sports, and a highly developed system of symbols. In the use of symbols, the Pioneers and the Komsomol differed. As an adult organization, the Komsomol disdained uniforms, salutes, and so forth, but such things were considered appropriate for children. When a child joined the organization — after a two-month probationary period — he took an oath. "I, Young Pioneer of the USSR, in front of my comrades, solemnly swear: (1) I shall be firm in the struggle for the cause of the working class and in the struggle for the liberation of the workers and peasants of the entire world. (2) I will honestly and with constancy carry out the laws and customs of the Young Pioneers."[87] He joined a link that had a name, for example, Red Flyer, Metalist, Bees, and Hammer and Sickle.[88] On joining, he received a little badge on which there was a Red Flag with hammer and sickle. Within the sickle there was a campfire with five logs burning with three flames. The emblem also contained the slogan "Be ready." It was explained to the child that the five logs represented the five continents and the three flames the Third International. The Pioneer was entitled and expected to wear a three-cornered red kerchief. The three corners stood for the Party, the Komsomol, and the Pioneers.[89] The uniforms, the slogans, and the symbols remind one of the Fascist organizations. It is unlikely, however, that the Russians considered it necessary to borrow from the Italians or Germans; similar needs in similar circumstances led to similar results.

The children went on excursions and, whenever possible during the summer, to camps. Playing sports, walking, getting acquainted with nature, and building campfires no doubt gave the Pioneers a great deal of pleasure. The guidebook for Pioneer leaders even provided discussion materials for campfire talks. It recommended the biography of Lenin, anecdotes from the history of the revolutionary movement, and so forth as suitable topics.[90]

The Pioneers encouraged the children's interest in nature, and the time spent in camps and excursions seemed to be appropriate for developing such an interest. Within the Pioneer organization, the regime created a "Young Naturalist" group, which by 1925 had 15,000 members. How single minded the regime was in making the Pioneer organization serve a useful purpose can be seen from a November 1925 circular written by the Komsomol Central Committee to its provincial committees:

The circles study mosquitoes and germs in order to fight disease. However some of the work has no social or practical significance. Such work is detached from life. It is necessary to direct the work into the proper channels. Therefore: The study (a) should concern the natural resources and productive strength of the USSR and the best way to use them in order to develop the national economy; (b) should concern work, such as problems of health, e.g., fighting malaria; (c) should concern work, such as questions of materialism based on the study of nature with respect to antireligious agitation.[91]

If the leaders of the regime had their way, few things could have continued to exist for their own sake.

The leaders of the Party and of the Komsomol were not fully satisfied with the work of the Pioneer organization. They had difficulty in finding enough willing and talented leaders of children. Not enough Komsomol youth volunteered for this particular type of social work. Playing with children had low prestige among Komsomol activists, and those who did volunteer were often unsuitable. It takes a special talent to gain the confidence and respect of children. The Smolensk Archives are full of complaints about lack of attention of the part of Komsomol cells to the youngest generation.[92]

The greatest obstacle to the development of the Pioneer organization was a lack of resources. Studying the children's movement in the 1920s, one is struck again and again by the appalling examples of poverty. Nowhere was the evidence of the exhaustion of society, as a result of war, revolution, and famine, more evident than in the deplorable condition of children. In the mid-1920s bands of orphans and abandoned children still roamed the streets of cities and the countryside, living off petty thievery. The hopes of the Soviet regime to teach "Soviet morality" to these children with the aid of the Pioneers were obviously unrealistic. But not only the orphaned and the abandoned were poor. Reports of doctors who examined Pioneers in camps painted a most depressing picture.[93] In one camp, 80 percent of the children examined suffered from anemia. The children were so weak that the authorities had to limit physical excerises to three times a week. A quarter of the children had no shoes. The report also noted that as a result of the poor material circumstances the relationships of children with one another and with adults were unsatisfactory. Under these circumstances, no indoctrination could be carried out. The children did not even know what the Bolshevik Party was.[94]

Such examples contradict the picture of the regime as a well-functioning propaganda machine. The Soviet Union was a heterogeneous society; in most places there was a large gap between intentions and achievement, between ideals and reality.

CHAPTER 9

The golden age of the Soviet cinema

The Western European public quickly came to appreciate the great Soviet filmmakers of the silent era. The film, and of course especially the silent film, is an international medium, and therefore the works of Vertov, Pudovkin, Dovzhenko, and above all Eisenstein attracted the interest of contemporaries. As time went on this interest not only did not decline but increased; an ever larger segment of Western opinion came to regard cinema as a major form of art and a medium that had a special significance in shaping the twentieth-century mind. The film and the study of film became fashionable, and in the mushrooming film histories the great Soviet figures usually received their due.

The communist ideology of the artists and the fact that they served the Soviet regime did not at all harm their reputation. Indeed, in the 1930s and once again since the 1960s the adjective "revolutionary" had a positive connotation among Western intellectuals. They looked on the Soviet directors as creators of the "revolutionary cinema."

Revolutionary cinema is an ambiguous phrase; different people at different times have attributed different meanings to it. Often it refers to innovative filmmaking. Eisenstein and his colleagues, of course, made great contributions to the development of the special language of the cinema and therefore they were revolutionary in this sense, but so are all other great artists at all times and everywhere.

In a trivial sense revolutionary cinema means nothing more than choosing revolutions as subject matter. Soviet directors in the 1920s often selected their topics from the history of the revolutionary movement, and, naturally, invariably depicted revolutionaries in a favorable light.

In the most meaningful sense, revolutionary films are those that are subversive to the values of the society in which they are created. According to this definition the Soviet directors were not revolutionary at all. They accepted with seeming enthusiasm the values of the state and were content to propagate such values. The Soviet state described itself as revolutionary, and to its tremendous advantage succeeded in persuading both friends and enemies to accept its self-definition. However, such manipulation of words should not prevent us from seeing that what was remarkable about Soviet directors was not that they were "revolutionary" but, on the contrary, that they were willing to serve the state and a prescribed ideology to a hitherto unparalleled extent. How successful they were as propagandists is another matter. In fairness to the Soviet directors it must be said that film by its very nature is not a revolutionary medium; it is almost always used to reinforce values and therefore the status quo. The difference between the Soviet directors and others was only that the Soviets were both more self-aware and more obedient.

It is not surprising that the Soviet state was the first to embark on the organization of a large-scale indoctrination network that would include the film in its aresenal. The Soviet leaders, instinctive propagandists that they were, had a prescient and impressively clear appreciation of the possibilities inherent in the medium. Lenin, Trotsky, and Stalin, among others, repeatedly expressed their faith in the future of film as a propaganda weapon. Party congresses one after another paid lip service to the necessity of using film for the purposes of indoctrination. As this chapter will demonstrate, however, a wide gap remained between intentions and reality.

Because Soviet leaders and publicists have always insisted that movies were primarily instruments of propaganda, a study of Soviet mass-indoctrination methods cannot ignore this subject. Film history, however, fits only uneasily within the framework of this book. Other topics discussed, such as the Komsomol, political education, the newspapers, and even the literacy drive, were primarily aimed toward indoctrination, and therefore it does not seem unfair to approach them from the point of view of the history of propaganda. It is different with movies of the period. To look at the work of Soviet directors purely as an exercise in propaganda is to miss what is truly interesting in their work. The seeming paradox of Soviet film is that in its golden period it failed to please the regime. Only after the artistic vitality of film was destroyed in the 1930s did it become a successful instrument of propaganda. The study of film as an agent of indoctrination in the 1920s is ultimately — and fortunately from the point of view of art — a study in failure.

The history of the movie life of the NEP period should be divided into two periods. Up to the end of 1924 studios did not turn out many interesting works; the purpose of the regime was to protect itself from subversion inherent in foreign and prerevolutionary films. During the second half of the 1920s the Soviet Union enjoyed a remarkable abundance of talent and an impressive flourishing of a new art form. At this time the Communists worked to influence artists to create usable films and to exploit whatever propaganda potential there was in the available films.

The organization of the film industry

The First World War and the Civil War devastated Russia. It was evident to contemporaries, and is indisputable in retrospect, that extraordinary efforts had to be made to rebuild the national economy. The Party could not avoid giving concessions to the peasants and to the bourgeoisie in order to rekindle private initiative. The toleration of private enterprise was distasteful to the Bolsheviks on ideological grounds: They hated to watch their enemies grow stronger.

Party activists believed that at a time when they had to give their enemies free rein, it was especially important to strengthen propaganda work. In fact, it was impossible to do so. Propaganda required money, and an essential feature of the new economic order was the return to financial orthodoxy, which called for stringent conservation of resources. The Party had to cut back on propaganda work when it was most needed. Perhaps nowhere was the Party's dilemma more evident than in its handling of the film industry. The regime tolerated questionable activities in the hope of making a profit. Soviet history had many moments of great danger, and the early NEP period was one of them.

The Civil War destroyed the film industry: Studios were idle, the distribution system stopped functioning, and the film theaters shut down. Moscow, for example, had 143 theaters operating before the World War, but in the fall of 1921 not a single one remained in operation.[1] During the worst period in 1921 film showings in Soviet Russia were limited to the exhibition of agitational films (agitki) at agitational stations (agitpunkty) and to infrequent and haphazard showings of agitki at public places in the open air, such as railroad stations. Some of the agitational trains continued to operate, carrying with them a few outdated agitki and showing them often in remote villages with the aid of old projectors, which frequently broke down.

Commercial theaters could not reopen because the supply of electricity was unreliable and the halls could not be heated. The cinemas were taken over by workers' clubs and by other organizations and used as offices. The British journalist Huntley Carter, who visited Soviet Russia several times in the 1920s, described Moscow movie houses as poorly lit, lice infested, and equipped with wooden benches in place of the previously comfortable seats. He found the situation in Moscow far worse than in Petrograd, where the damage was more quickly repaired.[2] It testifies to the power of the cinema that in these miserable times the Russian audiences had a pent-up hunger for it. In late 1921 the first commercial movie house opened in Moscow on the Tverskaia. It operated from 8 o'clock in the morning until midnight. It exhibited old films, the first one being *Quiet, My Sorrow, Quiet*. The performances lasted only for an hour, and yet people waited in long lines for admission.[3]

Both private entrepreneurs and Soviet organizations quickly realized that

197

there was money to be made. Especially in Moscow and in Petrograd, but also in the provincial cities, in the course of 1922 the revival of film life was astoundingly rapid. In early 1923 in Moscow, there were 90 functioning movie theaters, and in Petrograd 49. In Moscow 35 were privately owned, 45 were leased from the government by private entrepreneurs, and the others were operated by governmental organizations.[4]

The cinema managers did not always acquire their films legally. In 1919 the Soviet state nationalized and attempted to confiscate all the films in the country. The government had no means to enforce this measure, and like so many other acts of this time, it remained an empty gesture. In fact, the new economic policies superseded the nationalization edict. As a result, film after film reappeared rather mysteriously. In the early days, the theaters' program was made up almost exclusively of prerevolutionary films and foreign imports. The speed and volume with which foreign films came to Soviet Russia is striking. Distributors had a large number of foreign films that had been shown profitably in Western Europe and in the United States and had never appeared on the Russian screens. It was a situation in which many people could quickly make a lot of money.

Soviet film historians like to stress how bad these films were, and they quote with relish from contemporary newspapers. *Daughter of the Night* was advertised in this way: "Grand American picture. Full of head-turning tricks." The advertisement of *Cagliostro's Life* said: "Rendition of the life of the world's greatest adventurer. Based on historical facts as collected by Robert Liebman. Colossal mass scenes. Accurate description of the style of the epoch. The film was shot in the royal palace of Schoenbrunn. The furniture, carriages, and other props were taken from the collection of the Austrian Imperial Family." Other titles were *The Skull of the Pharaoh's Daughter* and *The Sovereign of Animals*.[5] There is no question that the Russians were able to see and were attracted to all sorts of cheap, second-rate foreign films. But it would be wrong to conclude that only such films appeared. Russian audiences could also see the best films produced abroad. *Dr. Mabuse* and *The Cabinet of Doctor Caligari* came to Russia soon after they were made.[6]

Why did the Party allow the importing of foreign films and the showing of prerevolutionary ones, which brought no ideological benefits? The answer is clear. The leaders deeply desired the revival of Russian filmmaking but did not want to spend the necessary money. The regime hoped to benefit from the people's addiction to poor films. This was a risky game. Non-Soviet films almost invariably included at least a bit of ideological poison. Further, the movies influenced people's taste. Indeed, all through the 1920s, even when Soviet industry was able to produce first-rate films, Russian audiences remained enamored of foreign products.

The Bolsheviks were overly ambitious, and in the process they almost killed the goose that was to lay the golden egg. The government squeezed the industry too hard. In 1922 and in 1923, it set such high rental charges on films, and such high taxes on tickets, that moviegoing became almost impossibly expensive. As a result, attendance started to fall, and theaters that had just opened were forced to close. The number of functioning movie theaters diminished all over the country, and many cities were left without movie houses altogether. Despite the high taxes, government revenues started to fall.[7]

Huntley Carter, who examined the movie situation at the time, wrote:

The managers all had the same story, they were glad to be in business again. But what a time they were having. No money for new films. Not allowed to show what they liked. Rents and taxes running into milliards of rubles. Their houses were falling to pieces, with no hope of repairing them at present. Prices? Well, they tried to make ends meet by putting up prices. At the Palace seats cost two million, 800,000 and 600,000 rubles. At the Art Kino 1,100,000, 700,000 and 600,000 rubles. At the Mirror 2,000,000, 900,000 and 700,000 rubles. One film a night was shown, a serial, or four act drama, comedy or farce. There were four houses of one hour each, 5 p.m., 7.30, 9.00 and 10.00. And not withstanding the prices, the brevity, the proletarians rolled up.[8]

Bolshevik thinking on movies can be clearly seen in a letter that Lenin wrote in early 1922 to E. A. Litkens, Lunacharskii's deputy in Narkompros.

Narkompros should organize supervision of all [movie] exhibitions and systematize the matter. All films exhibited in the RSFSR should be registered and numbered by Narkompros.

All movie exhibition programs should include a certain percentage: (a) films of amusement, especially for advertisement (attracting an audience) and for profit. (naturally without obscenity and counterrevolution) and (b) under the heading "from the lives of all people" pictures of especially propaganda character: such as the colonial policy of England in India, the work of the League of Nations, starving in Berlin, etc., etc. . . .

It is necessary to show not only films but also photographs that are interesting from the point of view of propaganda, with appropriate subtitles. Movie houses that are in private hands should give sufficient income to the government in forms of rent. We must give the right to entrepreneurs to increase the number of films and to bring in new films, but always under the condition of maintaining the proper proportion of films of amusement and films of propaganda character, under the heading "From the lives of all people." This should be done in such a way that the entrepreneurs would be interested in the creation and making of new films. They should have, within these limitations, broad initiative.

Films of propaganda character should be given for evaluation to old Marxist and literary people in order to make sure that such unfortunate events in which propaganda has backfired are not repeated.

Special attention should be given to the organization of movies in villages and in the East where this matter is a novelty, and therefore our propaganda should be especially successful.[9]

Lenin's letter was deeply revealing of the mentality of the great leader. The letter shows first of all his remarkable practicality. He was interested in making money. He wanted to allow managers to show the films of Charlie Chaplin, Mary Pickford, Douglas Fairbanks, and other Western stars in order to enrich themselves and in the process enrich the government. He saw that it was necessary to attract audiences to the movies not only to make money but also to show them propaganda. He never believed that the people, after having listened to several points of view, would be able to decide correctly for themselves. Experienced people, such as old Marxists, had to decide for them. Censorship and propaganda were related, and Lenin attributed the greatest significance to them. It is interesting that when Lenin looked for examples of propaganda, he chose only foreign ones. In January 1922, at the height of famine, Lenin wanted to show the Russians that people were starving – in Berlin.

As on so many other occasions, most of the ideas of Lenin's fertile mind remained unrealized. The government did not have the means to set up a network in the villages or in the East. Government control was so weak that it could not compel the showing of propaganda films. Indeed, at that time such films hardly existed. The government could not even carry out successful censorship. Weakness and confusion protected liberty. When the local organs prohibited the exhibition of one film or another, the private distributor simply sent the film to some far-away place where it was likely to escape the attention of the authorities. In 1922, for example, a certain private distributor, Poliakov, attempted to show in Ekaterinburg a film entitled *The Fall of Nations*. When the local Narkompros office forbade the showing, he exhibited the film in outlying districts of Siberia.[10]

Naturally, the Bolshevik leaders understood that things were not going well on the cinema front. Since they had neither the money nor the personnel to bring about real change, they were reduced to tinkering with the existing system. In the early 1920s, there were constant discussions of the proper organization of film matters, and the regime changed the institutions in a dizzying fashion.

The Soviet movie industry and distribution system came under the authority of Narkompros. Following the nationalization of the industry in August 1919, the government set up an All-Russian Photo-Movie Department (VKFO) within Narkompros, responsible for the production and distribution of films. A year or two later, similar departments were established within the commissariats of enlightenment of the future constituent republics of the Soviet Union.[11] Although the VFKO accomplished little, it would be unfair to blame it. The studios lay in ruins, and there was no film stock.

The situation changed with the introduction of NEP. Now that there was money to be made, private, government, and semigovernment agencies scrambled for the business. To the great dismay of Soviet leaders, Russian film organizations even competed against one another to get rights for showing foreign films and thereby bid up the cost. In this respect, for awhile Soviet Russia operated almost like a capitalist country.

In 1921 and 1922, P. Voevodin, head of the VFKO, constantly petitioned Sovnarkom for money. The filmmakers especially desired convertible currency to buy film and equipment from abroad. Without such purchases, the studios could not operate. Sovnarkom refused to make the investment, still hoping that the film industry itself would generate the necessary capital. How this should be accomplished was discussed by a committee headed by Voevodin. On the basis of the committee's report, in December 1922, Sovnarkom abolished the VFKO and in its place set up the Central State Photographic and Cinematic Enterprise, Goskino.[12] Like its predecessor, Goskino was located within Narkompros. Its first director was L. A. Liberman, who had considerable independence from Narkompros supervision.

The work began under inauspicious circumstances.[13] Goskino's tasks included the importation of films, the organization of the revival of film studios, and the enforcement of the monopoly of rentals. Once again, the imposition of central control was difficult, indeed impossible. In the previous months a number of film organizations had come into being, many with strong protectors in the Soviet hierarchy. Goskino had no authority outside the Russian republic, while the revival of filmmaking in Georgia, and especially in the Ukraine, was faster than within Russia itself. The strongest film organization in Russia was Sevzapkino, which had the best studio and also the largest distribution network. Although Sevzapkino was based in Petrograd, its Moscow office controlled a larger network of theaters than Goskino itself. The educational department of the Moscow Soviet also had a film office, Kino-Moskva, which wanted to defend its autonomy. The Petrograd Soviet protected Kinosever. The Red Army's political-education department, PUR, supported the film organization Krasnaia zvezda, and the trade unions maintained Proletkino primarily to supply workers' clubs.[14]

In addition, the NEP allowed the formation of the private joint-stock companies. Of these, the two most important were Rus and Mezhrabpom, which were later to form Mezhrabpom-Rus. Mezhrabpom was a remarkable organization, something that could exist only in the confused, ambiguous world of the early 1920s. Mezhrabpom was an acronym for International Workers' Aid, an organization that was established in Germany in 1921 by proSoviet and procommunist elements. Its original task was to help Soviet Russia fight famine. Once the initial emergency passed, the accumulated capital was used to help the nascent Soviet film industry.[15] This capital was an essential source for buying the necessary equipment and film abroad. Although the Mezhrabpom was reorganized and its German ties became less significant, all through the 1920s, it remained a useful link between Russia and Western Europe. Mezhrabpom-Rus made a great contribution to making the work of Soviet directors known first in Germany and later in the rest of Europe. The studios of Mezhrabpom-Rus also turned out some of the most interesting films produced in the Soviet Union. After 1923, all private film companies with the exception of Mezhrabpom-Rus were closed down.

Since Goskino had a monopoly on film rentals, other film organizations had to enter into contractual relations with it. This setup was such that conflicts could hardly be avoided. Goskino demanded 50 percent of the profit. Its leaders realized that it was essential to revive Russian filmmaking, and because the government was unwilling to contribute, it had to squeeze rental organizations. On the other hand, the army, the trade unions, and even Sevzapkino were strong enough to resist. They each wanted more money. Goskino, to lessen the competition, wanted to close the Moscow offices of Sevzapkino; however, the government refused; and Sevzapkino remained a thorn in the side of Goskino.[16]

Goskino was unable to generate the capital, and Sovnarkom repeatedly refused to help, so the film industry could be revived only with private capital, domestic or foreign.[17] At the recommendation of the government, Goskino entered into negotiations with a number of firms. Discussions with the American Fox and German Springer film companies were fruitless. Negotiations went furthest with the domestic private company of L. Azarkh, and an agreement was even signed, with the approval of Narkompros. In this contract, L. Azarkh promised: (a) to put up the capital of half a million gold rubles, (b) to give Goskino 53 percent of the shares, (c) to produce a yearly profit of 50,000 gold rubles, and (d) to make at least twenty feature films yearly. In exchange, Goskino agreed to allow Azarkh to use the only functioning Moscow studio, the ex-Khanzhonkov studio. Perhaps more important, by implication, Azarkh was able to take advantage of the monopoly enjoyed by Goskino. The agreement, however, remained only on paper. The government soon accused Azarkh of not observing its share of the bargain and repudiated the deal. From the available sources, it is impossible to establish whether Azarkh was in fact at fault, but it is clear that the government officials had second thoughts.[18] Giving up the Khanzhonkov studios meant that the government, at least for the time being, could not even hope to make the kind of films it wanted to have. The Communist leaders feared losing control over the final product. Filmmaking was obviously a sensitive matter; the role and function of private capital was more complicated that in the case of other industries.

Within a few months of its establishment, it was already evident that Goskino could cope with its problems no better that its predecessor. In April 1923, Lieberman was replaced by E. S. Kadomtsev as head of the organization, but a mere change in leadership did not make much difference.

The leaders of Goskino considered the very high taxes on cinema one of the greatest problems of the industry. They believed that without alleviating that burden, filmmaking could not revive. They therefore turned to Sovnarkom for help. Evidently the government had little confidence in the judgment of Goskino's leaders, because instead of granting this reasonable request, it set up a commission to study the problem.[19]

In the next two years, two major commissions dealt with the problems of the industry; these problems were discussed at the Thirteenth Party Congress in May 1924; and Sovnarkom also devoted considerable time and attention to them. The first commission, which worked from April to September 1923, was headed by N. N. Adveev and included representatives from Narkomfin (People's Commissariat of Finance), Narkompros, and Rabkrin (People's Commissariat of Workers' and Peasants' Inspection). These people acknowledged that the situation was deteriorating. They noted that aside from the government, local organizations, which were constantly in need of money, levied taxes on cinema tickets. The Moscow Soviet, for example, levied a 30 percent tax; in the Ukraine, theatergoers paid republic and local taxes and 10 percent extra to allow Red Army soldiers to go free.[20] Adveev's commission recommended lowering taxes.

In September 1923, Sovnarkom appointed another commission. This one was headed by A. V. Mantsev. It reported to Sovnarkom in November. Its recommendations went much further than those of the previous group. It recommended lowering ticket prices, eliminating taxes, and establishing a new organization to start work with a substantial government loan. It took, however, another year and long discussions before the recommendations were realized.

Sovnarkom set up Sovkino in December 1924, and the new organization began its work in January 1925. It was a joint-stock company in which all shares were held by government organizations: VSNKh got 15 percent; Narkompros and the Petrograd and Moscow soviets together 55; and Narkomvneshtorg 30.[21] That the largest single bloc of shares was given to the foreign-trade agency shows the decisive importance of imports at the time. The establishment of Sovkino did not mean the immediate dissolution of Goskino. That organization survived as a production unit until 1926. The new arrangements finally brought stability to the movie industry, which was a precondition for later accomplishments.

The constant reorganizations betrayed an impatience and concern on the part of Bolshevik leaders about how the cinema was fulfilling its educational and propaganda roles. The leaders had reasons for dissatisfaction.

Between the introduction of NEP and the establishment of Sovkino, the most valuable products in respect to political education, and also perhaps artistically, were newsreels. The regime concentrated its scarce resources on making newsreels. Lebedev, a young Communist activist in the film industry, reported that in 1921 and in early 1922, it was the newsreel section of the Moscow studios that alone showed any signs of life. In this section worked E. Tisse, the future collaborator of Eisenstein; G. Giber; A. Levitskii; and, most important, D. Vertov.[22] Vertov had been making newsreels since the early days of the Civil War, but the first in his famous series *Kino-Pravda* appeared only in May 1922. Working conditions were extremely difficult. Cameramen had to work with outdated and inadequate equipment. Worst of all, in the middle of the winter, they had to do their cutting and editing in totally unheated studios, working in their overcoats.[23]

According to Lebedev, the artistic quality of the early newsreels was low. Action was photographed from a single point of view. The cameramen did not know how to find significant details that would have emotionally involved the viewer. The newsreels constantly compared the "terrible past" with the "hopeful present." Lebedev observed that this particular characteristic of early propaganda newsreels came to be an important influence on Vertov's and Eisenstein's ideas about clashing montage, a montage of opposites.[24]

Aside from the newsreels, the studios made agitki. In artistic conception, length, and style, these were closely related to the newsreels. The main difference was that in the agitki, actors, not always professional ones, assumed roles. In 1921, the worst year, only four agitki were made in Moscow, two in Petrograd, three in the Ukraine, and one in Georgia.[25]

The most ambitious of these films was the *The Sickle and the Hammer,* directed by V. Gardin and photographed by Tisse.[26] V. Pudovkin played the main role. The film's misfortune was that its main agitational point became irrelevant before it was first shown. The film attempted to justify forced collection of food from the peasants by showing starving workers and by showing how peasants and workers fought together against the oppressors. The NEP, however, repudiated forced collection of food, and so the film was never widely distributed. In one respect the film contained a characteristic of many later products: The wicked kulak wanted to take advantage of the virtuous wife of a worker. As in other Soviet films of the future, the enemy was more highly sexed.[27]

A shorter but more successful work was *Hunger, Hunger, Hunger,* also directed by Gardin and shot by Tisse.[28] The film was largely assembled from documentary footage taken by Tisse in the famine-devastated Volga region. It was widely used abroad for soliciting famine relief. The appeal of the film comes from the inherent strength of the material. In the most easily measurable terms of money collected, this film was surely one of the most effective propaganda works ever made for foreign consumption.

The first film that can be more or less described as entertainment was *The Miracle Worker,* made in 1922 by Panteleev. This was a historical, antireligious film that contained some of the features of the agitki. At the time of Nicholas the First, a young serf, a trouble maker, is given by his master to serve in the army. The young soldier steals a diamond from an icon and then pretends that the Virgin Mary gave it to him. The authorities are put in a quandary when the news of the "miracle" spreads all over Saint Petersburg. Should they undermine the faith of the simpleminded by revealing that the "miracle" was phony, or should they let the scoundrel get away with his crime? The film has a happy ending: Boy gets girl, and the sly peasant lad has outwitted the authorities. The story is presented in an overly theatrical fashion, and there is little pretense of portraying reality, but the film is not without simple charm. The life of the soldiers and even of the serfs is not depicted in a somber fashion.

A film similar in its level of sophistication and propaganda is *Kombrig Ivanov*, made in Moscow in 1923. The movie tells the story of a Communist officer, Ivanov, falling in love with the daughter of a priest, and after some difficulties, persuading her to dispense with a church wedding. The criticism of the church is not particularly harsh: The priest is an obsequious fool but not really wicked. The Communist is not really a positive hero: He boasts, he falls in love, and he enjoys luxury. The film is silly and primitively made; the heroine flutters her eyelids excessively, and the intertitles are interminably long and boring.

In 1923 and 1924, Soviet film finally surpassed the level of agitki. One of the most successful films of the 1920s in terms of audience appeal was *The Little Red Devils*, made by Perestiani in 1923. This film, like many others before and since, manages at the same time to satirize and exploit the adventure genre. It is about three adolescents during the Ukrainian Civil War. One of them, rather incongruously, is an American black. The movie anticipated others in its most cavalier disregard for historical facts. In the course of their adventures, the children capture Anarchist chief Makhno and hand him over to the Red troops of Budenny. This incident was a figment of the imagination of the scenarist, for Makhno died in his bed many years later in Paris. The director also made the Ukraine mountainous in order to make it more picturesque. Once again, the wickedness of the villain is shown by the fact that he lusts after women. Among the many crimes of Makhno, this was the one that struck the imagination of filmmakers. The audience enjoyed the fast-moving action and the good performance of the young actors, and the critics approved of selecting the Civil War as a background for fabulous adventures.

Another important film of 1923 was not nearly as successful. This movie, *The Chancellor and the Metal Worker*, directed by Gardin, was based on a Lunacharskii play. The action takes place in a mythical country during the First World War; however, the story is a transparent allegory of the Russian Revolution. The ire of the filmmakers is concentrated not so much on the representatives of the old regime as, in proper Bolshevik fashion, on the Kerensky figure, who "betrays the Revolution." Once again, his wickedness is conveyed by his seduction of women. The story is confused, the characters are stereotyped, and the film is clumsily directed. *The Chancellor and the Metal Worker* received universally bad reviews in the press. Writing in *Pravda*, Lebedev went so far as to express concern that such a bad film made out of a decent play might set back the cause of filmmaking.[29]

Aelita, made by I. A. Protazanov, was incomparably more interesting. This first Soviet science-fiction film was based on A. Tolstoi's novel. In it, a Soviet engineer dreams of a trip to Mars, at least partially to escape his earthly problems. He arrives on Mars just in time to witness the revolution of the exploited. Although the constructivist sets for the action on the alien planet are striking, the action in NEP Russia is more interesting, at least in retrospect. The film was praised by critics for its technical accomplishments but was attacked for showing the young Soviet Union in an overly critical fashion.[30] One was not supposed to wish to escape from Communist Russia – even as a joke.

The finest comedy of the decade was *The Extraordinary Adventures of Mr. West in the Land of the Bolsheviks,* made by Kuleshov in 1924. The film was made to ridicule Western rumors about Bolshevik Russia. Mr. West, a rich American, comes to Moscow on business. Because he has heard many fantastic tales about life in the Soviet Union, he decides to bring a bodyguard, a cowboy. In spite of his precautions, he falls into the hands of a group of bandits who take advantage of his naivete. Naturally, the film ends happily: The authorities destroy the bandit group, and Mr. West can now become acquainted with the happy and civilized life of the Russian people.

The satire is double edged. Although it is true that the rumors are exaggerated, the Soviet Union is still depicted as a country in which a group of bandits can take on the regime more or less as equals. The film parodies the conventions of the American Western; however, much of the excitement and its appeal to the audience is based on the exploitation of the very same conventions. It is a loving satire of the genre.

Films, 1925–9

In the second half of the 1920s, the Soviet film industry greatly expanded. Sovkino opened a new studio in Leningrad, Mezhrabpomfilm started one in Moscow, and the Ukrainians built studios in Kiev, Odessa, and Yalta. In addition, the national minorities started to make films in Baku, Erevan, and Tashkent.[31] In 1928, the country had thirteen functioning studios. Four of these, Sovkino, VUFKU (the Ukrainian organization), Gruzkino, and Mezhrabpomfilm, produced over 80 percent of the movies.[32]

The number of films registered in the Catalog of Soviet Feature Films indicates the magnitude of the growth.[33] In 1921, there were 9 titles; in 1922, 16; and in 1923, 26. The great jumps took place in 1924, when 68 films were made; in 1926, 102; and in 1927, 119. The peak was reached in 1928, when the Soviet Union produced 123 films. In the following year, the number fell to 91. These numbers do not even show the full extent of the growth, for during the early years the studios made almost exclusively short agitki. Moviegoing in the Soviet Union was obviously popular. In 1928, 300 million tickets were sold. An average film was seen by 2.5 million people.[34]

In perspective, the great improvement is self-evident, but contemporary film directors bemoaned the continued poverty of the industry. They envied their Western colleagues, who had incomparably superior equipment. Indeed, conditions were poor. Since the Soviet Union did not manufacture raw film, it had to be bought abroad with precious convertible currency. Consequently, there was a continuous shortage, and film directors often could not afford the luxury of taking a scene over again. In addition, the film factories did not have proper lighting or good-quality chemicals for developing the films.[35]

Fortunately, however, beyond a certain minimum level, the quality of the equipment has little to do with artistry. The late 1920s were the golden age of the Soviet cinema. A remarkable flowering of many talents took place within a few years. One might assume that people who came to maturity more or less at the same time, who worked under similar difficult material conditions, and who at least ostensibly shared the same political ideology would develop similar styles. In the West, where Eisenstein's work became much better known than that of anyone else, it was often assumed that other directors made films like Eisenstein's. In fact, this was not the case. Different talents and different artistic credos produced a multiplicity of styles. Soviet directors influenced one another not so much by imitating each other's techniques, though that happened, but, more importantly, by providing negative models for each other. Artists found their individuality in juxtaposition to the work of their contemporaries.

The Soviet Union is enormous. The Bolsheviks, who were great centralizers, paradoxically built no Hollywood, and the country had many film centers. Leningrad competed with Moscow; the Georgians and the Ukrainians, who were the first among the national minorities to establish film industries, fairly soon developed different and characteristic styles. For example, the greatest of the Ukrainian directors, Dovzhenko, was a nationalist and a true original. Obviously, people operating in the very different cultural milieu's of the Caucasian republics or of Central Asia made very different films.

Among the famous Russian directors, there was obviously a gap between those who came to maturity before the establishment of Soviet power and those who started their work only in the 1920s. There were directors (like Gardin, Protazanov, and Zheliabuzhskii) who were willing to use technical innovations developed by others but were not particularly experimental themselves. There were also directors (like Vertov, Kuleshov, Eisenstein, and Pudovkin) who were natural innovators. Even the camp of the innovators was deeply divided. Eisenstein, on the one hand, and Kuleshov and Pudovkin, on the other, had altogether different views on the proper use of montage.

The relatively free artistic discussions and the competing talents produced an impressive film industry. The question arises of whether the artistic innovations were at all connected with the political innovations that were taking place at the same time. Russia had a great Revolution, and a short time later it enjoyed the flourishing of a new art. Were these two facts connected? It certainly never occurred to anyone to give credit for the great talents of Tolstoy, Dostoevsky, Turgenev, and Chekhov to the particular tsarist social and political system in which the artists worked. The issue, however, may be more complicated with the film industry. Bolshevism cannot claim credit for the almost mysterious convergence of so many first-rate artists in such a short time; on the other hand, the Bolshevik regime, by setting political goals, did at least partially free some of the directors from commercial considerations. It is unlikely that a capitalist studio would have financed Eisenstein's first artistic experiments because his work could not possibly have appealed to a large audience. Further, the regime and the artists tacitly cooperated: The regime provided the myths and the artists the iconography. Each benefited.

Between 1925 and 1929, the studios made 514 films.[36] These differed so much in subject matter and style that it is difficult to make generalizations. A few observations, however, can be made. First of all, with only a few exceptions, the films were made to serve the interests of the state. Some were made to popularize sports or the state lottery, or to help the fight against venereal disease, but the great majority were political. Even in these relatively liberal days, the Soviet regime rarely and barely tolerated a film that was made either to entertain or to give nothing but aesthetic pleasure.

Artists dealt with the pressures differently. Some convinced Bolsheviks naturally made the type of film that was expected of them. Others cared little about ideologies and were perfectly happy to serve any master that allowed them to make films. Lebedev, who worked in the early 1920s, talked to cameramen who made newsreels. He found that they were professionals who saw little ideological significance in their work. One of them said to him: "Our task is small: We just turn the handle. Where and what to photograph are matters that will be decided by the bosses."[37] Many of the directors compromised. They made the film that they wanted to make and appended the necessary political message as a price to be allowed to do their work. There were few Soviet films from this period that were completely without political propaganda.

One outstanding example is Kuleshov's *By the Law*, made in 1926. Since the studio did not approve the script, it was made as an "experiment" and had to be done on a shoestring.[38] There were only five actors and one interior set, a ramshackle cabin. The extreme simplicity of means actually adds to the power of the film. The script was based on a Jack London story of gold prospectors in the Yukon Territory. One of them goes berserk and starts to shoot his comrades in order to acquire more gold. A couple, however, manages to restrain him. Since the husband and wife believe that it is their duty to hand him over to the authorities, they keep him as a prisoner. The bulk of the film deals with the relationship of the three people. To make the film palatable, some of Kuleshov's friends argued that it was about capitalist greed. Kuleshov, in fact, was heavily attacked for his apoliticism. He never again made a first-rate film.[39]

Another characteristic of Soviet film was that none could give a realistic description of life. Unlike the 1930s, at this time directors could still deal with real issues that interested people. However, the approach was almost invariably stylized. The wicked were very wicked, and the good a little too good. Films had a fairy-tale quality, with one outstanding exception. This was *Three Meshchanskaia Street,* named abroad *Bed and Sofa,* made by Abram Room in 1927.

This film is a modest slice-of-life drama. A working-class couple live in a small, one-room apartment. The husband is a construction worker, and the wife, steeped in petit bourgeois mentality, stays home. The construction worker's friend, a printer, comes to town and finds a job. But because of the terrific apartment shortage, he is forced to move in with the couple. When the construction worker goes out of town on assignment, the wife, who is bored and has been neglected, easily enters into a relationship with the tenant. When the husband returns, it is he who has to sleep on the sofa. The woman becomes pregnant, and she herself does not know who the father is. The two men together try to persuade her to have an abortion. At this point she repudiates both her previous petit bourgeois existence and her two men, and she decides to start a new life for herself with her baby.

There were no films made in the Soviet Union until the 1960s in which average people were depicted in such a nonjudgmental fashion. There were certainly no Soviet films in which sex was treated so matter-of-factly. The film was greeted with a storm of abuse. Soviet critics did not want to see films about life as it was.[40] Room's talent was minute observation of little people, and of revealing details. He could never make another film of comparable quality. Soviet film was still defining itself; directors were still searching for the limits of the permissible. Soviet directors continued to make dramatizations from classics, historical costume dramas, and films that escape categorization, but the majority of films dealt with the history of the revolutionary movement or with current, NEP Russia.

Out of the 514 films, the history of the revolutionary movement was the subject matter of 144.[41] If we consider only full-length films, the proportion would certainly reach at least one-third. Admittedly, at times it is hard to put movies into one group or another. In some cases, the Revolution is there only as a distant background. At other times, movies that purported to depict the hard life of the workers in the past could easily be placed among the revolutionary films. Exact numbers, however, do not matter. It is indisputable that a very large proportion of Soviet films of the time dealt with this subject.

Among the revolutionary films, we might establish a subcategory that in the absence of a better term might be called revolutionary spectacle. Prime examples of the revolutionary spectacle are the first three films of Eisenstein, *Strike, Battleship Potemkin,* and *October;* Pudovkin's *End of Saint Petersburg;* and Dovzhenko's *Arsenal.* What these movies and other similar ones have in common is a lack of interest in story and in character, in fact the absence of recognizable human beings. What we have instead are types, symbols, and gestures.

Although only a few of the revolutionary films fall into this subcategory,

Plate 12. Poster advertising *Battleship Potemkin,* 1926.

they are important. Indeed, in the West, and even in Russia, when one talks about Soviet political cinema, these are the films one thinks of first. It was here that Soviet cinema was most original and innovative. No one had made revolutionary spectacles before Eisenstein, and not many have made them since. These films impressed some segments of the Western public so much that many unconsciously came to believe that all Soviet films were like *Potemkin.*

Eisenstein was the decisive figure in the development of the genre. His intellectual development was influenced by three different sources. First and most important, he learned from the thinkers of the Proletkul't. He accepted their view that the art of the working classes should be the art of the collective. This art must not emphasize individual heroes but, on the contrary, must show that in history only the masses mattered.

Second, Eisenstein, like most directors of the twenties, came under the influence of Dziga Vertov. Vertov was a true radical who believed that the Russian Revolution was merely an aspect of the renewal of everything in human life. He rejected literature, plays, and acting. As he put it: "Movie drama – this is the opium for the people. Movie drama and religion are the most deadly weapons in the hands of the capitalists." Elsewhere he said: "The very term art is in essence counterrevolutionary."[42] Vertov made documentaries because he believed that this was the only acceptable form of filmmaking in the proletarian era. Vertov did not like Eisenstein's work, because Eisenstein used scenarios and did tell something of a story. The two articulate avant-garde artists polemicized against one another. Eisenstein denied that he was influenced by Vertov, and indeed it is self-evident that the two directors had different artistic credos.[43] Nevertheless, it was at least partially because of Vertov that in the mid-1920s films without a particularly interesting story line, without actors, and without individuals somehow seemed more "revolutionary" and "antibourgeois."

In retrospect, it is an amazing example of self-deception that avant-garde artists believed that because they were antibourgeois they represented the working classes. There was never the slightest evidence to support such belief. If there was anyone who paid attention to artistic experimentation — and there were not many — these were bourgeois intellectuals. Of all the first-rate artists, none had more trouble in filling a movie house than Vertov.

Third, Eisenstein learned from the Japanese kabuki theater. He already had an interest in kabuki in his youth. He learned the technique of building effects and the notion of attraction of opposites, which came to be the most significant aspect of his montage.[44] But most important, he learned from the Japanese the importance of gestures and stylization. One is tempted to describe Soviet movie spectacles of the 1920s as revolutionary kabuki theater.

Eisenstein's first film, *Strike,* made in 1925, already contained all the important characteristics of his later works. The film tells the story of a strike. The workers are oppressed, they take heroic and collective action, and they are defeated. Eisenstein's "intellectual" montage is already in evidence here. As the soldiers put down the workers — the capitalist squeezes a lemon. As the soldiers fire on the workers — Eisenstein cuts to a scene in which bulls are slaughtered.

Battleship Potemkin, first shown in 1926, was Eisenstein's most influential film. It is based on the story of a mutiny on a tsarist ship in 1905, and street demonstrations in Odessa. The hero of the film is the battleship.

When the director worked on his next film, *October,* made for the tenth anniversary of the Revolution, he had a reputation to live up to. Eisenstein did not resist the temptation of gigantomania. Although his previous two films had dealt with well-defined, relatively small-scale events, the story of the October uprising could not be simply told. The film is sprawling, and unlike *Strike* and *Potemkin,* it lacks artistic unity. Although Eisenstein's montage is always obtrusive, in this film it is particularly so.

Eisenstein's admirers pointed out that *Potemkin,* and especially *October,* were taken by contemporaries and by later generations as documentary accounts. It is true that even historians have had trouble in escaping the impact of the pictorial presentation of events. This result, however, does not testify to Eisenstein's artistry. *October* gives the effect of a documentary, because no real documentaries exist of the taking of the Winter Palace, because the film has no actors, and because, with the lavish support of the Soviet state, Eisenstein used thousands of extras. By creating pseudoevents, by making the October 1917 events in Petrograd more large-scale and therefore more heroic than they really were, Eisenstein produced useful propaganda. This most ambitious film about the October Revolution was not ready to be shown for the celebration of its tenth anniversary. Trotsky's final defeat in the internecine struggle necessitated his removal from *October*. We have no reason to think that Eisenstein objected to the use of his film for such an immediate and small-scale political goal. He was happy to serve the regime in any way he was asked to. Not being a deeply political person, he drew no distinction between serving the lofty aims of communism and the far less lofty purposes of Stalin.

Pudovkin, Eisenstein's not always friendly rival, was ready for his anniversary offering. His *End of Saint Petersburg* was one of the most impressive films of the 1927 season. Pudovkin, unlike Eisenstein, was interested in individuals. At the center of the film, there is a story of a peasant lad becoming a worker and then finally a conscious revolutionary. It is characteristic of the genre, however, that we never learn his name. He is always referred to in the titles as "lad." Clearly, here we are dealing with a case of symbolism.

Aleksandr Dovzhenko was much more drawn to symbols than Pudovkin. His fine revolutionary spectacle *Arsenal,* made in 1929, was steeped in symbolism. The film was loosely built on a small-scale strike in Kiev, in 1918. However, the uninitiated viewer can follow the story line only with the greatest difficulty. Dovzhenko wanted to present images and did so in a ballad-like fashion. These images are haunting, and they remain with the viewer. *Potemkin*'s hero was the battleship; Pudovkin chose everyman, the little person who sided with the Revolution; *Arsenal*'s hero is the Ukrainian worker, who is unconquerable, whose strength reaches mythic proportions. In the famous ending of this film, Timosh, the central character, bares his breast in front of the firing squad, but bullets cannot kill him.

That artists as different in temperament and style as Eisenstein, Pudovkin, and Dovzhenko made films that shared so much, shows that the appearance of the revolutionary spectacle in the late 1920s was not the consequence of the individual director's predilection. The period created this genre.

What ideological message did the Soviet people get from these revolutionary spectacles? The films mentioned in this section all legitimized the Revolution and thereby legitimized the child of the Revolution, the regime. The films portrayed the Revolution not as a series of contingent events but as something predetermined. Good and evil clashed, and good inevitably won. In the film version of the events, political issues were not decided by the behavior of ordinary mortals, full of foibles, prejudices, and self-interest. The films removed the Revolution from the realm of the ordinary.

These films were a step toward socialist realism. They pointed to the

Plate 13 Scene from Dovzhenko's film *Arsenal*, 1929. Timosh the Ukrainian worker is in front of the firing squad. Bullets cannot kill him.

future by repudiating realism and in its stead assuming heroic, romantic stance. They showed a contempt for events as they really happened and for human beings as they really were. To be sure, before reaching socialist realism several important steps still had to be taken. The notion of the nameless hero, the collective, the little man as a decisive force had to be abandoned in the age of Stalinism. More important, artistic experimentation, which makes these films impressive at a distance of five decades, was not to be tolerated in the new age.

Most people did not want their revolutionary heroics straight. There are no audience statistics available, but the evidence suggests that films such as *Potemkin* and *Arsenal,* however much they impressed foreign critics, did not appeal to Russian audiences, and that is not at all surprising. Most people wanted to be entertained: They wanted a story, they wanted characters with whom they could identify. The great bulk of the revolutionary films at least attempted to entertain while instructing.

Revolutionary movies can be placed on a continuum. At one end of the spectrum, the revolutionary message was central to the film; on the other, the Revolution was there to make the film modish or to provide an interesting background for romantic and other adventures. In Pudovkin's two great films *Mother* and *The Heir of Gingis Khan,* made at the end of the 1920s, the revolutionary message was central. Both films, as well as *The End of Saint Petersburg,* were about the development of class and revolutionary consciousness. *Mother,* made in 1926 and based on M. Gorky's book, was Pudovkin's first great success. In the film, as in Gorky's book, a mother decides to follow her son's footsteps and joins the revolutionaries in their struggle. *The Heir of Gingis Khan* is one of the best films of the decade. In an exotic locale, a young Mongolian, reputed to be a descendant of the great conqueror, is picked by the British to play the role of the puppet. However, when the young man learns about the nefarious dealings of the imperialists and their cruelty, he decides to lead his people against the exploiters.

The theme of *Mother* was that in the new world it is the old who must learn from the young. This theme came to be very popular among Soviet directors. *Two Days,* a Ukrainian film made by Stabovoi in 1927, makes the same point. During the Civil War, when members of the upper classes escape from Bolshevik rule, an old servant hides his master's young son, who was left behind by accident. The old man does not even tell his Bolshevik son what he is doing. When the Whites return, the young upper-class boy, a little snake, informs on the servant's Bolshevik son, who is then killed. Now the old man finally understands that in the struggle of classes any feeling of pity for the enemy is misplaced. The enemy is merciless and so it must be fought mercilessly. The old man takes it on himself to burn down the manor house while the White officers and his treacherous young master are in it.

The argument that class interest supersedes other causes and other human feelings was also expressed in one of the most popular revolutionary films, Protazanov's *Forty First,* made in 1927. This is a Civil War love story with fable-like qualities. A Bolshevik woman soldier and a White officer are stranded on a desert island. They fall in love. When an enemy ship appears on the horizon, the class-conscious woman realizes that the ship would rescue the officer, and to avoid helping the enemy, she shoots her man. He is her forty-first kill. What makes the film better than Stabovoi's is that Protazanov at least hints at a moral complexity. The woman, without doubt, does the "right thing," but the viewer is not absolutely sure that Protazanov approves.

Many directors chose foreign and therefore exotic locales for their revolutionary stories. Room's *The Ghost That Will Not Return* was set in a Latin American country. Kozintsev and Trauberg's *New Babylon* dealt with the Paris commune. What these films had in common was a totally unrealistic portrayal of a non-Russian environment. Dovzhenko's first full-length film, *Diplomatic Pouch,* made in 1927, was almost comic in this respect. The British "political police" behave very much like Russians. All British workers and sailors are class-conscious proletarians who happily risk their lives in the service of the Soviet cause. The enemy is decadent and corrupt. We can tell that the representatives of the enemy are decadent because they dance with scantily dressed women. Class-conscious proletarians, on the other hand, are able to resist the allure of such females. There is very little in this dreadful film that would betray Dovzhenko's considerable talent.

In many a "revolutionary" film, the Revolution was there only for decoration. Kozintsev and Trauberg's visually interesting but confused film, *The Club of the Big Deed,* is one example. The directors did not seem to be interested in the history of the Decemberist rising, which is the ostensible topic of the movie, nor did they care much about such abstract subjects as the nature of injustice or why people become revolutionaries. The film is full of unusual angle shots, lights photographed through night fog, and interesting reflections. The story is built on fantastic, overdrawn characters, who are not placed in any definite period of history. Films such as this one hardly strengthened anyone's revolutionary consciousness.

Films dealing with the contemporary world usually had a more complex message and expressed a more complex world view than the "revolutionary" films. Directors who distinguished themselves in making revolutionary spectacles were not particularly adept in dealing with the contemporary scene. Eisenstein, for example, in his entire career made only one film about his own times. This film, *The General Line,* was undoubtedly his worst. He attempted to apply his methods when describing the life of the modern peasantry. Dealing with symbols and types, rather than with more or less believable characters seemed incongruous in a contemporary village setting. The film's greatest human-interest story is a marriage between — cattle.

The most interesting films about NEP Russia were made not by the famous directors Eisenstein, Pudovkin, and Dovzhenko but by Room, Protazanov, and Ermler. These men shared an interest in real people and in their foibles. It was their ability to bring human beings to the screen that attracted the audience.

Their films, with the exception of Room's *Three Meshchanskaia Street,* were not true-to-life dramas. Silent-film makers even outside Russia rarely attempted unvarnished realism. Soviet directors mercilessly caricatured – and often in the process unwittingly glamorized – wicked NEP men. They attacked bureaucracy. They warned their viewers against the evils of bourgeois decadence. Nevertheless, the problems that the directors discussed and the characters they caricatured were exaggerated and distorted versions of something real. On rare occasions, the Soviet people had the pleasure of getting glimpses of people like themselves. In the usual contemporary film, first some wrong or injustice was presented, which at the end was righted: The police arrived just in time; the Party understood the problem; the Komsomol intervened. Before reaching the end of the film, the director delivered some stinging observations about his society. The happy ending was always the least believable part.

Protazanov, the most senior and prolific of the Soviet directors, was primarily the portraitist of the village and little town. Because he left Russia at the end of the Civil War in 1920 and returned only in 1924, there is no reason to believe in his original commitment to communism.[45] He was not a deeply political person and was not particularly interested in technical innovations. He was perfectly happy to adopt techniques developed by others. His strength was his ability to observe the minutiae of life, his interest in character and in telling a story.

After the rather hostile reception of *Aelita,* Protazanov made *His Call* in 1925. In *Aelita* the recently returned emigrant showed Mars to be a more interesting place than Soviet Russia and in general depicted Soviet reality in somber colors. By contrast, *His Call* was, from a political point of view, much more acceptable. The story concerns a vicious emigrant who returns to Russia incognito to look for his hidden jewels. To accomplish this nefarious purpose, he pretends to fall in love with a young textile worker who is living in the place where the valuables were hidden. The plot enabled the director to show what was called at the time "new Soviet life," that is, the introduction of electricity, the kindergarten, the workers' club, and the library.[46] The young man soon exhibits his wickedness, and he is, of course, unmasked. The last reel of the film is in no obvious way connected with the rest of the story. Into this little town comes the sad news that the leader of the world proletariat, Lenin, has died. This is the time for the workers to show their redoubled commitment to the Leninist cause and join the Party. The young woman who fell for the capitalist rat feels herself unworthy of such an honor. Nevertheless, the Party is forgiving and she is redeemed. This film was a step in the development of the Lenin cult, and in this respect, if in no other, it was ahead of its time.

Protazanov's next film, much less ambitious, was far more attractive. *The Tailor from Torzhuk,* made in 1925, is about a lost and regained lottery ticket. The central character is an archetypical little man who when he wins a lot of money can dream only a very bourgeois dream of owning his own elegant tailor shop. The film is without true villains. Protazanov gently warns his peasant viewers that they must watch out for the sharp dealings of the city folk.

The Tailor from Torzhuk was a slight comedy. By contrast, Protazanov's 1927 film *Don Diego and Pelegaia* was a "problem" film and a biting satire. It was made to attack the heartlessness of Soviet bureaucracy. Its story was based on a feuilleton that had appeared in *Pravda.* An old peasant woman is jailed for the ridiculously insignificant offense of crossing the railroad tracks at the wrong place. She is treated most uncaringly by domineering, stupid little men. Her husband, an old peasant, turns to everyone for help. In the process, we get a strikingly realistic description of some aspects of Soviet life. The representatives of the city, who lord it over the peasants, cannot tell a beet from a potato. The old peasant is befuddled not only by the problems but even by phrases that are incomprehensible to him. When someone suggests to him that he should apply for amnesty on international women's day, he answers: "Kakaia zhe mezhdunarodnaia – ona derevenskaia!" ("What are you talking about, 'international' – she is a village woman!") The film was meant to be funny, but what one remembers is the genuine tragedy of simple people caught up in a machine that they do not understand. Finally, of course, there is a resolution. The Komsomol cell learns about the problem, and the young people take it on themselves to help and intervene. When the old woman is freed – she joins the Komsomol.

F. Ermler also made a film about the village Komsomol, *The Parisian Cobbler,* but he is better known for his films about Petrograd. One of these, *Katka's Reinette Apples,* made in 1926, is a most interesting portrayal of early NEP urban society. Katka, a young peasant girl, comes to Petrograd to earn enough money to buy a cow, but she cannot find a job at a factory and is forced to sell apples on the street. Private trade is the first step toward degeneracy and criminal life. She gets mixed up with a wicked villain, Semka, and she becomes pregnant. However, she is still basically good and therefore realizes the wickedness of the man, and she breaks with him.

The film acquaints us with the society of street vendors. In Ermler's scheme of values, Katka is preferable to Semka's new girlfriend, Verka, because Katka trades in apples and Verka in foreign goods. The street vendors, illegal little business people, also have their sense of community. They hire someone, Vadka, an unemployed intellectual, to look out for the police. We learn how loathsome Verka really is when she refuses to contribute to Vadka's meager compensation. In this bustling, exciting, but very poor world, Soviet power seems very remote. There is no mention of Lenin, of the Party, or of the noble goals of communism. The authorities exist only in the form of the police, who seem none too capable.

Plate 14. Scene from the film *Don Diego and Pelegaia* by Protazanov, 1927. The heartless Soviet bureaucrat arrests the innocent old peasant woman for crossing the railroad tracks at the wrong spot.

The most remarkable character in the movie is not the grotesquely over-drawn Semka, or even the prototype of the strong Soviet woman figure, Katka, but the unemployed intellectual, Vadka. Here is a man who is incapable of taking care of himself under the new circumstances. He cannot even properly kill himself: He jumps into shallow water. He returns to the bridge to find that his only jacket has been stolen. Katka saves the unfortunate fellow several times. She takes him in and she gives him something to do: take care of her new baby while she is out working. Vadka is a thoroughly decent man. In the climactic scene of the movie, he confronts, fights, and defeats Semka. The happy ending is inevitable. Katka gives up her shady job and becomes a worker. She marries the deserving and loving Vadka, and the alliance of working classes and honest intelligentsia is reaffirmed.

The films of Ermler and Protazanov, and of other directors who attempted to portray contemporary life, were often attacked by critics. Party activists hardly wanted moviemakers to hold up a mirror to their society. It was this genre that suffered the most and indeed disappeared in the 1930s when the political climate changed.

The audience

In 1923, Trotsky wrote an article titled "Vodka, the Church, and the Cinema" for *Pravda*. In it he said:

The fact that we so far, i.e., in nearly six years have not taken possession of the cinema shows how slow and uneducated we are, not to say, frankly, stupid. This weapon, which cries out to be used, is the best instrument for propaganda, technical, educational, and industrial propaganda, propaganda against alcohol, propaganda for sanitation, political propaganda, any kind of propaganda you please, a propaganda which is accessible to everyone, which is attractive, which cuts into the memory and may be made into a possible source of revenue.[47]

Trotsky went on to argue that the cinema should compete with and defeat both the barroom and the church.

The Commissar for War held conventional views concerning the propaganda significance of the cinema. Communist leaders at Party congresses and in editorials repeatedly affirmed the importance of movies for Communist education; the idea that the Party must control and exploit the film industry became a cliché.

When Trotsky spoke about movies competing with vodka, he had in mind a competition in two different senses: Films would draw workers away from the barroom by giving them healthy entertainment and education, and the film industry would take the place of alcohol as a source of revenue for the government. Stalin, at the Fifteenth Party Congress in 1927, introduced exactly the same idea.[48] (In fact, the Soviet government never came close to achieving this goal. At the end of the 1920s, the yearly income from the vodka monopoly was approximately a half-billion rubles, while movies brought in a paltry 15 million.)[49]

Should the movie industry be developed as a source of revenue or should it be an instrument of political education? To us it is evident that the two goals called for different policies. One could obscure the contradiction between the two goals only by assuming that the people wanted and were willing to pay for seeing films that were "good for them." All evidence showed that this was not the case. The Soviet people, like people elsewhere, wanted entertainment, and heavy doses of propaganda bored them. The Party leaders, however, were predisposed to overlook the obvious. It was hard to admit that the taste of the workers and peasants was, if anything, more petit bourgeois than the preference of the petite bourgeoisie and that, by disregarding reality, they could avoid making hard investment decisions. The illusion that Communist education would somehow pay for itself and would even bring in money was irresistible.

Today one marvels at the artistic effervescence of the Soviet cinema in the late 1920s. Therefore it is surprising that in contemporary discussions on film there was no tone of self-congratulation. On the contrary, everyone was talking about impending crisis. The film industry did not satisfy its critics because the Party set impossible tasks for the industry. The Party leaders wanted the directors to make films that were artistically worthwhile, politically beneficial, and also popular. On occasion, a director satisfied two of the three requirements, but no one managed to satisfy all three.

Sovkino, which was responsible for production and distribution of films in the late 1920s, drew heavy criticism.[50] It was widely attacked both in the daily press and in professional literature for being commercially minded. This was unfair, for the regime was unwilling or unable to invest in the industry but expected it to make money.

The charge of commercialism was made in two areas: its policy of importing films, and its alleged unwillingness to provide films for the countryside.

It was inevitable that the Soviet regime would make a sustained attempt to use the technological wonder of the cinema to bring political enlightenment to the peasants. Every Bolshevik knew that the Party was weak in the countryside and that the peasants had only a vague understanding of Communist goals and methods. Party congresses reaffirmed the need to improve propaganda among the peasants, and film was an obvious weapon. It could be used among illiterates, and the medium itself was attractive. Peasants, like everyone else, were curious to see the new invention. The use of transportable projectors was so obvious that it was "discovered" early in the Civil War. The peasants who would not sit through a political lecture came to see movies, whatever movies, with excitement.

As in so many other areas in the history of Soviet propaganda, the gap between intentions and reality was wide. it is clear that the failure was due to underestimating the value of the medium. The Bolsheviks could not achieve more because they lacked money and cadres. In addition, they were harmed by a particular Bolshevik flaw of the time, overoptimism, which made them imagine that it was possible to do much with little. Such overoptimism on occasion made it less likely that the scarce resources would be used wisely.

From the reports sent by Party functionaries traveling with projectors in the mid-1920s, we can form a picture of the difficulties. First of all, there were never enough projectors. In the middle of 1925, there were said to be only 900 machines for the entire country.[51] The number soon increased to 1,500, which was still not enough.[52] Moreover, a large percentage of the projectors was made before the war by foreign companies. Naturally, given the age of the projectors, the difficult conditions while traveling, and poor maintenance, the machines often broke down. By the mid-twenties, foreign companies stopped making projectors with built-in generators. Consequently, the Russians had to manufacture their own, and these were of poor quality. According to an estimate in the middle of 1926, half the projectors lay idle because they could not be easily repaired.[53]

Political-education workers equipped with projectors and films took one- or two-month-long trips through the countryside. According to a report from Irkutsk province, in the course of a journey, they visited 15 to 20 villages. In each they gave two performances. First they showed a feature film, and then a collection of shorts. They served approximately 5,000 people on a trip. Although the peasants were charged admission, 15 to 20 kopeks, only one out of three trips financed itself. One of the problems, it seems, was that there were not enough large halls in the villages. Often people came from neighboring settlements, as they heard news of the showing, but they could not be accommodated.[54]

Aside from unreliable projectors, the difficulties in traveling (which in Siberia, where settlements were small and far from one another, must have been considerable), and the lack of proper halls for the show, the greatest difficulty was a lack of trained personnel. The Party needed people who were mechanically minded, and, above all, politically trained and tactful. Often they had to read the intertitles aloud for an illiterate audience. At times, they had to explain some aspects of the film that the peasants could not understand. Such people were in short supply.

Also, there were not enough films for peasant audiences. The Bolsheviks, who had a patronizing attitude toward the peasants, assumed that films suitable for city viewers were not suitable for villagers. It was undoubtedly true that people who had no previous exposure to movies reacted negatively to experimental techniques, to quick cuttings, to strange juxtapositions — all characteristic of, for example, Eisenstein's work. The peasants preferred their films as realistic as possible, with long uninterrupted action. Some observers even suggested that the peasants would enjoy films more if projection speeds were slowed down.[55]

However, the Bolsheviks were concerned primarily with political content. In the debates that took place in the mid-1920s, it was even argued that the peasants should see nothing but educational films and newsreels.[56] Even the "liberals" assumed that films the slightest bit critical of Soviet reality could not be shown in the countryside. The showing of *Three Meshchanskaia Street,* for example, was out of the question. Dramatizations of classics, such as Kozintsev and Trauberg's *Overcoat,* could not be shown; *Aelita* was also considered too critical of Soviet life. The decade's commercially most successful film was *The Bear's Wedding* by Eggert. The scenario of the film was written by Commissar of Enlightenment Lunacharskii, on the basis of a Prosper Mérimée story. The film script, among other things, has scenes depicting a nineteenth-century feudal lord taking advantage of peasant women. This was considered too risqué for village people, and so they were not allowed to see the film.[57]

In matters of access to information and cultural events, the Bolsheviks at the beginning of their regime set up a rigidly hierarchical system. The large cities, especially the two capitals, were at the top. In the commercial movie houses of Leningrad and Moscow during the 1920s, audiences could enjoy a remarkably varied fare. Workers' clubs, by contrast, constantly complained that Sovkino did not care about them and was sending them old films, films that were not particularly popular. The situation was worse in the provincial cities, where distribution was haphazard.[58] In a small town it would take several years before even such a classic as *Potemkin* would appear. The peasants were least favored.

We have a glimpse of what the peasants actually saw in a report from Irkutsk province in 1926.[59] The writer complained that before setting out, he and his comrades looked through dozens of films but found almost none suitable. The regional office of Sovkino sent them films such as *How Snooky Became a Capitalist* (Snooky was an ape) and educational films such as *Cooperatives in Normandy,* a boring, outdated film that had nothing to do with the lives of the Russian peasants.

On each trip they took only one feature film and some newsreels and educational films. On the first trip they exhibited a film called *Evdokiia Rozhnovskaia;* on the second, *Khveska;* and on the third, *The Wolf's Duty. Evdokiia Rozhnovskaia* was made in 1924, but *Khveska* was made in 1920 and *The Wolf's Duty* in 1921. None of the films had artistic pretensions. *Evdokiia Rozhnovskaia* received reasonably wide distribution in the cities, but the other two films were practically unknown. All three were Civil War stories and took place in the countryside.

Of the films considered suitable for the peasants, not enough copies were available. As a result, even functioning projectors often were idle. Bringing political enlightenment to the peasantry through cinema was a Herculean task. The regime's accomplishments were not negligible, but they were not truly impressive.

Those who attacked Sovkino for not taking care of the needs of the countryside were usually the same people who disapproved of the agency's import policies.

Clearly, the Soviet people, if given a chance, preferred foreign, especially American, films. Foreign hits, such as *Robin Hood* or the *Mark of Zorro*, both with Douglas Fairbanks, played in the capital for months and were seen by many more people that *Potemkin*.[60] Even K. A. Mal'tsev, an opponent of the import policy of Sovkino, had to admit that on the average, a foreign film brought in ten times as much profit as a domestic one.[61] That audiences preferred American films did not in itself reflect poorly on the quality of Russian products. The Russians' love for the works of Hollywood require no special explanation. Everywhere in Europe the public taste was dominated by Hollywood. People all over the world enjoyed the adventures, the glamorous stars, and the spectacles Hollywood was able to manufacture. It made no difference that intellectuals deplored the effects of American films, often in terms not too dissimilar from those of Bolshevik critics. The difference between Soviet and non-Soviet critics was, of course, that the Bolsheviks did not have to stop at criticism. They could control what entered the country, and they were equipped with a world view that allowed them to give to the people not what the people wanted but what was "good for them."

Under the circumstances, what is surprising is that the Soviet state continued to import foreign products. The explanation should be sought in the particular organization of the Soviet film industry. Sovkino was motivated to import. Since the regime wanted to create a film industry and since it was unable or unwilling to provide the studios with enough money, Sovkino hardly had a choice. The Russian people enjoyed the luxury of seeing what they wanted to see, above all because their state was still too poor to provide them with what they should have wanted to see.

Indeed, in the course of the 1920s, the Soviet Union, as it produced more films of its own, gradually restricted imports. Imported films, and the profit from them, exceeded domestic products for the last time in 1926–7. In that year, 51 percent of the films were imported.[62]

Soviet critics believed that *all* foreign films were to some extent harmful because they were filled with a "hostile class ideology." From the Soviet point of view, however, the damage was not limited to the direct influence of an alien ideology. As long as films were imported, Russian directors had to compete for an audience; they had to put into their films those elements that attracted people to foreign products.[63]

As long as the regime allowed the importation of foreign films, it could have no control over the domestic industry. The great change occurred with the introduction of collectivization. A corollary of the altered political atmosphere was the stopping of imports. Now the directors did not have to compete any longer. They had a captive audience.

CHAPTER 10

Press and book publishing in the 1920s

Newspapers

A casual observer looking at a Soviet newspaper from the 1920s is likely to be struck by the dull format and style and by the thin and repetitious content. It is hard to reconcile these papers with our image of the Bolsheviks as master propagandists. Could such predictable and boring articles ever win over a reader? It is, of course, impossible to know whether a single article or a series of articles ever convinced many people. But notwithstanding the dullness of the press, it is evident that the network of newspapers played a decisively important role in the establishment and functioning of the Soviet regime. The newspaper network was the blood-circulation system of the body politic: It carried esential information everywhere rapidly – at least after the difficult years of crisis. The average citizen learned what were the legitimate public issues as defined by the leaders and learned the verbiage of political discourse. For the activist and for the Party functionary, reading the newspaper diligently was even more important. They found out how they had to act in small and large matters and learned how to discuss political and even nonpolitical issues with their fellow citizens.

The problems of increasing circulation. In the short run the introduction of the NEP was a disaster for the Soviet press. Under war communism a most peculiar system existed: Newspapers received what they needed free and in turn, they distributed their product also without payment. How many copies and which newspapers appeared depended on the availability of paper. How the extremely scarce paper supply was distributed depended above all on the strength of the sponsoring agency. During the Civil War, for example, the military press flourished; under war conditions the Red Army was a powerful agency, and its needs were well protected.

Under such circumstances it was impossible to know how well the news-

224

papers were doing their business. Indeed, it was impossible to know how widely they were read. The distribution system, understandably, functioned abysmally: We have a report, for example, from the village of Klinskaia from March 1921. The village librarian reported that he had just received a large package of newspapers from 1919 to 1920.[1] The newspapers had few responses from workers. In the editorial offices of the land, journalists had reason to doubt that anyone was receiving their message. The system of war communism was obviously a wasteful one.

Free newspapers, clearly, could not be reconciled with the principles of the NEP. The demand for cost accounting, that is, the requirement to become self-supporting, or at least more or less so, led to a precipitous decline in circulation figures. On January 1, 1922, there were 312 national and provincial papers and 490 local (uezd) publications with a combined circulation of 2,661,189. In the first half of 1922 there was a decline in every category. The bottom was reached in August. In that month only 163 national and provincial papers and 138 local ones came out. Their combined circulation was under 1 million (993,050).[2] This meant that in half a year the number of newspapers published in Soviet Russia declined by two thirds.

The leaders of the Party were acutely aware of the crisis. At a time when the significance of propaganda was clear to every Party activist, at a time when the enemy seemed to be gaining strength every day, the Bolsheviks could not reach the people through the printed word. Although the situation was bad everywhere, the position of the local press was particularly depressing. The local papers had always been the weakest, both in form and content, and now they seemed to be disappearing altogether.

From August on, the situation gradually improved. By March 1923, there was once again a larger number of papers – 293 national and provincial ones and 235 local ones, with a combined circulation of 1,753,720.[3] The Soviet leadership had reason to take satisfaction in overcoming the crisis. Not only did the press become a much smaller burden on government finances, but also the newspapers that survived were the better ones. The government continued to give some subsidies to local papers and also to the press of the national minorities, but by and large the major newspapers became and remained self-supporting.

One method of overcoming the financial crisis of the press was particularly appropriate in the capitalist world of the NEP. Lenin and other Bolshevik leaders had always been impressed by the power of advertising. During the twilight period of the free press in late 1917 and early 1918 the young Soviet state denied the right to bourgeois newspapers to carry commercial notices in the hope of undermining their financial strength. Now advertising was used to buttress the Soviet press. In 1922 and 1923, at the time when the Soviet press carried the largest amount of commercials, advertisements in the major national newspapers took up as much as one-eighth to one-quarter of their space. Unfortunately, this method of financ-

225

ing helped those papers the most that needed help the least. In the villages and small towns of the land there were not enough enterprises with the need or resources to advertise. Indeed, even in the major cities it was the state-owned enterprises, theaters and cinemas, that supported the press this way.

A far more important method of restoring the economic health of newspapers was soliciting subscriptions. The Eleventh Party Congress affirmed that every Party member must be a reader and a subscriber (individual or collective) of the Party press. The Twelfth Congress, which met in April 1923, restated this decision. The next Party congress, in the following year, once again turned to this matter: "The task of the next year should be to make every Party member a subscriber to the Party press, and to achieve that every working man and woman and Red Army soldier read a newspaper. We must send 2 million copies of newspapers into the villages, not less than one copy for every ten households.[4]

Of course, the Party's interest in persuading its members and sympathizers to subscribe to and to read newspapers was not primarily economic. Nevertheless, by defining the task of reading newspapers as a political one, it managed to restore the economic health of the press in an impressively short period. The growth in circulation figures was remarkable: In January 1923, 411 papers appeared in printings of 1.5 million copies. In November of the same year, there were 590 papers with a combined circulation of over 2 million. In the following years, the number of papers did not increase, but their combined circulation continued to grow. In January 1925, that figure was over 7 million; in January 1927, over 8 million. At the end of the NEP period in January 1929, the Soviet Union claimed a combined circulation of almost 12 million for Soviet newspapers.[5] The Soviet accomplishment was undoubtedly impressive. We must remember, however, that the Soviet authorities changed the definition of a newspaper in such a way as to overstate the growth.

They included in their terminology periodical publications. For example, out of the approximately 600 "newspapers" that appeared in 1928, only about 200 were dailies. This was a much smaller number than what had existed before the outbreak of the war.[6] Soviet statistics simply added the circulation figures of all periodical publications, often making no distinction between dailies and weeklies. On the basis of such statistics publicists proudly compared the Soviet Union with tsarist Russia, where circulation figures never reached 3 million.[7] Despite this change in the method of assessing circulation, it is clear that at the end of the 1920s more newspapers were available to more Russians than ever before.

The most important task of the Soviet press was to provide enough copies for the people. But it was almost as important to be able to appeal to every segment of the population by using different languages, by discussing different issues, and by addressing topics of particular interest to different target audiences. The Soviet regime was the first in the world with the task and opportunity to build an entire press network. In a capitalist society, the problem of how to cater to special audiences is resolved by the market mechanism. Publishers produce newspapers for those willing to pay for them; conversely, to sell as many papers as possible they put out papers that the people want to read. In the Soviet Union the problem was not so simple. Just how exactly the papers should differ from one another and what should be their relationship to one another were topics discussed by Bolshevik journalists almost from the time of the regime's creation. In 1919, the first congress of journalists passed a resolution that spoke of "mass" and "leading" papers. This resolution, however, did not end the discussion. Some prominent Bolsheviks, most important among them N. I. Bukharin, the editor of *Pravda,* expressed concern that if his paper were a "leading" one, it might lose touch with the workers. Nevertheless, distinctions clearly made sense, and they were very much in the spirit of Bolshevism. Communist leaders always thought in hierarchical terms. Since, in their view, the interpretation of political and social events was a science, it made sense to treat those who were more "advanced" differently from the rest. Accordingly, for example, movies and books that were appropriate for city dwellers were harmful for the less educated peasants.

The person who spoke up most often for differentiation was I. Vardin, the head of the press subsection of the agitprop department of the Central Committee of the Party. He said to a congress of journalists:

We have serious, leading organs, and we have a fighting, mass-popular press. We have come to this differentiation in a more or less hit-or-miss fashion. This took place not without some resistance on the part of some "conservative" comrades who supposed that *Pravda* and *Izvestiia* can take the place of popular newspapers. The conservatives, of course, are mistaken. The differentiation of newspapers should be introduced strictly and decisively. Our press should address every stratum of the population in a different form, but in the same, Communist language. We should have a newspaper for everyone (*Izvestiia VTsIK*), we should have a newspaper for the avant-garde of the working classes (*Pravda*). We need fighting, mass papers penetrating into the working classes, such as (*Rabochaia gazeta*), and into the peasantry (*Bednota*). In the localities we need provincial papers, such as *Rabochaia Moskva,* and in the countries, mass, peasant papers.[8]

The Twelfth Congress reaffirmed the position championed most strongly by Vardin.

By design and by experimentation, the press network created during the NEP period was differentiated vertically; that is, there were national, provincial, and local newspapers. It was also differentiated horizontally: Each important institution of the Soviet system had its own press. The Party, the government, the trade unions, the Komsomol, the Zhenotdel, (women's sections), the pioneer movement, and so forth, all put out their publications. Contemporaries, rather confusingly, at times spoke of "leading" and "mass" papers, and on other occasions of peasant and worker papers. The worker papers by and large were more "leading" than the peasant papers, but there were distinctions among worker papers also. The local press, except in industrial districts, was oriented toward the peasantry. Because the Party was the most important institution within the Soviet polity, its paper, *Pravda,* was the primary newspaper of the Soviet Union. It was the only newspaper whose editor, Bukharin, was a figure of major importance within the Soviet hierarchy. *Pravda* printed the most authoritative editorials, published the most extensive excerpts from important speeches at Party congresses and conferences, and devoted the largest amount of space to theoretical and practical questions of Party life. *Izvestiia,* the government's paper, on the other hand, had a more extensive coverage of foreign affairs in the 1920s than did *Pravda.*

It was easiest to provide the cities with newspapers. The Party had the greatest strength here, distribution presented few problems, and the workers were interested in reading the daily press far more than the peasants. Naturally, the revival of the press after the crisis of 1922 was forecast in the urban areas. By contrast, providing the countryside with papers during the first years of the NEP period seemed almost an insoluble problem. The major peasant paper of the time, *Bednota,* was completely unable to overcome the difficulties. Although the paper paid special attention to the problems of agriculture, it was not written in a style attractive to a peasant audience. The paper was read mostly by Bolshevik activists working in the countryside. Vardin presented evidence at the fourth congress of journalists in 1922 that clearly showed the extent of failure in attempting to penetrate the villages. He said that although the Ukraine was much better supplied than the rest of the Soviet Union, even there the daily circulation of peasant papers was a ridiculously low 9,000. This meant that there were more villages in the Ukraine at the time than copies of newspapers.[9]

The Bolsheviks made extraordinary efforts to overcome their weakness. First they had to face the total inadequacy of the distribution system. It was relatively easy to supply villages on a railroad line, but far-away settlements were seemingly beyond reach. Here the press depended on the postal service for delivery, but not every district even had such a service. Under such circumstances delivery was at times delayed for a month or longer. Even as late as November 1923, *Pravda* wrote that only 5 percent of all newspapers distributed were peasant papers, and these more often than not went to village soviet offices and not to the simple peasants.[10]

The distribution system gradually improved by slowly overcoming the faults of the postal system and by organizing a special agency. This new agency, *Sviaz,* worked from 800 drop points around the country. It delivered papers from the railroad stations to village soviet offices or, on occasion, to individual subscribers.[11] Soviet authorities instructed their supporters in the countryside, Party and Komsomol members, and workers of the village soviet to help disseminate the press. The great political significance of the task was evident.

A major turning point was the appearance of a new peasant "mass" newspaper, *Krestianskaia gazeta* (Peasant newspaper). This newspaper, which first came out in November 1923, was a weekly but soon expanded to appear three times a week.[12] The popularity of this peasant paper grew remarkably. Within a short time it became the largest newspaper in the Soviet Union, with a circulation of between 1 and 2 million. It far outdistanced its rival, *Bednota*. In contemporary terminology *Bednota* was a "leading" paper in contrast to *Krestianskaia gazeta*, which was a "mass" paper. That is, *Krestianskaia gazeta* was written for the little-educated peasant reader, whereas the other newspaper was meant to serve the needs of Communist activists in the countryside. The new paper took the task of the education and political education of peasants on itself. It participated in the literacy campaign by publishing in every issue, from March 1925 on, a page from a literacy textbook. The paper sent a folder to each subscriber to encourage him to create his own textbook.[13] The popularity of *Krestianskaia gazeta* was one of the great successes of the Bolshevik Party in its efforts to establish its influence among the peasantry.

Bolshevik publicists well understood that it was not enough to put out a national paper, however successful. The regime needed local newspapers, because only these could truly respond to the immediate concerns of the peasants. The strengthening of the local press was a difficult task indeed. The Party at this time did not possess reliable and experienced people capable of putting together interesting and, at the same time, ideologically sound, publications. Further, the economic base was missing for small newspapers, and therefore these had to continue to depend on government subsidies. The Party repeatedly instructed its executive committees (provincial and district) to continue to regard the publication of local, peasant papers as major political tasks. The quality of the provincial and district papers, however, remained weak: They frequently reprinted articles from the national press and wrote about local affairs in a stilted fashion.

Establishing newspapers for special audiences such as soldiers and youth was an incomparably easier task than serving the peasantry. After the end of the Civil War, the Party assigned relatively low priority to military papers. Only in the mid-twenties did the situation change. *Krasnaia zvezda*, the centerpiece of the network, started to appear in January 1924.[14] In the course of the 1920s its circulation never went beyond a few tens of thousands. In addition, the Party aimed to establish small papers in each military district. The goal of these newspapers, of course, was to improve the political education of the soldiers.

The Komsomol press grew much faster. The central paper of the organization, *Komsomolskaia pravda*, started to appear in May 1925.[15] The paper quickly acquired a readership, and by the end of the year it had a circulation of over one hundred thousand. The paper was among the liveliest ones in the Soviet Union.

In the course of the 1920s the Bolsheviks managed to build an all-encompassing network of newspapers and to increase the circulation of their press impressively. Their real innovation, however, was not in the character of the press network but in the newspapers themselves.

As the Bolshevik publicists of the period put it, theirs was a press of a new type. Even a most casual observer could see that Soviet newspapers were like no others. Perhaps the most obvious, but superficial, difference was that Soviet papers were extremely thin. Most papers in the twenties appeared in four-page issues, though on occasion there were six- or even eight-page ones. On the other hand, a major "leading" paper, such as *Bednota*, in the middle of the decade most often consisted of only two pages. A considerable portion of the scarce space, especially in the first half of the twenties, was taken up by advertisements.

The lack of space, however, did not result in concise journalism. On the contrary. Newspapers reprinted an endless series of boring speeches given at congresses, conferences, and on festive occasions. These were extremely repetitious. In addition, space in the papers was taken up by printing laws and regulations. Several times a week "leading" papers, such as *Pravda, Izvestiia,* and *Bednota,* published "theoretical" articles, in which the current leadership expressed its point of view on some question of the day. Little space was left for what anyone could describe as the news.

Nevertheless, foreign news coverage in the 1920s was superior to what was to come. At this time the Soviet leaders still believed that a knowledge of the world was part of education and culture and that therefore, somehow, such knowledge would contribute to building socialism. A random and admittedly cursory comparison of *Pravda* and the *New York Times* for September 1923 reveals that the Soviet paper did mention the most important matters happening around the world. The inferiority of the Soviet coverage had three sources. First of all, a lack of space prevented discussion in depth. Most of the news items appeared in the form of telegraphic dispatches. In this respect *Izvestiia* was slightly better, but only slightly. The second source of weakness was that the Russians had almost no foreign correspondents but had to rely on foreign wire services. Only on unusual occasions, for example, when Russian diplomats appeared at the Genoa conference, did Soviet papers send their own people abroad. As a result, some of the reporting was wildly inaccurate. *Pravda* and *Izvestiia* went on for days about the millions of victims of the Tokyo earthquake, for example, when the *New York Times* in its first account from Japan immediately correctly identified the number of dead as between one hundred and one hundred fifty thousand. Third, and most important, the press presented its stories almost invariably in a didactic fashion. Trotsky, in a 1923 *Pravda* article in which he argued against misleading headlines, in passing gave a good example of such coverage:

A simple report on a second-rate strike is often headlined "It's Begun!" or "The Denouement Is Approaching," whereas the cable itself talks briefly about a movement of railwaymen, without mentioning causes or aims. On the next day there is nothing about this event; nor on the day after. The next time the reader sees above a dispatch a headline "It's Begun!" he already sees in this a frivolous attitude toward the matter, cheap newspaper sensationalism, and his interest in cables and newspapers fades.[16]

Foreign news was presented by Soviet journalists in such a way as to show the superiority of the Soviet system and the weaknesses of capitalism. Understandably, strikes in capitalist countries received extensive coverage.

The main difference, however, between Soviet and non-Soviet newspapers was not in covering foreign affairs but in dealing with domestic news. Soviet society in the NEP period faced basic social, political, economic, and foreign problems. These problems came to be intertwined with the internecine struggle within the top circles for leadership. The Soviet press, however, reflected these struggles most inadequately. Those in the know, and historians with the benefit of hindsight, could understand the significance of references and the use of some catch phrases in speeches and articles. But the average reader learned only about the outcome of the struggle. Once Trotsky and later Zinovev and Kamenev lost, and the newspapers were safely in the hands of their political enemies, the people could find out about the magnitude of the fight that had just taken place. The defeated leaders were mercilessly vilified. But the Soviet press, even when the leaders were divided, never presented social, political, and economic issues in terms of alternatives. It never calmly discussed the advantages and disadvantages of a proposed course of action.

Remarkably, the Soviet press had no reporters. Although the Soviet leaders seemed to believe that the people should have the opportunity to learn about the world, though they made sure that the presentation of events would be done from a "correct" political point of view, they had no interest in letting the Soviet people know what in fact was happening in their own country. Under the circumstances, the profession of the reporter, a person who traveled to find out and describe conditions, was an impossibility. What should enter the public sphere could not be left to reporters. Because Soviet papers did not compete with one another, they did not need reporters to get "scoops." The place of reporters was taken by correspondents, by editors, and by the Soviet news agency, which was called Rosta during the first half of the decade and Tass during the second.

Not only weighty domestic-news items but also human-interest stories were missing from the press. It is not immediately evident why this should have been so. Trotsky, for example, wrote:

A newspaper does not have the right not to be interested in what the masses, the people in the street, are interested in. Of course, our newspaper can and must throw light on facts, since it is called upon to educate, elevate, develop. But it will only reach the goal if it starts off from facts, thoughts and moods that really affect the mass reader. There is no doubt, for example, that trials and so called "events" – accidents, suicides, murders, dramas of jealousy, etc. greatly excite the thoughts and emotions of broad circles of the population. This is not surprising; they are all brilliant bits of vivid life. But our press, as a general rule, shows a great lack of attention to this, commenting at best in a few lines of small type. As a result the people in the street get their news from lower quality sources, and along with the news, lower quality elucidations.[17]

The Soviet press did not heed Trotsky's advice. As time went on, such "frivolous" matters completely disappeared, and Trotsky, even decades after his complete political defeat, continued to be attacked for his position.[18] One can only speculate why the Soviet press abjured human-interest stories. First, it had no need to publish them, since the newspapers did not have to compete for readership. But more important, discussions of the messy aspects of life did not lend themselves easily to a didactic treatment. Such stories would have spoiled the picture Soviet journalists wanted to create. Those who learned about the world entirely from Soviet newspapers must have believed that everything happened either through the efforts of the regime or through the dirty machinations of the enemy.

Soviet newspapers were high-minded and almost never deviated from their serious tone. In spite of all the discussions about the need for differentiation, for an outsider, at least, they were striking in their uniformity. Each had regular sections. The size and importance of the section varied according to the newspaper. Naturally, *Pravda* had a larger "Party life" section than other papers, and in *Krestianskaia gazeta,* for example, the largest section was given to news from the villages. A typical newspaper had a section entitled "workers' life" that was largely based on reports from factory correspondents. In the major, national papers there was a department called "In the republics" that reported on such news as the visit of a Politburo member to Kiev, the prospects for the next harvest in Stavropol province, and so forth. In addition newspapers contained regular columns on life in the army and on the judiciary. The papers also printed cultural news, including brief theater reviews and, from the middle of the decade, movie reviews. The sport column gave chess a disproportionately large share.

A Westerner who looks at Soviet newspapers of the 1920s will be struck by how much poorer, how much more boring, these were than, let us say, American papers published at the same time. The technical quality was low, the arrangement of articles and advertisements betrayed a lack of imagination, and very few illustrations or pictures relieved the monotony. It would be wrong to conclude, however, that the press failed to carry out its assigned tasks within the Soviet system. We know that the peasants read *Krestianskaia gazeta* with great interest.[19] We have figures from 1924 showing that the workers were avid newspaper readers. According to a survey, 90 percent of male workers read a paper regularly, spending a surprising forty-five minutes average on this activity every day. The workers must have been slow readers. But even if we are skeptical about the daily forty-five minutes, we have no reason to doubt that people were interested in their newspapers.[20] Female workers, who aside from their jobs also had to do housework, and who were more likely to be illiterates, spent much less time reading newspapers. Only one-third of them claimed to be regular readers.[21]

From the regime's point of view, the press was vitally important. It defined the terms of political discourse and established the limits of the public sphere. Without such a press, a Soviet-type system would have been unthinkable; indeed, the two were born at the same time. The boundaries of the public sphere varied. A larger number of issues were discussed publicly in the 1920s than in the period that followed; but boundaries have always existed. What made the Soviet Union different from pluralist societies was that the boundaries could be consciously changed and manipulated by a political elite and that the public sphere even in the 1920s was remarkably narrow.

The newspapers were particularly important for Party activists. Even if they lived in the most remote corners of the land, the press enabled them to remain in constant touch with their government. From it they learned how to interpret events around the world and even around themselves. The newspapers created their language. They determined how Party members talked to one another and how they talked to the rest of the population.

The worker correspondent. In an important article printed in 1901, "Where to Begin?," Lenin wrote: "The newspaper is not only a collective propagandist and collective agitator, it is also a collective organizer."[22] Ever since the Revolution, Bolshevik propagandists have quoted this sentence ad nauseam. It certainly has become Lenin's best-known thought on the subject of the press. What Lenin had in mind was that the very process of putting together a newspaper would help to create a socialist party, which, at the time, he considered to be the most important goal for the Russian Marxists. Although his insight concerned an immediate and practical matter, it clearly had wider implications. Lenin saw that carrying out propaganda could be an excellent opportunity for organizing. But how should the press carry out this task under Soviet rule? Obviously, different circumstances demanded different policies. The Party created the worker-peasant correspondents' movement in order to bring Lenin's idea up to date. (The Russian abbreviation *rabsel'kor* comes from worker-village correspondent.)

There was nothing new about newspapers printing letters from readers or attempting to help them with their problems. Such correspondence has existed in the Russian press before, and it was not limited to the press of the revolutionary parties. Therefore it is ridiculous for Soviet historians to claim that the worker-peasant correspondents' movement has existed since the creation of the Bolshevik Party.[23] The movement was born because the Soviet authorities gave great encouragement to it and, more specifically, because they devised for it an organizational form. It was the organized nature of the letter writing that made it specifically Soviet.

The Bolshevik leaders had many reasons for being enthusiastic about the

233

movement. During the Civil War they became concerned that the press had come to be isolated from the readers. In a capitalist society such a problem rarely arises. When a point of view advocated by a newspaper is very much out of tune with that of its readers, people simply turn to another. The message is powerful and quick in coming. In the Soviet Union such correctives do not exist. The Soviet leaders have always been deeply concerned about what the people thought, how they saw the world, and what they considered to be their most important problems. But how could the Party leaders find out about the mood of the people? Waiting for election results was obviously not an answer. The great advantage of the worker-peasant correspondents' movement was that through it, the Bolshevik leaders believed, they could learn about the mental world of workers and peasants. Indeed, the Party activists followed the content of the letters most conscientiously. The newspapers periodically sorted the letters according to topic and summarized their content for the use of higher organs.[24]

Also, regularly publishing letters from readers saved money. Although the correspondents were paid for the letters that were actually printed, the newspapers saved money by not having to pay reporters' salaries. In any case, such "reporting" as the worker-peasant correspondents were capable of doing was very much the type that Soviet papers wanted. In an influential article in 1919, Lenin encouraged the press to stay close to "real life." By this admonition he meant that the press should not address itself to large and therefore political issues of the day but rather it should talk about concrete problems in concrete factories.[25]

The correspondents extended the Party's reach. Workers who wrote about wrongdoings in their factories provided a service. To the extent that such reporting undermined worker solidarity against the "bosses," that is, the Party, it was so much the better. This was particularly true in the countryside, where the regime had very little strength. If people worried that their anti-regime activities would be revealed by occasionally nameless correspondents, the regime obviously benefited.

Perhaps most important, some if not all the Bolshevik leaders supported the movement because they genuinely believed in workers' spontaneity and assumed that the correspondents expressed such spontaneity. As editor of *Pravda,* Bukharin played a crucial role in encouraging workers and peasants to write. He regarded the "voluntary" organization of correspondents as an essential part of the Soviet system and as a protection against bureaucracy, whose power many Bolshevik leaders feared. In his view this movement, and the many voluntary organizations that existed at the time (such as the Society against Illiteracy, Society of Godless, Society against Alcoholism, etc.), filled a vacuum between the Party-state and the people.[26] Ultimately such hopes were bound to be illusory. Bukharin and his comrades desired workers' spontaneity, but at the same time they demanded that the workers on their own arrive at the "correct" solution. Such an attitude allowed only a pretense of self-expression but was inimical to genuine self-reliance.

The Party control of this movement, and other movements like it, was never in question, and this control made sure that the correspondents never for a moment violated the Party's interest. Indeed, in publishing letters from workers and peasants, the regime faced not the slightest risk. The newspapers, after all, were not obliged to print representative letters, or even the most interesting ones. The editors chose those that supported the points that they themselves wanted to make. By having unknown workers and peasants express a point of view, the newspapers could create the impression that they were the mouthpiece of the people. When necessary and desirable, this method of communication could also absolve them from taking responsibility for positions that were unpopular.

The leaders of the Party appreciated the value of workers and peasants writing to their newspapers already during the Civil War. One can talk about the existence of an organized movement, however, only after the crisis year of 1922. In fact, the encouragement and organization of the movement were part of the effort to overcome the crisis. Editors hoped that publishing letters from readers would make their papers more interesting and help to sell them.

Remarkably, a great incentive for the development of the movement was a tragic murder of a correspondent in early 1922. A certain Spiridonov, who had unmasked irregularities in his factory in a letter to a newspaper, was killed by a man suspected to be insane. The director of the factory, a Communist, was also implicated in the murder.[27] Nevertheless, the press managed to depict the affair in such a way as to make Spiridonov a victim of the class enemy. Partially as a result of the well-publicized trial, the political significance of writing to newspapers became better known.

Like the growth of the press, the growth of this movement was impressive. Numbers, however, can be misleading. After all, who was a correspondent? Should the person who wrote a single letter be counted the same way as one who regularly informed the press about what was going on in his place of work? A person who wrote to more than one newspaper was likely to be counted several times, since the figures came from the newspapers.[28] Nevertheless, the magnitude of the increase was evident. At the end of 1924, 100,000 people considered themselves members of this movement. In March 1926, the estimate rose to 125,000, and at the end of the following year to 400,000.[29]

Given the nature of Soviet politics, it was inevitable that the regime would go further than merely encourage readers to write their newspapers. "Spontaneity" waited to be organized. Such organization means the holding of congresses and conferences, the publication of newspapers, and Party leadership and supervision of the movement. In carrying out this task, *Pravda* played a central role. Bukharin, the editor, was particularly interested in the matter. So was his ideological comrade, M. I. Ulianova, Lenin's sister.[30] She was on the editorial board of *Pravda* and headed the "workers life" section. Because of her official position, the task of leadership fell on her. In the spring of 1923 she organized a club of correspondents of *Pravda* in which the workers listened to speeches of Party functionaries and received instructions concerning how they could make an even greater contribution.[31]

In 1923 the peasant press was still in poor condition and the correspondent movement was limited to workers. When the first congress met in November 1923, under Ulianova's leadership, only forty-two participated, representing seventeen newspapers. The delegates discussed the issue: How should one become a correspondent? Should such people be elected or appointed? The congress sensibly decided that the movement, in order to be successful, must be voluntary.[32]

The second congress took place less than a year later, in October 1924. This was a much larger gathering: There were 353 delegates.[33] The delegates passionately debated the proper organizational form for the movement. The majority maintained that it was best to organize the writers into circles attached to newspapers. People argued that the correspondents, especially in the villages, must act as links between the readers and the editorial board. The minority, represented by Zinovev's followers in *Leningradskaia Pravda*, at the congress and later denounced the majority position as syndicalist and advocated a territorial organization that would be attached to Party committees.[34] The ostensible issue was obviously trivial. That it aroused such passions can be explained by remembering that it took place at a time of struggle for leadership. The Bukharinist, majority position implied a relatively greater confidence in the "spontaneity" of the "masses" and a greater desire to involve non-Party people in the work of building the new society. The debate was not resolved until Zinovev's final defeat. In 1926 the followers of Zinovev were removed from *Leningradskaia Pravda*.[35]

The buildup of the corps of correspondents in the villages started in 1924. In this area also, a sensational murder played the role of catalyst. In March 1924 in the village of Dymovka in the Ukraine a correspondent, G. Malinovskii, was killed. In an article Malinovskii had denounced two of his comrades in his Party cell for various illegal activities. The press once again portrayed the crime as the work of the class enemy.

Whoever was responsible for the murder of Malinovskii, there is no question that the correspondents faced danger, especially in the villages. To expand the circulation of newspapers and to create an army of people who were willing to serve the interests of the regime by writing letters was part of a major effort to penetrate the countryside. This took place at a time when the Soviet regime had overcome the famine and the discrepancy between agricultural and industrial prices and when Trotsky was accused by his fellow leaders of underestimating the significance of the peasantry. To extend its reach, the Party sent reliable people from the cities into the villages to act as correspondents. That these people found hostility could be taken for granted.[36] According to incomplete data, in 1924 8 people were killed, in 1925, 25, and in 1926, 96, for writing letters to newspapers.[37]

By the time the third congress of correspondents took place in May 1926, there were more village than worker correspondents. *Krestianskaia gazeta* came to receive more letters than any other newspaper in the country.

One of the functions of the correspondents' movement was a police function. We know, for example, that in 1927 alone as a result of letters sent to *Krestianskaia gazeta,* 461 people were fired from their jobs, judicial proceedings were initiated against 522, and 65 were excluded from the Party.[38] Another use of the correspondents was in the struggle to improve the economy. Already in 1923, before the first congress took place, *Pravda* under M. I. Ulianova's leadership initiated a competition for best factory director. Workers were asked to describe the work of the directors of their factories in their letters to newspapers, and the person who was judged best received a prize.[39] This idea was later expanded, and competitions took place for best village reading room (izba chital'nia), best teacher, best village Party cell, and so forth.

At the time of the fourth congress, which took place in November 1928, in which delegates represented a half-million people, the new campaign was to carry out "raids."[40] Correspondents carried out raids for surveys of entire branches of industry. The newspapers printed columns entitled: "Before the Raid," in which they published letters that described the problems and shortcomings. A little later the same newspapers under the heading "After the Raid" told readers how the various shortcomings had been surmounted. This idea fitted well into the spirit of the time. The country was just embarking on its large-scale industrialization effort. The regime wanted to use every means to mobilize the people for the great work.

Wall newspapers. Another unusual institution of the Soviet press was the wall newspaper. Although it is perhaps not immediately evident, the underlying idea of the wall paper and of the worker-peasant correspondents' movement was the same: the pretense of spontaneity.

Wall newspapers first played an important role during the Civil War. At the time, when there was a shortage of paper and when the communication network stopped functioning, it made sense to put the news of the day, admonitions, instructions, and so forth, on the walls in telegraph-dispatch-like articles. The institution of the wall newspaper was thus born, and it quickly spread to army barracks, schools, factories, and Soviet offices. In the world of the NEP, this instrument turned out to be an excellent propaganda weapon: It was cheap and flexible.

The Soviet conception of wall newspaper was well expressed in one of the resolutions of the Thirteenth Party Congress:

Wall newspapers are acquiring an ever-greater significance in our press network, as weapons affecting the masses and as forms of the expression of the activity of the masses. Factory newspapers are already playing a large role in the area of improving productivity and in the construction of a new form of life, in the struggle against illiteracy and against religious prejudices. The work with the wall newspapers in the enterprises should take place with the aid and leadership of the Party cell and of the Komsomol. The Party committees should improve their leadership over the wall newspapers. The wall newspaper in the village should become one of the most important forms of work of the local Party and Komsomol cells. It should struggle for the improvement of agriculture, for cooperatives, for raising the cultural level of the village, for the interests of the powerless peasants, against the exploitative tendencies of the kulak, and against the malfeasance of administrators. It is essential to connect the wall newspaper in the village with the library hut, with organs giving agricultural information, and with the school.[41]

It is evident that the purpose of the wall newspaper was not to spread news and information. The intellectual level and form of the wall newspapers, as one might expect, greatly varied. At some places the articles were handwritten and simply pasted on a board; by contrast, at other institutions, for example at universities or large factories, the wall newspaper was a rather elaborate matter, with pictures, decorations, and typed articles. Clearly, in the villages Party and Komsomol committees faced a more difficult task editing their paper than in urban institutions. The Party cell usually turned for help to the director of the library hut, to the teacher, and as it was frequently advised, to demobilized and literate Red Army soldiers. Both in the villages and in the cities the worker and peasant correspondents were expected to play a major role in writing and editing wall newspapers.

What is perhaps most striking about the wall newspapers of the 1920s is how closely the Party supervised them. They were the most extraordinary examples of organized "spontaneity." In 1930 the agitprop department published a pamphlet to help those who wanted to start a wall newspaper.[42] In this short brochure the Party gave detailed directions for properly organizing the work. First of all, the pamphlet made it clear that the purpose of the wall newspaper and also of the worker-peasant correspondents' movement was to draw the masses into political and social work.[43] This conception of the task explained a great deal about the organizational methods recommended. Those methods were extremely complex: The brochure advised electing a five-to-eleven member editorial board, establishing a special bureau of "accomplishments," and appointing people to be constantly on duty. One suspects that a main and not explicitly stated purpose of the wall newspaper was to give jobs to as many people as possible. Those who took their social jobs seriously were very busy people, indeed.

The pamphlet advised the activists how to proceed, step by step: First, it was necessary to consult with the local Party committee, to make sure that proper supervision was extended from the very beginning. The activists also had to ask advice and leadership from the worker-peasant correspondents' section of their local newspaper. The next step was to request aid from the factory committee in getting the necessary funds for paper, typewriter, and other supplies. At this point the activists had to form a provisional editorial committee. The future editors were advised even about the selection of a proper name: It was best to initiate a competition among the workers for the best title, to increase mass involvement.[44] The brochure went on for thirty pages, giving instructions about such matters as the proper format, the correct way to organize the meeting for the election of the editorial committee, and the content of articles. Lenin's notion concerning the organizational function of newspapers was thus realized.

Book publishing

The history of Soviet book publishing in the 1920s shows that the Soviet leaders were willing to make sacrifices and invest scarce resources. That the Bolsheviks did not achieve as much as they hoped to was not the result of a lack of will but the consequence of their weakness.

The revival of the industry. The principles of the NEP were introduced into publishing with some delay. The Soviet leadership feared that allowing freedom for private enterprise in the trade and production of books would cause ideological and therefore political damage. Yet the existing system obviously could not continue. The Civil War greatly harmed publishing. The shortage of paper, the deterioration of printing presses, and the disruption of the distribution network led to a precipitous decline in both the number of titles and the number of copies that came to the market. Furthermore, the notion of distributing books free was incongruous in the cost-conscious early 1920s. War communism was dreadfully wasteful of scarce resources. The task of the NEP was to limit the waste by establishing a connection between the kind of books people wanted to read and what in fact came off the printing presses.

The Moscow City Soviet took the first step. Its presidium in August 1921 rescinded a previous decree concerning municipalization of books and allowed free trade. It also promised to license private publishers. The significance of publishing was so great that the Politbureau of the Party considered it necessary to discuss the matter.[45] In September 1921, the highest Party organ instructed agencies of state control to keep a strict account of books printed and sold and to prevent the distribution of harmful literature. Under this heading came religious books, pornography, and counterrevolutionary works. It is evident that at this time the Bolshevik leaders feared most of all not the writings of White generals and other enemies of socialism but the works of Socialist Revolutionaries; that party seemed still dangerous at the end of the Civil War. The Socialist Revolutionaries retained considerable strength within the cooperative movement, which had traditionally controlled much of the book trade in the villages. The stipulation that cooperatives could publish and sell books only with the previous permission of Narkompros was meant to protect the peasants from harmful Socialist Revolutionary influences.[46]

239

THE BIRTH OF THE PROPAGANDA STATE

Learning from the experiences of the capital, in October Narkompros drew up a project that was to govern the book trade in the new world of the NEP. On the basis of this project, on November 28 Sovnarkom published a decree that allowed books to be sold. Newly printed books were to be sold at prices established by the government.[47]

Like other branches of Soviet industry at the time, publishing included both private and state enterprises. The share of private business, however, was always small, and as time went on it declined even further. In Soviet terminology, producing books was one of the commanding heights of the economy, which the state never relinquished. The state made the work of private firms difficult: They needed permission to publish, and they could not always get paper from state-owned supplies. But perhaps an even more important reason for the failure of capitalism to flourish was that book publishing in the 1920s was not a very good business. The cost of production was high and the reading public small.

From Soviet figures it is difficult to get a clear picture of the importance of private firms. Under the heading "private," these figures included publishing ventures of numerous Soviet voluntary societies, which in no sense were independent of the Soviet state. On the other hand, the figures did not count cooperative publishers, which were independent. According to contemporary Soviet estimates, only about 60 percent of the "private" publishing houses were owned by individuals.[48] Soviet statistics reported a decline in the absolute number of private publishers and an even greater decline in their share of the market. In 1922 there were 223 private publishers; in 1923, 218; in 1924, 141; and in 1925, only 111. Later in the decade this decline continued. Although private companies printed 25 percent of all copies in 1922, they produced only 5.8 percent in 1925.[49] By the end of the NEP period, the contribution of private publishers to the total output shrank to insignificance.

The importance of private publishers, however, was somewhat greater than these modest figures indicate. In areas in which the state had no interest in encouraging work, for example, philosophy and psychology, private firms' share of the market was quite large. Since state enterprises neglected to print books for children, this task also largely fell on private firms. In addition, as late as 1925 these companies published about one-quarter of belles lettres titles. The private firms printed a particularly large number of translations. Furthermore, especially in the immediate post–Civil War period, a large segment of the intelligentsia was so hostile to the Soviet state that it did not want to have anything to do with Gosizdat. Many authors refused to part with their manuscripts in 1919 and 1920; when the introduction of the NEP made this possible, they sought out private firms.[50] Private publishers considerably expanded the variety of books available for the Soviet reader in the 1920s.[51]

How the state could best carry out its responsibility to provide books for the Russian people was the subject of a great deal of experimentation. The industry oscillated between centralization and decentralization. The advocates of centralization believed that this was the only way to prevent parallelism and the waste of resources. People on the other side argued, however, that the building of one large bureaucracy would lead to the stifling of initiative and to the creation of a giant firm that could not well respond to the needs of the individual reader. In any event, various Soviet institutions, commissariats, voluntary organizations, and so forth, wanted to have their own publishing houses and acted as counterpressure to the centralizing tendencies inherent in the Soviet economy. As a result, the centralization of war communism gave way to a certain proliferation during the NEP period.

Even at this time, however, the state publishing house, Gosizdat, remained a giant. Undoubtedly it was the largest publishing firm in the world. Especially in the first years of the NEP, Gosizdat carried out tasks that went beyond printing books. Private publishers, for example, according to a regulation of 1921, needed the permission of Gosizdat to print books.[52] In districts where Gosizdat had no office, the local soviets had the right to authorize the printing of books. A year later, however, Gosizdat was relieved of the task of censorship, and a Committee for the Press was established within Narkompros to oversee private publishers.[53] An important task of the state publishing house was the creation and maintenance of the book-distribution network. Private houses remained dependent on Gosizdat for the sale of their books. In 1923, to alleviate the chronic shortage of paper, Gosizdat took over a paper-producing factory. This factory came to provide the state publisher with 80 percent of its needs.[54]

At the time of the introduction of the NEP, Gosizdat regarded itself as the agent of Narkompros and therefore as responsible for the education of the Soviet people. It acknowledged no boundaries for its publishing activities but strove for the enlightenment of the people in all fields. At this time the technical facilities of the enterprise were limited. Therefore, when Gosizdat considered the publication of a book necessary but could not arrange it in its own printing shops, it contracted with private firms to do the job. On such occasions the private company was given precious paper for the task. Within a couple of years, however, the situation improved and Gosizdat had no need for subcontractors.[55]

A primary responsibility of Gosizdat was to provide the country with textbooks. The Party leaders well understood the political significance of educational materials, and to assure that the correct ideological line would be communicated to the students they gave monopoly to the state publisher for the printing of textbooks in 1921. Although the monopoly was lifted later, Gosizdat still provided almost three-quarters of all texts in 1920, and these made up over half the production of Gosizdat. The desperate need to equip the students with books put Gosizdat in a dilemma: On the one hand, there were not enough ideologically acceptable textbooks that could be reprinted; on the other, it was impossible to wait. Under the circumstances, Gosizdat tinkered with the available texts. Editors eliminated offending paragraphs and appended ideologically correct messages. This was hardly a satisfactory solution. When in October 1923 a Narkompros commission examined the newly published textbooks, it found that almost a third of them were "harmful" and recommended their removal from the market.[56] The printing of textbooks was a considerable burden on Gosizdat, and the government did not always provide the necessary funds. In 1923, for example, Gosizdat received only one-third of the money it considered necessary for the production of textbooks.[57]

The second-largest percentage of the state publisher's output was classified as social and economic literature, which included propaganda pamphlets and printed materials used for the political-education network. This category also included the "classics" of Marxism. Aside from the works of Marx and Engels, the state publisher issued in very large quantities the writings of Lenin, Bukharin, Stalin, and Trotsky. Social and economic literature in the first half of the decade made up about 20 percent of the total volumes printed. By contrast, the share of belles lettres did not go above 15 percent.[58]

Gosizdat remained by far the largest publisher, producing approximately one-half of all books printed in the Soviet Union in the course of the 1920s.[59] During the first years of the NEP, however, a number of other state-owned publishing houses came into being. Krasnaia nov', established in 1922, was the publishing arm of Glavpolitprosvet, and specialized in printing agitational, antireligious, and other Marxist literature.[60] Novaia derevnia, also created in 1922, catered to the peasant reader. In addition the Komsomol had its own publisher, Molodaia gvardiia. Smaller firms specialized in technical and scientific literature, books of regional interest, and so forth. Although in the middle of the decade more than two thousand publishers existed, the twenty largest of these printed 90 percent of all copies.[61]

That the Party leadership was not fully satisfied with the consequences of the proliferation of publishers can be seen from a resolution of the Twelfth Congress:

It is necessary to note that the cost accounting enlivened publishing and gave the publishing houses an opportunity to work on firm and healthy foundations. On the other hand, their commercial independence brought a lack of coordination into their work. As a consequence, on the market appeared many unnecessary books and others that were poorly prepared. This led to a contraction of the book market and to a waste of material means.[62]

To respond to the Party's concern, the publishing industry in 1923 formed a bureau with the task of coordinating the work of state publishers and helping every one of them to develop its own particular profile.

As the resolutions of Party congresses testify, the Bolshevik leadership was deeply concerned with publishing. The leaders did not hesitate to invest scarce resources to help the reconstruction. As a result, in terms of quantity, publishing recovered remarkably quickly, considerably quicker in fact than other branches of industry.

The Soviet Union in the 1920s produced an abundant set of statistics concerning the production of books. Russian data, for example, are richer and more easily available than U.S. figures for the same period. The leaders needed the data to see how the publishing houses were carrying out their politically important assigned tasks. Also, because publishing was either in the hands of the state or closely supervised by state agencies, it was relatively easy to assemble the figures.

Imperial Russia was a major producer of books. In 1913, after Germany, it stood second place in the world in number of titles printed (34,000). Not surprisingly, during the Civil War there was a drastic decline. Soviet Russia in 1918 printed a few more than 6,000 titles; in 1919, 3,700; and in 1920, the worst year, only 3,326.[63] The gradual improvement coincided with the introduction of the NEP. In 1921, a few more than 4,000 titles came out. In the following year, the number passed 9,000.[64] In 1925, the Soviet Union produced over 20,000 titles.[65] In 1928, the Soviet Union surpassed the prewar number of 34,000.[66]

How many different books were published in a year is an interesting measurement, but one open to manipulation. It is clear, for example, that during the Civil War and also in the early 1920s a very large number of brochures and pamphlets were printed, many of which hardly deserved to be called books. Consequently, when Soviet historians and publicists boast that already in the desperately poor 1920s the Soviet Union far outpaced the incomparably richer United States, such comparisons must be taken with a grain of salt.[67] The total number of copies printed is perhaps a more meaningful figure, but even here some caution is in order. After all, how is one to decide how many copies of tiny pamphlets are the equivalent of a genuine book? But even if one approaches the Soviet figures with due skepticism, the magnitude of the achievement is beyond doubt. Before the war, Imperial Russia printed 133 million copies. In 1918, the number fell to 77 million; in 1919, to 54 million. In 1920, the country produced only 33 million; in 1921, 28 million. This was followed by an impressive improvement. In 1922, there were 37 million copies; in 1923, 64 million.[68] In 1925, the country comfortably surpassed prewar standards, and by the end of the decade, in 1928, it issued 270 million copies; that is, it more than doubled the achievement of Imperial Russia.[69]

The Soviet economy dealt with the problems of production better than with the problems of distribution. Tsarist Russia was hardly advanced in this respect, yet it took a very long time for the Soviet regime to match prewar standards. Before the Revolution, the cities were far better supplied than the villages. In cities readers could buy what they wanted in shops and in kiosks. In the countryside the situation was more haphazard. Some general stores sold books, but most of them were distributed through the cooperative movement, zemstvos, churches, and schools. In addition itinerant peddlers brought books with them and at times they were sold at fairs.[70]

As in other respects of Soviet life, the Revolution and Civil War further widened the gap between city and village. Although it was a manageable task to reopen the bookstores in the major cities of the country, to bring books to the peasants seemed exceedingly difficult. In 1922, for example, only 12 percent of the book trade took place in the provinces.[71] Of the 600 prewar railroad kiosks, only 112 remained in operation in 1922.[72]

Gosizdat, once again, had the major burden of responsibility. It established a trade section, which organized the wholesale trade for the entire country. The first task of the section was not to sell new books but to dispose of the supplies acquired from private owners at the time of nationalization. The trade section had the task of separating "useful" books from "harmful" ones. The great bulk of the "useful" books came to be distributed among small provincial libraries; the "harmful" ones were destroyed. The Soviet leaders certainly had no taboo against destroying books.[73]

The government tried to overcome the difficulties: Gosizdat established fourteen wholesale book-distribution centers in major cities; the trade section persuaded the cooperative network, which had over twenty thousand stores around the country, to stock books; and, in the middle of the decade, the government organized a company, Kniga–derevne (Book to the village), to help out in this important task. Nothing seemed to help, however. The Kniga–derevne organization functioned poorly.[74] The cooperative stores were allowed to make no profit from selling books, and therefore the managers resented having to give up shelf space.[75] Aside from textbooks, these stores sold few copies.

Partially as a result of the poorly functioning distribution network, a large percentage of the books remained unsold. In 1923, for example, at a time when the country suffered the most dire poverty and the young Soviet state had to make extraordinary sacrifices to revive the printing trade, only 60 percent of the textbooks, 40 percent of the popular-science books, and 37 percent of the belles lettres copies were sold.[76] In the course of the 1920s books that came to the villages came not to individual purchasers but to libraries, to Party and Komsomol cells, and to schools. Periodically the warehouses pulped their accumulated unsalable inventories.

The distribution system deserved only a part of the blame for the unsatisfactory situation. The main problem was that the Soviet regime did not print books that the bulk of the people wanted to read. Although the NEP introduced market principles into the economy, the Soviet leaders never meant to expand those principles fully into publishing. Furthermore, the industry faced serious economic problems. It was difficult and expensive to replace the aging, foreign-made printing presses. The paper-producing industry was slow to recover, and it reached prewar standards only at the very end of the decade. As a result, books remained expensive and worker, and especially peasant, readers could not afford them. The Party was well aware of the problem, and by subsidizing the industry it aimed to lower prices. But it still never succeeded in restoring the prerevolutionary relationship between book and agricultural prices.

The total output of Soviet publishers in the 1920s is impressive because it shows the regime's commitment to bring books to the people. It is somewhat less impressive when one considers how well the task was accomplished.

The Soviet reader. Soviet historians and publicists have often measured the achievements of the publishing industry in the 1920s in terms of the number of copies produced. A far more meaningful, albeit more elusive, measurement would be to establish how well the publishers satisfied the needs of the Soviet public. "Needs" are inevitably subjective. Furthermore, one cannot easily generalize about the Soviet reader because the reading public was extremely heterogeneous. The spectrum from the sophisticated urban intellectual to the barely literate peasant was broad, indeed. Paradoxically, the "worker-peasant" state, anxious to educate the underprivileged, in fact did far better in giving books to the educated than in satisfying the needs of the ordinary workers, especially peasants.

If our measure of censorship is the variety of books that could be printed, we must conclude that the hand of the censor in the 1920s was light. It is not that the Bolshevik leaders had a commitment to "formal" freedoms. On the contrary. All Bolshevik leaders admitted the necessity of censorship, though some did so defiantly and proudly, whereas others were more hesitant. Lenin and his ideological comrades seemingly enjoyed talking about the subject because it appeared to them that that was a manifestation of a firm, revolutionary line. The Leninists spoke with great fervor in favor of censorship at the crucial November 1917 meeting of the Soviets' Executive Committee, and indeed introduced a system that allowed only one interpretation of the news. Gosizdat, and later the press bureau of Narkompros, assumed explicit censorship functions. By contrast, leading figures such as Lunacharskii evidently felt uncomfortable in the new and unaccustomed role of censor. The commissar of enlightenment in a most interesting article wrote in 1921:

The person who tells us that censorship is necessary, even when it prevents the publication of great works of art when these hide obvious counterrevolution, is correct. So is the one who says that we must choose, and we must give only third, or fourth, priority to undoubtedly necessary works in comparison with books for which we have the greatest need. But the person who says "Down with all those prejudices about the freedom of expression. State leadership in literature corresponds to our new, Communist order. Censorship is not a terrible component of our time of transition, but a regular part of socialist life," the person who draws the conclusion that criticism should be turned into some kind of denunciation and that artistic work should be turned into primitive, revolutionary slogans, he only shows that under the Communist exterior, if you scratch him a bit, will find in reality, "Derzhimorda."[77]

Lunacharskii's words come as close to a defense of the freedom of expression as any Bolshevik leader was to make in the early 1920s.

Under Lunacharskii's ultimate authority – Gosizdat was a part of Narkompros – few manuscripts were rejected. In Petrograd, for example, private publishers submitted 190 manuscripts in the course of the first three months of 1922, of which only 10 were rejected. In Moscow, Gosizdat disallowed 31 out of 813 manuscripts.[78] Admittedly, the rejection rate is an unreliable standard of measurement, because perhaps many authors, realizing that their manuscripts could not be printed in Soviet Russia, never submitted them. Looking at *Krasnaia letopis'* (Red chronicle), an inventory of Soviet publications, however, convinces one that an impressive array of books appeared in Soviet Russia in those early days. A few examples must suffice: Gosizdat published Merezhkovskii, N. O. Losskii, and S. L. Frank. The works of Berdaev and Bulgakov were also printed. Although Lenin denounced Kautsky bitterly, the writings of the German Socialist leader continued to be translated and printed in very large numbers.[79]

Philosophers, sociologists, economists, and artists, as long as they did not touch on an immediate political issue, could freely express their anti-Marxist views even as late as 1922. As normality returned, however, and order was imposed on Soviet intellectual life, freedom of expression came to be more constrained. During the NEP period, the anti-Marxist opinions that appeared in print, appeared in covert forms.[80]

It is not that Bolsheviks altogether failed to notice what was happening. For example, a middle-level Party figure, Vareikis, writing in 1926, described the social-economic literature that had appeared in the previous two years as 50 percent good Marxist, 30 percent mixed, and 20 percent harmful. In the harmful category he placed authors such as Chaianov, Litoshenko, and Sukhanov. He discerned in the writings of others expressions of neopopulism, slavophilism, and other anti-Marxist tendencies. He went on to say:

Although the percentage of unacceptable books goes no higher than 20, these books are in the position to undermine the ideological-educational work that we must carry out. This social-economic literature is not without some influence on the Soviet intelligentsia, even including some Party circles. This is especially true in the provinces.[81]

Vareikis was correct. The non-Marxist books by their very existence influenced the intellectual-political atmosphere, and, from the point of view of a non-Bolshevik, for the better.

The authorities made no attempt to prevent the importation of books printed abroad. In the 1920s Russian émigrés in various European cities established publishing houses that brought out a large variety of works. Many of these in a remarkably short time found their way into the Soviet Union.

The question inevitably arises, Why did the regime tolerate hostile books, whether printed in the Soviet Union or abroad? Just like the ministers in the tsar's government before 1905, the leaders of the regime believed that erudite books, published in small numbers for an obviously limited readership, could not do much damage. The regime was not yet ready to break with the old, prewar intelligentsia, which, even at the end of the NEP period, continued to occupy the top positions in academic life. Further, many if not all Bolshevik leaders continued to have a respect for scholarship, as they had respect for "culture." They continued to hope that the values of culture and socialism were compatible and that one could work for both at the same time.

Looking at the attainments of Soviet science and art in the 1920s, it is evident that the degree of freedom necessary for creative work was still present. Soviet journals, for example, *Krasnaia nov'* (Red virgin soil), *Novyi mir* (New world) and *Pechat' i revoliutsiia* (The press and revolution), discussed cultural developments in the West often knowledgeably and intelligently. A cultured Russian did not yet need to feel that he or she was cut off from the civilized world.

By contrast, the semiliterate peasant had received very little. The literacy drive in the villages before the introduction of large-scale collectivization was only moderately successful. Those who knew the alphabet found that there was little for them to read that interested them. This was so, at least in part, because the regime failed to construct a well-functioning distribution system. But a more important reason was that Communist officials believed that the type of literature the peasants had read before the Revolution "was not good for them" and therefore did not deserve reprinting and distribution. In fact, state agencies destroyed large quantities of popular and religious books that came into their possession after the Revolution.[82]

How little the regime succeeded in bringing books to the countryside can be seen from contemporary figures. In the mid-1920s the yearly share of the peasant household budget for books was twenty kopecks. Since this figure included expenditures on calendars and textbooks, it is hardly an exaggeration to say that peasants bought no books.[83] To the extent books came to the peasants, they came through village libraries. It is therefore remarkable to find that in the late 1920s the combined holdings of village libraries were only half those of the prewar period. An average village library had between 1,000 and 2,500 books. Even this figure greatly overstates the available books because a large proportion of the libraries' holdings were made up of works of political literature that were rarely checked out. In the sample districts examined by *Kommunisticheskaia revoliutsiia*, the per capita book holdings varied from district to district between

0.15 and 0.2.[84] A main source of the problem was that library expenditures came out of the district budgets. Whenever financial problems arose, the local leaders were tempted to economize at the expense of the libraries. Because of the constant struggle for money, only 40 to 45 percent of the libraries had full-time paid employees. At other places the village teacher or some other literate person filled the position.[85] Socialist Soviet Russia, anxious to educate its people, evidently did less in this field than the tsarist Empire.

The officials of the regime removed from the peasants' reach not only light adventure stories and religious books but also literature that could be conceived as hostile to a Marxist, materialist world view. Their unstated assumption was that the ignorant peasants, unlike their better-educated fellow Russians, could not be trusted to handle criticism. In the early days of the Civil War and during the first years of the NEP, chaos prevailed. The Commissariat of Enlightenment sent out circulars to village libraries informing them what books they should remove and what should be kept. It seems, however, that at places overzealous librarians went to ridiculous lengths, and it is reported that on occasion even the writings of Lenin, which had been published under a pseudonym, had been taken off the shelves. At other places, to the annoyance of the authorities, nothing happened and the offending books remained in place. Krupskaia, who as head of Glavpolitprosvet was responsible for purging libraries, was dissatisfied and perhaps embarrassed by the extremely lengthy list of proscribed books, which included such authors as Plato and Kant. Her apologia in an article in *Pravda*, on April 9, 1924, betrays, however, a most far-reaching condescension toward the peasant readers:

In the circular there was no "defect", yet a "defect" was there all the same. To the circular was affixed a thoroughly unfortunate list of books, a list compiled by the Commission for the Reexamination of Books, attached to the circular I had signed, without my knowledge. As soon as I saw this list I cancelled it. Why was this list unfortunate? In the first place because it was beside the mark. In it it was said that it was necessary to remove from the mass libraries Plato, Kant, Mach – in general, idealists. That idealist philosophers are harmful people is beyond question. But their presence in a library for peasants or the worker masses is not harmful at all, it is senseless: a man of the masses will not read Kant. Hence the "list" did not alter matters in any way. Much worse was the fact that the list of books to be removed in the field of "religion" was extremely limited.[86]

An interesting aspect of the library purge was the removal of political materials. A 1923 circular from the propaganda section of the Central Committee of the Party instructed the libraries that they should withdraw not only "counterrevolutionary" books but also "out of date agitational and informatory material of Soviet origin (1918, 1919, 1920) on questions which are at present regulated differently by the Soviet power (agrarian question, system of taxation, question of free trade, food policy, etc.)."[87]

Soviet Russia already in 1923 was disowning its utopian past. Clearly, pamphlets from the period of war communism did not make good agitational material during the years of the NEP.

The libraries removed material that was politically unsatisfactory; removed books that the Soviet authorities looked down on, such as adventure stories, cheap romances, and other types of light literature that the peasants had enjoyed; and of course removed books that were in any way connected with religion, such as tales of pilgrims, lives of saints, and so forth. The trouble was that the libraries did not have much to take the place of the old and – from the Bolshevik point of view – unsatisfactory books. Only a tiny percentage of the total output of books was aimed at the peasant reader.[88] Those that were printed were clearly not what the peasants wanted. Prerevolutionary library surveys, for example, showed that the peasants checked out 60 percent books of literature, 17 percent histories, and approximately 7 percent religious books. In the middle of the twenties, the share of literature titles went down to about 50 percent, largely because the books the peasants liked and wanted were not available.[89] Only 14 percent of the books aimed at the peasant reader were belles lettres. (In the country's total output, literary titles made up almost exactly the same percentage.)[90] Clearly, there was no coincidence of supply and demand.

The Bolsheviks were acutely aware of the problem. They carried out periodic surveys of peasant readers to find out what the peasants wanted. One study of rural readers found that the peasants resented the condescension inherent in books directed at them. They did not like to be called "muzhiks." They found the imitation of peasant language laughable. Such misguided efforts by untalented propagandists lowered the peasants' respect for books and for the regime. Such well-founded criticisms were aimed both at books of literature and books of popular science and agronomy. Books in the last category were not as useful as representatives of the regime hoped, because the agronomists, writing for a countrywide audience, failed to distinguish between regions. As a result, their recommendations often did not work, and the peasants came to be disillusioned concerning the claims of scientific agriculture.[91]

An attempt to understand the peasant reader was made by the publisher Krasnaia derevnia, which specialized in books for peasants. It decided to create a five-person "peasant editorial committee" to pass on proposed publishing projects.[92] It is unclear whether this committee made much of a difference, for no Soviet publishing house was willing to print what the readers really wanted.

The basic problems besetting Soviet publishing remained unsolvable: At a time of a shortage of funds, how could they produce enough books? How could they get the books to the readers? How could they persuade the peasants to read what the Party leaders believed they should read? How could they produce books that were both ideologically useful and at the same time written in a language the peasants found attractive? Where could they find enough cadres who could write books for village readers? During the NEP period the Soviet regime succeeded in depriving the peasants of books it considered harmful. It did not yet have the strength to make the peasants read what it wanted them to read.

Conclusion and epilogue

The Soviet methods of mobilization

The Bolsheviks built an extraordinary propaganda apparatus and spent a great deal of time, energy, and scarce resources to indoctrinate the Soviet people. But did they make the correct investment? Did the huge indoctrination apparatus make a difference? Did the hundreds of thousands of agitators, the unabashedly biased newspapers, the innumerable "volunteer" organizations, the repetitious mass meetings help to influence the course of history? Although many contemporaries believed that the indoctrination campaigns failed to achieve their purpose, the majority of observers, on the contrary, have been greatly impressed by Soviet methods. Indeed, some hostile commentators have regarded the very essence of the Soviet evil as insidious brainwashing.

There can be no easy answers to the questions posed. The basic difficulty is that it is impossible to separate the results of indoctrination from the consequences of other aspects of the Soviet system. Who can say to what extent the people endorsed their government because they agreed with the goals of the regime and came to regard them as their own and to what extent they did so because they were afraid of the consequences of dissent? Similarly, did the Soviet people accept the goals of the regime because they found those goals attractive, or, did they support the regime to the extent they did as a result of clever manipulation of opinion? Such matters can never be fully resolved.

It can be stated with assurance, however, that the particular, Leninist-Stalinist methods of mass mobilization and indoctrination came to be essential aspects of the propaganda state. On the one hand, one cannot imagine the Soviet regime functioning without its mass-mobilization system; on the other, the various propaganda methods the Bolsheviks used made sense only in the given political environment. The entire social-political system could be and was copied; the propaganda methods in isolation, however, could not flourish on foreign soil.

There was nothing particularly clever about Soviet techniques of propaganda. The Communists had not found new and powerful ways to influence opinion. From a purely technical point of view, the Soviet leaders had much to learn from Westerners in the field of mass communication and almost nothing to teach them. The evaluation of the performance of the propaganda machinery, however, must not be reduced to an examination of the cleverness of propaganda tricks. Soviet propaganda has been successful because the Soviet regime was successful; it has survived. And in achieving that primary goal, survival, the propaganda system played as vital and indispensable a role as industrialization and coercion. The first conclusion that one can draw from this study of Soviet propaganda is that ideological struggle, indoctrination, propaganda, whatever it is called, does matter.

The history of Soviet propaganda begins with a dramatic irony. The Bolsheviks came to power with the belief that their indoctrination work was to bring to people the "true" view of the world and that thus they needed no bourgeois obfuscations, lies, and deceptions. It was this belief that allowed them proudly to call themselves propagandists. However, this same world view brought from their revolutionary past combined with the immediate press of circumstances to predispose them to build repressive institutions once they formed a government. Utterly convinced of the righteousness of their cause, without the slightest faith in pluralism or interest in protecting the rights of those who held different beliefs, they introduced repression and censorship strikingly soon after coming to power.

Within two weeks after the Revolution, the Central Executive Committee of the Soviets repudiated the principle of freedom of the press, and indeed by the middle of 1918 all non-Bolshevik newspapers had disappeared. Because the Bolsheviks knew how important ideas were in motivating people, they were determined to prevent the spread of hostile views. Although they professed to believe that material conditions determined political views, in fact they left nothing to chance. Lenin and his comrades often used the metaphor that ideas are weapons, which must be denied to the enemy. The revolutionaries' willingness, and often eagerness, to suppress was the other side of the coin of being good propagandists.

Of course, during a war no government likes to tolerate hostile criticism. The Whites were hardly liberals, and they by no means protected freedom of expression. However, the situations in Bolshevik and anti-Bolshevik Russia were altogether different. The terror was equally bloody on each side; however, the ex-tsarist generals, who never understood the significance of ideas but regarded the struggle as primarily military, satisfied themselves with haphazard repression of opinion. It never occurred to them to impose one and only one interpretation on all political events.

Once the Bolsheviks introduced censorship, they never relented for a moment. During the decisive days of the bitter Civil War and in the peaceful and liberal 1920s, the government's monopoly over the press remained complete. The peculiar characteristics of the Soviet press followed from the fact that Bolshevik journalists had no competition. They did not need to compose exciting human-interest stories, and they did not need to reveal wrongdoing and corruption to win the allegiance of the readers. The Party had the means and will to exclude topics from discussion. To employ the term used by Hannah Arendt in her *The Human Condition,* the public realm gradually but drastically narrowed. The people could not become acquainted with the crucial issues facing their society by reading their newspapers.

It is impossible to say whether Soviet newspapers lied more often than the Western press. In the Soviet case, the deceit was perpetrated by omission. Instead of genuine issues, the newspapers devoted columns more and more often to pseudoissues. Instead of discussing the difficulties of grain procurement, for example, the press wrote about the campaign organized to celebrate the anniversary of Lenin's decree on literacy.

The second conclusion that can be drawn from this study is that the main achievement of the Soviet regime was something negative: It succeeded in preventing the formation and articulation of alternative points of view. The Soviet people ultimately came not so much to believe the Bolsheviks' world view as to take it for granted. Nobody remained to point out the contradictions and even inanity inherent in the regime's slogans. In circumstances where only one point of view can be expressed, the distinction between belief and nonbelief and truth and untruth is washed away.

The Communists suppressed not only the freedom of expression but also the freedom of association. Indeed, one could not exist without the other. Very soon after coming to power, the Communists in territories under their control destroyed other political parties, first the nonsocialist ones and then the socialists. From the Bolshevik point of view, however, it was not enough to outlaw political organizations that might have competed for power. It was also necessary to remove any organization that had an independent existence.

The Orthodox Church, which claimed to be outside politics, was a particularly dangerous opponent, and the Communists had reason to fear the influence of the priests over the people. It is natural that the churchmen found materialist Marxism reprehensible. Furthermore, the official church had been an integral part of the old regime, and it would have been indeed surprising if now the priests had abandoned the endangered social-political order without a struggle. The church was an implacable enemy. It, unlike the White movement, did possess a national network, able to reach that segment of the Russian people on whose support the outcome of the struggle depended.

Lenin and his fellow leaders handled this ideological enemy with great skill. As long as the Civil War continued, the Communists attempted to avoid any head-on confrontation. They understood that the tactless behavior of local activists made martyrs out of priests and thereby caused a great deal of damage. The campaign against religion accelerated during the 1920s. The regime organized a "volunteer" atheist society, published newspapers and pamphlets, and used mass organizations such as the Komsomol to combat the continued influence of the church. It is hard to say how successful the antireligious campaigns were. Without a doubt, there was a backlash against the crude forms of atheist agitation among the peasantry. On the other hand, the young generation, particularly those who hoped to make a good career in the new system, abandoned the church seemingly with little struggle.

The Communists did not limit themselves to attacks on organizations that had obvious political significance, such as the church. They closed down sport clubs, singing societies, and even the boy scouts. In the course of the 1920s, however, the suppression of independent institutions and independent thought was not complete. Foreign films could be shown, "apolitical" novels and even non-Marxist philosophy published. The universities, the Academy of Sciences, and, more importantly, thousands of peasant communes retained a smaller or larger degree of autonomy. Only when all such autonomy was lost, and the grudging toleration of cultural heterogeneity ended, could one talk about the establishment of a totalitarian society.

After destroying independent organizations, whether they were hostile or only neutral, the Bolsheviks hastened to fill the gap. They created new ones and camouflaged them as independent and voluntary. The pretense was superficial, and it is unlikely that many took it seriously. A characteristic of Soviet life in the 1920s was the abundance of movements, societies, and organizations, in which each had the task of advancing one or another goal of the regime. Some had particular tasks such as helping the navy, or acquainting people with flying or chemistry, or fighting illiteracy or alcoholism. Others aimed to bring a section of the Soviet people into "socialist construction," such as the Zhenotdel or the Komsomol.

My third conclusion is that an important factor in the success of Soviet propaganda was an ever-increasing atomization of society. The regime substituted pseudoorganizations for genuine ones. These "voluntary" organizations benefited the regime in many ways: They circumvented spontaneity; they worked for ostensible goals that were desirable from the government's point of view; and they gave an outlet to those who had genuine enthusiasm. But perhaps their most important benefit was that they gave tasks and responsibilities to millions of citizens.

The fourth conclusion is closely related to the previous one. Soviet propaganda may not have convinced the masses but it succeeded in reinforcing the commitment of the propagandists. For example, young people who joined the Komsomol often had only the vaguest understanding of Marxist philosophy or even the immediate goals of the regime. Yet, while carrying out political tasks, most of them insignificant in themselves, they came to regard themselves as trusted and important citizens.

It seems there is no better way to convince people than to ask them to agitate. It is, therefore, naive to think of propaganda as the product of a small and self-conscious group of people who act on the people as a whole. The Soviet propagandists were not cynical; they spoke the same language among themselves as they did in their work. Before they could make any impression on their listeners, first of all they had to distort their own picture of reality. One might say that they were their own first victims.

The Soviet state that aimed to bring about economic equality was based on political inequality. The Bolsheviks built an exquisitely refined hierarchy. In this hierarchy, standing between the paid Party functionaries and the common people (itself divided into groups with political implications: workers, peasants, class aliens), stood a large class of activists. These were members of the Party, or active participants in the various mass organizations. For their work, and often the work was strenuous, they received the satisfaction of being able to think of themselves as active builders of a new society. In addition, the regime rewarded their contributions by helping them in their careers. One of the important sources of success of the Soviet experiment was the ability of the regime to advance social mobility, to bring into politics large groups of people who hitherto had been excluded. To understand the working of Soviet society, we must realize that the newly mobilized often possessed great enthusiasm. These people threw themselves with abandon into social work, which was almost always some form of agitation. Among other reasons, the country needed the enormous propaganda apparatus to give the hundreds of thousands of activists something to do.

Did the activists then succeed in convincing their fellow citizens? If one thinks of convincing as a process of presenting rational arguments that demolish the intellectual resistance of the listener, then the answer must be no, they did not succeed. However, this is not the way propaganda influences people. My fifth and last conclusion is that Soviet propaganda taught people a political language and a pattern of behavior. First the people came to speak a strange idiom and adopt the behavior patterns expected of them, and only then did the inherent ideological message seep in. The process of convincing proceeded not from inside out but from outside in. That is, people came to behave properly, from the point of view of the regime, not because they believed its slogans but because by repeating the slogans they gradually acquired a "proper consciousness."

It is not a mere figure of speech to say that the Soviet people came to speak a new language. In 1928 a Soviet linguist, Selishchev, published a book on linguistic changes under the new regime. He pointed out that contemporary Russian usage contained a large number of words from the military vocabulary. Newspapers and orators spoke of struggle, war, avant-garde, muster, battalion, storming, besieging, "war communism," workers' army, commanding heights, Leninist guards, the "Comintern as the general staff of the world revolution," fronts, foreposts, and so on and on.[1]

The new bureaucracy created a bewildering variety of abbreviations and neologisms. Much of the new vocabulary remained incomprehensible to the peasantry. A Soviet publicist, Ia. Shafir, in 1923 visited several villages to test the peasants' understanding of political verbiage. The peasants did not know even the most frequently used abbreviations, such as USSR and Sovnarkom. Many of the misunderstandings were rather amusing. The peasants confused plenum and prisoner (plen in Russian), initiative and nationality, production front and struggle against the authorities, and so forth. The peasants complained to Shafir that they needed a translator to understand the newspapers.[2]

In the 1920s city dwellers were exposed to incomparably more Soviet verbiage than the peasants. This did not mean, however, that the workers made a great deal more sense of what was presented to them than the peasants. Indeed, many of the speeches did not deserve the listener's attention. The utterances had a symbolic significance only. Selishchev, for example, quoted from *Pravda:*

Three or four years ago Lloyd George was the dominant figure in our newspapers. He was more popular in our press than the most popular Soviet leaders. Lloyd George, this was not a personal name, it was a collective name. It was the name of a phenomenon. This was Millerand, and Wilson, and Noske, and Mussolini, and Pilsudski – in one word "the vampire of imperialism." Then war was declared on Lloyd George, in the name of agricultural loan, in the name of the struggle against illiteracy, in the name of cooperation, and in the name . . . of the chicken. Evidently, raising chickens became a high-priority goal.[3]

As orators repeated phrases such as "We will storm the bastion of illiteracy!" hundreds of times, it is evident that words had been emptied of their meaning. These sentences were not meant to be understood but incanted. Soviet propaganda had substituted meaningless verbiage for discussion of issues facing society.

Epilogue

Soviet historians on the one hand, and determined opponents of the October Revolution on the other, like to stress that the basic features of the Soviet regime have been present from the very beginning. By contrast, those who found the promises of a socialist revolution attractive and Stalin repulsive emphasize the great differences between the era of Lenin and the time of Stalin.

It is evident that collectivization and industrialization meant a change not only in economic policies but also a thorough overhaul of the entire social and political order. At the same time it would be misleading to think that the system that existed in the 1930s was a simple repudiation of the old. Stalinist Russia was built on the achievements of the previous decade. It was during the Civil War and during the years of the NEP that the instruments of power were created, and it was at this time that the manipulative Bolshevik mentality, characterized by condescension toward the Russian people and contempt for their way of life, first exhibited itself.

The 1930s brought relatively few changes in the organizational methods or in the underlying principles of indoctrination. How were the thirties different? First of all, the system was greatly expanded. Second, the regime drastically curtailed the subjects that could be openly discussed. Third, the themes and tones of Soviet propaganda changed.

Although in the 1920s the Party made frantic efforts to bring its message to the people, the bulk of the population remained almost untouched. At this time in the villages the government seemed infinitely remote. A few thousand library huts, a few million Komsomol members did not make enough difference. Collectivization radically changed the situation. To force the peasants to accept the new order, the Party sent into the villages thousands of activists, who, among other things, acted as agitators. The new collective farms gave the Party an organizational base. Now the peasants attended one mass meeting after another; they were constantly exposed to that remarkable Soviet invention, the loudspeaker, which, for practical purposes, was never turned off. Given the furious resistance of the peasantry, given the misery and starvation that prevailed in this period, we have every reason to doubt that the peasants were won over by propaganda. Nevertheless, it was at this time that the peasants came to use an inimitably stilted, Soviet form of speech. For the first time, they truly became Soviet citizens.

How much better the government was able to reach the peasantry is clearly shown by the history of the literacy campaign. The Party had attributed great significance to literacy since it came to power in 1917; however, it was not able to reach those who were most likely to be illiterate. Furthermore, the Soviet government lacked the means to introduce compulsory schooling. Under these circumstances, in spite of the constant talk, in the 1920s there were almost as many adolescent illiterates added to the population as there were adults able to be taught by the regime.

In the new environment of the 1930s, the government was able to compel teachers to stay where they had been sent. As archival materials show, the lot of these people, who arrived at remote places that were totally unprepared to accommodate them, was usually dreadful. Teachers who came from Moscow and Leningrad with their families often did not even get their own rooms.[4] Nevertheless the Party possessed both the means and strength of will to coerce. Furthermore, through the collective farms, it was relatively easy to set up schools for illiterate adults. Learning to read and write, the peasants also learned "political literacy." As literate members of the community, they were exposed to the printed medium. By the end of the decade, four out of five Soviet citizens under the age of fifty could read and write. After the slow start of the 1920s this was an impressive achievement.

Many ceased to be peasants; millions migrated to the cities and took jobs in the newly built factories. The percentage of the population in the cities grew between 1926 and 1939 from 18 to 33. It was a major task for the regime to teach the new workers industrial discipline and political conformity. In the early days of the industrialization drive, the Party did not have enough trained agitators, that is, graduates of Soviet-Party schools, to carry out individual, oral agitation. Under the circumstances, the cheapest and simplest method of indoctrination was the mass meeting. The leaders of the Party, skilled propagandists that they were, well understood that mass meetings in which domestic and foreign enemies were regularly denounced and in which people were exhorted again and again to work harder did not do a great deal of good. Compelling people to attend meetings, however, was the best the regime could do on this front for the time being.

The Soviet regime greatly expanded the political-education network. As a result, by the second half of the thirties it once again had enough trusted and trained people to address small meetings, to lead reading circles, and even to engage in organized political conversations with single individuals. Newspaper-reading circles became regular features of Soviet factory life. Workers had to sacrifice a part of their lunch break or come early to work. One may assume that this extra burden was a source of considerable, if silent, resentment.[5]

The goal of industrialization was fantastically ambitious. The First Five-Year Plan period, like the Civil War, was a utopian time. Utopianism in this context meant a lack of balance between goals and means. The leaders of the regime attempted to remake society, expand the economy, increase the standard of living, and improve the defenses of the country. They wanted to accomplish all these worthwhile goals at the same time and in a great hurry in a poor country, which lacked trained and educated personnel and which suffered cruelly from famine. Their far-reaching goals and their impatience demanded extraordinary efforts of mobilization. These mobilization efforts meant improved organization, expanded coercion, and a much broader definition of the enemy. In the new and harsh world of the 1930s, the regime imposed a hitherto unparalleled straitjacket on the arts and scholarship.

The history of the Soviet film industry is a small illustration of this development. During the 1920s Soviet Russia not only made films that touched on genuine problems of the Soviet people and therefore interested them but also allowed the importation of foreign films. At the end of the twenties the number of imports gradually diminished and then finally at the time of collectivization stopped altogether. This move not only cut off audiences from the rest of the world but also very quickly changed the character of Soviet films. Now the directors had no need to compete. Gradually reality disappeared from Soviet screens. From the mid-thirties on, directors escaped into making historical costume dramas to fuel resurgent Russian nationalism. Or, if they did deal with the contemporary period, they depicted a never-never land with not even the remotest connection to reality. Happy peasants sang in the fields, and the best tractor driver got the prettiest woman, who was also the best worker. A typical Soviet film of the period depicted an uneducated Soviet woman textile worker who through sheer force of character and intelligence overfulfilled her norm several hundred percent. As a reward, she was able to meet Comrade Stalin. Not even the great Eisenstein was able to make a film about a genuine issue. His film *Bezhin's Meadow* was to be about Pavlik Morozov, the martyr-hero boy, who had denounced his father as an enemy of the people and was therefore killed by relatives. Although, needless to say, Eisenstein's political approach to his unsavory hero was absolutely orthodox, he was still not allowed to complete his work.[6] It is not an exaggeration to say that from the mid-thirties to the outbreak of the World War not a single film was made in the Soviet Union that commented, however obliquely, on any genuine issue facing the country.

Other branches of art fared no better. Music and painting were reduced to unsophisticated propaganda tools and novels, like movies, ceased to have anything to do with reality. However, fortunately for the people of the Soviet Union, the regime allowed almost without hindrance the enjoyment of the great classics of nineteenth-century Russian literature.[7] Soviet citizens, unlike the Chinese during their cultural revolution, were never deprived of the enjoyment of first-rate literature.

As artistic freedom was extinguished and as coercion increased, the slogans of Soviet propaganda acquired a new and menacing tone. The Bolsheviks always favored martial similes: Their speech often included references to "fronts," "campaigns," "marches," and so forth. Even in the 1920s the Bolsheviks spoke of "storming the fortress of illiteracy" and the "battle against the enemy: backwardness." Now, however, propaganda pamphlets ominously talked about "deserters from the proletarian army." A 1930 Komsomol pamphlet said this about illiteracy: "No organization that signed the agreement [about teaching a certain number of illiterates] has the right to repudiate the responsibilities undertaken. We must look on such occurrences as desertion under fire in the cultural revolution. The smallest delay in carrying out responsibilities must be looked at as a gross violation of discipline."[8] The errant Komsomol leaders had cause to be frightened. In the new world no one committed errors; there was only sabotage. In this deadly serious atmosphere there was no room for the occasionally good-natured humor found in the antichurch and antikulak pronouncements of the 1920s.

At the time of the Great Purge trials, not surprisingly, a major theme of Soviet propaganda was vigilance. One might say that the purge trials themselves were literature composed to drive home to the people this theme. Novels, films, and plays taught Soviet men and women that the enemy was lurking everywhere and that often those who looked the least suspicious were the most deadly opponents of the system.

The basic message of Soviet propaganda, however, remained what it had been in the previous decade. This message was that it was necessary to work hard to overcome backwardness. From the moment of their victory, the Bolsheviks well understood that socialism presupposed an industrial society. Lenin and his colleagues looked enviously on the prosperous West, where workers knew what labor discipline was and where productivity was far higher than in backward Russia. Even during the Civil War, when the survival of the regime was in question, the entire political-education system hammered on the theme of the importance of hard work. Understandably, at the time of the industrialization drive, when the regime assumed responsibility for running the entire economy and when the government and people made extraordinary efforts to build industry, the theme of productivity became the dominant one.

Soviet artists depicted heroes who overcame natural and human obstacles and reached miraculous levels of performance. The regime selected a group of workers and helped them to overfulfill their norms 1,000 to 1,500 percent, in order to hold them up as examples. Once again the Communists created a blend of literature and reality. As in the case of the purge trials, reality was fashioned to make propaganda points. The Party's control of politics, the society, and the economy enabled it to transform the country into a stage.

The regime created the Stakhanovist movement, named after a miner, who supposedly overfulfilled his norm 1,400 percent. The movement was almost entirely a propaganda exercise. It brought considerable benefits: It took advantage of the genuine enthusiasm that existed among the Soviet people for the cause of the socialist transformation of their land; it stratified the working class and showed to many that they too could live well by hard work; and it enabled the regime to raise the work norms for every worker and thereby squeeze people harder.

The supreme test for Soviet society was the Second World War. It passed that test. The country was prepared not only militarily and economically but also politically. The propaganda system played a major role. That system was flexible enough to adjust quickly to the changed circumstances. Propaganda helped to maintain national unity under very difficult circumstances, and it channeled the deeply felt patriotism of the Russian people into the immediate task of winning the war.

Notes

INTRODUCTION:
THE SOVIET CONCEPT OF PROPAGANDA

1 Jacques Ellul, *Propaganda: The Formation of Men's Attitudes* (New York: Knopf, 1965). Ellul, an enemy of mass democracy, describes propaganda as the cause of the illness in modern human beings and as a direct attack on him. See expecially p. xvi.

2 Herbert Marcuse, *One Dimensional Man: Studies in the Ideology of Advanced Industrial Society* (Boston: Beacon Press, 1964). In Marcuse's view, propaganda creates a self-contained system of beliefs in which the genuine aspirations of people are distorted. This system allows no development and offers no possibility for reform. It must be destroyed.

3 V. I. Lenin, *Polnoe sobranie sochinenii,* (hereafter abbreviated PSS), 5th ed., 55 vols. (Moscow: Gosizdat polit. lit., 1967–70), vol. 6, p. 30.

4 Ibid., p. 38.

5 That there was a tension between the Bolsheviks' professedly egalitarian ideology on the one hand and elitism on the other has been noted by many scholars. See a recent and lucid discussion of the problem in Paul Hollander, *Political Pilgrims* (New York: Oxford University Press, 1981), pp. 59–65.

6 Ibid., pp. 66–7.

7 Harold D. Lasswell, *Propaganda Technique in World War I* (Cambridge, Mass.: M.I.T. Press, 1971), p. 195.

8 Ibid., pp. 206–7.

9 See Riazanov's speech to the tenth Party Congress. *Desiatyi s"ezd Rossiiskoi kommunisticheskoi partii: Stenograficheskoi otchet. 8–16 marta, 1921 g.* (Moscow: Gosizdat, 1921), p. 84.

10 See the volume edited by Robert Tucker, *Stalinism: Essays in Historical Interpretation* (New York: Norton, 1977).

11 This is the point of view of Steven F. Cohen as presented in *Bukharin and the Bolshevik Revolution: A Political Biography, 1888–1938* (New York: Knopf, 1973).

12 Alex Inkeles, *Public Opinion in Soviet Russia* (Cambridge, Mass.: Harvard University Press, 1950).

13 Roger Pethybridge, *The Social Prelude to Stalinism* (New York, St. Martin's Press, 1977).

14 Ralph T. Fisher, *Pattern for Soviet Youth: A Study of the Congresses of the Komsomol, 1918–1954* (New York: Columbia University Press, 1959).

15 Richard Taylor, *The Politics of Soviet Cinema, 1917–1929,* (Cambridge: Cambridge University Press, 1979).

16 V. A. Kumanev, *Revoliutsiia i proshveshchenie mass* (Moscow: Nauka, 1973).

17 A. I. Nazarov, *Oktaibr' i kniga* (Moscow: Akad. Nauk, 1968).

18 A. Z. Okorokov, *Oktaibr' i krakh russkoi burzhuaznoi pressy* (Moscow: Mysl',. 1970).

CHAPTER I

THE PRESS

1 *Russkaia periodicheskaia pechat'* (hereafter abbreviated *RPP*) (*1859–Okt. 1917*) *Shornik* (Moscow, 1957), pp. 8–9.

2 J. Walkin, *The Rise of Democracy in Pre-revolutionary Russia: Political and Social Institutions under the Last Three Tsars.* (New York: Praeger, 1962), p. 119.

3 B. I. Esin, ed., *Iz istorii russkoi zhurnalistiki: Kontsa xix nachala xxv* (Moscow: Izd. Moskovskogo Universiteta, 1973), pp. 7–8.

4 Ibid., p. 10.

5 Ibid., p. 11.

6 Ibid., p. 14.

7 *Entsiklopedicheskii slovar',* Published by F. A. Brokgauz and I. A. Efron, vol. 74, p. 962.

8 Esin, p. 9

9 I. P. Belokonskii, *V gody bezpraviia* (Moscow: 1930), pp. 18–19. Belokonskii's description of this incident is marvelously vivid. "In connection with some sort of trial that was taking place in a Zhitomir court, my wife wrote an editorial. On the same theme, concerning the same issues someone else wrote another editorial, expressing completely contradictory views. The old man (the editor), somewhat confused, mechanically united the two articles, in which the second half was not distinguished from the first but simply appeared to be the continuation of the article written by my wife. She was amazed when she read it next morning and went to protest and demand that the newspaper print a note about this misunderstanding. But the editor did not agree. 'Nonsense,' he smiled in good humor, consoling my wife, 'there are different views. Some will like the first half, some will like the second.' 'But people will think this is from the same author! . . .' 'Nonsense! Who is there to think!' "

10 Walkin, pp. 116–20.

11 A. I. Denikin, *Staraia armiia,* 2 vols. (Paris: Rodnik, 1929–31), vol. 1, p. 115.

12 *Krasnyi arkhiv,* vol. 105 (1941), pp. 149–50.

13 *Krasnyi arkhiv,* vol. 10 (1925), p. 332. The Provisional Government demanded that the newspaper return this money.

14 *RPP,* pp. 17–18.

15 Lenin, *PSS,* vol. 5, p. 11. In this article, Lenin anticipated the argument he later developed in *What Is to Be Done?*

16 Ibid., pp. 11–12.
17 Ibid., vol. 6, pp. 160–71.
18 *RPP*, p. 38.
19 Ibid., p. 145.
20 Ibid., pp. 177–80.
21 *Krasnyi arkhiv*, vol. 81 (1937), p. 36. "*Zvezda* i *Pravda* i tsarskaia tsenzura."
22 Of the many books on the history of prerevolutionary *Pravda*, the best is S. A. Andronov, *Bol'shevistskaia pechat' v trekh revoliutsiiakh* (Moscow: Politizdat, 1978).
23 *RPP*, p. 199.
24 B. Wolfe, *Three Who Made a Revolution* (New York: Dial Press, 1948), p. 564.
25 *RPP*, p. 199.
26 Ibid.
27 Andronov, p. 138.
28 Wolfe, p. 562.
29 See, e.g., Lenin, *PSS*, vol. 48, pp. 94–5, 97–9.
30 Ibid., vol. 22, pp. 258–70.
31 N. K. Krupskaia, *Memories of Lenin (1893–1917)* (London: Lawrence and Wishart, 1942), pp. 179, 195–6.
32 Lenin, *PSS*, vol. 48, pp. 173–4.
33 *RPP*, p. 195.
34 E.g., a group of student revolutionaries put out a newssheet, *Listok pravdy* (Truth sheet), which contained a single article. The police immediately arrested the leaders, and very few copies appeared in the streets. I. Kuznetsov and A. Shumakov, *Bol'shevistskaia pechat' Moskvy* (Moscow, Moskovskii Rabochii, 1968), pp. 276–7. A partial exception to the complete repression was the Bolshevik-controlled *Voprosy strakhovaniia* (Problems of insurance), a weekly. This journal started to appear before the war as an outgrowth of a department of *Pravda*. It was suppressed with other revolutionary publications but was allowed to publish again in March 1915.
35 Robert P. Browder and Alexander F. Kerenski, eds., *The Russian Provisional Government: 1917: Documents,* 3 vols. (Stanford: Stanford University Press, 1961), vol. 1, p. 192.
36 Ibid., pp. 228–30.
37 Ibid., vol. 2, pp. 97, 978–9.
38 N. N. Sukhanov, *The Russian Revolution,* 2 vols. (New York: Oxford University Press, 1955), vol. 1, p. 208.
39 Lenin, *PSS*, vol. 34, pp. 209–10.
40 Okorokov, p. 40.
41 The central paper of the Socialist Revolutionaries was *Delo naroda* (The people's cause), but the party also published *Volia naroda* (The people's will), *Trud* (Labor), and Narodnoe slovo (The people's world), each representing a different political point of view. The Left Socialist Revolutionaries published *Znamia truda* (The banner of labor). The Mensheviks published, among other papers, *Edinstvo* (Unity), edited by Plekhanov, and *Rabochaia gazeta* (The worker's gazette). Two other papers deserve special attention. *Izvestiia petrogradskogo soveta rabochikh i soldatskikh deputatov* (The news of the Petrograd Soviet of Workers' and Soldiers' Delegates) was, as its title indicates, the

organ of the Socialist Revolutionary and Menshevik majority of the Petrograd Soviet. Gorki's *Novaia zhizn'* (New life) was important not because of its circulation figures but because of its high quality. The paper, which counted among its editors Maxim Gorky and N. N. Sukhanov, expressed an internationalist, leftist Menshevik position.

42 *RPP,* pp. 261, 251, 242, 269.

43 V. N. Zalezhskii, "Pervyi legalnyi Peka," *Proletarskaia revoliutsiia,* vol. 13 (1923), pp. 144–5.

44 P. Frank and B. C. Kirkham, "The revival of *Pravda* in 1917," *Soviet Studies* vol. 20 (1969), pp. 366–8. A Soviet source mentions 200,000 copies for the first issue. V. P. Budnikov, *Bol'shevistskaia pechat' v 1917 godu* (Kharkov: Izd. Kharkovskogo Universiteta, 1959), p. 13.

45 F. Raskol'nikov, "Priezd tov. Lenina v Rossiiu," *Proletarskaia revoliutsiia,* vol. 13 (1923), p. 221.

46 Budnikov, p. 53.

47 Ibid., p. 68.

48 Ibid., p. 69.

49 There is a large literature on the importance of German money in the Russian Revolution. See George Katkov, *Russia, 1917: The February Revolution* (London: Longmans, 1967) and S. P. Melgunov, *Zolotoi nemetskii kliuch k bol'shevistskoi revoliutsii* (Paris: Dom Knigi, 1940).

50 Budnikov, p. 88.

51 Kuznetsov and Shumakov, pp. 294–5.

52 Ibid., p. 323.

53 Ibid., pp. 326–7.

54 Kh. M. Astrakhan and I. S. Sazonov, "Sozdanie massovoi bol'shevistskoi pechati v 1917 godu," *Voprosy istorii,* no. 1 (1957), p. 89.

55 *RPP,* p. 237.

56 Astrakhan and Sazonov, p. 90.

57 Budnikov, p. 106.

58 Ibid., p. 107.

59 Kuznetsov and Shumakov, pp. 386–7.

60 Astrakhan and Sazonov, p. 92.

61 Kuznetsov and Shumakov, p. 361.

62 Alexander Rabinowitch, *The Bolsheviks Come to Power: The Revolution of 1917 in Petrograd* (New York: Norton, 1976), pp. 18–20.

63 Budnikov, p. 131.

64 Lenin, *PSS,* vol. 5, pp. 39–40.

65 Astrakhan and Sazonov, p. 95.

66 Ibid., p. 98.

67 Lenin, *PSS,* vol. 5, pp. 39–41.

68 Ibid., vol. 12, p. 101.

69 Ibid., pp. 99–105. See also discussions by Soviet scholars of this article. E. P. Prokhorov, "Leninskaia kontseptsiia svobody pechati," *Voprosy teorii i praktiki massovy sredstv propagandy,* 4 vols. (Moscow, 1971), vol. 4, pp. 5–40. According to Prokhorov, Lenin regarded freedom as an understanding of the laws of history and the recognition of necessity. See also G. Kunitsyn, *V. I. Lenin o partiinosti i svobode pechati* (Moscow: Gospolitizdat, 1971), pp. 92–101.

70 Lenin, *PSS,* vol. 34, pp. 208–13.

71 Ibid., pp. 236–7.
72 Okorokov, p. 168.
73 Ibid., pp. 168–70.
74 Ibid., p. 172.
75 *Pravda,* Oct. 28, 1917.
76 L. Schapiro, *The Origin of Communist Autocracy,* 2d ed. (Cambridge, Mass.: Harvard University Press, 1977), p. 69.
77 John Keep, trans. and ed., *The Debate on Soviet Power: Minutes of the All-Russian Central Executive Committee of the Soviets. Second Convocation, October 1917– January 1918* (Oxford: Clarendon Press, 1979). p. 75.
78 Ibid., p. 76.
79 Ibid., p. 70.
80 Ibid., p. 71.
81 Unfortunately, this crucial sentence is mistranslated in Keep. In his version: "If we are moving toward social (ist) revolution, we cannot reply to Kaledin's bombs with bombs of falsehood" (p. 75). See Lenin, *PSS,* vol. 35, p. 54.
82 Keep, *Debate on Soviet Power,* p. 76.
83 Ibid., p. 70. It is perhaps not necessary to add that no party or political group, aside from the Bolsheviks and Left SRs, ever received any of the confiscated goods.
84 Ibid., p. 78. D. Riazanov; N. Derbyshev, commissar of press affairs; I. Arbuzov, commissar of the state printing works; K. Iurenev, commissar of Red Guards; G. Fedorov, head of the labor-conflict department in the Commissariat of Labor; and Iu. Larin also resigned. A. Shliapnikov expressed agreement with those who resigned without himself doing so.
85 *Petrogradskii Voenno-Revoliutsionnyi Komitet: Dokumenty i materialy,* (hereafter abbreviated *PVRK*), 3 vols. (Moscow: Nauka, 1966–7), vol. 1, p. 530. See also discussion in Okorokov, p. 193.
86 *PVRK,* vol. 2, p. 144.
87 In the meeting, Dzerzhinskii, Sverdlov, Ioffe, Lashevich, and Skrypnik badgered the delegation of printers. They accused them of trying to break the unity of the proletariat. The majority of the delegation was unmoved, but a minority indicated that they would not go along. Relative strength among the printers could be seen from the election results to the Second Congress, which took place in Dec. Of the 75 delegates, the Bolsheviks could count only on 15. The Mensheviks lost their hold over the printers' union only at the end of 1919.
88 A. A. Goncharov, "Bor'ba sovetskoi vlasti k kontrrevolitsionnoi burzhuaznoi i melkoburzhuaznoi pechatiu (25 okt.–iul 1918 g.)," *Vestnik MGU: Zhurnalistika,* no. 4 (1969), p. 16.
89 Okorokov, p. 271.
90 Goncharov, p. 14.
91 Goncharov, p. 14; and *PVRK,* vol. 1, p. 130.
92 Lenin, *PSS,* vol. 34, pp. 208–13.
93 Okorokov, pp. 222–9.
94 *PVRK,* vol. 3, p. 232.
95 Lenin, *PSS,* vol. 44, p. 200.
96 Okorokov, pp. 251–5.
97 Ibid., pp. 253–5.

98   Ibid., pp. 258–9.
99   Ibid., p. 261.
100 *PVRK*, vol. 1, pp. 162–3.
101 Okorokov, p. 325.
102 A. L. Mishuris, *Pechat' rozhdennaia Oktiabrem* (Moscow: M.G.U., 1968), p. 17.
103 N. L. Meshcheriakov, "O rabote gosudarstvennogo izdatel'stva," *Pechat' i revoliutsiia,* no. 1 (1921), p. 9.
104 D. Lebedev, *Shest' let moskovskoi pechati, 1917–1923* (Moscow: Novaia Moskva, 1924), pp. 22, 27.
105 C. S. Sampson, "The Formative Years of the Soviet Press: An Institutional History, 1917–1924" (Ph.D. dissertation, University of Massachusetts, 1970), p. 126.
106 Leon D. Trotsky, *Sochineniie,* 21 vols. (Moscow: Gosizdat, 1925–7), vol. 21, p. 243. Also in Sampson, p. 96.
107 *Pravda,* Oct. 27, 1918.
108 *Perepiska sekreteriata Ts.K. RSDRP(b) s mestnymi organizatsiiami. Noiabr' 1917 g. fevral' 1918 g.* (Moscow: Izd. polit. literatury, 1957).
109 See, e.g., M. Zernitskii, "Belorusskaia gazeta *Zvezda* v 1918 godu," *Voprosy zhurnalistiki,* vol. 2, no. 1 (Leningrad, 1960), pp. 45–7.
110 D. Lebedev, *Shest'let,* p. 79.
111 A. Berezhnoi, *K istorii partiino-sovetskoi pechati* (Leningrad: Izd. Leningradskogo Universiteta, 1956), p. 6.
112 A. S. Iakushevskii, *Propagandistskaia rabota bol'shevikov sredi voisk interventov v 1918–1920 gg.* (Moscow: Nauka, 1974), p. 68.
113 *Vosmoi s"ezd RKP(b) Mart 1919 goda: Protokoly* (Moscow: Gosizdat, 1959), pp. 295–6.
114 Ibid., pp. 436–7.
115 A detailed description of the congress and its resolutions can be found in I. V. Vardin (Mgeladze), *Sovetskaia pechat': Sbornik statei* (Moscow: Rabotnik prosveshcheniia, 1924), pp. 126–30.
116 Ibid., pp. 130–2.
117 Lenin, *PSS,* vol. 37, pp. 89–91.

CHAPTER 2
THE STRUGGLE FOR THE PEASANTS

1   John Keep, "October in the Provinces," in Richard Pipes, ed., *Revolutionary Russia: A Symposium* (Cambridge, Mass.: Harvard University Press, 1968), p. 231.
2   V. D. Bonch-Bruevich, *Na boevykh postiakh feval'skoi revoliutsii,* 2d ed. (Moscow: Izd federatsii, 1931), pp. 117–21. Soviet historian I. S. Smirnov argued that Lenin's decrees were instruments of agitation. He quoted from Lenin to show that the Soviet leader was conscious of this use. I. S. Smirnov, *Lenin i Sovetskaia kultura* (Moscow: Izd. Academii nauk SSR, 1960), p. 174.
3   Smirnov, p. 162.
4   M. Fofanova, "Reshaiushchie dni," *Oktiabr',* Nov. 1956, p. 121.
5   "Kak pisal Vladimir Ilich dekret o zemle" appeared several times in different versions. First it came out in *Gudok* in Nov. 1927. Then it was republished

in 1930 in a collection of articles entitled *Na boevykh postiakh fevral'skoi i oktiab'rskoi revoliutsii* (Moscow: Federatsiia, 1930). This book came out in a second edition in 1931. The article appeared in a startlingly different version in the collected works of Bonch-Bruevich, *Izbrannye sochineniia*, 3 vols. (Moscow: Akad. Nauk, 1959–63), vol. 3. The same version is reprinted in V. D. Bonch-Bruevich, *Vospominaniia o Lenine* (Moscow: Nauka, 1969). Some of the differences between the earlier and later versions are easy to explain. Not surprisingly, in the later editions Trotsky is edited out. It is odd, however, that the early versions do not include the episode about the old calendars. It is hard to believe that Bonch-Bruevich recalled this story only in his old age. The British historian Roger Pethybridge fell victim to the confusion. In his book *The Spread of the Russian Revolution: Essays on 1917* (New York: St. Martin's Press, 1972), p. 154, he footnotes the story to the Bonch-Bruevich book of 1931, where in fact it did not appear.

6   Bonch-Bruevich, *Vospominaniia o Lenine*, p. 127.

7   V. M. Selunskaia, *Robochii klass i Oktiabr' v derevne* (Moscow: Mysl' 1968), pp. 60–1.

8   Ibid., p. 68.

9   Ia. Burov, *Organizuite derevniu* (Petrograd: Izd. Sold. i Krest. bib. 1918). Burov later became the head of the agittrain section of VTsSK.

10 Ibid., pp. 26–31.

11 Ibid., p. 34.

12 Ibid., pp. 37–43.

13 *Perepiska sekreteriata Ts.K.*, p. 349.

14 *Petrogradskii voenno-revoliutsionnyi komitet: Dokumenty i materialy*, 3 vols. (Moscow: Nauka, 1966–7), vol. 2, p. 541.

15 Ibid., vol. 3, p. 390.

16 Selunskaia, pp. 66–7.

17 N. K. Krupskaia, *Leninskie ustanovki v oblasti kultury* (Moscow: Gosizdat, 1934), p. 129.

18 Kumanev, *Revoliutsiia*, pp. 304–5.

19 *Vneshkolnoe obrazovanie*, no. 1 (1919), p. 7.

20 D. I. Erde, *Negramotnost' i bor'ba s nei* (Kharkov: Proletarii, 1924), p. 245.

21 *KPSS v resoliutsiiakh i resheniiakh s"ezdov, Konferentsii i plenumov Ts. K. 1898–1954* (hereafter abbreviated *KpSS*) (Moscow: Gospolitizdat, 1953–60), vol. 1, p. 129.

22 Instructions, Party work in Smolensk *raion*, Nov. 27, 1918, Smolensk Archives, WKP, reel. 2.

23 TsGAOR, f5451, 02, d347.

24 TsGAOR, f5451, 03, d471.

25 Sheila Fitzpatrick, *The Commissariat of Enlightenment: Soviet Organization of Education and Arts under Lunacharskii, October 1917–1921*. (Cambridge: Cambridge University Press, 1970), p. 243.

26 L. M. Maksakova, *Agitpoezd "Oktiabrskaia revoliutsiia," 1919–1920 gg.* (Moscow: Akad. nauk, 1956), p. 9.

27 Ts. Gofman, "K istorii pervogo agitparakhoda VTsIK "Krasnaia zvezda'," *Voprosy istorii*, no. 9 (1948), p. 63.

28 B. Sergeev, ed., "Agitpoezdki M. I. Kalinina v gody grazhdanskoi voiny," *Krasnyi arkhiv*, vol. 86 (1938), p. 96.

29 Maksakova, p. 19.
30 Sergeev, p. 98.
31 Richard Taylor, "A Medium for the Masses: Agitation in the Soviet Civil War," *Soviet Studies*, April 1971, p. 568.
32 Ibid.
33 Sergeev, p. 144.
34 Ibid., pp. 110–14.
35 Gofman, p. 65.
36 N. K. Krupskaia, "Po gradam i selam Sovetskoi respubliki," *Novyi mir*, no. 11 (1960), pp. 113–30.
37 Maksakova, p. 12.
38 Ibid., p. 14.
39 I described the South Russian White movement in great detail in my two books *Civil War in South Russia, 1918* (Berkeley: University of California Press, 1971), and *Civil War in South Russia, 1919–1920* (Berkeley: University of California Press, 1977). On the propaganda organization, see especially pp. 71–80 and 278–9 in the second volume.
40 Intelligence report, Oct. 28, 1919 (O.S.). Wrangel Military Archives, file 146, pp. 58–61.
41 Nikolai Ross, *Vrangel' v Krymu* (Frankfurt/Main: Possev, 1982), pp. 270–4.
42 J. S. Curtiss, *The Russian Church and the Soviet State 1917–1950* (Boston: Little, Brown, 1953), p. 101.
43 Ibid., p. 38.
44 Ibid., p. 38.
45 Ibid., p. 41.
46 Bonch-Bruevich, *Na boevykh postiakh*, p. 206.
47 Ibid., pp. 209–11.
48 Kenez, *Civil War in South Russia, 1919–1920*, p. 79.
49 Ibid., p. 80.
50 J. Bunyan and H. H. Fischer, eds. *The Bolshevik Revolution, 1917–1918* (Stanford: Stanford University Press, 1934), pp. 590–1.
51 Curtiss, p. 46.
52 Ibid., p. 45.
53 Ibid., p. 45.
54 Bonch-Bruevich, *Na boevykh postiakh*, pp. 211–13.
55 E. Ia. Liagushina, "Nauchno-ateisticheskaia propaganda v pervye gody sovetskoi vlasti," *Voprosy istorii*, no. 9 (1967), p. 98.
56 Ibid., p. 97.
57 P. A. Krasikov, *Na tserkovnom fronte (1918–1923)* (Moscow: Iurid. izd.-vo., 1923), p. 14.
58 Liagushina, p. 96.

CHAPTER 3

LIQUIDATING ILLITERACY IN REVOLUTIONARY RUSSIA

1 O. Anweiler, *Geschichte der Schule und Pedagogie in Russland vom Ende des Zarenreiches bis zum Beginn der Stalin-Ära* (Berlin: Osteuropa Institut, 1964), p. 78.
2 Krupskaia, *Memories of Lenin*, p. 2.
3 A. V. Lunacharskii, *Lenin i prosvesnhchenie mass* (Moscow: Gosizdat, 1924), p. 68.

4 Lenin, *PSS*, vol. 44, p. 174.

5 On literacy according to the 1897 census, see A. G. Rashin, *Naselenie Rossii za 100 let* (Moscow: Gos. statisticheskoe izd., 1956), pp. 284–93; and I. M. Bogdanov, *Gramotnost' i obrazovanie v dorevoliutsionnoi Rossii i SSSR* (Moscow: Statistika, 1964), pp. 58–74. See also the interesting discussion of the meaning of the data in Gregory Guroff and S. Frederick Starr, "A Note on Urban Literacy in Russia, 1890–1914," *Jahrbucher fur Geschichte Osteuropas,* vol. 19, no. 4 (1971), 520–31; and V. A. Kumanev, *Revoliutsiia i prosveshchenie mass* (Moscow: Nauka, 1973), pp. 50–61.

6 *Gramotnost' v Rossii* (Moscow: TsSU SSSR, 1922), p. 7.

7 Rashin, pp. 309–10.

8 Ibid., pp. 293, 297.

9 Ibid., p. 299.

10 Ibid., p. 304.

11 Kumanev, *Revoliutsiia,* p. 83.

12 Bogdanov, p. 132.

13 Fitzpatrick, *Commissariat of Enlightenment,* p. 11. On Krupskaia, see also R. H. McNeal, *Bride of the Revolution* (Ann Arbor: University of Michigan Press, 1972).

14 V. A. Kumanev, *Sotsialism i vsenarodnaia gramotnost'* (Moscow: Nauka, 1967), p. 33.

15 A. I. Fomin, "Sozdanie sovetskogo apparata narodnogo prosveshcheniia po mestakh," *Voprosy istorii,* no. 9 (Sept. 1979), pp. 25–7.

16 Smirnov, *Lenin i sovetskaia kul'tura,* pp. 214–24.

17 N. K. Krupskaia, *Pedagogicheskie sochineniia v desiati tomakh,* 10 vols. (Moscow: Institut pedagogii A.P.N. RSFSR, 1957–63), vol. 2, p. 88.

18 Erde, pp. 17–18.

19 Lenin, *PSS,* vol. 38, p. 331.

20 Erde, p. 18.

21 Anweiler, p. 214.

22 Erde, pp. 20–3.

23 The decree is reprinted in Kumanev, *Revoliutsiia,* pp. 311–12.

24 *Vneshkol'noe obrazovanie,* no. 2–3, p. 95. This journal was published by Krupskaia's department in 1919.

25 D. Iu. El'kina, *Na kul'turnom fronte* (Moscow: Gosizdat, 1959), pp. 39–40.

26 Kumanev, *Revoliutsiia,* p. 101.

27 Ibid., p. 117.

28 D. Iu. El'kina, "Likvidatsiia negramotnosti v Krasnoi Armii na frontakh grazdanskoi voiny," *Narodnoe obrazovanie,* no. 12 (1957), pp. 52–6.

29 Kumanev, *Revoliutsiia,* p. 113.

30 V. V. Maiakovskii, *Polnoe sobranie sochinenii v 13 tomakh,* 13 vols. (Moscow: Gosizdat khudozhestvennoi literatury, 1955–61), vol. 2, pp. 92–5, 500.

31 Kumanev, *Revoliutsiia,* p. 135.

32 Erde, p. 23.

33 TsGAOR, f5451, 04, d333.

34 Ibid.

35 Erde, p. 24.

36 Ibid.

37 TsGAOR, f2314, 01, d37.

38 TsGAOR, f5451, 01, d333.
39 Erde, p. 39.
40 Ibid., p. 25; and Kumanev, *Revoliutsiia,* p. 142.

CHAPTER 4
THE KOMSOMOL IN THE CIVIL WAR

1 There is a large literature on the Zhenotdel. The best book on the subject is R. Stites, *The Women's Liberation Movement in Russia: Feminism, Nihilism and Bolshevism, 1860–1930* (Princeton: Princeton University Press, 1978.)
2 A. Shokhin, *Kratkaia istoriia VLKSM* (Moscow: Molodaia Gvardiia, 1928), pp. 41–2.
3 Fisher, p. 5.
4 Balashov and Nelepin, *VLKSM za 10 let v tsifrakh* (Moscow and Leningrad: Molodaia gvardiia, 1928), p. 5.
5 The main spokesman on youth organizations was M. M. Kharitonov. It was he who introduced the resolution that was adopted by the congress. See the extensive discussions on this issue in *Shestoi s"ezd RSDRP Avgust 1917 goda; Protokoly* (Moscow: Gosizdat, 1958), pp. 181–91. The resolution is printed on p. 267.
6 Balashov and Nelepin, p. 5.
7 Shokhin, *Kratkaia istoriia,* p. 56.
8 *Slavnyi put' Leninskogo Komsomola,* 2 vols. (Moscow: Molodaia gvardiia, 1974), vol. 1, pp. 117–18.
9 Shokhin, *Kratkaia istoriia,* p. 58.
10 Ibid., p. 60.
11 *Slavnyi put' Leninskogo Komsomola,* p. 159.
12 Balashova and Nelepin, p. 6.
13 Fisher, p. 19.
14 Ibid., p. 18.
15 *Slavnyi put' Leninskogo Komsomola,* p. 159.
16 Ibid., p. 14.
17 Lenin, *PSS,* vol. 41, pp. 298–318.
18 *Slavnyi put' Leninskogo Komsomola,* p. 174.
19 Shokhin, *Kratkaia istoriia,* p. 77.
20 Smolensk Archives, Roll 51, WKP 467.
21 Ibid.
22 Shokhin, *Kratkaia istoriia,* p. 74.
23 *Slavnyi put' Leninskogo Komsomola,* p. 179.
24 Fisher, p. 49.
25 I. E. Liubimov, *Komsomol v sovetskom stroitel'stve 1917–1927.* (Moscow and Leningrad: Molodaia gvardiia, 1928), pp. 41–52.
26 *Slavnyi put' Leninskogo Komsomola,* pp. 199–200.
27 V. Ganichev, *Boevoi opyt komsomol'skoi pechati, 1917–1925* (Moscow: Moskovskii mabochii, 1973), pp. 17–18.
28 Balashov and Nelepin, p. 6.
29 Theses on work among youth in the coming summer. Approved by the Smolensk Provincial Committee of the Russian Communist Party, April 23, 1920. In Smolensk Archives, roll 51, WKP 467.

CHAPTER 5
THE POLITICAL USE OF BOOKS, FILMS, AND POSTERS

1   V. Slavskaia, "Kniga i revoliutsiia," *Kniga i revoliutsiia*, no. 3–4 (1920), p. 4.
2   Nazarov, *Oktiabr'*, p. 9.
3   Slavskaia, p. 4.
4   N. F. Ianitskii, *Knizhnaia statistika sovetskoi Rossii, 1918–1923* (Moscow: Gosizdat, 1924), p. 5.
5   Nazarov, *Oktiabr'*, p. 65.
6   Slavskaia, p. 5.
7   *Knizhnaia letopis'*, Jan. 1918, nos. 132, 133.
8   Nazarov, *Oktiabr'*, p. 133.
9   E. Dinershtein, *Izdatel'skoe delo v pervye gody Sovetskoi vlasti* (Moscow: Kniga, 1972), p. 7.
10 V. Polianskii, "Nachalo sovetskikh izdatel'stv," *Pechat' i revoliutsiia*, vol. 7 (1927), p. 233.
11 *Izdatel'skoe delo v pervye gody sovetskoi vlasti (1917–1922) Sbornik dokumentov i materialov* (Moscow, 1972). Decree of the Central Executive Committee on government publishing, pp. 14–16.
12 Polianskii, p. 233.
13 Keep, *Debate on Soviet Power*, p. 253.
14 Keep, in fact, makes this point in his notes. Ibid., pp. 408–9.
15 Polianskii, p. 236.
16 Ibid., p. 237.
17 A. I. Nazarov, *Kniga v sovetskom obshchestve* (Moscow: Nauka, 1964), p. 98.
18 Dinershtein, *Izdatel'skoe delo*, pp. 158–9.
19 Ibid., p. 13.
20 Ibid.
21 Ibid., p. 14.
22 Ibid., pp. 34–6.
23 Vardin, pp. 128–9.
24 Dinershtein, *Izdatel'skoe delo*, p. 21.
25 Ibid., p. 18.
26 Ibid.
27 Ibid., p. 160 n. 32.
28 Nazarov, *Kuiga*, pp. 139–40.
29 Dinershtein, *Izdatel'skoe delo*, p. 33.
20 Nazarov, *Kniga*, p. 149.
31 Dinershtein, *Izdatel'skoe delor*, pp. 34–5.
32 Nazarov, *Kniga*, p. 197.
33 Dinershtein, *Izdatel'skoe delo*, p. 37.
34 Ibid., p. 55 (Sovnarkom's decree on the distribution of paper).
35 Meshcheriakov, "O rabote gosudarstvennogo izdatel'stva," pp. 9–10.
36 Nazarov, *Kniga*, p. 176.
37 Ibid., p. 154.
38 A. Voronskii, "Iz proshlego," *Prozhektor*, no. 6 (1927), p. 19.
39 Nazarov, *Oktiabr'*, p. 134.
40 Dinershtein, *Izdatel'skoe delo*, p. 72 (Sovnarkom decree on nationalization of book collections, April 20, 1920).

41 Slavskaia, p. 101.
42 N. L. Meshcheriakov, "O rabote gosudarstvennogo izdatel'stva v novykh uslo-viakh," *Pechat' i revoliutsiia*, no. 1 (1922), p. 164.
43 N. A. Lebedev, *Ocherki istorii kino SSSR, Vol. 1: Nemoe kino, 1917–1934* (Moscow: Iskusstvo, 1965), pp. 43–4.
44 N. A. Lebedev, *Ocherk istorii kino SSSR* (Moscow, 1947), p. 13.
45 S. S. Ginsburg, *Kinematografiia dorevoliutsionnoi Rossii* (Moscow: Iskusstvo, 1963), p. 157.
46 N. Lebedev, *Ocherk*, pp. 20–9.
47 Ginsburg, p. 11.
48 Ibid., pp. 180–1.
49 N. Lebedev, *Ocherk*, p. 58.
50 *Samoe vazhnoe iz vsekh iskusstv: Lenin o kino* (Moscow: Iskusstvo, 1963), p. 124.
51 N. Lebedev, *Ocherk*, pp. 64–6.
52 L. Akselrod, "Dokumenty po istorii natsionalizatsii russkoi kinematografii," *Iz istorii kino*, no. 1 (1958), pp. 25–6.
53 Ibid., p. 29.
54 N. Lebedev, *Ocherk*, p. 68.
55 V. Listov, "U istokov sovetskogo kino," *Iskusstvo kino*, no. 3 (1969), pp. 3–4.
56 Akselrod, p. 27.
57 Listov, pp. 8–9.
58 S. Bratoliubov, *Na zare Sovetskoi kinematografii* (Leningrad: Iskusstvo, 1976), p. 24.
59 Listov, p. 12; and V. T. Ermakov, "Ideinaia bor'ba na kul'turnom fronte v pervom gode sovetskoi vlasti," *Voprosy istorii*, Nov. 1971, p. 19.
60 N. Lebedev, *Ocherk*, p. 68. Our basic source of knowledge about Soviet films is the massive four-volume catalog *Sovetskie khudozhestvennye fil'my: Annotirovan-nyi katalog* (hereafter abbreviated *S.kh.f.*), 4 vols. (Moscow: Iskusstvo, 1961–8). This catalog does not include films made during the Civil War by private companies.
61 Jay Leyda, *Kino: A History of the Russian and Soviet Film* (New York: Collier Books, 1960), pp. 423–4.
62 Ibid., p. 424.
63 Ibid., and N. Lebedev, *Ocherk*, pp. 68–71.
64 This film is available at the Pacific Film Archive in Berkeley, Calif.
65 Leyda, pp. 111–20.
66 Akselrod, p. 34.
67 N. Lebedev, *Ocherk*, pp. 76–9.
68 N. Lebedev, *Ocherki*, pp. 108–16.
69 N. Lebedev, *Ocherki* and *S.Kh.f.*, vol. 1, p. 15.
70 *S.Kh.f.*, vol. 1, p. 11.
71 Ibid.
72 Ibid., p. 14.
73 Ibid., p. 13; and N. Lebedev, *Ocherki*, p. 133.
74 *S.Kh.f.*, vol. 1, p. 10.
75 Ibid., pp. 5–19.
76 Ibid.
77 N. Lebedev, *Ocherk*, pp. 79–83.
78 There is disagreement among writers on the subject concerning the impor-

tance of the native tradition. B. S. Butnik-Siverskii attributed great significance to native examples in developing Soviet poster art: *Sovetskii plakat epokhi grazhdanskoi voiny: 1918–1921* (Moscow: Izd. knizhnoi palaty, 1960), pp. 7–16. Polonskii, by contrast, believed that native traditions played no role; "Russkii revoliutsionnyi plakat," *Pechat' i revoliutsiia,* no. 2 (1922), pp. 58–61. To me, Polonskii's arguments seem more convincing. In an interesting article, Stephen White distinguishes four native sources: (1) *lubok,* an illustrated peasant broadsheet, popular in the nineteenth century, (2) Russian satirical journals, (3) commercial posters, and (4) icons; "The Political Poster in Bolshevik Russia," *Sbornik: Study Group on the Russian Revolution* (Leeds: Study Group on the Russian Revolution, 1982), pp. 28–37.

79 Polonskii, p. 61.
80 Ibid.
81 D. S. Moor, *Ia Bolshevik* (Moscow: Sovetskii khudoztrik, 1967), pp. 7–14; N. M. Chegodaeva, "Plakat," in I. E. Grabar, ed., *Istoriia russkogo iskusstva,* 13 vols. (Moscow: Akad. nauk., n.d.), vol. 11, p. 58.
82 Chegodaeva, p. 64.
83 Robert C. Williams, *Artists in Revolution* (Bloomington: Indiana University Press, 1979), p. 80.
84 Butnik-Siverskii, p. 77. On Rosta, see N. A. Bryliakov, *Rossiiskoe telegrafnoe* (Moscow: Mysl', 1976).
85 M. Cheremykh, "Maiakovskii v Rosta," *Iskusstvo,* no. 3 (1940), p. 39.
86 White, p. 31.
87 Maiakovskii, vol. 3, p. 472.
88 Polonskii, p. 60.

CHAPTER 6
POLITICAL EDUCATION

1 See, e.g., the speeches of E. A. Preobrazhenskii and D. B. Riazanov to the Tenth Party Congress. *Desiatyi s"ezd Rossiiskoi kommunisticheskoi partii, Stenografieheskii otchet, 8–16 marta, 1921 g.* (Moscow: Gosizdat, 1921), pp. 74–87.
2 *Izvestiia Tsentral'nogo Komiteta,* no. 28 (1921), p. 13. See also N. N. Krestinskii's speech to the Tenth Congress. *Desiatyi s"ezd, p. 30.*
3 *Izvestiia Tsentral'nogo Komiteta,* no. 28, p. 16.
4 The establishment of Glavpolitprosvet is described in detail in Fitzpatrick, *Commissariat of Enlightenment,* pp. 175–86.
5 Ibid., pp. 243–4.
6 *Izvestiia Tsentral'nogo Komiteta,* no. 28 (1921), p. 13.
7 *Desiatyi s"ezd,* pp. 74–98.
8 Ibid., p. 84.
9 Ibid., pp. 74–82.
10 Ibid., pp. 84–7.
11 Ibid., pp. 95–8.
12 Ibid., pp. 82–4.
13 V. I. Lenin, " 'Novaia ekonomicheskaia politika i zadachi politprosvetov' Doklad na II vserossiiskom s"ezde politprosvetov. Oct. 17, 1921," *PSS,* vol. 44, p. 174.
14 *Desiatyi s"ezd,* p. 86.

15 The expression is from Sheila Fitzpatrick, *Education and Social Mobility in the Soviet Union, 1921–1934* (Cambridge: Cambridge University Press, 1979), p. 68.

16 E. H. Carr, *Socialism in One Country, 1924–1926*, 3 vols. (New York: Macmillan, 1960), vol. 2, p. 168, and Carr, *Foundations of a Planned Economy, 1926–1929* 3 vols. (New York: Macmillan, 1971), vol. 2, p. 151.

17 On Communist universities, see L. S. Leonova, *Iz istorii podgotovki partiinykh kadrov v sovetsko- partiinykh shkolakh i kommunisticheskikh universitetakh (1921–1925 gg)* (Moscow: Izdatel'stvo Moskovskogo Universiteta, 1972), p. 26.

18 Zev Katz, "Party Political Education in Soviet Russia," *Soviet Studies*, vol. 7 (Jan. 1956), p. 241.

19 *Agitatsionno-propagandistskaia rabota Glavpolitprosveta: Materialy k XII s"ezdy partii* (Moscow: Glavpolitprosvet, 1923), p. 18.

20 S. N. Harper, *Civil Training in Soviet Russia* (Chicago: University of Chicago Press, 1929), p. 285.

21 Katz, p. 245.

22 Carr, *Socialism in One Country*, vol. 2, p. 190.

23 Carr, *Foundations of a Planned Economy*, p. 155.

24 *Agitatsionno-propagandistskaia rabota Glavpolitprosveta*, pp. 6–7.

25 Carr, *Foundations of a Planned Economy*, vol. 2, p. 156.

26 *Agitatsionno-propagandistskaia rabota Glavpolitprosveta*, p. 20.

27 Ibid., p. 21.

28 Ibid.

29 Ibid., p. 20.

30 Ibid., p. 19.

31 Ibid., p. 18.

32 *Komsomol'skaia politshkola II stupeni. Programma, ob"iasnitel'naia zapiska, literatura* (Moscow and Leningrad: Molodaia gvardiia, 1926), p. 12.

33 *Agitatsionno-propagandistskaia rabota Glavpolitprosveta*, p. 17.

34 "Ob itogakh i perspektivakh raboty derevenskikh shkol politgramoty" (Decisions of Agitprop Section of Central Committee and meeting of leaders of agitprop of Party committees). March 15–17, 1926. In Appendix to *Kommunisticheskaia revoliutsiia* (hereafter abbreviated *Kom. rev.*), no. 8 (1926), pp. 3–4.

35 *Agitatsionno-propagandistskaia rabota Glavpolitprosveta*, p. 17.

36 Harper, p. 281.

37 "Ob itogakh i perspektivakh," p. 1.

38 The model curriculum is reproduced in ibid., pp. 12–41.

39 G. Baklaev, "O nedostatkakh v rabote shkol politgramoty," *Kom. rev.*, March 1925, pp. 14–19.

40 B. Chistov, "Opyt i vyvody odnogo obsledovaniia," *Kom. rev.*, Feb. 1927, pp. 66–73.

41 E. O. Kabo, *Ocherki rabochego byta* (Moscow: VTsSPS, 1928), p. 192.

42 Ibid., p. 195.

43 T. A. Remïzova, *Kul'turno-prosvetitel'naia rabota v RSFSR (1921–1925 gg)* (Moscow: Akad. nauk, 1962), p. 228.

44 Ibid., p. 236.

45 *Agitatsionno-propagandistskaia rabota Glavpolitprosveta.* p. 33.

46 Circular of Seniushkin, head of cultural department of VTsSPS to cultural sections of unions, Jan. 1, 1926, f5451, 010, d476.

47 Ratmanov, secretary of Ts.K. SRKKh, to union locals, Aug. 26, 1926, f5451, 010, d476.
48 T. H. Rigby, *Communist Party Membership in the USSR, 1917–1967* (Princeton: Princeton University Press, 1968, p. 116.
49 Carr, *Foundations of a Planned Economy,* p. 179.
50 *Pedagogicheskaia entsiklopediia,* 3 vols. (Moscow, 1927–30), vol. 3, p. 359.
51 Ibid., pp. 369–72.
52 Ibid., p. 362.
53 For the development of the Lenin worship and for the quasireligious aspect of the cult, see Nina Tumarkin's *Lenin Lives! The Lenin Cult in Soviet Russia* (Cambridge, Mass.: Harvard University Press, 1983).
54 *Izba-chital'nia* (monthly journal published by Glavpolitprosvet), May 1924, p. 49.
55 *Pedagogicheskaia entsikolpedia,* vol. 3, p. 367.
56 *Izba chital'nia,* May 1924, p. 10.
57 Ibid., Nov. 1924, p. 35.
58 S. Syrtsov, "Politprosvetrabota v derevne," *Kom. rev.,* March 1925, p. 4.
59 Ibid. Syrtsov mentions two extreme examples: In Zlatoust in the course of two years personnel changes were made 25 times. In an uezd of Viatka province, 17 times.
60 V. Meshcheriakov, "Politicheskoe prosveshchenie krestianstva," *Kom. rev.,* Dec. 1927, p. 34.
61 G. Rylkin, "Gorod izbachi Politprosvetskoi gubernii," *Kom. rev.,* May 1927, p. 39.
62 Ibid.
63 V. Meshcheriakov, "Politicheskoe prosveshchenie krestianstva," p. 36.
64 *Pravda,* Dec. 5, 1924.
65 *Pravda,* Dec. 30, 1924.
66 *Pravda,* Nov. 23, 1924.
67 *Pravda,* Dec. 20, 1924.
68 Rylkin, p. 36.
69 *Pedagogicheskaia entsiklopediia,* vol. 3, p. 371.
70 S. Syrtsov, "Politprosvetrabota v derevne," *Kom. rev.,* Nov. 1927, p. 54.
71 Ibid., p. 4.
72 G. Shibailo, "Kul'turnaia rol' shefov v derevne," *Kom. rev.,* Nov. 1927, p. 54.
73 Ia. Burov, *Rabochie obshchestva dlia shefstva nad derevne* (Moscow: Moskovskii Rabochii, 1925), p. 19.
74 Shibailo, p. 54.
75 Meeting of Elnink uezd Agitprop section, July 19, 1924, Smolensk Archives, item 10, reel 2.

CHAPTER 7

THE LITERACY CAMPAIGN

1 Harvey Graff, *The Literacy Myth: Literacy and Social Structure in the Nineteenth-Century City* (New York: Academic Press, 1979).
2 Lenin, *PSS,* vol. 44, p. 174.
3 S. G. Strumilin, *Khozaistvennoe znachenie narodnogo obrazovaniia* (Moscow and Leningrad: Ekonomicheskaia zhizn, 1924), p. 18.

4 Erde, p. 217.
5 Lenin, *PSS*, vol. 44, p. 174.
6 Kumanev, *Revoliutsiia*, p. 168.
7 Erde, p. 39.
8 Minutes of the Second All-Russian Congress for Liquidation of Illiteracy, May 20–4, 1923, TsGAOR, f5451, 07, d446.
9 May 20, 1924. Report of Revel'skii. Ibid., f5451, 07, d446.
10 Protocols of the meeting of the organizational bureau for Third All-Russian Conference for Liquidation of Illiteracy, April 17, 1924, f5451, 08, d387.
11 Protocol of meeting at Glavpolitprosvet concerning work of VChK/1b, Sept. 28, 1923. Report of Boguslavskaia, f5451, 07, d447.
12 Ibid.
13 Resolutions of the First All-Russian Congress of the Workers of the Anti-illiteracy Campaign, f5451, 06, d465.
14 D. A. Bondarev, *Likvidatsiia negramotnosti: Tsifry, fakty, perspektivy* (Moscow and Leningrad: Gosizdat, 1929), p. 42.
15 E.g., Letter of Union of Metal Workers to Cultural Department of VTsSPS, Jan. 16, 1923; Report from Miners, Jan. 16, 1923; Report from construction workers, Jan. 11, 1923; Report of local transport workers, Jan. 13, 1923; Report from Railroad workers, Jan. 25, 1923; Report from workers in paper-making industry, March 25, 1923; All the reports are in f5451, 07, d448; See also Report of Isaev, a leader in Cultural Department in VTsSPS (undated, but originated sometime in early 1923), f5451, 07, d446.
16 Report of Isaev, f5451, 07, d446.
17 Ibid.
18 Protocol of the meeting of the organizational bureau for the Third All-Russian Conference for the Elimination of Illiteracy, April 17, 1924, f5451, 08, d387.
19 Report of Kremenchug miners to Cultural Department of VTsSPS, May 31, 1921, f5451, 05, d602.
20 Report of local transport workers, Jan. 13, 1923, f5451, 07, d448.
21 Report from construction workers, Jan. 11, 1923, f5451, 07, d448.
22 Report from metal workers, Jan. 16, 1923, f5451, 07, d448, in 1923–4.
23 Report of the textile workers' union on literacy work to Cultural Department of VTsSPS, f5451, 08, d388.
24 Protocol of meeting of representatives of various unions in Cultural Department of VTsSPS, June 13, 1924, f5451, 08, d388.
25 Report of Ivanovo-Voznesensk Provincial ODN [Obshchestvo "Doloi Negramotnosti"; "Down with Illiteracy" Society], March 21, 1925, f5451, 09, d522.
26 Letter of Menzhinskaia, head of VChK/1b, to VTsSPS, Dec. 15, 1921, f5451, 05, d602.
27 Goriachev, secretary of workers in paper-making trade, to Cultural Department of VTsSPS, Feb. 17, 1923, f5451, 07, d448.
28 Agreement between Cultural Department of VTsSPS and VChK/1b on literacy work, Feb. 8, 1923, f5451, 07, d446.
29 Circular from Isaev, Cultural Department of VTsSPS to all unions, Sept. 4, 1924, f5451, 08, d388.
30 Protocol of meeting, Jan. 24, 1923, f5451, 07, d446.

31 Bondarev, p. 10.
32 E.g., Kumanev, *Revoliutsiia,* p. 170.
33 A review of the composition and work of ODN from Dec. 1923 to Oct. 1924, f5451, 08, d387.
34 Protocol no. 1, Founding meeting of the "ODN," Sept. 2, 1923, f5451, 07, d446.
35 Doloi negramotnost', *K pervomy vserossiiskomu s"ezdu obshchestva Doloi Negramotnost'* (Moscow and Leningrad: ODN, 1926), pp. 5–6.
36 A review of the composition and work of ODN from Dec. 1923 to Oct. 1924, f5451, 08, d387.
37 Report of the Archangel Provincial ODN on activities from Sept. 1924 to Jan. 1925, f5451, 09, d524.
38 Politprosvet report on ODN work in Briansk province, f5451, 00, d524.
39 Report from Irkutsk province on ODN work up to Jan. 1925, f5451, 08, s387.
40 Report on the work of ODN cells in the villages, Jan. 1925, f5451, 09, d522.
41 A review of the composition and work of ODN from Dec. 1923 to Sept. 1924, f5451, 08, d387.
42 Report of the Archangel Provincial ODN on activities from Sept. 1924 to Jan. 1925, f5451, 09, d524.
43 Letter from Central ODN to Seniushkin, Cultural Department of VTsSPS, Feb. 9, 1925, Concerning Penze provincial ODN, f5451, 09, d524.
44 Kumanev, *Revoliutsiia,* pp. 191–201.
45 Bondarev, p. 10.
46 Ibid., pp. 14–18.
47 Ibid., p. 13.
48 Ibid., p. 10.
49 Kumanev, *Revoliutsiia,* p. 193.
50 Bondarev, pp. 37–42.
51 *Pedagogicheskaia entsiklopediia,* vol. 3, p. 352.
52 Kumanev, *Revoliutsiia,* p. 193.
53 *Pedagogicheskaia entsiklopediia,* vol. 3, p. 352.
54 Ibid.
55 Bondarev, p. 42.
56 Ibid., p. 15.
57 Ibid., p. 63.
58 S. Fischer-Galati, ed., *East Central Europe under the Communists: Romania* (New York: Praeger, 1957), p. 56.
59 Bondarev, p. 62.
60 "People want to send their children to school, but the state cannot yet satisfy everyone. The kulaks take advantage of this opportunity and agitate against the teaching of adults. The correct class line is to teach poor peasant adults." Bondarev, p. 19.
61 Instructions for conducting a three-day campaign for the liquidation of illiteracy, May 1–3, 1925; signed by representatives of Glavpolitprosvet, VChK/1b, and ODN; f5451, 09, d522.
62 D. A. Bondarev, *Obshchestvenno-politicheskoe vospitanie v shkole gramoty* (Moscow: Gosizdat, 1930), pp. 14–15.

63 A. M. Bolshakov, *Derevnia 1917–1927* (Moscow: Rabotnik prosveshcheniia, 1927), p. 231.
64 Ibid., p. 231.
65 Ibid., p. 233.
66 Erde, pp. 125–6.
67 *V pomoshch likvidatoru: Prakticheskie rukovodstvo po programme i metodiki voprosam likvidatsii negramotnosti i malogramotnosti* (Orel: Orel Gub. ONO, 1926), pp. 5–6.
68 T. A. Remizova, *Kulturno-prosvetitelnaia rabota v RSFSR* (Moscow: Akad. nauk, 1972), p. 64.
69 Kumanev, *Revoliutsiia*, pp. 152–3.
70 Remizova, p. 64.
71 A. V. Kol'tsov, *Kul'turnoe stroitel'stvo v RSFSR v gody pervoi piatiletki 1928–1932* (Moscow and Leningrad: Gosizdat, 1960), p. 64.

CHAPTER 8
THE KOMSOMOL IN THE 1920S

1   Shokhin, *Kratkaia istoriia*, p. 115.
2   For statistics of Party membership, see Rigby.
3   Shokhin, *Kratkaia istoriia*, p. 116.
4   Balashov and Nelepin, p. 10.
5   Rigby, p. 361.
6   On the Ukrainian deviation, see Shokhin, *Kratkaia istoriia*, pp. 93–4. See also P. Smorodin's reply to the critics of the Central Committee: *II Vserossiiskaia konferentsiia* (Moscow, 1922), p. 63.
7   Shokhin, *Kratkaia istoriia*, p. 94.
8   *Slavnyi put' Leninskogo Komsomola*, vol. 1, p. 256.
9   Carr, *Socialism in One Country*, vol. 2, p. 133.
10 Shokhin, *Kratkaia istoriia*, p. 117.
11 Rigby, p. 116; and Balashov and Nelepin, p. 16.
12 Shokhin, *Kratkaia istoriia*, pp. 117–18.
13 *Slavnyi put'*, vol. 1, p. 259.
14 Ibid., p. 260.
15 See the speech given by L. Shatskin to the Second Komsomol Conference: *II Vserossiiskaia konferentsiia*, pp. 108–9.
16 See same speech by Shatskin, ibid., pp. 130–1.
17 Shokhin, *Kratkaia istoriia*, p. 110.
18 *Piatyi vserossiiskii s"ezd RKSM, 11–19 okt, 1922 goda* (Moscow and Leningrad, 1927). See Smorodin's speech, p. 105.
19 *II Vserossiiskaia konferentsiia*, p. 52.
20 Balashov and Nelepin, p. 17.
21 Bolshakov, p. 334. The same point is made by A. Shokhin, *Komsomolskaia derevnia* (Moscow: Molodaia gvardiia, 1923), p. 2.
22 Balashov and Nelepin, pp. 12–14.
23 Ibid., p. 19.
24 V. Zof, *Komsomol i Krasnyi Flot* (Moscow: Novaia Moskva, 1924), pp. 29–31.
25 *Slavnyi put'*, p. 105.
26 Ibid., p. 290.

27 Levgur, *Obiazannosti komsomoltsa* (Moscow: Novaia Moskva, 1924), pp. 3–4.
28 Fitzpatrick, *Education and Social Mobility*, pp. 104–5.
29 Balashov and Nelepin, p. 22.
30 Ibid., p. 21.
31 Ibid.
32 Shokhin, *Komsomolskaia derevniia*, p. 41.
33 *IV s"ezd RKSM: Stenograficheskii otchet, 21–28 sentiabria 1921 goda* (Moscow and Leningrad, 1925), p. 344.
34 Shokhin, *Kratkaia istoriia*, p. 167.
35 Fisher, p. 410.
36 *Desiatyi s"ezd Rossiiskoi kommunisticheskoi partii* [hereafter abbreviated RKP]: *Stenograficheskii otchet 8–16 marta, 1921 goda.* (Moscow: Gosizdat, 1921), p. 86.
37 Balashov and Nelepin, p. 11.
38 Shokhin, *Kratkaia istoriia*, pp. 130–1.
39 Ibid., p. 134.
40 Shokhin, *Komsomolskaia derevniia*, p. 7, and Merle Fainsod, *Smolensk under Soviet Rule* (Cambridge, Mass.: Harvard University Press, 1958), p. 410. Fainsod quotes from the archives of the Smolensk district, which shows great decline.
41 *Piatyi s"ezd RKSM* (Moscow, 1922), pp. 113–15.
42 *Desiatyi s"ezd RKP*, p. 86.
43 S. Shul'man and V. Reznik, "Komsomolskoe politobrazovanie v derevne," *Kom. rev.*, June 1925, p. 16.
44 Ibid.
45 *Piatyi s"ezd RKSM*, p. 97.
46 Shul'man and Reznik, p. 18.
47 The Smolensk Archives provide abundant evidence – see WKP 402, 403, 404.
48 Circular of the Smolensk Provincial Committee to Komsomol cells on the subject of exploiting parties. Item 67, WKP 401.
49 Item 28, WKP 403.
50 Ibid.
51 Piatyi s"ezd RSKM, p. 125.
52 *Kommunisticheskaia Partiia Sovetskogo Soiuza v resoliutsiiakh i resheniiakh s"ezdov, konferentsii i plenumov Ts.K, 1898–1954*, 4 vols. (Moscow: Gospolitizdat, 1954), vol. 2, p. 51.
53 Ibid., p. 329.
54 O. Adamovich, *Za Kul'turnyi rost derevni* (Leningrad: Priboi, 1928), p. 12.
55 I. Liubimov, *Komsomol v sovetskom stroitel'stve, 1917–1927* (Moscow and Leningrad: Molodaia gvardiia, 1928), pp. 153–4.
56 Bolshakov, p. 332.
57 The debates are well described by Joan Delaney, "The Origins of Soviet Anti-religious Organizations," in Richard H. Marshall, Jr. et al., eds., *Aspects of Religion in the Soviet Union 1917–1967* (Chicago: University of Chicago Press, 1971), pp. 103–29.
58 Ibid., p. 121.
59 *Komsomolskaia paskha* (Moscow: Novaia Moskva, 1924).
60 Ibid., p. 94.
61 Ibid., p. 97.

62 Liubimov, p. 149.
63 Bocharov makes this point. See his reminiscences, op. cit., p. 63.
64 *Izvestiia Tsentralnogo Komiteta RKP*, no. 27, (July 20, 1925), p. 4.
65 Bolshakov, p. 334.
66 I. Razin, ed., *Komsomolskii byt: Sbornik* (Moscow and Leningrad: Molodaia gvardiia, 1927), p. 304.
67 Bocharov, pp. 70–5.
68 *Izvestiia Tsentralnogo Komiteta RKP*, no. 17–18, (May 11, 1925), pp. 15–16.
69 This was a most interesting and thoughtful speech given by Bukharin. *Piatyi s"ezd RDSM*, pp. 113–32.
70 Levgur, p. 27.
71 Ibid., pp. 27–8.
72 Ibid., p. 30.
73 *Izvestiia Tsentralnogo Komiteta RKP*, no. 1 (Jan. 5, 1925), pp. 2–4.
74 Bocharov writes: "The lecturer talked about Trotsky and about his anti-Party position and demanded a resolution about the removal of all Trotsky's followers from posts in the Red Army. I, as others, came to the meeting little understanding the struggle of Party leaders and the Trotskyist opposition. We thought: Such are the circumstances, so they should be. We had already heard several times that Trotsky's relationship to the peasantry was hostile. Therefore, we as one, voted for the expulsion of Trotskyists from the Red Army." Bocharov, p. 73.
75 Smolensk Archives, WKP 259, press bulletin no. 12 (Moscow, April 6, 1929).
76 On the early history of the Communist children's movement, see Shokhin, *Kratkaia istoriia*, pp. 126–30; Harper, pp. 61–6.
77 Shokhin, *Kratkaia istoriia*, p. 126.
78 *VLKSM v resoliutsiiakh ego s"ezdov i konferentsii 1918–1928* (Moscow and Leningrad, 1929), pp. 121–4.
79 Balashov and Nelepin, pp. 34–7.
80 Harper, p. 67.
81 Balashov and Nelepin, p. 36.
82 *Iunyi pioner: Posobie dlia instruktora* (Moscow: Novaia Moskva, 1924), pp. 47–51.
83 *VLKSM v resoliutsiiakh*, p. 177.
84 For an example of the dissatisfaction for the lack of political work among children, see Smolensk Archives, WKP 404, Report on the Viazma pioneer organizations, Nov. 21–Dec. 2, 1925.
85 *Izvestiia Tsentralnogo Komiteta RKP*, no. 15–16 (April 21, 1925), p. 32.
86 Harper, p. 84.
87 *Iunyi pioner*, p. 57.
88 Ibid., p. 50.
89 Ibid., p. 54.
90 Ibid., pp. 74–6.
91 Directive issued by the Central Committee of the Komsomol to all regional and district committees on the subject of supervising youth groups, Nov. 16, 1925, Smolensk Archives, WKP 133.
92 See, e.g., discussions of the district bureau of young pioneers, Oct. 14, 1926. Report on the Pioneer organizations of Iartsevo, Smolensk Archives, WKP 281.

93 E.g., Doctors' report on the Young Pioneer health service, March–Sept. 1925, Smolensk Province Komsomol Committee, Smolensk Archives, WKP 400. In one group examined (328 children), one-third suffered some kind of lung disease, 44% were anemic, etc. Children who returned from the camps showed a slight improvement in their physical conditions.

94 Report of the district committee on the Viazma pioneer camp, March 1925, Smolensk Archives, WKP 402, pp. 47–9.

CHAPTER 9
THE GOLDEN AGE OF THE SOVIET CINEMA

1 Huntley Carter, *The New Theater and Cinema of Soviet Russia* (London: Chapman and Dodd, 1924), p. 238; and N. Lebedev, *Ocherk,* vol. 1, p. 87.

2 Carter, pp. 238–9.

3 N. Lebedev, *Ocherk,* p. 87.

4 Carter, p. 238.

5 N. A. Lebedev, "Boevye dvadtsatye gody," *Iskusstvo kino,* no. 12 (1968), p. 88. *The Skull of the Pharaoh's Daughter* was a mistranslation; the German title was *The Skull of the Pharaoh's Wife.* But such minor inaccuracies did not matter to the audience.

6 Carter, p. 250.

7 A. Gak, "K istorii sozdaniia Sovkino," *Iz istorii kino,* vol. 5 (Moscow, 1926), p. 136.

8 Carter, p. 241. It is impossible to give the value of a million rubles at the time. Inflation was extremely rapid.

9 Lenin, *PSS,* vol. 44, pp. 360–1.

10 Gak, p. 133.

11 N. Lebedev, *Ocherk,* p. 72.

12 Gak, p. 131. The establishment of Goskino is also discussed in detail in Taylor, *Politics of the Soviet Cinema,* pp. 71–2.

13 Gak, pp. 132–3.

14 Ibid., p. 133.

15 Iu. A. Fridman, "Dvizhenie pomoshchi mezhdunarodnogo proletariata Sovetskoi Rossii v 1921–1922 godakh," *Voprosy istorii,* no. 1 (1958), p. 100. Also Taylor, *Politics of the Soviet Cinema,* p. 73.

16 Gak, pp. 133–4.

17 Ibid., p. 134.

18 Ibid., pp. 134–5.

19 Ibid., p. 139.

20 Ibid.

21 Ibid., pp. 141–4.

22 N. Lebedev, "Boevye," p. 95.

23 Ledya, pp. 161–2.

24 N. Lebedev, *Ocherk,* pp. 104–5.

25 *S.Kh.f.,* vol. 1, pp. 27–31.

26 Most of the films that I mention in this chapter I saw at the Pacific Film Archives, Berkeley, Calif. I saw *Kombrig Ivanov* at the Hoover Institution Archives, Stanford, Calif. For the films that I could not see, I base my

descriptions on those given in *S.kh.f.* I shall note only those films for which my source was the Soviet catalog.

27 *S.kh.f.*, vol. 1, p. 30.
28 Ibid., p. 29.
29 *Pravda*, Dec. 13, 1923.
30 Ibid., Oct. 1, 1924.
31 N. Lebedev, *Ocherk*, p. 144.
32 K. Mal'tsev, "Sovetskoe kino na novykh putiakh," *Novyi mir*, May 1929, p. 244.
33 *S.kh.f.*, vol. 1, p. 30.
34 Mal'tsev, p. 243.
35 Denise Youngblood, "On the Kino Front: The Evolution of the Soviet Cinema in the 1920's" (Ph.D. dissertation, Stanford University, 1980), pp. 88–90.
36 *S.kh.f.*
37 N. Lebedev, "Boevye," p. 95.
38 Leyda, p. 213.
39 See, e.g., the review in *Pravda*, Dec. 4, 1926.
40 Youngblood, pp. 228–32.
41 *S.kh.f.*
42 N. Lebedev, *Ocherk*, p. 106.
43 Youngblood, p. 160.
44 Marie Seton, *Sergei M. Eisenstein* (New York: A. A. Wyn), 1952, p. 38.
45 N. Zorkaia, "Iakov Protazanov i Sovetskoe kinoiskusstvo 20kh godov," *Voprosy kinoiskusstva*, no. 6 (1962), p. 166.
46 *Izvestiia*, Feb. 19, 1925.
47 L. Trotsky, "Vodka, the Church and the Cinema," in his *Problems of Everyday Life* (New York: Monad Press, 1973), p. 33.
48 *Piatnadtsatyi s"ezd VKP(b): Dekabr' 1927 goda: Stenograficheskii otchet* (Moscow: Gosizdat, 1962), p. 60. Also see Taylor, *Politics of the Soviet Cinema*, p. 105.
49 Mal'tsev, p. 243.
50 The polemics are described well and in detail by Youngblood.
51 "Kino dlia derevni," *Izvestiia Tsentralnogo komiteta Rossiiskoi Kommunisticheskoi Partii(b)*, no. 28 (July 27, 1925), p. 4.
52 Taylor, *Politics of the Soviet Cinema*, p. 89.
53 Ibid.
54 P. Rudenko, "Novyi derevenskii agitator," *Kom. rev.*, March 1926, p. 44.
55 N. Khrenov, "K probleme sotsiologii i psikhologii kino 20kh godov," *Voprosy kinoiskusstva*, 1976, p. 171.
56 Youngblood, pp. 100–10.
57 *S.kh.f.*
58 A. K., "Kino rabota v Donskom okruge," *Kom. rev.*, March 1926, pp. 49–50.
59 Rudenko, p. 44.
60 Taylor, *Politics of the Soviet Cinema*, p. 95.
61 Mal'tsev, pp. 243–8.
62 Mal'tsev, p. 243; and Taylor, *Politics of the Soviet Cinema*, p. 96.
63 A small but amusing example of how a director grappled with the problem of both repudiating and exploiting foreign films was Komarov's 1927 work *The*

Kiss of Mary Pickford. The film gently ridiculed the hero worship that surrounded foreign stars, but much of the appeal of the film came from the fact that Douglas Fairbanks and Mary Pickford appeared in it. The famous American couple came to Moscow for a visit. Komarov so cleverly built the newsreel accounts into his film that the Americans seemed to be willing participants.

CHAPTER 10
THE PRESS AND BOOK PUBLISHING IN THE 1920S

1 V. V. Uchenova, *Partiino-sovetskaia pechat' vosstanovitel'nogo perioda* (Moscow: Moskovskii Universitet, 1964), p. 5.
2 Vardin, p. 54.
3 Ibid.
4 *0 partiinoi i sovetskoi pechati: Sbornik dokumentov* (Moscow, 1954), p. 305.
5 Artur Just, *Die Presse der Sowjet Union* (Berlin: Duncker, 1931), p. 113.
6 Ibid., pp. 114–15.
7 I. M. Vareikis, ed., *Pechat' SSSR za 1924 i 1925 gg.* (Moscow: Gosizdat, 1926), p. 7.
8 Vardin, p. 40.
9 Vardin, p. 84.
10 Sampson, pp. 193–5.
11 Ibid., p. 205.
12 E. M. Fingerit and I. V. Kuznetsov, eds., *Gazetnyi mir Sovetskogo soiuza, 1917–1970* (Moscow, 1972), p. 157.
13 Ibid.
14 Fingerit and Kuznetsov, p. 161.
15 Ibid., pp. 194–6.
16 Leon Trotsky, "The Newspaper and its Readers," in Trotsky, p. 123.
17 Ibid., pp. 126–7.
18 A. Berezhnoi, *K istorii partiino-sovetskoi pechati* (Leningrad: Leningradskii Universitet, 1956), p. 76. Berezhnoi maintains that Trotsky advocated printing mildly pornographic stories, descriptions of scandals, and sensation mongering reports.
19 A. Kravchenko, *Derevenskie iacheiki partii i kul'turnaia rabota v derevne* (Moscow: ODN, 1925), p. 19.
20 E. O. Kabo, *Ocherki rabochego byta* (Moscow, 1928), p. 192.
21 Ibid., p. 208.
22 Lenin, *PSS,* vol. 5, pp. 11–12.
23 See, e.g., V. N. Alferov, *Vozniknovenie i razvitie rabsel'korovskogo dvizheniia v SSSR* (Moscow: Mysl', 1970).
24 Harper, p. 102.
25 Lenin, *PSS,* vol. 37, pp. 89–91.
26 S. F. Cohen, *Bukharin and the Bolshevik Revolution: A Political Biography, 1888–1938* (New York: Knopf, 1973), pp. 207–8.
27 Vardin, pp. 109–25.
28 The problem is mentioned in Vareikis, p. 29.
29 Alferov, pp. 103, 122, 115.
30 Cohen, pp. 226–7.

31 Alferov, p. 90.
32 Ibid., p. 94.
33 G. A. Kozhevnikov, "Bor'ba KPSS za razvitie rabsel'korovskogo dvizheniia v gody stroitel'stva sotsializma v SSSR," in *Partiino-sovetskaia pechat' v period bor'by za stroitel'stvo sotsializma* (Moscow, 1964), pp. 62–4.
34 Carr, *Socialism in One Country,* vol. 2, pp. 63–4.
35 Sampson, p. 272.
36 Carr, *Socialism in One Country,* pp. 195–8.
37 Just, p. 93.
38 Ibid., p. 91.
39 Alferov, pp. 90–1.
40 Ibid., p. 119.
41 *O partiinoi i sovetskoi pechati: Sbornik dokumentov,* p. 307.
42 *Kak naladit' rabotu stennoi gazety* (Moscow: Gudok, 1930).
43 Ibid., p. 26.
44 Ibid., pp. 3–4.
45 Lenin, *PSS,* vol. 44, p. 11.
46 Nazarov, *Oktiabr',* pp. 234–5.
47 Ibid., pp. 235–6.
48 Vareikis, p. 126.
49 Ibid., p. 127; and N. F. Ianitskii, *Knizhnaia statistika sovetskoi Rossii, 1918–1923* (Moscow: Gosizdat, 1924), p. 15.
50 N. L. Meshcheriakov, "O rabote chastnykh izdatel'stvakh," *Pechat' i revoliutsiia,* no. 6 (1922), p. 129.
51 Vareikis, pp. 126–30.
52 Meshcheriakov, "O rabote gosudarstvennogo izdatel'stva v novykh usloviakh," pp. 166–7.
53 Nazarov, *Oktiabr',* p. 241.
54 Ibid., p. 244.
55 Ibid., p. 266.
56 Ibid., p. 274.
57 Ibid.
58 Ibid., p. 267.
59 Vareikis, p. 52.
60 *KPSS,* vol. 1, p. 644.
61 Vareikis, p. 51.
62 *KPSS,* vol. 1, p. 737.
63 Ianitskii, p. 5.
64 Ibid.
65 Vareikis, p. 52.
66 Nazarov, *Kniga,* p. 143.
67 See, e.g., Nazarov, *Oktiabr',* p. 336.
68 Ianitskii, p. 5.
69 Nazarov, *Kniga,* p. 143.
70 Jeffrey Brooks, "Discontinuity in the Spread of Popular Print Culture, 1917–1927" (unpublished manuscript), p. 9. I have greatly benefited from Brooks's research in writing this chapter.
71 N. G. Malykhin, *Ocherki po istorii knigo-izdatel'skogo dela v SSSR* (Moscow, 1965), p. 340.

72 Meshcheriakov, "O rabote chastnykh izdatel'stvakh," p. 130.

73 Ibid., p. 339.

74 Vareikis, p. 94.

75 Nazarov, *Oktiabr'*, p. 368.

76 Malykhin, p. 342.

77 A. Lunacharskii, "Svoboda knigi i revoliutsiia," *Pechat' i revoliutsiia*, no. 1 (1921), p. 8.

78 Meshcheriakov, "O rabote chastnykh izdatel'stvakh," pp. 128-34.

79 See *Knizhnaia letopis'* for 1920-2.

80 Carr, *Socialism in One Country*, vol. 1, pp. 63-6.

81 Vareikis, p. 83.

82 V. Smushkov, "Raspredelenie proizvedenii pechati," *Pechat' i revoliutsiia*, no. 1 (1921), pp. 38-9. This point is also made by Brooks, p. 8.

83 N. Vanno, "Kniga–moguchii rychag kul'turnogo pod"ema derevni," *Kom. Rev.*, Dec. 1927, p. 52.

84 Ibid., p. 54.

85 Ibid.

86 I am taking this quotation, as well as the story of the purge of the libraries, from B. Wolfe's article, "Krupskaia Purges the People's Libraries," *Survey*, vol. 72 (1969), pp. 143-6.

87 Carr, *Socialism in One Country*, vol. 1, pp. 65-6.

88 S. Syrtsov, "Knigu v derevniu," *Kom. rev.*, March 1925, p. 3.

89 Vanno, p. 56.

90 Vareikis, p. 90.

91 Syrtsov, pp. 3-12.

92 Vareikis, p. 93.

CONCLUSION AND EPILOGUE

1 Ia. M. Selishchev, *Iazyk revoliutsionnoi epokhi* (Moscow: Rabotnik prosveshcheniia, 1928), pp. 85-91.

2 Ia. Shafir, *Gazeta i derevnia* (Moscow: Krasnaia nov' 1923). Also quoted by Selishchev, pp. 210-15.

3 Ibid., p. 24; *Pravda*, no. 101 (1926).

4 Archives of the workers of education, Moscow, f5462, 012, d135. Informational report about the mobilization of "2000," 1930. This report speaks not only of the incredible conditions in which teachers had to work but also about their resistance to "mobilization." One Leningrad teacher said: "I will not go to the village. Let them take me under guard." Another said: "Mobilization is exile." A third declared: "The Communists organized it – let them go."

5 Smolensk Archives, WKP 265. See, e.g., Vorobeva's report on reading newspapers in the Rumiantsev factory, Nov. 15, 1935. Vorobeva reported that some workers complained that they had so little time that they could hardly finish their lunch, and therefore the common reading of papers was a hardship.

6 Seton, pp. 351-78.

7 See, e.g., reports from libraries in Smolensk Archives, WKP 265. The reports are from 1935.

8 L. Rimskii, *Liudi kul'tpokhoda* (Moscow: Gosizdat, 1930).

Glossary

agitka	short agitational film
agitprop	agitation and propaganda
agitpunkt	agitational station
CEC	Central Executive Committee (of the Congress of Soviets)
Cheka	Chrezvychainaia komissiia (Extraordinary Commission; the name of the political police)
Glavbum	Glavnoe upravleniie bumazhnoi promyshlennosti (chief Administration of the Paper Industry)
Glavpolit-prosvet	Glavnyi politiko-prosvetitel'nyi komitet (chief Committee for Political Education)
Glavpolit-put'	Political Department of the Commissariat of Communications
gorkom	gorodnyi komitet (city committee)
Gosizdat	Gosudarstevnnoe izdatel'stvo (State Publishing House)
Goskino	Gosudarstevennoe kino (state film studio)
Gramcheka	Extraordinary Committee for the Elimination of Illiteracy; see VChK1/b
Iuk	Iunyi kommunist (Young Communist)
izba-chital'nia	reading hut
izbach	the person responsible for the reading hut
Kadet	member of the Constitutional Democratic Party
kolkhoz	kollektivnoe khozaiztvo (collective farm)
Komsomol	Kommunisticheskii soiuz molodezhi (Communist League of Youth)

KPSS	Kommunisticheskaia Partiia Sovetskogo Soiuza (Communist Party of the Soviet Union)
likbez	likvidatsiia bezgramotnosti (liquidation of illiteracy)
likpunkt	school for the liquidation of illiteracy
MRC	Military Revolutionary Committee
Narkomfin	Narodnyi komissariat finansov (People's Commissariat of Finances)
Narkompros	Narodnyi komissariat prosveshcheniia (People's Commissariat of Enlightenment)
Narkom-vneshtorg	Narodnyi komissariat vneshnei torgovli (People's Commissariat of Foreign Trade)
NEP	Novaia ekonomicheskaia politika (New Economic Policies)
ODN	Obshchestvo "Doloi Negramotnosti" ("Down with Illiteracy" Society)
ODVF	Obshchestvo Druzei Vozdushnogo Flota (Society of the Friends of the Air Fleet)
politprosvet	politiko-prosvetitel'nyi komitet (committee for political education)
politprosvet-rabota	political-education work
Proletkul't	Organizatsiia predstavitelei proletarskogo iskusstva (Organization of the Representatives of Proletarian Art)
PUR	Politicheskoe upravlenie revvoensoveta (Political Administration of the Revolutionary Military Council)
PVRK	Petrogradskii voenno-revoliutsionnyi komitet (Petrograd Military-Revolutionary Committee)
rabkor	rabochii korrespondent (worker correspondent)
Rabkrin	narodnyi komissariat rabochei i krestianskoi inspektsii (People's Commissariat of Workers' and Peasants' Inspection)
Rosta	Rossiiskoe telegrafnoe agenstvo (Russian telegraph agency)
RSDRP	Rossiiskaia Social-Demokraticheskaia Rabochaia Partiia (Russian Social-Democratic Labor Party)
RSFSR	Rossiiskaia Sotsialisticheskaia Federativnaia Sovetskaia Respublika (Russian Socialist Federal Soviet Republic)
sel'kor	sel'skii korrespondent (village correspondent)
shefstvo	sponsorship
Sovnarkom	Sovet narodnykh komissarov (Council of People's Commissars)
Ts.K.	Tsentral'nyi komitet (Central Committee) z
Tsentro-pechat'	Central agency for the distribution of printed matter

VChKl/b	Vserossiiskaia Chrezvychainaia Kommissiia lik/bez (All-Russian Extraordinary Committee for the Liquidation of Illiteracy)
VFKO	Vserossiiskii fotokinmatografichskii otdel (All-Russian Photographic and Cinematographic Section)
VLKSM	Vsesoiuznyi Leninskii kommunisticheskii soiuz Molodezhi (All-Union Leninist Communist League of Youth)
VSNKh	Vysshii sovet narodnogo khozaistva (Supreme Council of the National Economy)
VTsIK	Vsesoiuznyi tsentral'nyi ispolnitel'nyi komitet (All-Union Central Executive Committee)
VTsSPS	Vsesoiuznyi tsentral'nyi sovet prof-soiuzov (All-Union Central Council of Trade Unions)
Zhenotdel	Zhenskii odtel (Women's Section)

Bibliography

The subject matter of this book dictated the use of various primary sources.

I was able to work in the Soviet Union in TsGAOR (Central State Archive of the October Revolution). Here I had access to the archives of the trade unions, in particular, the papers of the Union of Workers of Enlightenment (Profsoiuz rabotnikov prosveshcheniia). Chapters 3 and 7 are based on these Soviet archival sources. Examining the correspondence of cultural sections of trade unions, one gains a better understanding of Soviet notions concerning political education.

Every scholar dealing with the first two decades of Soviet history must examine the Smolensk Archives. These archives, microfilmed and well cataloged, proved useful for every topic I discussed.

I benefited from using the pamphlet collections of the Lenin Library in Moscow, the Library of Congress in Washington, and the Institute for Social History in Amsterdam. I also found valuable material in the Samuel Harper Collection at the University of Chicago and in the Hoover Institution at Stanford University.

I have acquired my knowledge of Soviet films at the Pacific Film Archives of the University of California, Berkeley. This institution owns almost a hundred Soviet silent films, including all the most valuable ones. In addition, the Hoover Institution has a few feature films and also some interesting documentary footage.

Aside from documentary sources and pamphlets, my most important sources were contemporary newspapers and periodicals. I have examined a large number of these. Two stand out in importance. *Izvestiia Tsentralnogo Komiteta* speaks with the authoritative voice of the highest Party leadership. Even more important for my purposes is *Kommunisticheskaia revoliutsiia,* a journal aimed specifically at helping the Party activists. Here are discussed the daily problems and responsibilities of the Party worker in the countryside. Today the articles open a window for us into the world of the Soviet propagandist in the 1920s.

The organization of the bibliography that follows presented special problems. I have discussed such disparate topics in this book, and have drawn on such different literatures, that to present the entries in simple alphabetical order would make little sense. Therefore the bibliography is divided into six categories. The first and largest category includes books and pamphlets that deal with the large issue of propaganda. My other categories are self-explanatory: political education, illiteracy, the Komsomol, the press and book publishing, and film. A list of the newspapers and journals referred to is also included.

PROPAGANDA IN GENERAL

Barghorn, F. *Soviet Foreign Propaganda*, Princeton University Press., Princeton, 1964.

Baron, S. H. *Plekhanov: The Father of Russian Marxism*. Stanford University Press, Stanford, 1963.

Belokonskii, I. P. *V gody bezpraviia*. Moscow, 1930.

Blonskii, P. P. *Trudovaia shkola*. Literaturno-izdatel'skii otdel Narodnogo kom. po prosveshcheniiu, Moscow, 1919.

Bolshakov, A. M. *Derevnia 1917–1927*. Rabotnik Prosveshcheniia, Moscow, 1927.

Bonch-Bruevich, V. D. *Na boevykh postakh fevralskoi i Oktiabrskoi revoliutsii*. Izd. federatsii, Moscow, 1930.

Izbrannye sochinennia. 3 vols. Akad. Nauk, Moscow, 1959–63.

Vospominaniia o Lenine. Nauka, Moscow, 1969.

Bunyan, J., and H. H. Fisher, eds. *The Bolshevik Revolution, 1917–1918*. Stanford University Press, Stanford, 1934.

Odinnadtsatyi s"ezd RKP(b) Mart-Aprel' 1922 g. Stenograficheskii otchet. Gosizdat, Moscow, 1961.

Piatnadtsatyi s"ezd V.K.P.(b) Dekabr' 1927 goda. Stenograficheskii otchet. 2 vols. Gosizdat, Moscow, 1961–2.

Trinadtsatyi s"ezd RKP(b) Mai 1924 g. Stenograficheskii otchet. Gosizdat, Moscow, 1963.

Petrogradskii voennorevoliutsionnii komitet. 3 vols. Nauka, Moscow, 1966–7.

Carr, E. H. *The Bolshevik Revolution*. 3 vols. Macmillan, New York, 1951–3.

The Interregnum: 1923–1924. Macmillan, New York, 1954.

Socialism in One Country, 1924–1926. 3 vols, Macmillan, New York, 1960.

Foundations of a Planned Economy. 1926–1929, 3 vols, Macmillan, New York, 1971.

Claudin-Urondo, Carmen. *Lenin and the Cultural Revolution*. Humanities Press, Atlantic Highlands, N.J., 1977.

Cohen, S. F. *Bukharin and the Bolshevik Revolution: A Political Biography, 1888–1938*. Knopf, New York, 1973.

Communist Party of the Soviet Union. *Desiatyi s"ezd Rossiiskoi kommunisticheskoi partii. Stenograficheskii otchet. 8–16 marta 1921 g*. Gosizdat, Moscow, 1921.

KPSS v rezoliutsiiakh i resheniiakh s"ezdov, konferentsii i plenumov Ts.K. 1898–1954. Gospolitizdat, Moscow, 1953–60.

Perepiska Sekretariata Ts.K. RSDRP(b) s mestnymi partiinymi organizatsiiami. 3 vols. Izd. polit. literatury, Moscow, 1957.

Shestoi s"ezd RSDRP. Avgust 1917 goda: Protokoly. Gosizdat, Moscow, 1958.

Vosmoi s"ezd RKP(b). Protokoly. Gosizdat, Moscow, 1959.

Curtiss, J. S. *The Russian Church and the Soviet State: 1917–1950*. Little, Brown, Boston, 1953.

Daniels, R. V. *The Conscience of the Revolution*. Harvard University Press, Cambridge, Mass., 1960.

Denikin, A. I. *Staraia armiia*. Rodnik, Paris, 1929.

Ellul, J. *Propaganda*. Knopf, New York, 1965.

Entsiklopedicheskii slovar'. F. A. Brokgauz and I. A. Efron, St. Petersburg, 1890–4.

Ermolaev, Herman. *Soviet Literary Theories 1917–1934: The Genesis of Socialist Realism*. University of California Press, Berkeley, 1963.

Fainsod, M. *Smolensk under Soviet Rule*. Harvard University Press, Cambridge, Mass., 1958.

Fediukin, S. A. *Sovetskaia vlast' i burzhuanie spetsialisty*. Mysl', Moscow, 1965.

Velikii Oktiabr' i intelligentsia. Nauka, Moscow, 1972.

Fitzpatrick, Sheila. *The Commissariat of Enlightenment: Soviet Organization of Education and Arts under Lunacharskii, October 1917–1921*. Cambridge University Press, Cambridge, 1970.

Fofanova, M. "Reshaiushchie dni." *Oktiabr*, Nov. 1956.

Fotieva, L. A. *Iz vospominanii o Lenine*. Izd. polit. literatury, Moscow, 1964.

Fulop-Miller, R. *The Mind and Face of Bolshevism: An Examination of Cultural Life in Soviet Russia*. Knopf, New York, 1928.

Geyer, D. "Arbeiterbewegung und Kulturrevolution in Russland. 1917–1922." *Vierteljahrhefte fuer Zeitgeschichte*, 1962, pp. 43–55.

Gorkii, M. A. *Vospominaniia o Vladmire Il'iche Lenine*. Gospolitizdat, Moscow, 1956.

Nesvoevremennye mysli. Stat'ia 1917. Ed. G. Ermolaev. YMCA Press, Paris, 1971.

Harper, S. N. *Civil Training in Soviet Russia*. University of Chicago Press, Chicago, 1929.

Hollander, Paul. *Political Pilgrims*. Oxford University Press, New York, 1981.

Inkeles, A. *Public Opinion in Soviet Russia*. Harvard University Press, Cambridge, Mass., 1950.

Kalinin, M. I. *O voprosakh sotsialisticheskoi kultury*. Molodaia gvardiia, Moscow, 1938.

Karpov, G. G. *O sovetskom kul'ture i kul'turnoi revoliutsii v SSSR*. Gosizdat polit. literatury, Moscow, 1954.

Katkov, George. *Russia, 1917: The February Revolution*. Longmans, London, 1967.

Keep, John. *The Russian Revolution*. Norton, New York, 1976.

trans. and ed. *The Debate on Soviet Power: Minutes of the All-Russian Central Executive Committee of the Soviets. Second Convocation, October 1917–January 1918*. Clarendon Press, Oxford, 1979.

Kenez, Peter. *Civil War in South Russia, 1918*. University of California Press, Berkeley, 1971.

Civil War in South Russia, 1919–1920. University of California Press, Berkeley, 1977.

Browder, Robert P., and Alexander F. Kerensky, eds. *The Russian Provisional Government: 1917: Documents*. 3 vols. Stanford University Press, Stanford, 1961.

Kim, M. "O zakonomernostiakh kul'turnoi revoliutsii." *Voprosy istorii*, vol. 5 (1960), pp. 3–22.

Kolakovski, L. *Main Currents of Marxism*. 3 vols. Oxford University Press, Oxford, 1978.

Kol'tsov, A. V. *Kul'turnoe stroitel'stvo v RSFSR v gody pervoi piatiletki (1928–1932)*. Gosizdat, Moscow and Leningrad, 1960.

Krupskaia, N. K. *Leninskie ustanovki v oblasti kultury.* Gosizdat, Moscow, 1934.
Memories of Lenin. Lawrence and Wishart, London, 1942.
"Po gradam i selam Sovetskoi Respubliki." *Novyi mir,* vol. 11, 1960.
Kulturnoe stroitel'stvo SSSR: Statisticheskii sbornik. Gosstatizdat, Moscow, 1956.
Kurskaia, A. S. *Perezhitoe.* Moskovskii rabochii, Moscow, 1965.
Lasswell, H. O. *World Revolutionary Propaganda.* Knopf, New York, 1939.
Propaganda Technique in World War I. M.I.T. Press, Cambridge, Mass., 1971.
Lenin, V. I. *Polnoe sobranie sochinenii.* 55 vols. 5th ed. Gospolitizdat, Moscow, 1960–5.
Lenin ob ideologicheskoi rabote. Politizdat, Moscow, 1969.
Leonova, L. S. *Iz istorii podgotovki partiinykh kadrov v sovetsko-partiinykh shkolakh i kommunisticheskikh universitetakh (1921–1925 gg.).* Izdatel'stvo Moskovskogo Universiteta, Moscow, 1972.
Lunacharskii, A. V. *Lenin i prosveshchenie mass.* Gosizdat, Moscow, 1924.
Vospominaniia i vpechatleniia. Sov. Rossiia, Moscow, 1968.
Maiakovskii, Vladimir. *Polnoe sobranii sochinenii.* 13 vols. Gos. izd. khudozhestvennoi literatury, Moscow, 1955–61.
Marcuse, Herbert. *One Dimensional Man: Studies in the Ideology of Advanced Industrial Society.* Beacon Press, Boston, 1964.
McNeal, Robert. *Bride of the Revolution.* University of Michigan Press, Ann Arbor, 1972.
Medynskii, E. N. *Rol' rabochego klassa v razvitii sotsialisticheskoi kul'tury.* Moscow, 1967.
Melgunov, S. P. *Zolotoi nemetskii kliuch k bol'shevistskoi revoliutsii.* Paris, 1940.
Ozerskaia, F. S., ed. *Lunacharskii o narodnom obrazovanii.* Akad. pedagogocheskikh nauk RSFSR, Moscow, 1958.
Pethybridge, Roger. *The Spread of the Russian Revolution: Essays on 1917.* St. Martin's Press, New York, 1972.
The Social Prelude to Stalinism. St. Martin's Press, New York, 1974.
Petrograd Soviet. *Petrogradskii sovet rabochikh i soldatskikh delegatov. Protokoly zasedranii.* Gosizdat, Moscow, 1925.
Pipes, Richard, ed. *Revolutionary Russia: A Symposium.* Harvard University Press, Cambridge, Mass., 1968.
Rabinowitch, Alexander. *The Bolsheviks Come to Power.* Norton, New York, 1976.
Rashin, A. G. *Naselenie Rossii za 100 let.* Gos. statisticheskoe izd., Moscow, 1956.
Remizova, T. A. *Kul'turno-prosvetitel'naia rabota v RSFSR (1921–1925 gg.).* Izd-vo Akademii nauk, Moscow, 1962.
Rigby, T. H. *Communist Party Membership in the USSR, 1917–1967.* Princeton University Press, Princeton, 1968.
Lenin's Government: Sovnarkom 1917–1922. Cambridge University Press, Cambridge, 1979.
Ross, N. *Vrangel' v Krymu.* Possev, Frankfurt/Main, 1982.
Sbornik: Study Group on the Russian Revolution. Leeds, Study Group on the Russian Revolution, 1982.
Schapiro, Leonard. *The Communist Party of the Soviet Union.* Eyre & Spottiswoode, London, 1960.
The Origin of the Communist Autocracy. Harvard University Press, Cambridge, Mass., 1977.
Selunskaia, V. M. *Rabochii klass i Oktiabr v derevne.* Mysl', Moscow, 1968.

Smirnov, I. S. *Iz istorii stroitel'stva sotsialisticheskoi kul'tury v pervom periode Sovetskoi vlasti.* Gosizdat polit. literatury, Moscow, 1952.

Lenin i sovetskaia kultura. Akad. nauk, Moscow, 1960.

Sorenson, Jay. *The Life and Death of Soviet Trade Unionism: 1917–1928.* Atherton Press, New York, 1969.

Stites, Richard. *The Women's Liberation Movement in Russia: Feminism, Nihilism and Bolshevism, 1860–1930.* Princeton University Press, Princeton, 1978.

Sukhanov, N. N. *The Russian Revolution.* 2 vols. Oxford University Press, New York, 1955.

Taylor, Richard. "A Medium for the Masses: Agitation in the Soviet Civil War." *Soviet Studies,* April 1971, pp. 298–318.

Trifonov, I. *Ocherki istorii klassovoi bor'by v SSSR v gody NEPa (1921–1937).* Gospolitizdat, Moscow, 1960.

Trotsky, Leon. *Sochineniie.* 21 vols. Gosizdat, Moscow, 1927.

Problems of Everyday Life. Monad Press, New York, 1973.

Tucker, Robert. *Stalinism: Essays in Historical Interpretation.* Norton, New York, 1977.

Voprosy teorii i praktiki massovykh sredstv propgandy. 4 vols. Mysl', Moscow, 1971.

Walkin, Jacob. *The Rise of Democracy in Pre-revolutionary Russia: Political and Social Institutions under the Last Three Tsars.* Praeger, New York, 1962.

Williams, Robert C. *Artists in Revolution.* Indiana University Press, Bloomington, 1977.

Wolfe, B. *Three Who Made a Revolution.* Dial Press, New York, 1948.

Zeman, Z. A. B. *Nazi Propaganda.* Oxford University Press, New York, 1973.

POLITICAL EDUCATION

Abolin, A. *Agitatsiia i propaganda v derevne: Posobie dlia derevenskikh iacheek RKP i VLKSM.* Priboi, Leningrad, 1925.

Agitatsionno-propagandistskaia rabota glavpolitprosveta. Krasnaia nov', Moscow, 1923.

Aluf, A. S. *The Development of Socialist Methods and Forms of Labor.* Cooperative Publishing Society of Foreign Workers in the USSR, Moscow, 1932.

Beskin, O. M. *Kak prazdnovat' Oktiabr'.* Gosizdat, Moscow and Leningrad, 1925.

Burov, Ia. I. *Organizuite derevniu.* Izd. sold. i krest. bibl., Petrograd, 1918.

Rabochie obshchestva dlia shefstva nad derevnei. Moskovskii rabochii, Moscow, 1925.

Butnik-Siverskii, B. S. *Sovetskii plakat epokhi grazhdanskoi voiny: 1918–1921.* Izd. vsesoiuznoi knizhnoi palaty, Moscow, 1960.

Charques, R. D. *Soviet Education: Some Aspects of Cultural Revolution.* Hogarth Press, London, 1932.

Chegodaeva, N. M. "Plakat." In *Istoriia russkogo iskusstva,* 13 vols., ed. I. E. Grabar, vol. 11, pp. 54–79. Akad. nauk, Moscow, 1953–68.

Cheremykh, M. "Maiakovskii i Rosta." *Iskusstvo,* vol. 3 (1970), 39–44.

Dinershtein, E. A. *Izdatel'skoe delo v pervye gody Sovetskoi vlasti.* Moscow, 1972.

Dolinskii, S., and S. Bergman. *Kruzhkovaia rabota v klube.* Rabotnik prosveshcheniia, Moscow, 1925.

Duvakin, V. "Okna Rosta i ikh politicheskoe i literaturnoe znachenie." In *Tvorchestvo Maiakovskogo: Sbornik statei,* pp. 313–437. Akad. nauk, Moscow, 1952.

Ermakov, V. T. "Ideinaia bor'ba na kul'turnom fronte v pervym godakh sovetskoi vlasti." *Voprosy istorii,* no. 11 (Nov. 1971), pp. 16–31.

Fenner, H. *Die propaganda Schulen der Bolschewisten.* Verlag der Kulturliga, Berlin, 1920.

Fitzpatrick, Sheila. *Education and Social Mobility in the Soviet Union, 1921–1934.* Cambridge University Press, Cambridge, 1979.

Fomin, A. I. "Stanovlenie tsentral'nogo sovetskogo apparata gosudarsvennogo rukovodstva narodnym prosveshcheniem." *Voprosy istorii,* no. 12 (Dec. 1976), pp. 17–29.

"Sozdanie sovetskogo apparata narodnogo prosveshchenie po mestakh." *Voprosy istorii,* no. 9 (Sept. 1979), pp. 24–35.

Frid, L. S. *Ocherki po istorii razvitiia politikoprosvetitel'noi raboty v RSFSR 1917–1929.* Politprosvet inst., Leningrad, 1941.

Gerasmov, E. "Nesluchainye vstrechi." *Novyi mir,* vol. 11 (Nov. 1960), pp. 131–56.

Gofman, Ts. "K istorii pervogo agitparakhoda VTsIK 'Krasnaia zvezda'." *Voprosy istorii,* no. 9 (1948).

Gorodetskii, E. N. "Bor'ba narodnykh mass za sozdanie sovetskoi kultury (1917–1920 gody)." *Voprosy istorii,* no. 4 (1954), pp. 18–37.

Iakushevskii, A. S. *Propagandistskaia rabota bol'shevikov sredi voisk interventov v 1918–1920 gg.* Nauka, Moscow, 1974.

Iaroslavskii, E. *Protiv natsionalizma: Protiv religii.* Gosizdat, Moscow, 1931.

Ingulov, S. B. *Uchebnik politgramoty.* Partiinoe izdatel'stvo, Moscow, 1932.

Kabo, E. O. *Ocherki rabochego byta.* VTsSPS, Moscow, 1928.

Kalinin, M. I. *On Communist Education.* Foreign Languages Publishing House, Moscow, 1949.

Karel'skii. *Politodel'tsy.* Molodaia gvardiia, Moscow, 1934.

Katz, Zev. "Party political education in Russia, 1918–1935." *Soviet Studies,* vol. 7 (1956), pp. 237–47.

Khlebtsevich, E. "Chitatel'skie intersy kranoarmeitsev." *Pechat' i revoliutsiia,* no. 2 (1921), pp. 49–55.

Kim, M. *Kommunisticheskaia partiia – organizator kul'turnoi revoliutsii v SSSR.* Gosizdat polit. literatury, Moscow, 1955.

40 let sovetskoi kul'tury. Gospolitizdat, Moscow, 1957.

Kommunisticheskoe vospitanie v sovetskoi shkole. Akad. ped., Moscow, 1950.

Klochko, V. F. *Kul'turnoe stroitesel'stvo v sovetskoi derevne v gody vtoroi piatiletki.* Gosizdat kulturno-provetitel'noi literatury, Moscow, 1956.

Krasikov, P. A. *Na tserkovnom fronte (1918–1923).* Iurid. izd.-vo, Moscow, 1923.

Izbrannye ateisticheski proizvedeniia. Mysl', Moscow, 1970.

KPSS vo glave kul'turnoi revoliutsii v SSSR. Politizdat, Moscow, 1972.

Kratkii ocherk kul'turno-politicheskoi raboty v Krasnoi armii za 1918 god. Moscow, 1919.

Krupskaia, N. K. *On Education.* Foreign Languages Publishing House, Moscow, 1957.

Pedagogicheskie sochineniia. 10 vols. Institut pedagogii A. P. N. RSFSR, Moscow, 1957–63.

Kul'turnaia revoliutsiia v SSSR 1917–1965. Nauka, Moscow, 1967.

Lashin, A. G. *Kul'turno-vospitatel'naia deiatel'nost' Sovetskogo gosudarstva.* Gosizdat iurid. literatury, Moscow, 1955.

Lenin, V. I. *O kulture i iskusstve*. Iskusstvo, Moscow, 1956.

V. I. *Lenin i problemy narodnogo obrazovaniia*. Akad. ped., Moscow, 1961.

Liagushina, E. Ia. "Nauchno-ateisticheskaia propaganda v pervye gody sovetskoi vlasti." *Voprosy istorii,* no. 9 (1967), pp. 93–100.

Lilge, F. "Lenin and the Politics of Education." *Slavic Review,* vol. 2 (1968).

McClelland, James. "Proletarianizing the Student Body: The Soviet Experience During the New Economic Policy." *Past and Present,* Aug. 1978.

Maksakova, L. V. *Agitpoezd "Oktiabrskaia revoliutsiia" 1919–1920 gg.* Akad. nauk, Moscow, 1956.

Martynova, Z. V. *Bor'ba partii za kul'turnyi pod"em derevni v gody pervyi piatiletki (1928–1932).* Avtoreferat, Moscow, 1964.

Medynskii, E. N. *Kak organizovat' i vesti sel'skie prosvetitelnye obshchestva i kruzhki.* Soiuz prosvetitel'nykh organizatsii Nizhegorodskogo kraia, Nizhnii Novgorod, 1918.

Prosveshchenie v SSSR. Gos. uchebno-pedagog. Izdatel'stvo, Moscow, 1955.

Mitiaeva, O. I. "Kul'turno-prosvetitelnaia rabota v dervene v gody pervoi piatiletki (1928–1932)." *Istoriia SSSR,* vol. 5 (1958).

Moor, D. S. *Ia Bol'shevik.* Sovetskii khuozhnik, Moscow, 1967.

O kul'turno-prosvetitelnoi rabote, No. 1–8. Sovetskaia Rossiia, Moscow, 1968.

o sisteme politobrazovaniia. Molodaia gvardiia, Moscow, 1924.

Orekhanov, A. F. *Leninskie idei kul'turnoi revoliutsii.* Znanie, Moscow, 1961.

Paech, Joachim. *Das Theater der russischen Revolution.* Scriptor Verlag, Kronberg, 1974.

Petrov, A. A. *Pamiatka rabochego samoobrazovaniia.* Trud i kniga, Moscow, 1924.

Plaksin, R. Iu "Tserkovnaia kontrrevoliutsiia v dni Oktiabria." *Voprosy istorii,* no. 11 (1954), pp. 45–52.

Pomanskii, N. *Sotsialno-kul'turnoe stroitel'stvo derevni v piatiletke.* Gosfinizdat, Moscow, 1930.

Pozdniakov, P. B. *Effektivnost' kommunisticheskoi propagandy,* Politizdat, Moscow, 1975.

Reeder, Roberta. "The interrelationship of codes in Maiakovskii's ROSTA posters." *Soviet Union,* vol. 7 (1980), pp. 28–52.

Selishchev, Ia. M. *Iazyk revoliutsionnoi epokhi.* Rabotnik prosveshcheniia, Moscow, 1928.

Sergeev, B. "Agitpoezdki M. I. Kalinina v gody grazhdanskoi voiny." *Krasnyi arkhiv,* vol. 86 (1938), pp. 93–168.

Slavenson, V. "Sotsial'nyi plakat." *Kniga i revoliutsiia,* no. 6 (1920), pp. 11–15.

Sovetskii politicheskii plakat. Iskusstvo, Moscow, 1962.

Tumarkin, Nina. *Lenin Lives! The Lenin Cult in Soviet Russia.* Harvard University Press, Cambridge, Mass., 1983.

Voevodin, P. "Agitpoezd 'Oktiabrskaia revoliutsiia.'" *Partiinaia zhizn',* vol. 5 (1957).

Voprosnik k programme samoobrazovaniia kommunistov. Samarskii gubizdat, Samara, 1923.

ILLITERACY

Adamovich, O. *Za kul'turnyi rost derevni.* Priboi, Leningrad, 1928.

Agitatoru i propagandistu o XV-letii komsomola. Molodaia gvardiia, Moscow, 1933.

Avsent'evskii, D. A. *Kul'tpokhod za gramotu (opyt Ts. Ch. O.)*. Rabotnik prosveshcheniia, Moscow, 1930.

Blinnikov, A. *Obuchenie chteniiu i pis'mu negramotnykh vzroslykh*. Uchpediz, Moscow, 1931.

Bogdanov, I. M. *Gramotnost' i obrazovanie v dorevoliutsionnoi Rossii i v SSSR*. Izd. statistiki, Moscow, 1964.

Bogdanov, V. I. *Uchitel'stvo i sovetskaia vlast'*. Gosizdat, Moscow, 1919.

Bondarev, D. A. *Likvidatsiia negramotnosti: Tsifrykh, fakty, perspektivy ODN*. Gosizdat, Moscow and Leningrad, 1929.

Bondarev, D. A. *Obshchestvenno-politicheskoe vospitanie v shkole gramoty*. Gosizdat, Moscow, 1930.

Broido, G. I. *Za gramotnyi zavod*. Gosizdat, Moscow, 1930.

Brooks, Jeffrey. "Studies of the Reader in the 1920's." *Russian History*, vol. 9 (1982), pp. 187–202.

Budnyi, G. *Izba-chial'nia na shturm bezgramotnosti*. Moscow, 1931.

Byrnes, R. F., ed. *East Central Europe Under the Communists: Yugoslavia*. Praeger, New York, 1957.

Chto chitaiut vzroslye rabochie i slushashchie po belletristike. Trud i kniga, Moscow, 1928.

Chto govoriat massy o narodnom obrazovanii. Narkompros, Moscow, 1929.

Dellin, L. A. D., ed. *East Central Europe Under the Communists: Bulgaria*. Praeger, New York, 1957.

Elkina, D. Iu. "Likvidatsiia negramotnosti v krasnoi armii na frontakh grazhdanskoi voiny." *Narodnoe obrazovanie*, vol. 12 (1957), pp. 52–6.

Na Kulturnom fronte. Akademiia pedagogicheskikh nauk RSFSR, Moscow, 1959.

Erde, D. I. *Negramotnost' i bor'ba s nei*. Proletarii, Kharkov, 1924.

Lenin i negramotnost'. Proletarii, Kharkov, 1925.

Evdokimov, A. *Novaia sistema raboty v derevne*. Priboi, Leningrad, 1930.

Filkov. *Kak iacheiki ODN pomogaiut kollektivizatsii*. Moscow, 1931.

Fischer-Galati, S. A., ed. *East Central Europe Under the Communists: Romania*. Praeger, New York, 1957.

Goflin, N., and V. Konovalov. *Programa politchasa v shkolakh dlia malogramotnykh*. Gosizdat, Moscow and Saratov, 1930.

Graff, Harvey. *The Literacy Myth: Literacy and Social Structure in the Nineteenth-Century City*. Academic Press, New York, 1979.

Gramotnost' v Rossii. Central Statistical Bureau, Moscow, 1922.

Ivanova, A. M. *Chto sdelala sovetskaia vlast' po likvidatsii negramotnosti sredi vzroslykh*. Gosizdat, Moscow, 1949.

Likvidatsiia negramotnosti sredi vzroslykh SSSR (1917–1941 gg). Avtoreferat, Moscow, 1955.

Iz opyta raboty po povysheniiu obshcheobrazovatel'nyi gramotnosti sredi vzroslogo neseleniia. Otdel propagandy Penzenskogo oblastnogo komiteta, Penza, 1951.

Kiparisov, V. "Obzor literu ry po likvidatsii negrammotnosti." *Pechat' i revoliutsiia*. no. 1 (1921), pp. 66–8.

Kolodnaia, A. *V pomoshch' shkolam malogramotnykh*. Moscow, 1925.

Korol', B. *Gramotnyi, obuchi negramotnogo!* Novaia Moskva, Moscow, 1927.

Korostelev, A. I. *Uchitel' i revoliutsiia*. Rabotnik prosveshcheniia, Moscow, 1925.

Kravchenko, A. *Derevenskie iacheiki partii i kul'turnaia rabota v derevne.* ODN, Moscow, 1925.

Kul'turnyi pokhod i novye puti likvidatsii negramotnosti. Materialy k vserossiskomu s"ezdu po likbez. Iun 21–25, 1929., Glavpolitprosvet, Moscow, 1929.

Kumanev, V. A. "Massovyi kul'turnyi pokhod za likvidatsiiu negrammotnosti v sovetskoi derevne (1928–1932)." *Istoriia SSSR,* no. 5 (1958), pp. 92–110.

Sotsialism i vsenarodnaia gramotnost'. Nauka, Moscow, 1964.

Revoliutsiia i prosveshchenie mass. Nauka, Moscow, 1973.

Mochalov, I., and I. Abramov. *Pervye pobedy: Iz Ural'skogo optyta likvidatsii negramotnosti.* Gosizdat, Moscow and Leningrad, 1930.

Na bor'bu s negramotnost'iu: Sbornik agitmaterialov. ODN, Tula, 1924.

Obshchetvo Doloi Negramotnosti. *Doloi negramotnost': K pervomu vserossiskomu s"ezdu ODN.* ODN, Moscow and Leningrad, 1926.

Nozhnitskii, G. *Bor'ba mass za kul'tminimum.* Gosizdat, Moscow, 1930.

Kak organizovat' kul'tpokhod v derevne. Gosizdat, Moscow, 1930.

Orlik, Ia. M. *Kak dolzhna rabotat' iacheika ODN.* Gosizdat, Moscow, 1928.

Pamiatka likvidatora negramotnosti. Novonikolaevsk, 1924.

Rimskii, L. *Liudi kul'tpokhoda.* Gosizdat, Moscow, 1930.

Pechat' v pokhode. Narkompros, Moscow and Leningrad, 1930.

Likbezpokhod segodnia. Narkompros RSFSR, Moscow and Leningrad, 1931.

Romanov. *Osobye komissii i ODN.* Gosizdat, Moscow, 1930.

Rudenskii, P., and K. Geints. *Na novykh nachalakh.* Gosizdat, Archangel, 1931.

Shiraev, E. N. *Rabota s razrodnoi gruppoi v shkolakh i kruzhkakh malogramotnykh.* ODN, Moscow and Leningrad, 1927.

Stal', L. *Rabotat' po novomu, po revoliutsionnomu.* ODN, Moscow, 1929.

Vypolnim zavety Lenina na kul'turnom fronte. Gosizdat, Moscow, 1930.

Itogi i perspektivy raboty ODN. OGIZ, Moscow and Leningrad, 1931.

Rabotnitsa i krestianka v kul'tpokhode. OGIZ, Moscow, 1931.

Starr, F. S., and Gregory Guroff. "A Note on Urban Literacy in Russia, 1890–1914." *Jahrbuecher fuer Zeitgeschichte,* Dec. 1971, pp. 520–31.

Statisticheskii sbornik: K otchetu na II oblastnoi konferentsii. Leningrad, 1929.

Strumilin, S. G. *Khoziaistvennoe znachenie narodnogo obrazovaniia.* Ekonomicheskaia zhizn', Moscow and Leningrad, 1924.

Uspenskii, V. V. *Sovetskaia iacheika ODN v kul'tpokhode.* Gosizdat, Moscow, 1930.

Vdovina, E. A. *V pokhod za znaniiami: Komsomol srednei Volgi v bor'be za vseobshchuiu gramotnost' v 1928–1932 gg.* Kuibishev, 1971.

Vikhirev, N. *Razvernem massovoe dvizhenie v bor'be za kul'turu.* Novosibirsk, 1931.

Vorukhovich, I. *Politiko-prosvetitel'naia rabota sredi negramotnykh i malogramotnykh (Iz Saratovskogo opyta).* Gosizdat, Saratov, 1930.

Voskresenskii, V. D. *Planirovanie i uchet v shkolakh gramoty.* OGIZ, Moscow and Irkutsk, 1934.

V pervykh riadakh kul'tpokhoda, Gosizdat, Moscow and Leningrad, 1930.

V pokhod za gramotu. Ural sovet ODN, Sverdlovsk, 1929.

V pomoshch' likvidatoru: Sbornik. Vypusk 1–3. Orel gubono, Orel, 1927–8.

THE KOMSOMOL

Arkhangel'skii, V. *Petr Smorodin.* Molodaia gvardiia, Moscow, 1979.

Atsarkin, A. N. *Nasha rozhdenie: Sbornik vospominanii, statei, materialov i dokumentov po istorii vozniknovenia iunosheskogo dvizheniia v Moskve.* Molodaia gvardiia, Moscow, 1931.

Bocharov, N. "V uezdnom zakholust'e." *Komsomol sbornik statei,* Munich, 1960.

Delaney, Joan. "The Origins of Soviet Anti-Religious Organizations." In *Aspects of Religion in the Soviet Union, 1917–1967,* ed. Richard H. Marshall et al., University of Chicago Press, Chicago, 1971.

Detskoe kommunisticheskoe dvizhenie v SSSR. Statisticheskii sbornik o chislennom i kachestvennom sostave pioner-organizatsii za period s iulia po l ianvaria 1926 goda. Moscow, 1926.

Dudchenko, E. *Iz istorii komsomola Primor'ia (1920–1922).* Primorskoe knizhnoe izdatel'stvo, Vladivostok, 1960.

Evdokimov, A. *Bor'ba za molodezh'.* Priboi, Leningrad, 1929.

Fisher, Ralph T. *Pattern for Soviet Youth: A Study of the Congresses of the Komsomol 1918–1954.* Columbia University Press, New York, 1959.

Ganichev, V. *Boevoi opyt komsomol'skoi pechati, 1917–1925.* Moskovskoi rabochii, Moscow, 1973.

Gorshenin and Gal'ianov. *Voennaia rabota komsomola.* Molodaia gvardiia, Moscow, 1931.

Istoriia RKSM. Kurskii gubkom R. K. P. (b), Kursk, 1924.

Iunyi pioner. Novaia Moskva, Moscow, 1924.

Khanin, D. *Protiv komsomol'skoi oppozitsii: Stat'i.* Priboi, Leningrad, 1926.

Kirkizh, K. *Komsomol i trotskism: Doklad na Kharkovskom aktive LKSMU.* Proletarii, Kharkov, n.d.

Komsomol'skaia paskha. Novaia Moskva, Moscow, 1924.

Komsomol'skaia politshkola II stupeni: Programma, ob"iaznitel'naia zapiska, literaturo. Molodaia gvardiia, Moscow and Leningrad, 1926.

Komsomol'skoe rozhdestvo. Krasnaia nov', Moscow, 1923.

Kosarev, A. V. *Leninskomu komsomolu bol'shevistskii stil' raboty.* Molodaia gvardiia, Moscow and Leningrad, 1933.

Lavrikov, K. *Komsomol v kul'turnyi estafete.* OGIZ, Moscow and Leningrad, 1931.

Levgur. *Kak voznik komsomol.* Novaia Moskva, Moscow, 1924.

Obiazannosti komsomol'tsa. Novaia Moskva, Moscow, 1924.

Liubimov, I. E. *Komsomol v sovetskom stroitel'stve 1917–1927.* Molodaia gvardia, Moscow and Leningrad, 1928.

Mehnert, Klaus. *Youth in Soviet Russia.* Harcourt, Brace, New York, 1933.

Mushkin, V. *O rabote komsomola v shkole.* Moscow, 1936.

Naslednikam revoliutsii: Dokumentry partii o komsomole i molodozhi. Molodaia gvardiia, Moscow, 1969.

Nelepin and Balashov. *VLKSM za 10 let v tsifrakh.* Molodaia gvardiia, Moscow and Leningrad, 1928.

Nozhnitskii, G., and A. Iasnyi. *Komsomol v kul'tpokhode.* Gosizdat, Moscow, 1931.

O politicheskom obrazovanii komsomol'tsev: Sbornik. Molodaia gvardiia, Moscow, 1935.

Rivkin. *O Ocherki po istorii VLKSM.* Moscow, 1933.

Rogov, I. M. *Perspektivy iunosheskogo truda i zadachi ekonomicheskoi raboty RKSM.* Molodaia gvardiia, Moscow, 1924.

Samokhin, L. F. *Kommunisticheskoe vospitanie shkolnika v sem'e.* Gos. uchebno-pedagog. izdatel'stvo, Moscow, 1934.

Sbornik materialov po politprosvet rabotu RKSM. Gosizdat, Moscow, 1921.

Shokhin, Andrei. *Komsomolskaia derevnia.* Molodaia gvardiia, Moscow, 1923.

Kratkaia istoriia VLKSM. Molodaia gvardiia, Moscow, 1928.

Singalevich, S. P. *Leninism v shkole: Metodicheskoe rukovodstvo.* Rabotnik prosveshcheniia, Moscow, 1924.

Slavnyi put' Leninskogo Komsomola. 2 vols. Molodaia gvardiia, Moscow, 1974.

Slepnev, N. *Komsomolskaia pechat'.* Molodaia gvardiia, Moscow, 1926.

Stratonitskii, A. *Voprosy byta v komsomole.* Priboi, Leningrad, n.d.

Trushenko, N. V. *Partiia i komsomol, 1918–1920.* Gorkii, 1966.

Vasiutin, N. *Ocherednye zadachi detskogo kommunisticheskogo dvizheniia.* Molodaia gvardia, Moscow, 1924.

V edinom stroiu (Stranitsy istorii komsomola). LGU, Leningrad, 1968.

VLKSM v rezoliutsiiakh ego s"ezdov i konferentsii 1918–1928. Moscow, 1929.

Zamoskovretskii, V. *Klub rabochei molodezhi.* Novaia Moskva, Moscow, 1924.

Zof, V. *Komsomol i Krasnyi flot,* Novaia Moskva, Moscow, 1924.

THE PRESS AND BOOK PUBLISHING

Alekseev, V. P. *V. I. Lenin o partiinosti i svobode pechati.* Moscow, 1971.

Alferov, V. N. *Vosnikovenie i razvitie rabsel'korovskogo dvizheniia v SSSR.* Mysl', Moscow, 1970.

Andronov, S. A. *Bol'shevistskaia pechat' v trekh revoliutsiakh.* Politizdat, Moscow, 1978.

Astrakhan, Kh. M., I. S. Sazonov, and A. F. Berezhnoi. *Bol'shevistskaia pechat' v bor'be za vlast' sovetov: Mart–Okt. 1917.* Leninizdat, Leningrad, 1960.

Astrakhan, Kh. M., and I. S. Sazonov. "Sozdanie massovoi bol'shevistskoi pechati v 1917 godu." *Voprosy istorii,* no. 1 (Jan. 1957), pp. 87–98.

Baluev, B. P. *Lenin polemizuruet s burzhuaznoi pressoi.* Politizdat, Moscow, 1977.

Bel'skii, N. "Russkaia bumazhnaia promyshlennost'." *Pechat' i revoliutsiia.* vol. 1 (1921), pp. 18–25.

Berezhnoi, A. *K istorii partiino-sovetskoi pechati.* Izd. Leningradskogo universiteta, Leningrad, 1956.

Bliakhin, P. A. "Pechat' SSSR za 1924–1925 gg." *Pechat' i revoliutsiia,* 1926, pp. 122–6.

Brooks, Jeffrey. "Discontinuity in the Spread of Popular Print Culture, 1917–1927." Unpublished manuscript.

Bryliakov, N. A. *Rossiskoe telegrafnoe . . . ,* Mysl', Moscow, 1976.

Budnikov, V. P. *Bol'shevistskaia partiinaia pechat' v 1917 godu.* Izd. Kharkovskogo universiteta, Kharkov, 1959.

Bulgakova, Lidia. *Das studium der Presse in der USSR.* Komintern, Cologne, 1928.

Buzek, Anthony. *How the Communist Press Works.* Pall Mall Press, London, 1964.

Bystrianskii, V. "Gosudarstvennoe izdatel'stvo i ego zadachi." *Kniga i revoliutsiia,* no. 1 (1920), pp. 2–4.

Dementev, A. G. *Ocherki istorii russkoi sovetskoi zhurnalistiki, 1917–1932.* Nauka, Moscow, 1966.

Dinershtein, E. A. *Polozhivshie pervyi kamen: Gosizdat i ego rukovoditeli.* Kniga, Moscow, 1972.

Razvitie izdatel'skogo dela v soiuznykh i avtonomicheskikh respublikakh. Kniga, Moscow, 1973.

Izdatel'skoe delo v pervye gody sovetskoi vlasti (1917–1922) Sbornik dokumentov i materialov. Kniga, Moscow, 1972.

Esin, B. I., ed. *Iz istorii russkoi zhurnalistiki: Kontsa XIXv nachala XXv.* Izd. Mosk. univ., Moscow, 1973.

Fingerit, E. M., and I. V. Kuznetsov, eds. *Gazetnyi mir Sovetskogo Soiuza, 1917–1970.* 1972.

Goncharov, A. A. "Bor'ba sovetskoi vlasti s kontrarevoliutsionnoi burzhuaznoi i melkoburzhuaznoi pechatiu." *Vestnik MGU, Zhurnalistika,* vol. 4 (1969). x8

Ianitskii, N. F. *Knizhnaia statistika sovetskoi Rossii, 1918–1923.* Gosizdat, Moscow, 1924.

Ingulov, S. B. *Kul'turnaia revoliutsiia i pechati.* Moskovskii rabochii, Moscow and Leningrad, 1928.

Ionov, I. "Bumaga." *Kniga i revoliutsiia,* no. 2 (1920), pp. 4–5.

Jaryc, Marc. *Press and Publishing in the Soviet Union.* London University Press, London, 1935.

Just, Artur. *Die Presse der Sowjet Union.* Duncker, Berlin, 1931.

Kak naladit' stennoi gazety. Gudok, Moscow, 1930.

Kantor, M. "Gosizdat k desiatiletiiu oktiabria." *Pechat' i revoliutsiia,* no. 7 (1927), pp. 314–20.

Khlebtsevich, E. "Chitatel'skie interesy Krasnoarmeitsev." *Pechat' i revoliutsiia,* no. 2 (1921), pp. 49–55.

Kovalev, I. "Tsarism v bor'be s revoliutsionnoi pechatiu v 1905." *Krasnyi arkhiv,* vol. 105 (1941), pp. 140–5.

Kozhevnikov, G. A. *Partiia-organizator rabsel'korovskogo dvizheniia.* Izd. Saratovskogo universiteta, Saratov, 1965.

Kruglov, A. A. *V. I. Lenin i stanovlenie sovetskoi pressy.* Mysl', Moscow, 1973.

Krupskaia, N. K. *Lenin–redaktor i organizator partiinoi pechati.* Partiinoe izdatel'stvo, Moscow, 1932.

Kunitsyn, G. V. I. *Lenin o partiinosti i svobode pechati.* Gospolitizdat, Moscow, 1971.

Lebedev, D. *Shest' let moskovskoi pechati, 1917–1923.* Novaia Moskva, Moscow, 1924.

Lemke, M. "Ocherednye zadachi Gosudarstvennogo izdatel'stva." *Kniga i revoliutsiia,* no. 2 (1921), pp. 1–4.

Lenin, V. I. *O pechati,* Moscow, 1974.

Lenin i Izvestiia. Politizdat, Moscow, 1975.

Lunacharskii, A. "Svoboda knigi i revoliutsiia." *Pechat' i revoliustiia,* no. 1 (1921), pp. 3–9.

Meshcheriakov, N. L. "O rabote gosudarstvennogo izdatel'stva." *Pechat' i revoliutsiia,* no. 1 (1921), pp. 9–14.

"O rabote chastnykh izdatel'stvakh." *Pechat' i revoliutsiia,* no. 1 (1922), pp. 128–34.

"O rabote gosudarstvennogo izdatel'stva o novykh usloviiakh." *Pechat' i revoliutsiia,* no. 1 (1922), p. 163–8.

Mishuris, A. L. *Pechat', rozhdennaia Oktiabrem.* MGU, Moscow, 1968.

Nazarov, A. I *Kniga v sovetskom obshchestve.* Nauka, Moscow, 1964.

Oktiabr' i kniga. Akad. nauk, Moscow, 1968.

Novitskii, P. "Iz istorii Krymskoi pechati v 1919–1920 gg." *Pechat' i revoliutsiia,* no. 1 (1921), p. 54–63.

Okorokov, A. Z. *Oktiabr' i krakh russkoi burzhuaznoi pressy.* Mysl', Moscow, 1970.

ed. *V. I. Lenin o pechati.* Politizdat, Moscow, 1974.

"Podkup 'Novogo vremeni' tsarskim pravitel'stvom." *Krasnyi arkhiv,* vol. 21 (1927), pp. 223–6.

Polianskii, V. "Nachalo sovetskikh izdatel'stv." *Pechat' i revoliutsiia,* no. 7 (1927), pp. 233–40.

Polonskii, V. "Ocherednaia zadacha Gosudarstvennogo izdatel'stva." *Pechat' i revoliutsiia,* no. 1 (1921), pp. 14–18.

Prokhorov, E. P. "Leninskaia kontseptsiia svobody pechati." *Voprosy teorii i praktiki massovykh sredstv propagandy,* vol. 4 (1971).

Raskol'nikov. "Priezd tov. Lenina v Rossiiu." *Proletarskaia revoliutsiia,* vol. 1 (1923).

Russkaia periodicheskaia pechat' (1895–Okt. 1917) Sbornik, Gospolitizdat, Moscow, 1957.

Sampson, Charles B. "The Formative Years of the Soviet Press: An Institutional History, 1917–1924." Ph.D. dissertation, University of Massachusetts, 1970.

Satiukov, P. A. *Pechat' kommunisticheskoi partii v period podgotovki i provedeniia velikoi Oktiabrskoi Sotsialisticheskoi Revoliutsii.* Vysshaia partiinaia shkola pri Ts.K. KPSS, Moscow, 1953.

Savel'ev, M. "Pis'ma rabochikh v 'Zvezdu' i 'Pravdu.' " *Krasnyi arkhiv,* vol. 77 (1936), pp. 19–21.

"S"ezd Gosizdat (3–6 Okt. 1921 g.)." *Pechat' i revoliutsiia,* no. 1 (1921), pp. 138–41.

Shafir, Ia. *Gazeta i derevnia.* Krasnaia nov', Moscow, 1923.

"Razoblachitel'nye priemy 'Pravdi' v 1917." *Pechat' i revoliutsiia,* no. 2 (1927), 5–15.

Shchegolev, P. and M. Lemke. "Ocherednye zadachi Gosudarstvennogo izdatel'stva." *Kniga i revoliutsiia,* no. 1 (1920), pp. 7–9.

Shchelkunov, M. "Zakonodatel'stvo o pechati za piat' let." *Pechat' i revoliutsiia,* no. 2 (1922), pp. 172–8.

Shenderovich, M. "Poligraficheskaia promyshlennost i perspektivy no 1921 god." *Pechat' i revoliutsiia,* no. 1 (1921), pp. 25–37.

Shumakov, A., and I. Kuznetsov. *Bol'shevistskaia pechat' Moskvy.* Moskovskii rabochii, Moscow, 1968.

Slavskaia, V. "Kniga i revoliutsiia." *Kniga i revoliutsiia,* no. 3–4 (1920), pp. 4–6.

Stepanov, I. "Gosudarstvennoe izdatel'stvo, chastnye firmy i podriadnye predpriatiia." *Kniga i revoliutsiia.* no. 6 (1920), pp. 4–9.

Uchenova, V. V. *Partiino-sovetskaia pechat' vosstanovitel'nogo perioda.* Izd-vo Moskovskogo universiteta, Moscow, 1964.

Usagin, A. "Bol'shevistskaia pechat' v Moskve v epokhu Zvezdy i Pravdy." *Proletarskaia revoliutsiia,* vol. 14 (1923), pp. 401–17.

Vardin, I. V. *Sovetskaia pechat': Sbornik statei.* Rabotnik prosveshcheniia, Moscow, 1924.

Vareikis, I. M., ed. *Pechat' SSSR za 1924 i 1925 gg.* Gosizdat, Moscow, 1926.

Voronskii, A. "Iz proshlego." *Prozhektor,* vol. 6 (1927), pp. 19–20.

Wolfe, Bertram. "Krupskaia purges the peoples' libraries." *Survey*, vol. 72 (1969).
Zalezhskii, V. N. "Pervyi Legalnyi Peka." *Proletarskaia revoliutsiia*, vol. 13 (1923).
Zinovev, G. *Novyi velikii pochin: Rabkorovskoe i sel'korovskoe dvizhenie*. Gosizdat, Leningrad and Moscow, 1925.

FILM

Akademia Nauk SSSR. *Ocherki istorii sovetskogo kino, vol. 1, 1917–1934*. Iskusstvo, Moscow, 1956.
Iz istorii kino. Akad. nauk SSSR, Moscow, 1958.
Akselrod, L. "Dokumenty po istorii natsionalizatsii russkoi kinematografii." *Iz istorii kino*, vol. 1 (1958), pp. 25–37.
Bratoliubov, S. *Na zare Sovetskoi kinematografii*. Iskusstvo, Leningrad, 1976.
Carter, H. *The New Theater and Cinema of Soviet Russia*, Chapman and Dodd, London, 1924.
Cohen, Louis. *The Cultural Political Traditions and Developments of the Soviet Cinema, 1917–1972*. Arno Press, New York, 1974.
Ginzburg, S. S. *Kinematografiia dorevoliutsionnoi Rossii*. Moscow, 1963.
Khanzhonkov, A. *Pervye gody russkoi kinematografii*. Iskusstvo, Moscow, 1937.
Kinematograf: Sbornik statei. Gosizdat, Moscow, 1919.
Kleberg, Lars. "The Audience as Myth and Reality: Soviet Theatrical Ideology and Audience Research in the 1920's." *Russian History*, vol. 9 (1982), pp. 227–41.
Kresin, M. L. "Iz vospominanii starogo kinorabotnika," *Iz istorii kino*, vol. 1 (1958), pp. 92–6.
Lebedev, N. A. *Ocherk istorii kino SSSR*. Iskusstvo, Moscow, 1947.
Ocherki istorii kino SSSR. Vol. 1: nemoe kino 1917–1934. Iskusstvo, Moscow, 1965.
"Boevye dvatsatye gody." *Iskusstvo kino*, vol. 12 (1968), pp. 85–99.
Leyda, Jay. *Kino: A History of the Russian and Soviet Film*. Collier Books, New York, 1960.
Listov, V. "U istokov sovetskogo kino." *Iskusstvo kino*, vol. 3 (1969), pp. 2-15.
Malykhin, N. G. *Ocherki po istorii knigoizdatal'skogo dela v SSSR*. Kniga, Moscow, 1965.
Preobrazhenskii, N. F. "Vospominaniia o rabote VFKO." *Iz istorii kino*, vol. 1 (1958), pp. 85–91.
Rimberg, John D. *The Motion Picture in the Soviet Union*. Arno Press, New York, 1973.
Rimberg, John, and Paul Babitsky. The Soviet Film Industry. Praeger, New York, 1955.
Samoe vazhnoe iz vsekh iskusstv: Lenin o kino. Iskusstvo, Moscow, 1963.
Seton, Marie. *Sergei M. Eisenstein*. A. A. Wyn, New York, 1952.
Sobolev, R. *Aleksander Dovzhenko*. Iskusstvo, Moscow, 1980.
Sovetskie khudozhestvennye fil'my. 4 vols. Iskusstvo, Moscow, 1961–8.
Youngblood, Denise. "On the Kino Front: The Evolution of the Soviet Cinema in the 1920's." Ph.D. dissertation, Stanford University, 1980.
Zhdan, V. N., ed. *Kratkaia istoriia sovetskogo kino*. Moscow, 1969.
Zorkaia, N. "Iakov Protazanov i sovetskoe kinoiskusstvo 20-kh godov." *Voprosy kinoiskusstva*, vol. 6 (1962).

NEWSPAPERS AND JOURNALS

Bednota
Bezbozhnik
Birzhevaia vedomosti
Derevenskaia bednota
Derevenskaia pravda
Golos soldata
Gudok
Iskusstvo
Iskusstvo kino
Iz istorii kino
Izvestiia
Kniga i revoliutsiia
Kommunisticheskaia revoliutsiia
Komsomolskaia pravda
Krasnaia nov'
Krasnyi arkhiv
Luch
Narodnye prosveshchenie
Novaia zhizn'
Novyi mir
Pioner
Pravda
Proletarskaia revoliutsiia
Prozhektor
Trud
Vneshkol'noe obrazovanie
Vozhatyi

Index